CRUSADE AND MISSION

Princeton University Press
41 WILLIAM STREET
PRINCETON, NEW JERSEY 08540

At the suggestion of Benjamin Kedar, we
are sending you a copy of his book which
is new in paperback.

We hope you will let your colleagues and
students know that the book is now available,
and that you will consider adopting it as
assigned reading for classroom use.

Arlene Warren
Publicity Associate
(609) 452-4876

Publication: Crusade and Mission: European
               Approaches Toward the Muslims

Author: Benjamin Z. Kedar

Publication Date: 1989

Paperback Price: $14.95

   PUBLISHERS OF BOLLINGEN SERIES

BENJAMIN Z. KEDAR

Crusade and Mission

European Approaches
toward the Muslims

Donated by Fred A. Casel Jr.

PRINCETON UNIVERSITY PRESS

Property of
Charles A. Owen, Jr.
Medieval Studies Library

Limited Paperback Edition, 1988

Publication of this book has been aided by a grant from The
Andrew W. Mellon Foundation

This book has been composed in Linotron Galliard

Clothbound editions of Princeton University Press books are
printed on acid-free paper, and binding materials are chosen
for strength and durability. Paperbacks, while satisfactory
for personal collections, are not usually suitable for
library rebinding.

Printed in the United States of America by
Princeton University Press
Princeton, New Jersey

To my father,
Dr. Samuel Kraus,
healer unto Jew,
Christian, and
Muslim

CONTENTS

SOME INTRODUCTORY REMARKS

THE present work was not conceived as an addition to the rather over-burdened shelf of histories of the crusades or to the less extensive though still weighty one of surveys of Christian missionary activity. Rather it is an attempt at the clarification of one specific issue: the relationship between crusade and mission as two Catholic European approaches to the Muslims in medieval times. Did one supersede the other, the rising missionary idea gradually replacing the declining idea of the crusade? Were the two complementary or competitive, with mission implying a criticism of crusade and undermining support for it? Historians of the crusades have repeatedly touched upon these questions, usually assuming a move from crusade to mission, but have devoted little attention to the issue.[1] Nor were the related questions of the place of Muslim conversion among the aims of the crusades, the extent of Catholic missionizing and Muslim conversion in the Crusading Kingdom of Jerusalem, and the effect of criticism of the crusade upon the genesis of the idea of mission to the Muslims given much consideration.[2]

The original aim of this work was to delineate more clearly the relations between warfare, conversion, and mission in the history of the crusades and the Crusading Kingdom of Jerusalem. All three were carried out not only in the crusader East but also in the other theaters in which Catholics and Muslims clashed; indeed, as will be shown, warfare and conversion were already linked at the reduction, about 973, of the Muslim stronghold of Fraxinetum on the coast of Provence. It has therefore been considered expedient to compare pertinent developments along the Catholic-Muslim border in its entirety, with

---

[1] S. Runciman, "The Decline of the Crusading Idea," in *Relazioni del X Congresso Internazionale di Scienze Storiche*, vol. 3 (Florence, 1955), pp. 650–52; A. Waas, *Geschichte der Kreuzzüge*, 2 vols. (Freiburg, 1956), 2:71–78; P. Rousset, *Histoire des croisades* (Paris, 1957), p. 237. On crusade and mission as complementary or rival concepts, see the views of Cl. Cahen in a review article published in *Revue historique* 227 (1962): 230, and of J. Prawer, *Histoire du royaume latin de Jérusalem*, 2 vols. (Paris, 1969–70), 2:389–90; also H. E. Mayer, *The Crusades*, trans. J. Gillingham (New York and Oxford, 1972), pp. 221–22.

[2] For a short sketch of conversion and missionizing among the Muslims of the Crusading Kingdom see J. Richard, *La papauté et les missions d'Orient au moyen âge (XIIIᵉ–XVᵉ siècles)* (Rome, 1977), pp. 7–8, 41–44.

the intention of arriving at distinctions between general trends and regional particularities. It is true that, at present, studies of Catholic-Muslim relations in Spain, Sicily, and the crusader East are largely conducted in isolation from one another. (To give just one telling example, an eminent expert on the history of the kingdom of Valencia, undoubtedly confounding tenth-century Byzantines with crusaders, believes that the latter settled converts from Islam as military colonists in some border regions.) Obviously, any attempt to cover simultaneously so much ground is beset with pitfalls; but when a complex issue is involved, one should try, even in this age of overspecialization, to cope with as many of its ramifications as is feasible while remaining conscious of the possibility, nay the probability, of overlooking some of the pertinent literature, rather than overprudently writing off the comparative approach and the insights it is likely to yield. After all, if in the latter part of the twelfth century the Roman Curia was able to answer queries from Spain and the Crusading Kingdom concerning Muslim conversion (queries prefigured, as will be shown, by a decision in Norman Sicily a century earlier), why should not a present-day historian try to deal with such developments within a common framework? Besides, although the phenomenon under consideration occurs in a number of geographical areas within a sizable time span, it is of limited enough scope to allow in almost all cases for the consultation, or reconsideration, of the pertinent primary sources.

The belated appearance of Catholic missionary efforts aimed at Muslims, centuries after the first Catholic-Muslim encounter on the battlefield, is of considerable importance to the present examination. To test the plausibility of explanations for this lag, the range of inquiry has to be broadened once more to encompass the missionary activities of the other Christendoms that faced Islam during the same centuries. This line of investigation also permits placing in sharper relief the Catholic European stances vis-à-vis Islam. In addition, it leads to the realization that several hitherto unnoticed pieces of information about the Arabs and their religion found their way into Catholic Europe in early medieval times: One of these goes some way in explaining the protracted absence of Catholic missionizing among Muslims. Finally, it is in a ninth-century Latin poem that one finds the earliest rudiments of the link between Muslim conversion and anti-Muslim warfare that will become fully articulated by the mid-thirteenth century and harnessed for a novel purpose in the sixteenth. The delineation of the gradual unfolding and differential acceptance of this linkage that ultimately emerges from this inquiry seems to justify the work's somewhat meandering progress.

A novice to this subject is scarcely aware of the extent to which a sizable part of the relevant secondary literature is permeated with present-day attitudes and emotions. These interfere with the proper understanding of the issues in varying degrees. Sometimes the attitudes are so transparent as to be quite harmless, as when one writer considers it improbable that a message of the caliph ʿAbd al-Raḥmān III to Emperor Otto I contained insulting references to Christ, arguing with disarming naiveté that the caliph "was an acknowledged leader of the Muslim world, and it is not reasonable to suppose he would have offered such insults whether Otto had given some cause or not."[3] Again, when a writer seriously posits a "trans-historical relationship" between the offer of ordeal supposedly made by Francis of Assisi to the Muslims near Damietta and that of Muhammad to the Christians of Nadjrān, one can only shrug one's shoulders.[4] When another historian characterizes the views of the *Summa Halensis* on Jews and pagans as "a stray streak of medieval Christian theology of which one ought to be deeply ashamed today," and another concludes his colorful history of the crusades with the accusation that "the Holy War itself was nothing more than a long act of intolerance in the name of God, which is the sin against the Holy Spirit," or when still another states—at a scholarly colloquium in 1972—that Peter of Cluny "devised several clever arguments against Islamic doctrine which have proved convincing to this day," the cards are on the table, the reader knows exactly where the author stands, and no misunderstanding can arise.[5] Apologetic prefaces to learned surveys of Christian anti-Islamic polemic merely indicate how emotionally charged the subject remains, as does the fact that the translator of a fourteenth-century *itinerarium*, published in Dublin in 1960, simply skips over some of the more extreme anti-Islamic remarks.[6] Anachronistic nomenclature such as "Christian Arabs" instead

[3] A. A. El-Hajji, *Andalusian Diplomatic Relations with Western Europe during the Umayyad Period, 138–366/755–976: A Historical Survey* (Beirut, 1970), p. 212.

[4] B. Basetti-Sani, *Per un dialogo cristiano-musulmano: Mohammed, Damietta e La Verna* (Milan, 1969), p. 387.

[5] Elisabeth Gössmann, *Metaphysik und Heilsgeschichte: Eine theologische Untersuchung der Summa Halensis* (Munich, 1964), p. 366; S. Runciman, *A History of the Crusades*, 3 vols. (Cambridge, 1951–54), 3:480; J. Kritzeck, "De l'influence de Pierre Abélard sur Pierre le Vénérable dans ses oeuvres sur l'Islam," in *Pierre Abélard—Pierre le Vénérable: Les courants philosophiques, littéraires et artistiques en Occident au milieu du XIIᵉ siècle. Actes et mémoires du Colloque international de Cluny, 1972*, ed. R. Louis and J. Jolivet (Paris, 1975), p. 214.

[6] N. Daniel, *Islam and the West: The Making of an Image* (Edinburgh, 1960), p. v; A.-T. Khoury, *Les théologiens byzantins et l'Islam: Textes et auteurs (VIIIᵉ–XIIIᵉ s.)* (Louvain and Paris, 1969), p. 7; idem, *Polémique byzantine contre l'Islam (VIIIᵉ–XIIIᵉ s.)*

of "Arabic-speaking Christians" is dangerous only insofar as it may mislead the uninitiated.[7] More disconcerting are paraphrases of sources that more often than not tone down the militancy of the original statements. And because attitudinal undercurrents color almost imperceptibly the study of the issues proper, the present writer—personally about equidistant from the traditions of Christianity and Islam—considers it helpful to occasionally draw attention to them.

The term "mission" and its derivatives appear only in early modern times, but it would be pedantic to dispense with them here. But since the term is sometimes used to denote all attempts at Christianization, it may be useful to clarify that in this book the term refers only to peaceful efforts to cause the infidel to convert. Following the lead of Robert Lopez, I use the term "Catholic Europe," which is more exact than "Christian Europe"; but the Mozarabs, Catholic subjects of the Muslims in Spain, will be treated separately from their unsubjugated brethren. Whenever Latin or Greek texts are paraphrased, Muslims will be designated, as in the texts themselves, as "Saracens" or "Agarens"; elsewhere they will be spoken of as Muslims. The name of Muhammad will always be spelled as it is by the writer being discussed at the time, in order to show the manifold ways in which medieval Christians rendered the name of their great adversary.

I FIRST came to deal with crusade and mission in my M.A. thesis, written in Jerusalem in 1964–65 under the direction of Joshua Prawer, my first teacher in matters medieval. In 1966, while studying at Yale, I ransacked my Jerusalem thesis for a paper later delivered at a medieval studies colloquium, and I still remember the suggestions Robert Lopez made on that occasion. After a decade I returned to crusade and mission during my 1976–77 sabbatical. A stay at Sidney Sussex College, Cambridge, allowed for many profitable conversations with my host R. C. Smail and his pupils, especially Jonathan Riley-Smith. A fellowship from the Alexander von Humboldt Foundation permitted me to spend about sixteen months in Munich and make use of that medievalist's paradise, the twin libraries of the Monumenta Germaniae Historica and the Bayerische Staatsbibliothek.

In Jerusalem, Joshua Prawer was always ready to answer queries on crusader matters; Eliyahu Ashtor volunteered to translate some Arabic

(Leiden, 1972), p. 7; *Itinerarium Symonis Semeonis ab Hybernia ad Terram Sanctam*, ed. and trans. M. Esposito (Dublin, 1960), pp. 50–51, 54–55.

[7] N. Daniel, *The Arabs and Mediaeval Europe* (London and Beirut, 1975), pp. 114, 205 ("Christian Arabs"), 194 ("Arab Christians"); other terms of this kind are used throughout.

texts, check the translations of many others, and clarify several issues concerning Muslim-Christian relations; Nurith Kenaan advised me, inter alia, on aspects of art history; and the participants in my seminars on crusade and mission and on twelfth-century criticism of the crusades helped me to clarify my thoughts on those subjects at least as much as I was able to clarify theirs. In Munich, members of the Monumenta Germaniae Historica, especially Horst Fuhrmann, its president, and Alexander Patschovsky, as well as Hans Eberhard Mayer, were always generous with their time. So were the librarians Fräulein Dr. Hilda Lietzmann and Frau Christa Becker. Alois Madre of the Raimundus-Lullus-Institut in Freiburg im Breisgau, W. M. Grauwen (O. Praem.) of Meise, Dietlind Schack, Ludwig Schmugge, and Juliane C. Wilmanns proffered pertinent information or assistance. Josep Perarnau of Barcelona generously put at my disposal the typescript of his inventory of Ramon Llull's writings. Gabriella M.E.G. Airaldi of Genoa repeatedly advised me on matters of paleography.

Final additions to the book were made during a stay at the Institute for Advanced Study in Princeton in 1981–82, where I could profit from the critique of S. D. Goitein and A. L. Udovitch as well as of Robert Benson and Gavin Langmuir.

My assistant in Jerusalem, Reuven Avi-Yonah, offered manifold aid; Dr. Carol Bosworth Kutscher of Jerusalem and Ms. Susan Oleksiw of Beverly, Mass., attempted to improve my English; Mrs. Tilly Eshel (Jerusalem) and Mrs. Sandy Lafferty (Princeton) did the typing. Guido Clemente of Florence obtained the photograph of the *Christus militans* that appears on the jacket. Finally, my editor at Princeton University Press, Miss R. Miriam Brokaw, was always at hand with no-nonsense encouragement and advice. I would like to thank them all.

Jerusalem, May 1984

The publication of the paperback edition allows me to correct a few misprints and mistakes, to restate a facetious remark which one of my reviewers took at face value, and to slightly expand the list of works which appeared after the original typescript had gone to press. The Catholic treatment of the Muslims of medieval Hungary, undeservedly ignored in the present book, will be taken up elsewhere.

Jerusalem, March 1988

CRUSADE AND MISSION

ONE

The Early Centuries: The Muslims beyond the Bounds of European Mission and Polemics

THE history of Europe's relations with Islam begins with an enigma: Did a Roman pontiff attempt, some twenty years after the death of Muhammad, to convert Muslims to Christianity?

The Roman pontiff in question is Martin I (649–53), the fierce opponent of Monothelitism—the Christological formula propounded by the Byzantine emperors of his day—who was eventually abducted to Constantinople, charged with treason, and exiled to the Crimea. In a letter Martin wrote after his abduction, he intimates that his enemies accused him of dispatching to the Saracens letters, money, and "a so-called *tomus* [instructing them] in what manner they should believe."[1] Martin does not indicate whether the Saracens with whom he purportedly maintained relations were the new Saracen masters of the Levant, or the Saracens who briefly raided Sicily in 652. Whichever may be the case, the letter leaves no doubt that a pope was said to have tried to spread Christianity among Saracens around the year 650— that is, precisely when the authoritative text of the Koran was being established.

Although Martin categorically denied the charges, they were not necessarily trumped up. It is a fact that Martin endeavored to establish an anti-Monothelitic church in the patriarchates of Jerusalem and An-

---

[1] "Ego aliquando ad Saracenos nec literas misi, nec quem dicunt tomum qualiter credere debeant, aut pecunias unquam transmisi, exceptis dumtaxat quibusdam illuc venientibus servis Dei causa eleemosynae, quibus et modicum quid praebuimus minime ad Saracenos transmissum." Mansi, *Concilia*, 10:850. In this context, *tomus* means "a formulation of dogma": cf. *Le Liber Pontificalis*, ed. L. Duchesne, 3 vols. (Paris, 1955–57), 1:238, 253.

The extant text of Martin's letter, a ninth-century Latin translation by Anastasius the Librarian, whose knowledge of Greek was limited, may be corrupt: see C. de Boor's introductory remarks to his edition of Theophanes's *Chronographia*, 2 vols. (Leipzig, 1883–85), 2:415–16; P. Peeters, "Une vie grecque du pape S. Martin I," *Analecta Bollandiana* 51 (1933): 236; see also p. 247, where Peeters suggests that Anastasius pieced together this and another letter by carving passages from a fuller narrative.

tioch, and that he even appointed a special apostolic vicar, John of Philadelphia, authorizing him to install orthodox bishops, priests, and deacons in those Saracen-ruled areas.[2] Why should Martin not have also contemplated offering the orthodox faith to the Saracen conquerors themselves? It would not have been the papacy's first attempt at evangelizing a distant, barbarous nation; only half a century earlier, Gregory I had initiated the mission to the Anglo-Saxons. Martin, moreover, shared with the Saracens a common enemy: the Monothelitic emperor at Constantinople. (Reasons for attempting to convert the Saracen raiders of Sicily are even more obvious.) The accusation leveled at Martin, therefore, is not inherently improbable. But, in the absence of corroborative evidence, the possibility that a mid-seventh-century pope tried to convert Saracens must remain in the realm of conjecture. The hard fact is that such an attempt was ascribed to Pope Martin—obviously in order to brand him a traitor to the empire—and that he took pains to deny it.[3]

Another hard fact is that more than three centuries will pass before an attempt at Muslim conversion will again be alluded to in a European source, and more than five centuries before Europeans will launch a systematic missionary effort among the Muslims. This is a puzzling fact, since the very centuries in which Catholics abstained from attempts at evangelizing the Muslims abounded in Catholic missionary activities in the European north and east: These were the centuries in which the Christian faith was carried to the Frisians, the Danes and the Swedes, the Slavs, the Prussians and the Hungarians. The discrep-

[2] Mansi, *Concilia*, 10:805–32; cf. E. Caspar, *Geschichte des Papstums*, vol. 2 (Tübingen, 1933), pp. 561–62. Caspar, who believes that Martin's plan to establish an orthodox hierarchy in the East remained on paper, dismisses the charges against Martin as wild rumors, but gives no reason for his view (p. 566).

[3] It should be noted that the Byzantine chronicler and theologian Nicephorus (d. 829) relates that Cyrus, the patriarch of Alexandria at the time of the Arab conquest, suggested—probably in 640—that a daughter of the Byzantine emperor be given in marriage to ʿAmr b. al-ʿĀṣ, the future conqueror of Egypt, to induce him to convert to Christianity: *Nicephori patriarchae de rebus gestis post Mauricii imperium*, in PG 100:917–22. Butler and Caetani regard the story as highly improbable; Nau, who speculates that Cyrus might have attempted to convert Muhammad himself by sending him a noble Coptic girl, gives it full credence: A. J. Butler, *The Arab Conquest of Egypt and the Last Thirty Years of the Roman Dominion* (Oxford, 1902), p. 264; L. Caetani, *Annali dell'Islām*, vol. 4 (Milan, 1911), pp. 184–85; F. Nau, "La politique matrimoniale de Cyrus (Le Mocaucas)," *Le Muséon, Revue d'études orientales* 45 (1932): 1–17. On the other hand, the fact that Maximus the Confessor, Martin's ally in the struggle against Monothelitism, was accused at his trial of having handed Egypt and Africa to the Saracens (PG 90:111–12) may be adduced to support the view that the charge against Martin was a fabrication.

ancy between the assiduous missionizing in one geographical area and its total absence in another may best be exemplified by the life story of Willibald (ca. 700–787), the Anglo-Saxon monk who played a significant role in the Christianization of the south German tribes. Willibald, who was to traverse "through the uncultivated province of the Bavarians shoving the plough, sowing seeds, reaping the harvest," had gone on a pilgrimage to Jerusalem in the 720s. Yet in the detailed account of his sojourn in the land of the "Saracen pagans" (*pagani Sarracini*) there is nothing to suggest that the future cultivator of the Bavarians ever attempted to preach his faith to the Saracens he encountered. The nun Hugeburc, who committed to writing the story of Willibald's pilgrimage, does relate that he came close to being martyred in the East—not because he preached the Christian faith, but for smuggling some balsam through the customhouse of Tyre.[4]

Nor did the Muslims of Spain, so close to the heartland of Catholic Europe, become a missionary target. It is true that Archbishop Wilcharius of Sens, after having obtained the permission of Pope Hadrian I, consecrated about the year 790 a certain Egila as bishop, and dispatched him to Spain "for the preaching of the orthodox faith and the Holy Catholic Church." But Hadrian's letters to the bishops of Spain, and to Egila himself—the only sources for this mission—leave no doubt that Spanish Christians, who had adopted a number of unorthodox positions, were to be preached to, not the Saracens.[5] Charlemagne, a supporter of Egila's mission, exhibited a marked concern for the spiritual soundness of the Spanish Christians. In a letter of 794 to Elipand,

[4] *Vita Willibaldi episcopi Eichstetensis*, ed. O. Holder-Egger (1887), in MGH SS 15, 1:86–106 (*pagani Sarracini*: pp. 94–95; smuggling: p. 101; "reaping the harvest": p. 106). Bernhard Bischoff ingeniously extracted the nun's name from a cryptogram: "Wer ist die Nonne von Heidenheim?" *Studien und Mitteilungen zur Geschichte des Benediktiner-Ordens und seiner Zweige* NS 18 (1931): 387–88.

A recent writer has remarked that Boniface mentioned Saracens, Saxons, and Frisians in one breath and considered their missionizing the great task of his time: R. C. Schwinges, *Kreuzzugsideologie und Toleranz: Studien zu Wilhelm von Tyrus* (Stuttgart, 1977), p. 99. The mention, however, which appears in a letter of Pope Zacharias to Boniface, does not deal with missionizing at all: *Die Briefe des heiligen Bonifatius und Lullus*, no. 60, ed. M. Tangl (1916), in MGH Epp. sel. 1:123. Boniface, in a letter of 746–74 to King Aethelbald of Mercia, considers the Saracen invasions of Spain, Provence, and Burgundy a just punishment of the sinful inhabitants of these countries: *Die Briefe*, no. 73, p. 151 (=D.56 c.10).

[5] The papal letters, which reveal that Hadrian at one point believed that Egila himself had adopted heterodox teachings, were edited by W. Gundlach (1892) in MGH Epist. 3:636–48; the quotation appears on p. 644. For a discussion see E. P. Colbert, *The Martyrs of Córdoba (850–859): A Study of the Sources* (Washington, D.C., 1962), pp. 59–63.

the Adoptionist bishop of Muslim-ruled Toledo, and to other Spanish bishops, he declares that he is more deeply saddened by the straying of Spanish Christians from orthodoxy than by their oppression under the Saracens. Formerly, he writes, he and his people prayed for them and waited for the opportunity to liberate them from their servitude, but as long as they continue to stray, they deserve neither prayer nor help.[6] Thus it transpires that Charlemagne had played with the idea of liberating the Spanish Christians living under Muslim rule; but there is no hint that the ruler who forced Christianity upon the Saxons ever contemplated the Christianization of Spain's Muslims.

This is not to say that the fundamental Muslim opposition to Christianity went unnoticed. Already Bede (d. 735), who had witnessed from his Northumbrian vantage point first the Arab conquest of Spain and then the invasion of southern Gaul, in one of his Biblical commentaries placed the Saracens among the adversaries of the Church.[7] Later authors repeatedly described the Saracens as "enemies of Christ," "hateful to God," and the like.[8] But it is as enemies of Christianity that the Saracens were presented, not as targets of Christian missionary activity.

Why this long-lasting forbearance from attempts at Christianizing the Muslims? The question—like most questions about potential but unexploited courses of action—has not received much attention, but the following explanatory factors have been occasionally proffered: a) an ecumenical division of labor, which assigned the task of converting the Muslims to the Oriental Christians; b) the view that Muslims were heretics, thus closer to Christianity than were pagans, hence less in need of Christian missionizing; c) a tacit acknowledgment that the Christian duty to spread the Gospel did not extend to the Muslims; d) Europe's cultural inferiority vis-à-vis the realm of Islam, and superiority over the pagans of the north and northeast; and e) the location of Europe's traditional missionary frontier in the north and northeast, not in the south, where the Muslims made their appearance.[9]

---

[6] The letter was edited by A. Werminghoff in MGH Conc. 2, 1:157–64; see especially p. 159, lines 22–32; p. 162, line 18 through p. 163, line 8. For a discussion see Colbert, pp. 64–84.

[7] *Venerabilis Bedae Opera quae supersunt omnia*, ed. J. A. Giles, vol. 8 (London, 1844), p. 185.

[8] For example, MGH Capitularia regum Francorum 2:67; *Registrum Johannis papae VIII*, ed. E. Caspar (1928), in MGH Epist. 7:20, 29, 204, 267–68; *Liber Pontificalis*, 2:81.

[9] J. Richard, "La papauté et les missions catholiques en Orient au moyen âge," *Mélanges d'archéologie et d'histoire publiés par l'Ecole française de Rome* 58 (1941–46): 253–54; idem, *La papauté et les missions d'Orient au moyen âge (XIIIᵉ-XVᵉ siècles)* (Rome,

These explanations are hardly convincing. The first three are pure conjectures, with no foundation whatever in the sources. As to Europe's cultural inferiority, it is an objective fact that could have accounted for the failure of Catholic missionizing among the Muslims *had such missionizing been undertaken*; it cannot explain why Christianization was not ventured upon. (An equally objective fact is the indisputable vigor of Islam as a salvationist, monotheistic religion, a vigor that would have rendered ineffective any missionary effort. But since in early medieval times few, if any, Catholic Europeans had a coherent notion about the beliefs of the Saracens, this fact is also not explanatory. Nor could contemporaries have grasped that peaceful missions from one self-assured high culture to another are necessarily futile.) Finally, Europe's traditional missionary frontier lay indeed to the north and the east, and tradition probably played a role in the launching of subsequent missionary efforts in these directions, especially since missionaries there could have drawn upon experience gained while combating remnants of paganism among adjacent, previously Christianized tribes. But why did not the emergence of the Muslim realm—surely a momentous event—lead to a deflection of at least part of the missionary efforts from the traditional routes, a deflection that was to occur in the High Middle Ages? Of course, the Muslims first appeared on the European scene as a military threat, which called for a military response, and since Christian arms remained on the defensive for centuries, forcible Christianization of the vanquished—as practiced in Saxony and elsewhere—was not feasible either. But why were there no attempts at peaceful conversion, by missionaries individually operating among Muslims?

A seldom-noted source reveals that the Muslim refusal to convert to Christianity was observed at a very early state. In a poem written in about 826 in honor of Louis the Pious, Ermold the Black lets Louis deliver the following speech before launching his assault on Muslim Barcelona in 801:

> "Had this people [= the Saracens] worshiped God, pleased Christ, and received holy baptism,"—so Louis tells the leaders of his

1977), pp. 8, 12. But the fact that Oliver of Cologne implies that the Saracens *could* have heard the Gospel from Oriental Christians does not mean that he, or other Europeans, believed that "c'était donc aux chrétiens orientaux que devait revenir l'obligation d'instruire les Musulmans." For the views of H. G. Beck, P. Hübinger, R. Elze, and H.-D. Kahl, expressed in a discussion held at the 1964 convention of German historians, see the laconic summary of that discussion in *Geschichte in Wissenschaft und Unterricht*, Beiheft 1965: 23–24. A. Cutler, "Peter the Venerable and Islam (review article)," *Journal of the American Oriental Society* 86 (1966): 187.

camp—"we should have made peace with them, and kept that peace, in order to bind them to God through religion. But this people remains detestable; it spurns the salvation [which we offer] and follows the commandments of the demons. Therefore, God's compassionate justice prevails on us to subject it to servitude. Let's hurry now to the walls and the towers, O Franks, so that your former valor should revive!"[10]

The Carolingian poet is obviously aware of the Saracen unwillingness to convert to Christianity; moreover, he presents the Saracens' refusal as justification for waging war on them.[11] (A similar justification will be adduced in the age of the crusades, just as Ermold's description of cleaning the sites of demon worship in conquered Barcelona will be paralleled in the Song of Roland and sundry crusader chronicles.)[12] It is also noteworthy that Ermold's acceptance of the unlikelihood of Saracen conversion contrasts sharply with his confidence in the prospects of preaching Christianity to the pagan Danes.[13]

About a generation later, John Scotus Erigena (d. ca. 877), the outstanding Irish scholar active at the court of Charles the Bald, writes in one of his short poems that the Agarens (= Saracens) of the south and the pagans of the north "will bend their necks in subjection; Christ will reign everywhere; all submit to both King and God."[14] Here Saracens and Norsemen are on a par; both are expected to accept the rule of Christ. This expectation could, but may not necessarily, have been merely eschatological, for in Erigena's lifetime some Saracens did convert to Catholicism. The fact is mentioned in passing in a southern Italian treaty of 849, when Radelchi of Benevento promises to Siconolfo of Salerno not to admit any Saracens to his lands "excepting those who were [= became] Christian in the time of Lord Sicone and Sicardo, unless they have fallen into apostasy."[15] Thus in the days of

[10] See Appendix 4/a.

[11] According to Karl Heisig, the first to draw attention to the passage in this context, Ermold believed that the struggle between Christianity and Islam would continue until the Muslims converted: K. Heisig, "Die Geschichtsmetaphysik des Rolandliedes und seine Vorgeschichte," *Zeitschrift für romanische Philologie* 55 (1935): 11–12. This interpretation is not warranted by the text.

[12] For the description of the cleansing see MGH Poetae 2:21, lines 532–34; E. Faral, ed. and trans., *Ermold le Noir, Poème sur Louis le Pieux et épitres au roi Pépin* (Paris, 1932), p. 42.

[13] MGH Poetae 2:60–63; Faral, pp. 144–52.

[14] *Iohannis Scoti Carmina*, ed. L. Traube (1896), in MGH Poetae 3, 2:545.

[15] ". . . et amodo, ut dictum est, nullum Sarracenum recipiam vel recipere permittam, praeter illos qui temporibus domni Siconis et Sicardi fuerunt christiani, si magarizati non sunt." *Radelgisi et Siginulfi divisio ducatus Beneventani*, c. 24, ed. F. Bluhme (1868),

the Beneventan rulers Sicone (817–33) and his son Sicardo (833–39), a number of Saracens—at least on two different occasions, if the text is taken literally—converted to Christianity in that Lombard duchy, under circumstances that remain unknown. Their Catholic steadfastness must have been rather questionable, as Radelchi takes into account the possibility of their apostasy, that is, of their return to Islam. The significant fact is that Saracen conversion did occur, and therefore, at least in some regions of southern Italy, the Christianization of Saracens could not have been regarded as entirely impracticable. Equally important is that this conversion took place in a Christian-ruled country.

If there was a precedent of Saracens accepting Christianity, and they were not universally regarded as a people who could not be converted, then the absence of attempts at missionizing among them becomes even more puzzling. Or had some attempts taken place and their failure discouraged further efforts? The sources are mute on this point, although it is possible that Ermold's statement about the Saracens' unwillingness to convert reflects some such experience. The sources, however, contain other relevant references, which point to a more specific answer.

AN EFFECTIVE DETERRENT: THE INTERDICTION OF ATTACKS AGAINST ISLAM

Most Catholic Europeans knew little or nothing about Muslim internal affairs. And yet the sources suggest that one facet of Islam must have been surprisingly well known: the absolute prohibition of attacks against the Muslim creed. The ban is first mentioned in a little-known version of the Passion of George, Aurelius, and Nathalia. The three belonged to a group of Spanish Christians who sought martyrdom in the 850s by publicly attacking the religion of their Muslim rulers, and whose deeds were described by Eulogius of Cordova, one of the last of that group to be executed. In 858, two monks of St. Germain-des-Prés, Usuard and Odilard, brought to France some relics of George, Aurelius, and Nathalia, as well as a variant version of the chapter of Eulogius's work that tells their story. This version, most probably prepared for the Frankish monks by Eulogius himself, contains a remark absent from the work as it survives in Spain: "The Saracens think that

in MGH LL 4:224. For the possible background of the conversion see M. Amari, *Storia dei Musulmani di Sicilia*, ed. C. A. Nallino, 3 vols. (Catania, 1933–39), 1:446, n. 1; p. 492; for the date of the treaty see G. Musca, *L'emirato di Bari, 847–871* (Bari, 1964), p. 37.

only those who leave their sect and turn to the Christian faith, and those who utter blasphemies against their Legislator, deserve death."[16] This clear-cut statement, undoubtedly meant for an audience unfamiliar with life under Muslim rule, must have reached a number of trans-Pyrenean readers, for the variant version is extant in seven manuscripts, most of which originate from Parisian monasteries; one is from the ninth, two from the tenth, one from the eleventh, and three from the thirteenth or fourteenth centuries.[17]

The same Muslim prohibition is also mentioned by two northern writers of the second half of the tenth century. The first, John of Metz, some time after 974 wrote the Life of John of Gorze, the abbot whom Otto I sent in 953 on a mission to Muslim Cordova. While describing the vicissitudes of the mission, John of Metz remarks that the very first law of the Saracens forbids, upon pain of death, any attack whatsoever against their religion.[18] A similar statement appears in Hrotsvitha of Gandersheim's Life of Pelagius, the Galician youth whom the Muslims executed in Cordova in 925. Hrotsvitha (d. ca. 1000), the astonishing canoness who assumed the unlikely task of extolling the chastity of holy virgins in a fashion modeled on Terence, knew less than nothing about Islam: She is the first Catholic European to depict the Saracens as veritable polytheists who adore idols made of gold and marble. (About a century later Saracen idolatry will reappear in the Song of Roland, and then become a stock motif of the *chansons de geste*.) But even in her northern-German Gandersheim Hrotsvitha knows that the Christians of Spain are forbidden, on pain of death, "to blaspheme the gods made of gold which the [Saracen] ruler adores."[19]

[16] "Ipsos enim solum vident saraceni interimendos, qui relicta eorum secta, vertunt se ad Xpistianam fidem; vel qui blasphemias garriunt adversus legislatorem suum." R. Jiménez Pedrajas, "San Eulogio de Córdoba, autor de la Pasión francesa de los mártires mozárabes cordobeses Jorge, Aurelio y Natalia," *Anthologica Annua* 17 (1970): 567–68. Jiménez Pedrajas prints in parallel columns the variant version brought to France, here edited critically for the first time, and the well-known Spanish version, extant only in the heavily retouched printed edition of 1574 by Ambrosio de Morales. (In the Spanish version Nathalia is called Sabigotho.)

[17] On these manuscripts see Jiménez Pedrajas, pp. 474–79.

[18] *Vita Iohannis abbatis Gorziensis auctore Iohanne abbate S. Arnulfi*, ed. G. H. Pertz (1841), in MGH SS 4:371, lines 33–35. The author, a friend of John of Gorze, began this work after John's death in 974. On John's mission see N. Daniel, *The Arabs and Mediaeval Europe* (London and Beirut, 1975), pp. 64–69. The date of the mission has been established by E. Ashtor, *The Jews of Moslem Spain*, trans. A. Klein and J. Klein, vol. 1 (Philadelphia, 1973), p. 421, n. 20.

[19] *Passio S. Pelagii*, lines 56–58, in *Hrotsvithae opera*, ed. P. Winterfeld (1902), in MGH Scr. rer. Germ. 34:53; M. Gonsalva Wiegand, trans., *The Non-Dramatic Works of Hrotsvitha* (St. Meinard, Ind., 1936), p. 131. Hrotsvitha's depiction of Pelagius's Sara-

It is possible to assume that the Catholic abstention from efforts to convert the Muslims resulted to a considerable extent from an awareness of the Muslim prohibition of attacks against their religion, attacks that were bound to be intrinsic to Catholic missionary efforts of that age. True, work among the pagans of the north and the east could sometimes also lead to the missionary's death—it is enough to mention Adalbert of Prague or Brun of Querfurt—but capital punishment was not an omnipresent threat as it was in the realm of Islam.[20] Even so, candidates for missionizing among the pagans were not always easy to recruit: The days of the enthusiastic Irish and Anglo-Saxon missionaries of the sixth, seventh, and eighth centuries had passed. Thus, when Louis the Pious looked in 826 for a missionary willing to go to heathen Denmark, he was told by the prelates of the realm that "in no wise do they know a man so devoted as to assume a voyage so dangerous."[21] This was so although the mission in question—ultimately undertaken by Ansgar, the "Apostle of the North,"—was planned by Louis as a supplementary step to a Frankish-engineered restoration of a baptized Danish ruler to his possessions in Denmark.

If that was the case under relatively favorable conditions, one should not be surprised that missionaries did not leave for the lands of the Saracens. Indeed, the Norman chronicler Orderic Vitalis, albeit of the twelfth century, explicitly states that fear deterred Christian teachers from entering the Saracen realm. In 1125, he relates, the Spanish Christians who had lived under Saracen rule told King Alfonso I of Aragon that their knowledge of Christianity was wanting because, while subjected to the infidels, they had not dared ask Roman or French teachers to come to them, "and those did not come to us [of their own accord] because of the barbarity of the pagans to whom we had

---

cen executors as idolaters should be contrasted with the tenth-century *Vita vel passio S. Pelagii*, written in Spain by the priest Raguel. Here the Saracen ruler tells Pelagius: "Grandis te honoris fascibus sublimabo, si . . . nostrum volueris Prophetam verum esse dicere." *España sagrada*, ed. H. Florez, vol. 23 (Madrid, 1767), p. 233. The notion of Saracen idolatry may have reached Hrotsvitha from Byzantium (see below n. 41); it is also possible that her *Pelagius* is modeled on the lives of martyrs from the times of the pagan Roman Empire. In contrast to the Song of Roland and the *chansons de geste*, Hrotsvitha's Saracen idols bear no names.

[20] Cutler has not taken this basic difference into account in his discussion of the absence of missionizing among the Muslims: Cutler, "Peter the Venerable," p. 187, n. 10.

[21] *Vita Anskarii auctore Rimberto*, ed. G. Waitz (1884), in MGH Scr. rer. Germ. 55:26–27. The purpose of this passage was probably to underline Ansgar's courage and devotion, but it would not have been effective had missionizing under such circumstances not been perceived as dangerous.

been subservient." If "Romans" and "Frenchmen" were indeed afraid to teach Christianity to their brethren living under Muslim rule, they must have been all the more frightened to preach Christianity to the Muslims themselves. In fact, a thirteenth-century pioneer of missionizing among the Muslims explicitly maintains that the past unwillingness to confront the Saracen religion resulted from the Saracen refusal to grant access to preachers intent on assailing their creed.[22]

The relative importance of the knowledge of the Muslim prohibition as a factor explaining the absence of Catholic missionizing among Muslims in early medieval times can be more accurately assessed once Catholic Christendom is compared, from this point of view, with the other Christendoms that faced Islam: the Christendoms, from Mesopotamia to Spain, that were subjected to Muslim rule, and the Byzantine Christendom. The traditional missionary frontiers of these Christendoms were not necessarily in the north and east, and with the possible exception of the Spanish Christians, they can by no means be considered culturally inferior to their Muslim neighbors. Nevertheless, these Christendoms also failed to launch missionary efforts among the Muslims.

The abstention did not stem from a general lack of interest in missionizing. The Nestorians living under Muslim rule attempted to spread their faith most vigorously. The Nestorian patriarch Timothy (ca. 728–823) was an especially energetic organizer of missions; like his Carolingian contemporaries, he dispatched monks to preach the Gospel and to serve as bishops in the converted regions. But these missionary efforts, like those of the Carolingians, were directed at pagans, not Muslims. This was so even though the Nestorians—and the Jacobites—living under Muslim rule could look back to successful missionary efforts among pre-Islamic Arabs. They had converted not only nomads who lived on the borders of Mesopotamia and Syria but also Arabs of Nadjrān, deep in the Arabian peninsula, and of the western coast of the Persian Gulf; in 585, when Muhammad was a young boy, a Nestorian council took place in Qatar.[23] But after the rise of Islam,

[22] *Orderici Vitalis Historiae Ecclesiasticae libri tredecim*, XIII, 6, ed. A. Le Prévost, vol. 5, Société de l'Histoire de France, Publications 79 (Paris, 1855; reprint, New York, 1965), p. 13. Jacques de Vitry, *Historia Hierosolimitana*, in J. Bongars, *Gesta Dei per Francos*, vol. 1 (Hanau, 1611), p. 1063; ed. F. Moschus (Douai, 1597; reprint, Farnborough, 1971), p. 44: "Nec inventus est aliquis vir Catholicus, qui se murum pro domo Domini tantae pesti valeret opponere, eo quod Saraceni contra legem suam praedicatores non admittunt."

[23] On Christian missionizing among pre-Islamic Arabs see F. Nau, *Les Arabes chrétiens de Mésopotamie et de Syrie du VIIᵉ au VIIIᵉ siècle* (Paris, 1933); C. A. Nallino, "Ebrei e Cristiani nell'Arabia preislamica," in *Raccolta di scritti editi e inediti*, vol. 3 (Rome, 1941),

no Nestorian missionary efforts in these directions are heard of. Even as Patriarch Timothy sent his monks to convert the idolaters in the regions bordering on the Caspian Sea, and established metropolitans in Turkestan and Tibet, remarking in one of his letters that "many monks cross the seas to India and China with only a rod and a scrip," there is nothing to hint that he, or any other Oriental Christian, ever contemplated mounting a missionary campaign at the Muslims of the Arabian peninsula, or indeed at those of Baghdad, among whom he lived.[24]

The Byzantines also could look back upon successful missionary activities among pre-Islamic Arabs. As early as the 340s, Emperor Constans I sent a missionary, whose efforts met with considerable success, to the southwestern part of the Arabian peninsula. Later emperors promoted the Christianization of various northern Arab tribes; anchorites converted nomads among whom they lived; and the Monophysites of Byzantium initiated missions. Thus the Arabs who lived on the borders of the Byzantine Empire were gradually converted to Christianity. After the rise of Islam, the Byzantines abstained from sending missionaries to the Muslims, even though they did dispatch missionaries during the same period to the pagans of the north and northeast. The mission of the brothers Constantine-Cyril and Methodius to the Slavs of Greater Moravia is the best-known attempt in this direction, but the Byzantines were also active among the pagans of

---

pp. 87–156; C.D.G. Müller, *Kirche und Mission unter den Arabern in vorislamischer Zeit* (Tübingen, 1967).

[24] On Timothy's efforts see *The Book of Governors: The Historia Monastica of Thomas, Bishop of Margâ, A.D. 840*, ed. and trans. E.A.W. Budge, vol. 2 (London, 1893), pp. 467–513. (On one of the missionary monks who, like Boniface a few decades earlier, succeeded in his mission only after having axed down the "mighty oak tree" of the pagans, see pp. 511–13.) For the quotation see O. Braun, "Ein Brief des Katholikos Timotheos I über biblische Studien des 9. Jahrhunderts," *Oriens Christianus: Römische Halbjahrhefte für die Kunde des christlichen Orients* 1 (1901): 309–11; *Timothei patriarchae I epistulae*, ed. O. Braun, CSCO. Syri, 67 (1915), Letter 13, p. 70. For general accounts of the Nestorian mission see F. Nau, "L'expansion nestorienne en Asie," *Annales du Musée Guimet: Bibliothèque de Vulgarisation* 40 (1913): 193–388; L. E. Browne, *The Eclipse of Christianity in Asia: From the Time of Muhammad till the Fourteenth Century* (Cambridge, 1933), pp. 93–108; for a recent summary see W. Hage, "Der Weg nach Asien: Die ostsyrische Missionskirche," in *Die Kirche des früheren Mittelalters*, ed. K. Schäferdiek, vol. 1 (Munich, 1978), pp. 360–66, 539–41.

Timothy might have been guided by his conciliatory attitude toward Islam, which was not shared by all the Nestorians of his day. One of Timothy's pupils, as well as his secretary, wrote polemical tracts against Islam; see G. Graf, *Geschichte der christlichen arabischen Literatur*, vol. 2, *Die Schriftsteller bis zur Mitte des 15. Jahrhunderts*, Studi e Testi, 133 (Città del Vaticano, 1947), p. 118.

Bulgaria, Kiev Rus', the Crimea, and Khazaria.[25] It is true that a Byzantine hagiographical source does mention a case of preaching Christianity in a Saracen country: Elias the Younger (823–903), a Sicilian saint carried off in his youth to North Africa, is said to have persuaded a number of Saracens to convert to Christianity. But from the present point of view, it is significant that the Life of Elias portrays him not as coming to North Africa in order to spread the Gospel, but as having been forcibly abducted and taken there from his native Sicily.[26]

The fact that even those Christendoms that had sent missionaries to the Arabian south before the rise of Islam, and were undoubtedly capable of engaging in theological disputes with the Muslims, did not attempt to evangelize them enhances the probability that the Muslim prohibition against attacks on their religion was the underlying cause behind the Christian abstention from missionizing among them. Daunted by the Muslim interdiction, the Christians—Nestorians, Byzantines, and Catholic Europeans alike—chose the route of lesser resistance, dispatching missionaries to the less-refractory pagans of their respective norths and northeasts, where the danger seemed less and past gains held the promise of future success.

A Residual Possibility: Preaching by Invective

Only on the rare occasions when dread of punishment at the hands of the Muslims was surmounted could verbal attacks on Islam take place. But for the few individuals who overcame the barrier of fear, the quest of a martyr's death at the hands of the Muslims was far more important than the wish to actually convert them, and the superiority of Christianity was mainly proclaimed by publicly vilifying Islam. In the Orient, this provocative stance was assumed by the solitary figure of Peter of Capitolias, Trans-Jordan, a hermit who—according to his Life,

---

[25] On the Byzantine missions to the pre-Islamic Arabs see (in addition to the works quoted in n. 23) I. Engelhardt, *Mission und Politik in Byzanz: Ein Beitrag zur Strukturanalyse byzantinischer Mission zur Zeit Justins und Justinians*, Miscellanea Byzantina Monacensia, 19 (Munich, 1974), pp. 90–100, 158–62, 171–73. On the missions to the pagans, see G. Ostrogorsky, "The Byzantine Background of the Moravian Mission," *Dumbarton Oaks Papers* 19 (1965): 1–18. For a recent general survey, see Ch. Hannick, "Die byzantinischen Missionen," in *Die Kirche des früheren Mittelalters*, 1:279–359.

[26] *Vita di Sant'Elia il Giovane*, ed. and trans. G. Rossi Taibbi (Palermo, 1962), chaps. 16–17, 23–24, pp. 24–27, 32–37. Chapter 16 is of considerable importance for the history of the Christians of Muslim North Africa.

The Saracen invaders of the Peloponnesus in the tenth century were also said to have converted under the influence of a local saint; for that incident, see J. Meyendorff, "Byzantine Views of Islam," *Dumbarton Oaks Papers* 18 (1964): 131.

extant only in a Georgian translation—developed a vehement craving for martyrdom, and in 715 succeeded in bringing death upon himself by openly denouncing Muhammad and his creed. (Significantly, the Life reveals that the death penalty was passed reluctantly. The district commander—in strict accordance with Muslim legislation—first ordered that Peter's sanity be established and then offered him the chance to recant and escape punishment.)[27] In Muslim Spain, on the other hand, the same stance was adopted in the 850s by the fifty men and women (many of them offspring of mixed, Muslim-Christian marriages) who are known as the martyrs of Cordova.[28] There was also a Frank from Gaul named Vulfura who, yearning for martyrdom, came to Cordova, aroused the ire of the Saracens, and, after refusing to renounce Christianity, was executed in 931.[29]

[27] The Georgian text is summarized, not *sine ira et studio*, by P. Peeters, "La passion de S. Pierre de Capitolias," *Analecta Bollandiana* 57 (1939): 301–16. Peter of Capitolias is probably Peter of Maiumas mentioned in Theophanes's *Chronographia*, 1:416–17; cf. 2:271.

For the Muslim legislation on apostasy and blasphemy see E. Sachau, *Muhammedanisches Recht nach schafiitischer Lehre* (Stuttgart and Berlin, 1897), pp. 812, 843–46; T. W. Juynboll, "Apostasy (Muhammadan)," in *Encyclopaedia of Religion and Ethics*, vol. 1 (Edinburgh, 1908), pp. 625–26; idem, "Blasphemy," ibid., vol. 2 (Edinburgh, 1909), p. 672. Most jurists held that apostates should be encouraged to recant, and the following Oriental Christian Lives (as well as the Lives of the Cordovan enthusiasts; see below) indicate that this was followed in practice: Peeters, "La passion," pp. 330–33 (on the Armenian Vahan, d. 737); K. Schulze, trans., "Das Martyrium des heiligen Abo von Tiflis," in *Texte und Untersuchungen zur Geschichte der altchristlichen Literatur* NF 13, 4 (Leipzig, 1905), pp. 11–41 (Abo was executed in 786); F. Combefis, *Christi martyrum lecta trias* (Paris, 1666), pp. 100–112 (on the Palestinian Daḥḥāk-Bacchus, d. ca. 806, about whom see also PG 117:211–14). Vahan, Abo, and Daḥḥāk, unlike Peter of Capitolias, were punished for having converted to Christianity.

[28] The most exhaustive studies of the affair are those of F. R. Franke, "Die freiwilligen Märtyrer von Cordova und das Verhältnis der Mozaraber zum Islam (nach den Schriften von Speraindeo, Eulogius, und Alvar)," *Gesammelte Aufsätze zur Kulturgeschichte Spaniens* 13 (1958): 1–170, and E. P. Colbert, *The Martyrs of Córdoba*. See also A. Cutler, "The Ninth-Century Spanish Martyrs' Movement and the Origins of Western Christian Missions to the Muslims," *Muslim World* 55 (1965): 321–39, countered by J. Waltz, "The Significance of the Voluntary Martyrs of Ninth-Century Córdoba," ibid., 60 (1970): 143–59, 226–36; and N. Daniel, *The Arabs*, chap. 2.

[29] *Vita Argentee et comitum eius martyrum*, ed. A. Fabréga Grau, in *Pasionário hispánico (siglos VII–XI)*, 2 vols. (Madrid and Barcelona, 1953–55), 2:382–87; see also 1:238–39. The *Vita* does not explicitly state that Vulfura assailed Islam, but the phrases used to describe his zealous act and the Saracens' violent reaction and the customary choice given him between renouncing Christianity and death (2:385–86) suggest that he had done so. His companion, Argentea, was probably the daughter of 'Umar b. Ḥafṣūn, the rebel who converted to the Christianity of his forefathers in 899 and held his own for decades in southern Andalusia.

Paul Alvar, a Cordovan contemporary of the enthusiasts who went to their death in the 850s, presented their public avowals of Christianity and attacks on Islam as acts of preaching. Error, so writes Alvar in a key passage in his defense of these "Saints of God," should be openly attacked: That was the purpose of Christ's ministry, and the acts of the prophets and the Apostles. Moreover, according to Matthew 24:14, the End of the World will not come unless the Gospel be preached to all creatures; and this preaching Alvar interprets as the proclamation of the faith to the unbelievers, not the believers, a proclamation to be made at the risk of one's life even as the Apostles had done. But among the Saracens, no Christian preacher had appeared—until the Cordovan enthusiasts arose and preached the Gospel to them, rendering thereby the End of Days closer.[30]

It is true that Isaac, the first of the Cordovan "spontaneous martyrs"—the expression is Alvar's—did invite his Muslim judge to embrace Christianity, and that Eulogius, the chronicler of the events and a central figure, did preach the Gospel to the amir's councilors shortly before his execution.[31] But these were clearly acts of defiance, not attempts at persuasion. The few individuals of Muslim parenthood who, like the Cordovan enthusiasts Nathalia and Leocritia, converted to Christianity in that age did so under the secret influence of their Christian relatives, not because of public invectives or exhortations by the seekers of spontaneous martyrdom. Nor is there evidence that the enthusiasts' steadfastness in the face of death affected their Muslim contemporaries. "None of the Infidels was worthy to be called to the faith of Christ in that time," admits the anonymous author of the Passion of Nunilón and Alodia. (The two, daughters of a Muslim father and a Christian mother, were executed in 851 at Huesca for clinging to

---

[30] Alvar, *Indiculus luminosus*, c. 10, in *Corpus scriptorum Muzarabicorum*, ed. J. Gil, 2 vols. (Madrid, 1973), 1:281–82 (= PL 121:524–25). The crucial passage is "Puto quod in hac Ismahelitica gente nullus actenus extitit predicator per quod deuitores fidei tenerentur. Isti enim, ut ita dicam, apostolatus uicem in eosdem et euangelium predicatjonem inpleuerunt eosque deuitores fidei reddiderunt. . . ." (Gil, 1:282). I find no justification for Colbert's suggestion (*The Martyrs*, p. 278, n. 41) that *puto* here means *dubito*.

Again, Eulogius regards preaching as a binding duty: *Memoriale Sanctorum*, I, 25 (Gil, 2:389; PL 115:758).

[31] On Isaac, see Eulogius, *Memoriale Sanctorum*, prefatio in primum librum, c. 2 (Gil, 2:367; PL 115:736–37). On Eulogius, see Alvar, *Vita Eulogii*, c. 15 (Gil, 1:340; PL 115:717). For an English translation of Alvar's Life of Eulogius see C. M. Sage, *Paul Albar of Cordoba: Studies on His Life and Writings* (Washington, D.C., 1943), pp. 190–214. For similar cases see *Memoriale Sanctorum*, II, 13;. III, 10, 11 (Gil, 2:432–33, 451, 454).

their Christian faith.)[32] Yet Alvar—and Eulogius—did not really expect the Saracens to convert in the wake of the enthusiasts' public proclamations. The crucial fact was that the enthusiasts assumed the office of apostle (*apostolatus vicem*) to the Saracens. For Christ did not say that the End of the World would follow the *acceptance* of the Gospel by all creature; the necessary prerequisite was the *preaching* to all. Therefore, the enthusiasts hastened the Last Days and also rendered the Saracens 'debtors of the faith' (*devitores fidei*), who henceforward would suffer eternal damnation for having spurned it.[33] The Cordovan apostles to Islam were thus hailed for procuring the damnation of the Muslims rather than for securing their salvation.

Alvar's originality in pointing out the need for Christian preachers among the Saracens was matched by his pioneering advocacy of a holy war against them. (An early student of the Cordovan enthusiasts, von Baudissin, believed that it is Alvar's "unquiet Jewish blood" that is revealed in his ardor.)[34] Elaborating on one of Jerome's letters, Alvar argued that just as the prophet Elijah stood up against the prophets of Baal not only with words but also with the sword, Moses and Samuel were cruel to the worshipers of the golden calf and to Agag, and Peter and Paul severe to Simon Magus, Anania, and Sapphira, so now contempt of the Divinity should be countered by recourse to 'holy cruelty' (*sancta crudelitas*). "Piety for God," Alvar quotes approvingly from one of Jerome's epistles, "is indeed no cruelty."[35] And Eu-

[32] The text has been edited by J. Gil, "En torno a las Santas Nunilón y Alodia," *Revista de la Universidad de Madrid* 19, no. 74 (1970): 113–22; the quotation appears on p. 122. Because of the infidels' unworthiness, so argues the author of the Passion, God did not allow miracles to be performed through these martyrs. The author also states (p. 113) that in 851 the Saracen ruler *Abderrahaman* proclaimed that the offspring of mixed Christian-Saracen marriages must choose between renouncing Christianity and death. This proclamation should be considered one of the causes behind the wave of voluntary martyrdoms.

For a much shorter account about Nunilón and Alodia see Eulogius, *Memoriale Sanctorum*, II, 7 (Gil, 2:406–8; PL 115:774–76).

[33] See n. 30 above. On the culpability of the infidel who spurns Christian preaching see also Eulogius, *Memoriale Sanctorum*, I, 25 (Gil, 2:389; PL 115:758). Cf. Franke, "Die freiwilligen Märtyrer," p. 26. The idea, of course, goes back to Mark 16:15–16.

[34] W. W. von Baudissin, *Eulogius und Alvar: Ein Abschnitt spanischer Kirchengeschichte aus der Zeit der Maurenherrschaft* (Leipzig, 1872), p. 51.

[35] Alvar, *Indiculus luminosus*, c. 11 (Gil, 1:283–85; PL 121:525–27); cf. *Epistolae S. Hieronymi*, in PL 22:908 (Jerome's formulation made its way into C.23 q.8 c.13). Elsewhere Alvar writes, "Et certe plus est iuxta nos ut Elias gladio decertare quam lingua ut nostri heroes adversare." *Indiculus luminosus*, c. 6 (Gil, 1:278; PL 121:521). His advocacy of *sancta crudelitas* is echoed by the anonymous author of the *Crónica Albeldense*, who, writing in Christian Spain in the last third of the ninth century, remarks that the Spanish Christians fight the Saracens day and night, "dum predestinatio usque divina

logius, alluding to Samuel's execution of Agag, declares that were Muhammad still alive, Christians should not recoil from putting him to death.[36] Thus the embryonic contemplation of a Christian mission to the Muslims is accompanied by a rudimentary advocacy of holy warfare against them.

Holy cruelty, however, was not a practical proposition in ninth-century Cordova. And preaching, largely assuming the form of anti-Islamic invective, was taken up—in Cordova as in Capitolias—only by the few who were willing to suffer a martyr's death.

THE REASONS FOR CATHOLIC DISINTEREST: A COMPARATIVE APPROACH

Absence of organized missionary activity is not the shibboleth that distinguishes the Catholic European stance toward Islam from that of the Christendoms of the Orient, Byzantium, and Muslim Spain in the early Middle Ages. Catholic Europe of that age stands in sharp contrast to the other Christendoms by its lack of intellectual interest in Islam as a religion.

The Oriental Christians who lived under Muslim rule dealt with Islam in a large number of apologetic and polemical works, the earliest dating probably from the seventh century. These works took the form of epistles, tractates, single-theme dialogues in which the parties are summarily identified as "Christian" and "Saracen," full-scale discussions between prominent exponents of the two faiths, and the Apocalypse of Baḥīrā, which amounts to a Christian account of the rise of Islam. Most of the works are in Arabic; some are in Syriac or Greek, for example, John Damascene's influential chapter entitled The Deceptive Superstition of the Ishmaelites. Some of the writings attempt to prove the truth of Christianity by adducing Biblical quotations; some—like a Christian-Muslim dialogue partially preserved on an eighth-century papyrus—endeavor to do so by quoting from the Koran; other works, especially those by Yaḥyā b. ʿAdī (d. 974, Baghdad) and his

---

dehinc eos expelli crudeliter jubeat." M. Gómez-Moreno, ed., "Las primeras crónicas de la Reconquista: el ciclo de Alfonso III," *Boletín de la Real Academia de la Historia* 100 (1932): 601.

[36] Eulogius, *Memoriale Sanctorum*, I, 20 (Gil, 2:384; PL 115:753–54). Did Eulogius really say, in so many words, that "magni meriti esse credo subuertere impios, ecclesiae hostibus contraire, *bellum parare incredulis* et framea uerbi Dei concidere aduersarios fidei," or is it once more the heavy hand of the sixteenth-century editor Ambrosio de Morales? On the advocacy of violence see also Heisig, "Die Geschichtsmetaphysik," pp. 14, 16–17; Franke, "Die freiwilligen Märtyrer," pp. 26–27.

followers, use rational arguments. Attitudes toward Islam range from the conciliatory posture of the Nestorian patriarch Timothy, whose Parable of the Pearl sounds like an early prefiguration of the Parable of the Three Rings made famous by Boccaccio and Lessing, to the militant stance of the anonymous, probably tenth-century author of the letter attributed to al-Kindi, who urges his Muslim correspondent to admit that Islam is the Law of Satan, of wrongdoing and of evil, assails Muhammad's morality, and alleges that his repudiation of idolatry was less than total. The writer so bluntly derides Muslim rites that Sir William Muir, the Victorian summarizer of the letter, felt constrained to skip several passages he considered "both childish and indelicate," "gross and offensive," or even "at once silly and grossly improper." (It is symptomatic that the militant letter attributed to al-Kindi was translated into Latin in the twelfth century, and had a considerable impact on later Catholic European writers, whereas Timothy's conciliatory parable remained unknown in the West until the present century.)[37]

The Byzantine literary output, though less voluminous than the Oriental Christian, but almost as varied, includes hostile chronicle accounts of the rise of Muhammad and his religion, tractates and letters attempting to refute Islam, Christian-Muslim disputations incorporated into saints' Lives, a formula for the abjuration of Islam, and even

[37] A comparative study of Oriental Christian works dealing with Islam, irrespective of the language in which they were written, remains a desideratum. Most works are referred to or dealt with by G. Graf, *Geschichte der christlichen arabischen Literatur*, vol. 2; G. Troupeau, "La littérature arabe chrétienne du Xe au XIIe siècle," *Cahiers de civilisation médiévale* 14 (1971): 1–20; D. J. Sahas, *John of Damascus on Islam: The "Heresy of the Ishmaelites"* (Leiden, 1972); A. Baumstark, *Geschichte der syrischen Literatur* (Bonn, 1922), p. 211. Syriac and Arabic versions of the Apocalypse of Baḥīrā were edited and translated by R. Gottheil, "A Christian Bahira Legend," *Zeitschrift für Assyriologie* 13 (1898): 189–242; 14 (1899): 203–68; 15 (1900–1901): 56–102; 17 (1903): 125–66. For the dialogue preserved on an eighth-century papyrus see G. Graf, "Christlich-arabische Texte: Zwei Disputationen zwischen Muslimen und Christen," *Veröffentlichungen aus den badischen Papyrus-Sammlungen* 5 (1934): 1–24. For Timothy's Parable of the Pearl see A. Mingana, ed. and trans., "The Apology of Timothy the Patriarch before the Caliph Mahdi," *Bulletin of the John Rylands Library* 12 (1928): 224–25; see also L. E. Browne, "The Patriarch Timothy and the Caliph al-Mahdi," *Moslem World* 21 (1931): 38–45. (A comparative study of the motif, from Timothy to Lessing, is the subject of a forthcoming article of mine.) The twelfth-century Latin translation of the letter attributed to al-Kindi was edited by J. Muñoz Sendino, "Al-Kindi, Apología del Cristianismo," in *Miscelánea Comillas*, 11–12 (Comillas, Santander, 1949), pp. 337–460; partial translation into English by W. Muir, *The Apology of Al Kindy Written at the Court of Al Mamun in Defence of Christianity against Islam* (London, 1882), with Muir's observations appearing on p. 37, n. 1. See also G. Troupeau, "al-Kindī," in *Encyclopaedia of Islam*, 2d ed.

a poem in Arabic, sent to a caliph of Baghdad, that concludes with an attack on Muhammad.[38] Indeed anti-Islamic arguments seem to have spread among educated Byzantines from a relatively early date. Thus when the Muslims wrested the Sicilian town of Syracuse from the Byzantines in 878, and the captured bishop was led before the amir of Palermo, the following exchange, according to an eyewitness, took place:

Amir (speaking through his interpreter): Do you perform our prayer?

Bishop: No.

Amir: Why?

Bishop: Because I am a priest of Christ and a mystagogue of the rites of His beneficial sacrament, whom many prophets and just men did foretell.

Amir: Do we not also have prophets?

Bishop: Yours are prophets but in name, not in preachings and just ways; wicked they walk around.

Amir: Why do you visit blasphemies upon our Prophet?

Bishop: We priests do not blaspheme prophets, because we were not taught to speak against prophets but about them. But your prophet we acknowledge not.[39]

The bishop was evidently acquainted with some of the typical arguments against Muhammad's prophethood, namely, that his life and teachings fell short of the standards for a prophet and his mission was not foretold. Not surprisingly, the bishop's exhibition of familiarity with anti-Islamic argumentation led to his prompt relegation to prison.

[38] The most recent survey is by A.-Th. Khoury, *Les théologiens byzantins et l'Islam: Textes et auteurs (VIIIᵉ–XIIIᵉ s.)* (Louvain and Paris, 1969), idem, *Polémique byzantine contre l'Islam (VIIIᵉ–XIIIᵉ s.)* (Leiden, 1972). For the disputations appearing in saints' Lives, see notes 26 above and 101 below. For the Arabic poem see G. von Grünebaum, "Eine poetische Polemik zwischen Byzanz und Bagdad im X. Jahrhundert," in *Studia Arabica*, vol. 1. Analecta Orientalia, 14 (Rome, 1937), pp. 47–50, 53–59. Several Byzantine and Oriental Christian texts appear in French translation in the lively selection by A. Ducellier, *Le miroir de l'Islam: Musulmans et Chrétiens d'Orient au Moyen Age (VII–XI siècles)* (Paris, 1971).

[39] The pertinent passage of the report by the eyewitness, the monk Theodosius, survives only in two divergent Latin translations of the seventeenth century, printed in A. Piccoli, *De antico iure ecclesiae Siculae dissertatio* (Messina, 1623), p. 145, and in Muratori, *RR. SS. II.*, 1, 2 (Milan, 1725), p. 264. I follow the translation in Piccoli, which is evidently more reliable; cf. C. O. Zuretti, "La espugnazione di Siracusa nell'880: Testo greco della lettera del monaco Teodosio," in *Centenario della nascita di Michele Amari*, vol. 1 (Palermo, 1910), pp. 171–72. See also B. Lavagnini, "Siracusa occupata dagli Arabi e l'epistola di Teodosio Monaco," *Byzantion* 29–30 (1959–60): 267–79.

The most influential Byzantine anti-Islamic work was the Refutation of the Book Forged by Moámet the Arab, which Nicetas of Byzantium wrote in the middle of the ninth century. Nicetas was conversant with the Koran and criticized it in great detail, discussing suras 2 to 18 one by one, as well as several of the later chapters. But whether through genuine misunderstanding or otherwise, he asserted that the Koran presents God as "all-spherical" or "of hammer-beaten metal," and proceeded to deride the Muslims for adhering to so corporeal a conception of God.[40] Elaborating on a tradition that may be traced back to the first half of the eighth century, Nicetas also claimed that Muhammad commanded the Saracens to adore at Baka (= Mecca) an idol, purportedly patterned after Aphrodite, and concluded that the religion of Muhammad is idolatrous at bottom.[41] But there probably were Byzantines whose stance was more conciliatory, for Nicetas argues against the opinion that the Agarens (= Saracens) worship the true God.[42] A similarly conciliatory view may be discerned in a letter of 913 or 914 sent by Patriarch Nicholas of Constantinople, the de facto ruler of the empire at the time, to the caliph al-Muqtadir. In this oft-quoted letter the patriarch states that "we [he and the caliph] have obtained the gift of our authorities from a common Head," probably implying that both of them share the belief in one and the same God.[43] But only in the twelfth century did a Byzantine openly express the opinion that Christians and Saracens believe in the same God, a statement that led to a major internal clash.[44]

Even the Christians of Muslim Spain, who were probably closer

---

[40] *Nicetae Byzantini Philosophi confutatio falsi libri quem scripsit Mohamedes Arabs*, in PG 105:707–8, 775–76; cf. Meyendorff, "Byzantine Views of Islam," p. 122; Khoury, *Polémique*, pp. 338–41.

[41] PG 105:793B. For a discussion of this motif in the Greek works see W. Eichner, "Die Nachrichten über den Islam bei den Byzantinern," *Der Islam* 23 (1936): 234–41; see also Meyendorff, p. 119 (on the little-known statement by Germanus of Constantinople, ca. 725), and Khoury, *Polémique*, pp. 275–81, 341–44.
Already in the chronicle of John of Nikiu, the Coptic bishop who writes in the late seventh century, the Muslims are called idolaters: *The Chronicle of John, Bishop of Nikiu*, trans. R. H. Charles (London, 1916), chap. 121, p. 201. But did the term occur in John's original Greek text, or was it introduced by the translator into Arabic or Ethiopian?

[42] PG 105:801–2. Cf. Khoury, *Théologiens*, p. 161, n. 55.

[43] R.J.H. Jenkins and L. G. Westerink, ed. and trans., *Nicholas I, Patriarch of Constantinople: Letters* (Washington, D.C., 1973), pp. 3–4, 525–26. Cf. Meyendorff, p. 128, and Julia Gauss, "Toleranz und Intoleranz zwischen Christen und Muslimen in der Zeit vor den Kreuzzügen," *Saeculum* 19 (1968): 363 (but the unequivocal formulations by Meyendorff and Gauss are not warranted by the text; see also n. 89 below).

[44] See chap. 2 below.

culturally to their Catholic brethren north of the Pyrenees than to the Christians of the Orient or Byzantium, engaged in polemics with Islam. From the late eighth or early ninth century there existed in Muslim Spain a short, polemic text called Note on Mahmeth—thus is Muhammad's name spelled in two tenth-century manuscripts of this Latin account—which portrays the Prophet as a concupiscent heresiarch who called on "his brute Arabs" to abandon idolatry and adore a "corporeal God" (*Deum corporeum*) in heaven. (The last statement might be compared with Nicetas's assertion that the Koran presents God as "all-spherical.") Abbot Speraindeo, the teacher of Eulogius and Alvar of Cordova, wrote an anti-Islamic tract that seems to have consisted of Christian answers to Muslim objections; his writings exhibit remarkable parallels to a roughly contemporary work describing a Christian-Muslim disputation allegedly held in Jerusalem around the year 800. Eulogius and Alvar, while defending the Cordovan enthusiasts, frequently take issue with Islam, and the Cordovan abbot Samson (d. 890) mentions that he defended his faith in disputation with Christians, Jews, and Arabs.[45]

The Spanish Christian writers living under Muslim rule seem to have adopted, on balance, a more vehement tone than their Oriental counterparts. Whereas in the letter attributed to al-Kindi and in the Apocalypse of Baḥīrā, Muhammad's followers eventually find his putrid body after waiting for him to rise from the dead after three days, in the Spanish Note on Mahmeth dogs devour the putrid corpse.[46] Abbot Speraindeo brands the Saracen Paradise a brothel.[47] And several writers explicitly assert that the origin of Muhammad's revelations was diabolical.[48] But this radical stance, which probably paved the way for

[45] The Note on Mahmeth, which survives in two versions, has been edited by M. C. Díaz y Díaz, "Los textos antimahometanos más antiguos en codices españoles," *Archives d'histoire doctrinale et littéraire du Moyen Age* 45 (1970): 153, 157–59. The editor persuasively argues for a Mozarab origin of the work (pp. 154–56).

The four manuscripts that contain the longer version (three dating from the tenth and one from the twelfth century) have *Deum corporeum*. The 1574 printed edition has *Deum incorporeum*, but this may be an emendation by Morales (p. 157, apparatus). The parallels between Speraindeo and the Disputation of Jerusalem have been discovered by Franke, "Die freiwilligen Märtyrer," pp. 50–58; see also Colbert, *The Martyrs*, pp. 157–62. On Samson see *Samsonis Apologeticus*, II, 4 (Gil, 2:571); for the background, Ashtor, *The Jews*, pp. 91–92.

[46] Muñoz Sendino, "Al-Kindi," p. 410; Muir, p. 17; Gottheil, "Legend," *Zeitschrift für Assyriologie* 14 (1899): 215, 250–51; Díaz y Díaz, "Los textos," pp. 153 (version A), 159 (version B).

[47] Quoted by Eulogius in his *Memoriale Sanctorum*, I, 7 (Gil, 2:376; PL 115:745).

[48] Díaz y Díaz, "Los textos," p. 157 (for the Note on Mahmeth); Gil, "En torno a las Santas Nunilón y Alodia," p. 114; Alvar, *Indiculus luminosus*, c. 25: "demone illo qui

the outbreak of religious fervor in the 850s, was not adopted by all Spanish Christians living under Muslim rule. Indeed Eulogius had to defend the Cordovan enthusiasts against fellow Christians who claimed that they were not to be considered martyrs, because they had not been killed by pagans but "by men who worship God and acknowledge heavenly laws," and because they had been executed after having been invited, "not to the sacrileges of the idols, but to the cult of the true God."[49] These statements, unfortunately known only through the sixteenth-century, printed edition of Eulogius's works, indicate that there were Spanish Christians who, not unlike the Nestorian patriarch Timothy, regarded Islam as a religion containing some elements of truth.

The polemic and apologetic works of the Oriental, Byzantine, and Spanish Christians still await a systematic comparison.[50] But even a cursory examination reveals that a number of themes recur in all three geographical areas. One of these, which will quite surprisingly re-emerge under a different guise at a later stage of the present inquiry, is the repudiation of the Islamic Holy War, usually contrasted with the peaceful spread of Christianity. Nicetas of Byzantium bitterly rebukes Muhammad for having authorized the slaying of those who introduce an associate at the side of God, specifically the Christians, and insists that all slaughter be shunned.[51] Alvar juxtaposes Christ, who taught peace and forbearance, to Muhammad, who brought war and sword upon innocents, and whose followers seek to wage war upon all "as if by God's command."[52] In Oriental Christian literature, this theme is variously developed. For instance, in the Christian-Mus-

---

ei sub persona Gabrihelis apparuit" (Gil, 1:299; PL 121:540); also, c. 8 (Gil, 1:280; PL 121:523); Eulogius, *Memoriale Sanctorum*, I, 8 (Gil, 2:377; PL 115:746); Díaz y Díaz, pp. 163–64 (Gil, 2:709–10), for a text in which a wicked angel persuades the monk Ozim to adopt the name *Mahomad*. L. Vázquez de Parga ("Algunas notas sobre el Pseudo Metodio y España," *Habis* 2 [1971]: 152) believes that the last-mentioned text antedates the ninth century. For later Latin versions in which the monk and Muhammad are fused into one person see A. d'Ancona, "Il Tesoro di Brunetto Latini versificato," *Atti della R. Accademia nazionale dei Lincei: Memorie della classe di scienze morali, storiche e filologiche*, 4th ser., 4 (1888): 205–27.

[49] "praesertim cum ab hominibus Deum colentibus et caelestia iura fatentibus compendiosa morte perempti sunt." Eulogius, *Liber apostolicus martyrum*, 3 (Gil, 2:477–78; PL 115:854B). "Dicunt enim quod ab hominibus Deum et legem colentibus passi sunt, nec ad sacrilegia idolorum, sed ad cultum ueri Dei inuitati perempti sunt." *Liber apostolicus martyrum*, 12 (Gil, 2:481; PL 115:857C).

[50] The potentialities of such an approach are suggested by the studies of Franke, "Die freiwilligen Märtyrer," pp. 27–67, and Schwinges, *Kreuzzugsideologie*, pp. 68–104.

[51] PG 105:835–42; cf. Khoury, *Théologiens*, p. 133.

[52] Alvar, *Indiculus luminosus*, c. 33 (Gil, 1:311; PL 121:552).

lim disputation that allegedly took place in Jerusalem, the monk Abraham of Tiberias emphasizes that converts to Christianity took the faith, not out of fear or for the sake of worldly goods, but because of the tenets preached to them and the miracles they witnessed.[53] On a more abstract plane the theme is dealt with by the Nestorian physician and philosopher Ḥunayn b. Isḥāq (d. ca. 875) in the tractate entitled On the Manner of Recognizing the Truth of a Religion. Whether a religion be true or false, argues Ḥunayn, can be ascertained by examining the motives that originally led men to adhere to it. First among the reasons for adopting a false religion is violence and the hope for material advantages, whereas witnessing miracles is adduced as the first reason for embracing a true religion.[54] And in the letter attributed to al-Kindi, the author first emphasizes that the Apostles propagated their faith by spreading the Gospel, performing miracles, and leading an exemplary life, and then exclaims, "How different this from the life of thy Master and his Companions, who ceased not to go forth in battle and rapine, to smite with the sword, to seize the little ones, and ravish wives and maidens. . . . Look now at the lives of Simon and Paul, who went about healing the sick, and raising the dead, by the name of Christ our Lord; and mark the contrast."[55] (The contrast was duly marked by many Catholic European writers from the twelfth century onward. Even a well-known contemporary historian of the crusades writes that "unlike Christianity, which preached a peace that it never achieved, Islam unashamedly came with a sword.")[56]

The intellectual altercation with Islam in the Orient, Byzantium, and

[53] K. Vollers, trans., "Das Religionsgespräch von Jerusalem (um 800 D) aus dem Arabischen übersetzt," *Zeitschrift für Kirchengeschichte* 29 (1908): 63; see also p. 39. For similar Christian arguments see P. Peeters, "La passion de S. Michel le Sabaïte," *Analecta Bollandiana* 48 (1930): 72; *Gregorii Barhebraei Chronicon ecclesiasticum*, ed. and trans. J.-B. Abeloos and T. J. Lamy, vol. 3 (Paris and Louvain, 1877), p. 136.

[54] L. Cheikho, ed. and trans., "Un traité inédit de Ḥonein," in *Orientalische Studien Theodor Nöldeke zum 70. Geburtstag gewidmet*, ed. C. Bezold, vol. 1 (Giessen, 1906), pp. 284–90; on pp. 287 and 291 appears a similar argument by Abū Rā'iṭa, the Jacobite bishop of Takrit, Iraq, in the early ninth century. On Ḥunayn see also R. Haddad, "Ḥunayn ibn Isḥāq apologiste chrétien," *Arabica* 21 (1974): 292–302.

[55] Muir, *The Apology*, pp. 57–58. (The passage does not appear in the Latin translation: Muñoz Sendino, "Al-Kindi," p. 455.) At the other end of the continuum of Oriental Christian writings, the Nestorian patriarch Timothy praises Muhammad for having used force against the idolaters, and draws a parallel with Moses, who killed the worshipers of the golden calf: Mingana, "The Apology," p. 197 (translation of Syriac version); Browne, *The Eclipse*, p. 113 (translation of Arabic version).

[56] On the motif in Catholic writings, see N. Daniel, *Islam and the West: The Making of an Image* (Edinburgh, 1960), pp. 74–77, 123–27; for the quotation, see S. Runciman, *A History of the Crusades*, 3 vols. (Cambridge, 1951–54), 1:15.

Muslim Spain had no parallels whatever in early medieval Europe. The one man who exhibited some interest in polemics with Islam was Charlemagne. Some time in 799 he asked Alcuin for "the disputation of Felix with a Saracen." Alcuin, whose letter is the only source on the matter, answered that he had neither seen nor heard of it, but according to his men Bishop Laidrad of Lyons might have it, and he sent a messenger posthaste to fetch the work for the king. A disputation with a Jew, Alcuin added, he did hear when he passed through Pavia in his youth.[57] It remains unknown whether the text of Felix's disputation was ever found, but Alcuin's letter leaves no doubt that Charlemagne wanted to learn about Christian arguments against the beliefs of the Saracens. (It also suggests that Alcuin himself considered the religion of the Saracens a challenge somehow resembling that of Judaism.)[58] Yet in this respect, as in so many others, Charlemagne was head and shoulders above the men of his age: Not until the twelfth century will another Catholic European look around for a polemical work against Islam.

How should this absence of anti-Islamic polemics be explained? It has been claimed that lack of direct contact with the realm of Islam was the decisive factor.[59] But in reality there was no dearth of direct contacts. From the all-too-often misdated Battle of Tours-Poitiers of 733 onward, the two sides clashed in battle in southern Gaul, northern Spain, and various parts of Italy, including the immediate vicinity of Rome; Narbonne, where traces of what might have been a mosque were recently discovered, was in Muslim hands from 719 to about 759; Carolingian rulers exchanged embassies with Baghdad and Cordova; Hārūn b. Yaḥyā, a prisoner of war from Ascalon, made his way in the 880s to Rome and conversed there, inter alia, about the local

---

[57] *Alcuini Epistolae*, ed. E. Dümmler (1895), in MGH Epist. 4:284–85. Already W. W. von Baudissin made use of this important letter and ascribed the disputation to Felix, bishop of Urgel: von Baudissin, *Eulogius und Alvar*, p. 62. Felix of Urgel, who recanted at the Council of Aachen, 799, had to live thereafter in the custody of the bishop of Lyons: Colbert, *The Martyrs*, pp. 80–81. The proven connection between Felix of Urgel and Laidrad should dispel the hesitation of J. Gil (in the introduction to his *Corpus scriptorum Muzarabicorum*, I:xxxix, n. 88) to identify the Felix of Alcuin's letter with Felix of Urgel.

[58] Alcuin's consecutive references to Saracens and Jews should be compared with the statement of Prudentius of Troyes (d. 861), a Spaniard by origin, that the Christian convert to Judaism Bodo-Eleazar prompted the Saracens of Spain to force the Christians living under their rule *ad Iudeorum insaniam Saracenorumque dementiam: Annales de St. Bertin*, ed. F. Grat et al. (Paris, 1964), p. 54.

[59] Julia Gauss, "Anselm von Canterbury und die Islamfrage," *Theologische Zeitschrift* 19 (1963): 250.

shaving customs; Berta of Tuscany held at her mercy 150 captured Muslims for at least seven years, and in 906 entrusted their erstwhile commander, the eunuch ᶜAlī, with a confidential mission to the caliph of Baghdad; southern Italian city-states, especially Amalfi, maintained commercial and probably also political ties with Muslim countries; some Catholic pilgrims visited the Muslim-ruled Holy Land; a Muslim political entity, the emirate of Bari, existed on Italian soil from 847 to 871; a band of Muslims established themselves in the early 880s at Monte Garigliano, northwest of Naples, and ravaged the adjoining area until their defeat in 915; and on the Provençal coast east of Marseilles, a group of Muslims maintained the important base of Fraxinetum from the closing years of the ninth century until their expulsion about 973.[60] In sum, direct contacts with Muslims, whether on the battlefield or elsewhere, were not lacking; yet mere contact unsupported by more pressing motives rarely generates serious interest.

Ignorance of the Arabic language should also not be considered a factor that necessarily prevented an altercation with Islam.[61] Catholic

[60] For the date of the Battle of Tours-Poitiers, see M. Baudot, "Localisation et datation de la première victoire remportée par Charles-Martel contre les Musulmans," *Mémoires et documents publiés par la Société de l'Ecole des Chartes* 12, 1 (1955): 93–105. On the Carolingian embassies to the caliphate see the detailed survey by M. Borgolte, *Der Gesandtenaustausch der Karolinger mit den Abbasiden und mit den Patriarchen von Jerusalem*, in the Münchener Beiträge zur Mediävistik und Renaissance–Forschung, 25 (Munich, 1976). Hārūn b. Yaḥyā's account about the West—which includes also references to Venice and Pavia—appears in Ibn Rusteh, *Les atours précieux*, trans. G. Wiet (Cairo, 1955), pp. 143–46. On Berta of Tuscany and her Muslim prisoners see M. Hamidullah, "Embassy of Queen Bertha of Rome to Caliph al-Muktafi billah in Baghdad," *Journal of the Pakistan Historical Society* 1 (1953): 272–300; G. Levi della Vida, "La corrispondenza di Berta di Toscana col califfo Muktafi," *Rivista storica italiana* 66 (1954): 21–38; C. G. Mor, "Intorno a una lettera di Berta di Toscana al Califfo di Bagdad," *Archivio storico italiano* 112 (1954): 299–312. On Amalfi see A. O. Citarella, "The Relations of Amalfi with the Arab World before the Crusades," *Speculum* 42 (1967): 299–312, and C. Cahen, "Le commerce d'Amalfi dans le Proche-Orient musulman avant et après la Croisade," *Comptes-rendus de l'Académie des Inscriptions et Belles-Lettres*, 1977: 291–300. For a recent survey of pilgrimage to the Holy Land see J. Wilkinson, *Jerusalem Pilgrims before the Crusades* (London, 1978). On the Muslim enclaves in the West and their reduction see B. Luppi, *I Saraceni in Provenza, in Liguria e nelle Alpi Occidentali* (Bordighera, 1952); G. Musca, *L'emirato di Bari*, and E. Eickhoff, *Seekrieg und Seepolitik zwischen Islam und Abendland: Das Mittelmeer unter byzantinischer und arabischer Hegemonie, 650–1040* (Berlin, 1966). For an overenthusiastic interpretation of some archaeological finds see J. Lacam, *Les Sarrazins dans le haut moyen-âge français: Histoire et archéologie* (Paris, 1965). For a recent attempt at synthesis see P. Sénac, *Musulmans et Sarrasins dans le sud de la Gaule du VIIIᵉ au XIᵉ siècle* (Paris, 1980).

[61] Marie Thérèse d'Alverny adduces ignorance of Arabic as one of the main obstacles to the dissemination of information about Islam in Catholic Europe: "La connaissance de l'Islam en Occident du IXᵉ au milieu du XIIᵉ siècle," in *Settimane di studio del Centro italiano di studi sull'alto medioevo*, vol. 12 (Spoleto, 1965), p. 577. But Mlle. d'Alverny

Europeans could have enlisted the help of their brethren in Muslim Spain, not a few of whom knew Arabic well. Alvar lamented the fascination Arabic letters held for many Spanish Christians; by 946 parts of the Bible had been translated into Arabic in Cordova, evidently for the use of Arabic-speaking Christians; a tenth-century manuscript of a Latin work by Samson of Cordova has Arabic notes in the margins.[62] Perhaps the most telling evidence of the degree to which these Christians became Arabicized is a Latin translation of an Arabic calendar from Cordova that is so influenced by the Arabic original that even Jerusalem is once referred to by a hybrid form of one of its Arabic names, *domus almegdis*, a term then explained with the words *id est Ierusalem*.[63] But in the early Middle Ages, the Christians north of the Pyrenees did not draw upon this substantial reservoir of Latin-Arabic bilingual Christians, even though some made their way to Catholic Europe. Thus Bishop Recemund of Elvira, who wrote a book in Arabic, in 955 left for the court of Otto I as ambassador of Caliph ʿAbd al-Raḥmān III; Dúnala, from the vicinity of Cadiz, at about the same time passed through Rome on his way to Constantinople and Jerusalem.[64]

Neither can it be said that no information about the conquests, habits, and beliefs of the Muslims infiltrated Catholic Europe in the early Middle Ages. A scanning of the Latin sources of that period reveals an astonishing number of references that could have whetted the appetite of Catholic writers both north and south of the Alps had they wanted to preoccupy themselves with the Muslims and their religion. The earliest of these references appears in the Merovingian chronicle that goes under the name of Fredegar. The Latin of the anonymous, presumably Burgundian, author is startlingly confused; many of his facts smack of legend; and yet his account of the Saracen conquests, written about 658, probably antedates all extant Oriental descriptions, whether in Armenian, Syriac, Arabic, Ethiopian, or Greek. It also provides striking proof of the passage of Oriental themes into

---

was apparently not aware of much of the information about Islam that did trickle into Catholic Europe (see below).

[62] *Indiculus luminosus*, c. 35 (Gil, 1:314–15; PL 121:555); H. Goussen, *Die christlich-arabische Literatur der Mozaraber* (Leipzig, 1909), p. 9 (see also pp. 17–20); Colbert, *The Martyrs*, p. 370.

[63] *Le calendrier de Cordoue*, ed. R. Dozy and trans. Ch. Pellat (Leiden, 1961), p. 73.

[64] On Recemund's Arabic book as one of the sources of the Cordovan calendar, see *Le calendrier*, p. ix; on Recemund encouraging Liutprand of Cremona to write a history *totius Europae*, see *Liudprandi Antapodosis*, ed. J. Becker (1915), in MGH Scr. rer. Germ. 41:3–4. See also K. J. Simonet, *Historia de los Mozárabes de España* (Madrid, 1897–1903), pp. 606–18, and F. Fita, "San Dúnala, procer y mártir mozárabe del siglo X," *Boletín de la Real Academia de la Historia* 55 (1909): 433–42.

mid-seventh-century Gaul. The account opens with the statement that *Aeraglius emperatur*—this is how the so-called Fredegar spells *Heraclius imperator*—discovered, through the practice of astrology, that his empire was to be laid waste by circumcised races. He requested, therefore, that the Frankish king Dagobert baptize all the Jews of his realm, and passed like orders throughout his own empire, which was nevertheless soon invaded by another circumcised people, the Saracens. There follows a short description of the Saracen victory over Heraclius's army, and a later chapter reports the conquest of Jerusalem, Egypt, and the Roman province of Africa, and the tribute Emperor Constans II had to pay to the Saracens.[65]

Especially in its earlier part, this story has obvious legendary overtones, but they are not of Fredegar's making. Though Fredegar's modern editors have been unaware of the fact, a number of Oriental writers, both Muslim and Christian, present substantially the same story about Heraclius's foreknowledge of the imminent descent of a circumcised race. The earliest of these writers are ʿAbd al-Razzāq al-Ṣanʿānī (d. 827) and al-Buk̲h̲ārī (d. 870), both compilers of traditions concerning the Prophet.[66] Evidently the story originated in the East, sometime after the Arab conquests in the 630s, and made its way to Merovingian Gaul, where it was soon committed to writing, whereas in the Orient it continued as oral tradition for about two more centuries. Thus Catholic Europe possessed, at a very early date, a rudimentary account of the Arab conquests that was not elaborated for centuries but copied, with little or no changes, from one Latin chronicle to another. (Early in the fourteenth century, one Latin chronicle containing Fredegar's account was brought to Tabriz, the capital of Mongol Persia, and the account subsequently appeared in Persian translation in the History of the Franks by Rashīd al-Dīn, the vizier of the Il-Khans who attempted to write an all-Eurasian history.)[67]

[65] *Fredegarii et aliorum Chronica*, ed. B. Krusch (1888), in MGH Scr. rer. Mer. 2:153–54, 162; *The Fourth Book of Fredegar with Its Continuations*, ed. and trans. J. M. Wallace-Hadrill (London, 1960), pp. 53–55, 68–69. On the authorship and date see the view of Wallace-Hadrill in his introduction, pp. xiv–xxiv, and W. Goffart, "The Fredegar Problem Reconsidered," *Speculum* 38 (1963): 206–41. For another instance in which Fredegar records a contemporary Eastern tradition see S. H. Wander, "The Cyprus Plates and the *Chronicle* of Fredegar," *Dumbarton Oaks Papers* 29 (1975): 345–46.

[66] ʿAbd al-Razzāq al-Sanʿānī, *Al-Muṣannaf*, ed. Habiburrahman al-Aʿzami, vol. 5 (Beirut, 1972), p. 343; El-Bokhâri, *Les traditions islamiques*, trans. O. Houdas and W. Marçais, vol. 1 (Paris, 1903), p. 9. I would like to thank my student ʿAmikam Elʿad for having brought to my attention the passage in *Al-Muṣannaf*.

[67] *Die Frankengeschichte des Rašīd ad-Dīn*, trans. K. Jahn, Denkschriften der Österreichischen Akademie der Wissenschaften, 129 (Vienna, 1977), p. 72. Rashīd al-Dīn

Considerably more solid information about the Saracens appears in the Revelation of Pseudo-Methodius, a tract originally written in Syriac in northern Mesopotamia in the seventh century, soon translated into Greek, and, possibly by the early eighth century, rendered from Greek into Latin by a monk called Peter who lived somewhere in the Frankish kingdom.[68] Under the guise of a prophecy *ex eventu*—which, to use Paul J. Alexander's suggestive phrase, amounts to a chronicle written in the future tense—it presents a lengthy description of the Ishmaelites who will erupt from the desert of Ethribum (Yathrib = Medina), conquer the lands of the East, and attack Sicily and "those who live close to Rome." In the Orient, the conquerors will seek all possible sources of income and their crushing exactions will not stop at orphans and widows, the poor and the weak. All the trees of the woodland will be cut down, the shape of the mountains undone, towns deserted, regions made roadless, humanity diminished. This description of the impact of the Arab conquests on Near Eastern civilization—apparently overlooked by economic historians—extends also to matters spiritual. The Ishmaelites, so states the Revelation, will mock and deride all wise men; their own wisdom will freely come forth, and none will be able to change or contest their words. Theirs will be the rebellion that according to the Second Epistle to the Thessalonians 2:3, must precede the coming of Antichrist. The rebellion will take its toll of the conquered Christian population: "Many will deny the true faith, the life-giving cross of Christ and the holy mysteries; indeed without any coercion, torture and scourges they deny Christ and fol-

---

was one of the very few Muslims who showed interest in the history of Catholic Europe: B. Lewis, "Masʿūdī on the Kings of the Franks," in *Al-Masʿūdī Millenary Commemoration Volume*, ed. S. M. Ahmad and A. Rahman (Aligarh, 1960), p. 10; idem, *The Muslim Discovery of Europe* (New York and London, 1982), pp. 150–51, 209–10, 212. The Eastern and Western versions of the story about Heraclius's foreknowledge will be treated in a forthcoming study of mine.

[68] For the date see P. J. Alexander, "Byzantium and the Migration of Literary Motifs: The Legend of the Last Roman Emperor," *Medievalia et Humanistica* NS 2 (1971): 57. The Latin version was edited by E. Sackur, *Sibyllinische Texte und Forschungen: Pseudo-methodius, Adso und die Tiburtinische Sibylle* (Halle a.S., 1898), pp. 59–96. On the abbreviated Latin version, written some time between the mid-eighth and tenth centuries, see P. J. Alexander, "The Diffusion of Byzantine Apocalypses in the Medieval West and the Beginnings of Joachimism," in *Prophecy and Millenarianism. Essays in Honor of Marjorie Reeves*, ed. Ann Williams (London, 1980), pp. 65–67. On the value of the historical parts of medieval apocalypses see P. J. Alexander, "Medieval Apocalypses as Historical Sources," *American Historical Review* 73 (1967–68): 997–1018. For the Greek version see A. Lolos, ed., *Die Apokalypse des Ps.-Methodios*, Beiträge zur klassischen Philologie, 83 (Meisenheim, 1976).

low the transgressors."[69] Then, switching to genuine prophecy, the Revelation foresees that a Byzantine emperor will ultimately destroy Yathrib, utterly defeat the Ishmaelites, and subjugate them. The Latin translation of this work must have found a sizable readership in Catholic Europe: Four of the extant manuscripts probably date from the eighth century, and many others were copied in the following centuries.[70]

References to Muslim habits and beliefs may be encountered at quite unexpected junctures. In 786 two English synods forbade clerics to eat in secret during fasts, "because it is hypocrisy and [the manner] of the Saracens"—a remark that suggests that some of the synods' participants (possibly the papal legates George and Theophylact) had a notion of the Muslim method of keeping the fast, which Catholic writers from the twelfth century onward often describe as a caricature of true fasting.[71] In the Acts of the Synod of Paris in 825, which dealt with the issue of iconoclasm, there is a Latin summary of the statement by John of Jerusalem on the origins of the destruction of images in the Oriental churches, which originally had been read in Greek at the Second Council of Nicaea in 787. In this Latin summary, read in Paris in the days of Louis the Pious, appear the names of the Umayyad caliphs *Seleman* (Sulaymān, 715–17), *Humarus* ('Umar II, 717–20), and *Ezidus* (Yazīd II, 720–24), as well as the story of the iconoclastic edict of Yazīd II and its short-lived enforcement.[72] The leading theologian Pas-

---

[69] Sackur, pp. 80–89; the quotation appears on p. 86. The allusion to Christian conversion to Islam ties in with the unequivocal statements of John of Nikiu, the Coptic bishop who wrote in the late seventh century: *The Chronicle of John, Bishop of Nikiu*, chaps. 114, 121, pp. 182, 201. These texts militate against Claude Cahen's assumption that in the early days of Arab rule, Christian conversion to Islam was negligible: C. Cahen, "Note sur l'accueil des chrétiens d'Orient à l'islam," *Revue de l'histoire des religions* 166 (1964): 51–58.

Raoul Manselli presented the Revelation as a testimony of the Christian reaction to the emergence of Islam: R. Manselli, "La *res publica christiana* e l'Islam," in *Settimane di Studio del Centro italiano di studi sull'alto medioevo*, vol. 12 (Spoleto, 1965), p. 121. The Revelation's statements on the impact of the conquests are discussed in my "The Arab Conquests and Agriculture: A Seventh-Century Apocalypse, Satellite Imagery, and Palynology," *Asian and African Studies* 19 (1985): 1–15.

[70] For details on the four earliest manuscripts, see Sackur, p. 57; unfortunately, Sackur dispensed with listing all later manuscripts that came to his knowledge. See also M. B. Ogle, "Petrus Comestor, Methodius, and the Saracens," *Speculum* 21 (1946): 318–24.

[71] "Quia hypocrisis et Saracenorum est." *Councils and Ecclesiastical Documents relating to Great Britain and Ireland*, ed. A. W. Haddan and W. Stubbs, vol. 3 (Oxford, 1871), p. 451, and n. 1. For a critical edition of the text, which contains the exact date, see *Alcuini Epistolae*, ed. E. Dümmler, in MGH Epist. 4:19–29 (the quotation appears on p. 22, line 43). For the views of later writers on Muslim fasting, see N. Daniel, *Islam and the West*, pp. 220–22.

[72] *Concilium Parisiense, a. 825*, ed. A. Werminghoff (1908), in MGH Conc. 2, 1:519,

chasius Radbertus, in a short passage of his commentary on Matthew 24:14, probably written in the 850s, exhibits a definite awareness of Islam's monotheism, as well as of its relationship to Judaism and Christianity. The Christian faith, he remarks, had come in the past to the notice of the Saracens, but later they "were wickedly seduced by some pseudoapostles, disciples of Nicholas so to speak, and composed for themselves a law from the Old as well as from the New Testament, and so perverted everything under the cult of one God, unwilling to agree with us or with the Jews in any respect." Radbertus also knows of the Saracens' aspiration to subjugate the entire world, and of their indifference to the God the subjugated people worship, as long as these acquiesce in their rule. He adds that since the Saracens "had taken upon themselves, by God's just judgment, the Spirit of Error, perhaps, as many think, Antichrist will be taken up [or: begotten] by them."[73]

In 858, Usuard and Odilard of St. Germain-des-Prés brought from Cordova the Passion of George, Aurelius, and Nathalia, which mentions not only the Saracen prohibition of apostasy and attack against their Legislator but also refers to the study, by Saracen youngsters, of an *arabica litteratura* fraught with "the absurdities of a perverse doctrine" and "the demons' subtle deception." The text also states that "the nation of the Ishmaelites venerates that Pseudoprophet so greatly ... as if they accepted through him the path of salvation" (an explanation that appears only in the version earmarked for non-Spanish readers), and that the Saracens constitute a "sect." The ecstatic invec-

---

line 38 through 520, line 13. For the full statement read at Nicaea see Mansi, *Concilia* 13:197–200; English translation in A. A. Vasiliev, "The Iconoclastic Edict of the Caliph Yazīd II, A.D. 721," *Dumbarton Oaks Papers* 9–10 (1956): 28–30. Vasiliev also discusses the Paris Synod of 825 (pp. 36–37).

For doubts about the authenticity of Yazīd's edict see O. Grabar, "Islam and Iconoclasm," in A. Bryer and Judith Herrin, eds., *Iconoclasm: Papers Given at the Ninth Spring Symposium of Byzantine Studies, University of Birmingham, March 1975* (Birmingham, 1977), p. 46.

[73] See Appendix 1/a below. Radbertus's insistence that the Gospel had reached the Saracens in the past contrasts with Alvar's assumption that no Christian preacher had ever been active among them. Radbertus's awareness of the Saracen tolerance of other religions was later shared by John of Gorze and Hrotsvitha: *Vita Iohannis abbatis Gorziensis*, in MGH SS 4:372; *Passio S. Pelagii*, p. 53, lines 50–54.

It is puzzling that R. W. Southern, who claims that before 1100 Western writers "knew virtually nothing of Islam as a religion," ignores this important passage by Radbertus, even though he refers to Radbertus to demonstrate "the mild and academic thesis that the existence of Islam outside the Church did not prove that the last days were *necessarily* still far distant." R. W. Southern, *Western Views of Islam in the Middle Ages* (Cambridge, Mass., 1962), pp. 14, 27.

tive of the monk George, who came all the way from the Judean monastery of Mar Saba, informs the reader that the Master of the Saracens was Satan's disciple, a perfidious and worthless believer in the Devil, a minister of Antichrist and a labyrinth of all the vices, who not only plunged to hell but through his useless ordinances destined his followers to eternal flames; the one who had appeared to him in the guise of an angel of light had in reality been a demon.[74] Thus, but for the name "Muhammad," which goes unmentioned throughout the work, an attentive reader could have pieced together many of the elements of the image of the Prophet presented in the Spanish Note on Mahmeth, the Life of Nunilón and Alodia, and similar works.

The existence of Saracen literature could also have been deduced from a letter Pope Nicholas I sent to the Bulgarians in 866, in which he orders the burning of the "profane books" captured by the Bulgarians from the Saracens, because they are harmful and blasphemous.[75] The pope's decree may be compared with the answers of al-Awzāʿī (d. 774) and al-Shāfiʿī (d. 820), two leading Muslim jurists. When asked whether Greek books found in enemy territory should be burned or might be sold, al-Awzāʿī replied that they should be buried, not burned; they must not be sold, because their content was polytheistic. Al-Shāfiʿī, disclosing a better acquaintance with Greek literature, answered that the leader of the expedition should first have the books translated; then the books on medicine and other sciences could be sold, and those that were polytheistic in content must be slashed and only their bindings kept.[76]

The name of the Prophet appears in a decision of a southern Italian ecclesiastical council, probably held in the late ninth century. A prohibition of sexual relationships between clerics and their female slaves is followed by the remark that "the Agarens observe such a law and custom, which their pseudoprophet Muaméth, erroneously called Machameta, is said to have given them, namely, that they might lawfully use a female slave, no matter the manner in which she had been acquired."[77]

[74] Jiménez Pedrajas, "San Eulogio de Córdoba," pp. 486–87 (*arabica litteratura*), 494 (path of salvation), 557, 562 (sect), 569 (George's invective).

[75] *Nicolai I papae Epistolae*, ed. E. Perels (1925), in MGH Epist. 6:599. During the Byzantine *reconquista* of the tenth century, soldiers were ordered to gather copies of the Koran and burn them: Julia Gauss, "Toleranz," p. 373.

[76] M. Canard, "Quelques 'á-côté' de l'histoire des relations entre Byzance et les Arabes," in *Studi orientalistici in onore di Giorgio Levi della Vida*, vol. 1 (Rome, 1956), p. 118.

[77] "Sed talem legem et consuetudinem agareni [cus]todiunt, quam eis suus pseudopropheta muaméth qui [cor]rupto nomine machameta vocatur, tradidisse dici[tur] ut

After 873 Catholic Europeans could have read in Latin about the alleged idolatry of the Saracens, a theme most prominent in Byzantine anti-Islamic polemics and alluded to in the Oriental Christian Letter of al-Kindi.[78] This was so because in that year Anastasius the Librarian, a major and intriguing figure of mid-ninth-century Rome, translated from the Greek the Acts of the Seventh Ecumenical Council of 787. The translation contains not only the account of the Saracen role in the genesis of iconoclasm (an earlier Latin version had been read in Paris in 825) but also a letter, from about 725, in which Germanus of Constantinople advised his fellow Christians to counter the Saracens' charge of Christian idolatry by accusing them of worshiping an inanimate stone called Chobar in the desert. (A copy of Anastasius's translation, which contains other, vaguer references to the beliefs of the Saracens, was given in the tenth century to St. Rémi at Reims.)[79]

Finally, from the mid–870s onward there existed in Latin a narrative that included fairly detailed entries about the rise of Muhammad, the Arab conquests, and the history of the caliphate down to the struggle between the heirs of Hārūn al-Rashīd. The text also lists some of Muhammad's teachings—on the remuneration for the participants in a Holy War, on Paradise, on the duty to show compassion and extend help to the suffering—and presents his creed as a heresy. Originally written in Greek by the Byzantine chronicler Theophanes (d. 817), the narrative was translated into Latin by Anastasius the Librarian between 871 and 874 and incorporated into his *Chronographia Tripertita*.[80] This work was copied a number of times; the oldest extant manuscript dates from the tenth century; two others date from the

---

ancilla qualitercumque acquisita licite utant[ur]." A. Amelli, "Excerpta e codicibus Casinensibus," *Spicilegium Casinense*, vol. 1 (Monte Cassino, 1893), p. 390. Cf. D. G. Morin, "Un concile inédit dans l'Italie méridionale à la fin du IXᵉ siècle," *Revue Bénédictine* 17 (1900): 143–51. The text has been reprinted by C. J. Hefele and H. Leclercq (*Histoire des Conciles*, vol. 3, 2 [Paris 1910], pp. 1228–29), who did not point out Amelli's conjectural readings.

[78] Muñoz Sendino, "Al-Kindi," pp. 422–23; partial translation by Muir, *The Apology*, pp. 38–39. The theme is lightly touched upon also by Alvar, *Indiculus luminosus*, c. 25 (Gil, 1:298–99; PL 121:539–41); cf. Franke, "Die freiwilligen Märtyrer," p. 122.

[79] On the date of Anastasius's translation, see G. Laehr, "Die Briefe und Prologe des Bibliothekars Anastasius," *Neues Archiv der Gesellschaft für ältere deutsche Geschichtskunde* 47 (1927–28): 429. For the text of the translation see Mansi, *Concilia*, 13:197–200 (Saracens and genesis of iconoclasm), 12:110E (letter of Germanus); see also 12:358D. On the copy given to St. Rémi see MGH Epist. 7:415.

[80] Anastasius Bibliothecarius, Chronographia Tripertita, in *Theophanis Chronographia*, ed. C. de Boor, 2:31–346; the passage on Muhammad's rise and teachings appears on pp. 208–10. On the time span in which Anastasius compiled his chronicle see Laehr, "Die Briefe," p. 432.

eleventh and three from the twelfth century.[81] Anastasius's account about Muhammad, as well as many of his entries about the Saracens, was taken over almost verbatim for the compilation pieced together by Landulf Sagax, probably in Benevento sometime before 1023.[82] (It is noteworthy that whereas the extant manuscripts of the work of Theophanes and Anastasius tend to give Arabic names in Grecized forms like Muamed, Moamed, or Mauhias, the oldest manuscript of Landulf's compilation, probably written under his supervision, spells the names in much closer conformity with the Arabic pronunciation, for example, Muhammad, Muhauias, or Muhauie.)[83]

The amount of knowledge about the Arabs and their creed that infiltrated Catholic Europe in early medieval times in all probability exceeded that revealed by the extant sources. Thus, in a letter of 790 to Master Colcu of Clonmacnoise, Ireland, Alcuin mentions the extent of Saracen rule at that time and then goes on to remark that he had written Colcu some time earlier about the emergence of the Saracens[84]— and one is left wondering what Alcuin might have written in that earlier, no-longer-extant letter. Again, what were the contents of the *Historia Saracenorum*, which Abbot Theobald of Monte Cassino ordered copied in 1023?[85] And how much oral information reached Europe through ambassadors and pilgrims; fugitives like the North Africans who made their way to Rome, Thuringia, and perhaps even Ireland; exiles like Eulogius's brothers, who left Muslim Spain for Bavaria; merchants like the Amalfitans who lived in Cairo in numbers by 996 and the Venetians who sailed up the Nile to Cairo about 1026; or a hermit like Simon of Syracuse, who for seven years served as a pilgrim guide in Jerusalem, later spent a number of years in Bethlehem and in the Sinai, then sailed down the Nile aboard the above-mentioned Venetian ship, and finally made his home in a cell of Trier's Porta Nigra?[86]

---

[81] E. Perels and G. Laehr in MGH Epist. 8, 1:418–19.

[82] For a critical edition of this compilation see *Landulfi Sagacis Historia Romana*, ed. A. Crivelucci, 2 vols. (Rome, 1912–13). The two extant manuscripts date from the eleventh century; one was brought to Corvey, probably around 1050.

[83] Ibid., 2:128, 132–33, 135 (Muhammad), 138–52 (Muhauias and Muhauie).

[84] *Alcuini Epistolae*, in MGH Epist. 4:32.

[85] Theobald's order is mentioned in a list from Monte Cassino printed by G. Becker, *Catalogi bibliothecarum antiqui* (Bonn, 1885), p. 133.

[86] On North African fugitives see L. White, Jr., *Latin Monasticism in Norman Sicily* (Cambridge, Mass., 1938), p. 20, and n. 7; Eulogius's brothers: Gil, 2:497, 500; PL 115:845, 847; Amalfitans: C. Cahen, "Un texte peu connu relatif au commerce oriental d'Amalfi au Xᵉ siècle," *Archivio Storico per le Province Napoletane* NS 34 (1953–54): 61–67; Venetians and Simon: *Vita S. Symeonis auctore Eberwino abbate S. Martini Treviris*,

In any case, it is evident that a considerable amount of information about the Saracens did reach Catholic Europe between the mid-seventh and early eleventh century, and therefore it is inaccurate to describe this period—as Richard William Southern did in his well-known essay on Western views of Islam in the Middle Ages—as the age of ignorance. But it is equally evident that the various notices about Islam did not serve as points of departure for a preoccupation, to say nothing of an altercation, with it. The available building blocks remained dispersed and unused. For instance, the perceptive remarks of Paschasius Radbertus were not taken up by later writers, and the detailed and coherent account of the *Chronographia Tripertita* by Anastasius the Librarian, in existence since the 870s, did not exert an influence on transalpine chronicle-writing before the early twelfth century. Thus, lack of interest rather than ignorance characterized the Catholic European stance toward the religion of the Saracens in the period under discussion.[87]

What is the explanation for this centuries-long lack of intellectual interest? Why this total abstention from polemics with Islam in a period in which some Catholic Europeans were capable of producing anti-Jewish tracts and the other Christendoms invested considerable energy in religious altercation with Islam?

The main reason for the difference, in this respect, between Catholic Europeans and the Christians living under Muslim rule may very well be that for the latter Islam was a constant, daily challenge and threat that had to be warded off. Theodore Abu Qurra, a leading Oriental polemicist of the early ninth century, writes that "it is the habit of the hypocrite Saracens that upon meeting a Christian, they would not greet him, but say at once: 'Christian, this is the testimony—God is one, without an associate, and Muhammad is his servant and messen-

---

in AA. SS. Iun. I, pp. 86–92. Eberwin's description of a *navis de Venetia* that arrived in Cairo laden with goods is one of the earliest testimonies to Venice's commerce with Egypt. For a German translation see P. Thomsen, "Der heilige Symeon von Trier," *Zeitschrift des Deutschen Palästina-Vereins* 62 (1939): 149–56. The date can be approximated, since Simon, after leaving Egypt aboard the Venetian ship, made his way to Antioch, where he met Richard of St. Vanne, who probably passed through the city early in 1027. (For Richard's itinerary see H. Dauphin, *Le Bienheureux Richard, Abbé de Saint-Vanne de Verdun* [Louvain and Paris, 1946], pp. 306–8.)

[87] For R. W. Southern's position see his *Western Views*, chap. 1. A Christian lack of interest or curiosity has been noted by Norman Daniel (*The Arabs*, p. 62) and Dorothée Metlitzki (*The Matter of Araby in Medieval England* [New Haven and London, 1977], p. 14); but the authors, unaware of the available points of departure for intellectual concern, did not attempt an explanation. On the Muslim lack of interest in Catholic Europe see Lewis, *The Muslim Discovery*, pp. 76–77, 90–96, 142.

ger!'" A few decades later Eulogius of Cordova indignantly reports that the Saracens deride and stone Christian clergymen as they pass in the streets, hurling insults and curses when the Christian hour of prayer is announced. Under more benign circumstances the Christian religion could become the object of a tease. Yaḥyā b. ʿAdī, the prominent Oriental Christian philosopher of the tenth century, relates that when a vizier once proposed engaging a competent Christian secretary, a Muslim official objected on the grounds that the secretary could not count: "With him, one is three and three is one." The vizier laughed, but the jest prompted Yaḥyā to write a tract on God's unity and trinity. Occasionally a ruler would interrogate a Christian about his faith, or a Muslim query a Christian acquaintance about his belief.[88] Thus the Christians under Muslim rule had no choice but to engage in apologetics and polemics, since their self-preservation depended to a considerable extent on their ability to defend their faith against the pressure of the Muslim surrounding.

The discrepancy between Byzantium and Catholic Europe in the sphere of anti-Islamic polemics may be considered primarily the result of the difference between the Muslim forces each faced and the relationship each evolved with them. The Muslim power the Byzantines confronted along a broad, continuous front, and very often waged war with, was the caliphate, the empire that claimed the allegiance of all Muslims. Its centers were relatively close to the Byzantine frontier, and its political and economic vigor could not have gone unnoticed. Indeed, the caliphate came to occupy in Byzantine esteem the place that had been reserved for the Persian Empire, until the Arab conquests: that is, the caliphate had become the second great world power beside Byzantium itself. This is clearly expressed in the above-mentioned letter Patriarch Nicholas of Constantinople sent in 913 or 914 to Caliph al-Muqtadir. "There are two lordships, that of the Saracens and that of the Romans," writes Nicholas, "which stand above all lordship on earth, and shine out like the two mighty beacons in the firmament. They ought, for this very reason alone, to be in contact and brother-

---

[88] Abu Qurra, in PG 97:1544. Eulogius, *Memoriale Sanctorum*, I, 21 (Gil, 2:385–86; PL 115:754–55). A. Périer, *Petits traités apologetiques de Yaḥyā ben ʿAdī* (Paris, 1920), pp. 63–68. On interrogations by rulers see F. Nau, "Un colloque du Patriarche Jean avec l'émir des Agaréens et faits divers des années 712 à 716," *Journal asiatique*, 5th ser., 10 (1915): 225–64, differently dated and interpreted by H. Lammens, *Etudes sur le siècle des Omayyades* (Beirut, 1930), pp. 13–25; Maçoudi, *Les prairies d'or*, ed. and trans. C. Barbier de Maynard, vol. 2 (Paris, 1862), pp. 386–88. A good example of queries are those addressed to the Nestorian bishop Elias of Nisibis by a fugitive Egyptian vizier in July 1026: Browne, *The Eclipse*, pp. 48–49, 68, 72–73, 82–83, 123–25; Graf, *Geschichte der christlichen arabischen Literatur*, 2:177–82.

hood and not, because we differ in our lives and habits and religion, remain alien in all ways to each other, and deprive themselves of correspondence carried on in writing."[89] The susceptibilities of this second world power had to be taken into account; consequently, possibly by 717, consent was given to erect in Constantinople a mosque for the use of Muslim visitors or prisoners of war (Rome, it should be noted in passing, has no mosque to this very day).[90] Moreover, the rulers of this great power, following a custom allegedly initiated by Muhammad himself, repeatedly sent the Byzantine emperors letters inviting them to convert to Islam.[91] These official calls for conversion, issued before the eruption of hostilities or at the enthronement of a new caliph, sometimes containing elaborate attacks against Christianity, triggered Byzantine apologetic and polemical responses; two of these were composed by Nicetas of Byzantium at the behest of Emperor Michael III (842–67). The caliphate also comprised a large Christian population that had formerly been under Byzantine rule and continued, in part, to maintain religious and cultural ties with Byzantium. This facilitated the flow of information about Islam, and of Oriental anti-Islamic polemics, into the empire.[92] As for the Byzantines,

[89] Jenkins and Westerink, *Nicholas I, Patriarch of Constantinople: Letters*, pp. 2–3; cf. pp. 525–26. Cf. Gauss, "Toleranz," p. 363. It should be noted that when Nicholas writes to a Christian correspondent—the ruler of Amalfi—he chooses to speak of "the godless tyranny of the sons of Hagar": Jenkins and Westerink, pp. 460–61. Is this so because he refers in this letter to the Saracen band at Garigliano, or is he less than sincere in his letter to the caliph?

[90] On the mosques established in Constantinople see L. Bréhier, *La civilisation byzantine*, vol. 3 (Paris, 1950), pp. 312–13. It should be noted that the observation on the erection of a mosque in 717 appears only in the tenth-century *De administrando imperio*, in a passage the author purports to have taken from the chronicle of Theophanes, but does not appear in the chronicle's extant version: Constantine Porphyrogenitus, *De administrando imperio*, c. 21, ed. and trans. Gy. Moravcsik and R.J.H. Jenkins (Budapest, 1949), pp. 92–93. Rome's first mosque is scheduled to be erected in the mid–1980s: A. Barone, "Anche Roma avrà una moschea," *L'Islam, I problemi di Ulisse*, 83 (Florence, 1977), pp. 179–83.

[91] The initiating of the practice by Muhammad is characterized as a later tradition by F. Buhl, "Fasste Muḥammed seine Verkündigung als eine universelle, auch für Nicht-araber bestimmte Religion?" *Islamica* 2 (1926–27): 135–49. An offer of conversion Muʿāwiya extended to Emperor Constantine IV, about 640, is mentioned by the Armenian chronicler Sebeos in *Histoire d'Héraclius*, trans. F. Macler (Paris, 1904), pp. 139–40; for other calls for conversion to Islam see M. Canard, "Quelques 'à-côté,' " pp. 99–100; idem, "Les relations politiques et sociales entre Byzance et les Arabes," *Dumbarton Oaks Papers* 18 (1964): 36. On the necessity, according to Islamic law, of inviting the enemy to accept Islam, see M. Khadduri, *War and Peace in the Law of Islam* (Baltimore, 1955), pp. 96–98; see also Khoury, *Théologiens*, pp. 201–2.

[92] The influence of John Damascene on Byzantine anti-Islamic polemics is well known.

they probably felt the need for polemical tracts in order to confirm in their faith the Christians wavering in the face of Muslim pressure, as well as to aid in converting the Muslims who came under Byzantine rule in sizable numbers, especially in the tenth century.

Catholic Europe, on the other hand, faced, on a number of relatively narrow and discontinuous fronts, several minor Muslim powers, which came nowhere near the caliphate in might or pretension. The Umayyad Emirate of Cordova was the refuge of the dynasty defeated in the struggle for mastery of the caliphate; the ruler of the short-lived emirate of Bari sought recognition as governor of a province of the caliphate, "so that," as the contemporary chronicler al-Balādhurī puts it, "he may not be included in the category of usurpers."[93] And the Saracens at Fraxinetum were obscure pirates. Hence it is not surprising that none of the Muslim powers in the West loomed as large in the consciousness of Catholic Europeans as did the caliphate in that of the Byzantines, or that none of these minor Muslim powers took upon itself the religious duty of formally offering Islam to its Christian adversaries. (In the eyes of the caliphs of Baghdad, on the other hand, Catholic Europe must have appeared far too distant, and politically far too fragmentary, to warrant a call for conversion.) Only after ʿAbd al-Raḥmān III of Cordova proclaimed himself caliph in 928 might a change have taken place. A Spanish Muslim author, albeit a late one, relates that the caliph once showed a Koran, a saber, and fire to Christian envoys, telling them that Allāh ordered the Muslim to invite the unbelievers to conform to the Holy Book, or else constrain them by the saber and dispatch the slain to the fires of hell. An embassy of the same caliph, though seeking friendly ties and originally led by a bishop, delivered to Otto I a letter containing "several blasphemies against Christ."[94] It might have been interesting to compare this letter and Otto's vigorous reply with the Muslim offers of conversion to the rulers of Byzantium and the polemical responses they evoked, but unfortunately the exchange between ʿAbd al-Raḥmān and Otto has not

---

On the Oriental source, or sources, of Theophanes's account about Muhammad and the caliphate see Anne S. Proudfoot, "The Sources of Theophanes for the Heraclian Period," *Byzantion* 44 (1974): 384–86.

[93] *The Origins of the Islamic State: The Kitāb Futūḥ al-Buldān of al-Balādhuri*, trans. P. K. Hitti, vol. 1 (New York, 1916), p. 372.

[94] The Spanish author is Muḥyy al-Dīn b. al-ʿArabī (1165–1240). For a French translation of his account see E. Lévi-Provençal, *l'Espagne musulmane au Xème siècle: Institutions et vie sociale* (Paris, 1932), pp. 48–49. Ramon d'Abadal identified the envoys as coming from Barcelona, about 950: R. d'Abadal i de Vinyals, *Els primers comtes catalans* (Barcelona, 1958), pp. 315–16. On the embassy to Otto I see *Vita Iohannis Gorziensis*, in MGH SS 4:370.

survived. At any rate, the heyday of the Cordovan caliphate was soon over and no further overtures in this vein are heard of.

Charlemagne at one time hoped to liberate the Spanish Christians living under Saracen rule.[95] Theodulf of Orléans, in one of his poems, wishes Louis the Pious to "repress" Spain and overcome the Maurs and the Arabs.[96] And in a vision in 853, Audradus Modicus makes God promise that Charles the Bald will liberate Spain from the infidels.[97] Yet the ties between the Frankish Kingdom and the Christians of Muslim Spain were not as close as those between Byzantium and the Greeks living under Muslim rule. After all, Syria and Egypt had formerly been Byzantine territories, whereas Muslim Spain had been Visigothic, not Frankish. So it came about that the Greek polemics of Oriental Christians living under Muslim rule, especially the work of John Damascene, had a major influence on Byzantine polemics, while the Latin anti-Islamic works of the Christians of Muslim Spain failed to reach France before the eleventh century, the only exception being Eulogius's description of the three Cordovan enthusiasts, who were of immediate interest to the monks of St. Germain-des-Prés. (It is symptomatic that the Note on Mahmeth did reach the northern, Christian-ruled part of Spain, which together with the Muslim south had once constituted the Visigothic kingdom. From the present point of view, northern Spain may be considered Byzantium's occidental counterpart.)[98] Finally, during the early Middle Ages the Christian-Muslim

[95] See n. 6 above. According to the Life of Louis the Pious by the so-called Astronomer, one of the purposes of Charlemagne's Spanish campaign was "laboranti ecclesie sub Sarracenorum acerbissimo jugo Christo fautore suffragari." *Vita Hludovici imperatoris*, ed. G. H. Pertz (1829), in MGH SS 2:608.

[96] *Theodulfi Carmina*, ed. E. Dümmler (1881), in MGH Poetae 1:531, lines 7–9. Elsewhere (p. 461, line 13) Theodulf mentions the city of *Bagatat, Agarenis rebus onusta*, probably the earliest mention of Baghdad in a Latin source.

[97] It is noteworthy that while God tells Charles the Bald that he will liberate Spain "from the infidels," Louis the German is told that his dominion will extend "into the hitherto infidel people" who border on German territory: "do tibi, Karole, ut Hispanias duce beato Martino principe [i.e., the patron-saint of the Franks] (iterum) liberes ab infidelibus et tuo regno ad honorem nominis mei secundum libertatem fidelium meorum consocies. . . . et tu, Hludovice Germanorum rex . . . duce beato Paulo principe [i.e., the Apostle to the Gentiles] erit in gentes, quae sunt adhuc infideles apud Germanias, felicissima dilatatio tua." The vision has been edited by L. Traube, "O Roma nobilis: Philologische Untersuchungen aus dem Mittelalter," *Abhandlungen der philosophisch-philologischen Classe der kgl. Bayerischen Akademie der Wissenschaften*, vol. 19, Denkschriften, 64 (Munich, 1892), pp. 384, lines 22–24; 385, lines 9–12. Does the different phrasing reflect a differential evaluation of the prospects of Saracen versus pagan conversion?

[98] For knowledge of Muslim history in northern Spain see also the late-ninth-century *Crónica profética* in Gómez-Moreno, ed., "Las primeras crónicas de la Reconquista," pp. 624–27. For northern Spanish attitudes toward the Muslims, which resemble to some

frontiers in the West, unlike those in the East, remained relatively stable. Hence at no time during that period did a sizable Muslim population come under Catholic rule.

The decline of cultural contacts between Byzantium and Catholic Europe may also be regarded as a factor accounting for the Catholic European lack of interest in Islam. As long as Byzantine works were translated into Latin, relatively valuable information on the Muslims could reach the West, as the Latin versions of the Revelation of Pseudo-Methodius and of Theophanes's *Chronographia* prove. Had Greek works continued to be translated, some anti-Islamic polemics might have been rendered into Latin. But Anastasius the Librarian, the translator of Theophanes whose own command of Greek was already quite limited, found no followers, and so it happened that John Damascene's chapter on the heresy of the Ishmaelites, the only anti-Islamic Greek work to reach Catholic Europe in medieval times, was translated into Latin only in the thirteenth century.[99]

The potential importance of the Byzantine connection may best be demonstrated by examining the infiltration of Byzantine anti-Islamic polemic motifs into a Christendom that probably had fewer direct contacts with the Muslims than did Catholic Europe, but still maintained close ties with Byzantium—namely, the Slavic Christendom. In the Old Church Slavic Life of Constantine-Cyril, probably written a few years after the death of the apostle of the Slavs in 869, Constantine goes to the land of the Saracens to conduct a religious disputation in answer to their challenge. He is subsequently portrayed as attacking the prophethood of Muhammad at the court of the Khazar khan. Thus, even as Hrotsvitha of Gandersheim presented the Saracens as idolaters and Guibert of Nogent, one of the most cultured men of the early twelfth century, stated that he was unable to find a written account about *Mathomus*,[100] monks in Eastern Europe had information at hand about Islam in the Life of the founder of Slavic literature. Here they could have learned that the *prorok* ("prophet") *Mah'met'* praised Christ "in his books," considered him to have been a great prophet, and

---

extent those of the Byzantines, see R. Barkai, *Cristianos y musulmanes en la España medieval (El enemigo en el espejo)* (Madrid, 1984).

[99] B. Kotter, ed., *Die Schriften des Johannes von Damaskos*, vol. 4, *Liber de haeresibus: Opera polemica*, Patristische Texte und Studien, 22 (Berlin and New York, 1981), p. 16. (The translator was Robert Grosseteste.)

[100] Guibert of Nogent, *Gesta Dei per Francos*, in RHC. HOcc. 4:127. Cf. C. Cahen, discussing the lecture by Marie-Thérèse d'Alverny, "La connaissance de l'Islam en Occident," p. 800.

identified the Virgin Mary with Mary the sister of Moses. Here they could have read a close paraphrase of the Koranic verse (19:17) on the Spirit entering the Virgin, and become acquainted with some of the religious altercations between the Christians and Muslims of the Levant.[101]

Yet the decline in Europe's cultural contacts with Byzantium must necessarily be regarded as a subsidiary factor. Since even those passages in Byzantine texts that had been translated into Latin failed to arouse intellectual curiosity about Islam, it is plausible to assume that additional translations would have suffered a similar fate. More basically, Catholic Europeans failed to concern themselves with Islam because of the very character of early medieval Latin culture. The concentration on Scripture and patristic writings and the dependence on the summaries of knowledge compiled in late antiquity led to an emulation or continuation of past efforts and achievements, leaving little scope for seriously tackling the post-Biblical, postclassical, postpatristic—and from this viewpoint inherently marginal—phenomenon of Islam. The commentaries on the Biblical account of Ishmael and his descendants could, and did, serve as channels for some observations on this new phenomenon, but because of the prevailing cultural bent, these were only sparingly used.

THE EARLY awareness of the Muslim intolerance of attacks against their religion was a major deterrent to Catholic European as well as other Christian missionizing in Muslim lands. The absence of a Muslim religious challenge and of a subjugated Muslim population, the character of contemporary Latin culture, and the decline of cultural contacts with Byzantium account for the nonexistence of Catholic European polemics throughout the early Middle Ages. To what extent will things change with the start of Europe's counteroffensive against the realm of Islam, which will bring considerable numbers of Muslims under Catholic rule and coincide with a marked change in the temper of European culture?

[101] For 882 as the *terminus ad quem* of the Life of Constantine-Cyril see P. Meyvaert and P. Devos, "Trois énigmes cyrillométhodiennes de la 'Légende Italique' résolues grâce à un document inédit," *Analecta Bollandiana* 73 (1955): 435. For the pertinent passages (in Old Church Slavic and in a modern Latin translation) see *Constantinus et Methodius Thessalonicenses: Fontes*, ed. and trans. F. Grivec and F. Tomšič (Zagreb, 1960), pp. 103–5, 123–24, 178–82, 195–96. For a French translation see F. Dvorník, *Les légendes de Constantin et de Méthode vues de Byzance* (Prague, 1933), pp. 354–59; for a comparison of the anti-Islamic argumentation contained in the Life of Constantine-Cyril with that of Byzantine polemicists, see pp. 109–11.

TWO

Christian Reconquest and
Muslim Conversion

A Recurring Pattern: Fraxinetum, Spain, Sicily

During the night of July 21, 972, Abbot Maieul of Cluny was taken prisoner by the Saracens of Fraxinetum as he was crossing the Alps on the way back from Rome. Maieul's earliest biographer, Syrus, writing shortly after the abbot's death in 994, relates that when the more frivolous among his captors began to disparage the Christian faith, Maieul "pierced the enemies of Christ with the spear of God's word, showing Christianity to be good and true, and undertook to demonstrate with proven and most credible reasons that the one whom they worshiped as God could neither free himself from punishment nor help them in any way." The Saracens became so infuriated by these words that Maieul expected to be martyred, but instead was imprisoned under harsh conditions.[1]

Whether Syrus's story testifies once more to an awareness of the Muslim prohibition of attacks against their religion is a moot question. The vehement reaction to Maieul's speech might have been presented as an on-the-spot response of the particular Saracens involved, rather than as a manifestation of the general Saracen intolerance of such attacks. Regardless, this is undoubtedly the earliest known account of a Catholic European altercation with Islam, an account that suggests that either Maieul or his biographer believed that the Saracens worshiped Muhammad as God. Taken literally, it also indicates that Maieul attempted to discredit Muhammad by pointing to his inability to save himself from suffering, that is, by applying a mirror image of the age-

---

[1] "Protinus ergo beatus Maiolus, belligerator optimus, scutum fidei arripiens, cuspide verbi Dei perfodiebat inimicos Christi, christianae religionis cultum approbans, et eum quem Deum colebant nec se a supplicio liberare, nec illos in aliquo posse adjuvare, certis et evidentissimis aggressus est rationibus demonstrare." *Ex Syri Vita S. Maioli*, ed. G. Waitz (1841), in MGH SS 4:652. J.-T. Reinaud, one of the few writers to utilize this passage, believed that both *se* and *illos* refer to the Saracens: J.-T. Reinaud, *Invasions des Sarrazins en France, et de France en Savoie, en Piémont et dans la Suisse* (1836; reprint, Paris, 1964), p. 204. For the date see P. A. Amargier, "La capture de Saint Maieul de Cluny et l'expulsion des Sarrasins de Provence," *Revue Bénédictine* 73 (1963): 319.

old anti-Christian ridicule of Jesus' agony on the cross. But the main importance of Maieul's altercation lies in its purported effectiveness. After the monks of Cluny had ransomed Maieul, the outraged magnates of Burgundy and Provence descended on the Saracens of Fraxinetum, uprooted them completely, pursued them into the mountains, and captured there some who requested to be baptized, prompted as they were, reports Syrus, by the *disputatio* Maieul had held in captivity.[2]

Thus, the description of one of the earliest episodes of the Catholic European counteroffensive against the forces of Islam associates Christian conquest with Muslim conversion: Decisively routed, some Saracens opt for baptism. At the same time, Christian preaching and fighting are presented as complementary, since Maieul's "salutary words" to his Saracen captors bear fruit only after their total military defeat. Moreover, the preacher is portrayed as sustaining the warriors, for Syrus remarks that although Maieul had been physically absent from the battle, his merits had been present and therefore the victors allocated him a share of the spoils.[3]

Partial Muslim conversion in the wake of Christian conquest—the sequence described by Syrus—reappears in the main arenas of the European counteroffensive, though the temporal link between conquest and conversion is not always as close as in the example of Fraxinetum. Already in the early stages of the Spanish *reconquista* some Muslims accepted the faith of the expanding kingdoms of Aragon and Castile: Six Saracen serfs of Muñones and Lumberres who had turned Christian (*quod tornauerunt ad Christianisimo*) were accorded free status and

[2] MGH SS 4:653, lines 24–25; 654, lines 7–10.

[3] Ibid., p. 654, lines 14–17. The importance of the story has been hinted at by P. Lamma, *Momenti di storiografia cluniacense* (Rome, 1961), p. 135. Raoul Manselli, who believes that armed attack and attempt at conversion were the two lines along which the posture of Catholic Europe toward Islam developed from the end of the tenth century onward, presents the story of Syrus as a departure point of the second line: "La *res publica christiana*," p. 132. The passage about Maieul's share in the booty, however, leaves no doubt that in this story the two lines are in full harmony. See also E. Delaruelle, "The Crusading Idea in Cluniac Literature of the Eleventh Century," in *Cluniac Monasticism in the Central Middle Ages*, ed. Noreen Hunt (Hamden, Conn., 1971), p. 194.

Karl Heisig attaches much importance to the fact that the conversion of the Saracens does not appear in Aldebald's adaptation of Syrus's *Vita Maioli*: "Die Geschichtsmetaphysik," pp. 22–23. Nor is the conversion mentioned in Odilo's *Vita* of Maieul (PL 142:959–62) or in Glaber's well-known account of Maieul's captivity (Raoul Glaber, *Les cinq livres de ses histoires, 900–1044*, ed. M. Prou [Paris, 1886], pp. 10–12). The conversion is described at some length in the *Vita* written by the Cluniac monk Nalgodus in the early twelfth century: AA. SS. Maii II, p. 664.

full property rights by King Sancho Ramírez of Aragon in 1081; some Muslims of Toledo, conquered in 1085 by Alfonso VI of Castile, converted to escape enslavement; most of the Muslim slaves owned by the monastery of Sobrado, Galicia, at the end of the eleventh century, converted to Christianity—one Mafumat, baptized as Martinus Menendi, later became a lay brother—and all children of the few slaves who remained faithful to Islam accepted the Christian religion; and at the other end of the social scale, the "Mora Zaida," daughter-in-law of a Muslim ruler of Seville, was baptized in or after 1091, and became first the concubine of Alfonso VI and then the heroine of a Castilian *cantar*.[4] At the time of the first conquest of Valencia, in 1094, several of the Muslim warriors who fought under the Cid and other Christian chieftains abandoned Islam: Thus reports Abū Marwān ʿAbd al-Malik b. al-Kardabūs, a reliable African chronicler of the later twelfth century. And when the Pisans captured Majorca in 1114, a sister of the Muslim ruler chose to join the Pisan fleet on its way home, and was later baptized in Pisa together with her little son.[5]

The conversion of Spanish Muslims soon became an avowed aim of

[4] J. M. Lacarra, *Documentos para el estudio de la Reconquista y repoblación del valle del Ebro*, 3d ser. (Saragossa, 1952), doc. 288, pp. 515–16 [= *Estudios de Edad Media de la Corona de Aragón: Sección de Zaragoza* 5 (1952)]; G. Liauzu, "La condition des musulmans dans l'Aragon chrétien aux XIᵉ et XIIᵉ siècles," *Hespéris-Tamuda* 9 (1968): 188, 199. A. González Palencia, "Toledo en los siglos XII y XIII," in *Moros y cristianos en España medieval: Estudios historico-literarios* (Madrid, 1945), p. 205. The *Genealogia sarracenorum Sancte Marie Superaddi* is reproduced in Ch. Verlinden, *L'esclavage dans l'Europe médiévale*, 2 vols. (Brugge, 1955; Gent, 1977), 1:123, n. 56, and discussed on pp. 123–26. E. Lévi-Provençal, "La 'Mora Zaida,' femme d'Alphonse VI, et leur fils, l'infant don Sancho," in *Islam d'Occident: Etudes d'histoire médiévale* (Paris, 1948), pp. 137–51; R. Menéndez Pidal, *La España del Cid*, 2 vols., 4th ed. (Madrid, 1947), 2:760–64. Casilda, a Spanish saint believed to have been a contemporary of the "Mora Zaida," is presented as the daughter of a Muslim king who was baptized at Burgos: AA. SS. Apr. I, pp. 838–41. M. Alamo (*Dictionnaire d'histoire et de géographie ecclésiastiques*, 11:1282) and G. D. Gorrini (*Bibliotheca Sanctorum*, vol. 3 [Rome, 1963], p. 894) claim that the first documents to mention Casilda date from the fifteenth century. A fragment of her Life, however, appears in a thirteenth-century manuscript: M. C. Díaz y Díaz, *Index Scriptorum Latinorum Medii Aevi Hispanicorum*, vol. 1 (Salamanca, 1958), no. 849, p. 191.

An Arabic compilation of the early eleventh century relates that after the Christian occupation of Galicia in 749–50, all Muslims of that region who were uncertain in their faith became Christian: *Ajbar Machmuă (Colecion de tradiciones): Crónica anónima del siglo XI*, ed. and trans. E. Lafuente y Alcántara (Madrid, 1867), pp. 62 (text), 66 (translation). Claudio Sanchez Albornoz convincingly argues that the passage in question was interpolated by the eleventh-century compiler: *El "Ajbār Maŷmūʿa": Cuestiones historiograficas que suscita* (Buenos Aires, 1944), pp. 171–75.

[5] R. Dozy, *Recherches sur l'histoire et la littérature de l'Espagne pendant le moyen âge*, vol. 2, 3d ed. (Paris and Leiden, 1881), app. 2, pp. xxi (text), xxvi (translation). Cf.

prominent Catholic Europeans. Ordered by Pope Gregory VII and persuaded by Abbot Hugh of Cluny, the hermit Anastasius left for Spain, apparently in 1074, to preach there to the Saracens (*ad praedicandum Sarracenis*); so relates an otherwise unknown Galterus, whose Life of Anastasius is the only source on this mission. Galterus does not specify whether the hermit was to be active in the newly conquered areas or in Muslim-ruled Spain proper, but asserts that his offer to prove the truth of Christianity by ordeal of fire did not impress the Saracens and therefore he returned to Cluny.[6] If authentic, this account shows that already at an early stage of the Spanish reconquest, the pope and the abbot of Cluny were interested in the conversion of Spain's Muslims to the point of sending, for the first time, a missionary to them. True, the account is not corroborated by other sources, but this does not necessarily render it spurious. First, the offer to let an ordeal decide in matters religious—this will later reappear in Franciscan legend—accords with the temper of the age. According to the mid-twelfth-century *Crónica Najerense*, King Alfonso VI of Castile attempted to prove in 1077 the superiority of the Roman over the Mozarab, or Toledan, rite through a judicial duel between representatives of the two rites, and when the knight who fought for Toledo won, the king resorted to an ordeal by fire. (This fire ordeal literally misfired, for the volume containing the Toledan Divine Office escaped the flames, whereupon the king kicked it into the fire, thus definitely concluding

---

Menéndez Pidal, *La España del Cid*, 1:315. On the chronicler see Brockelmann, *GAL* 1, no. 345.

The Muslim warriors' conversion was not entirely uprecedented. For an *'ilḏj* (apostate from Islam) fighting with Christians against the army of al-Manṣūr, master of Muslim Spain in the closing years of the tenth century, see Lévi-Provençal, *L'Espagne musulmane au Xème siècle*, p. 147.

On the conversion of King Mortada's sister see *Gesta triumphalia per Pisanos facta de captione Hierusalem et civitatis Maioricarum*, ed. M. L. Gentile (1936), in RIS new ed. 6, 2:93. Earlier historians believed that the epitaph of a queen of Majorca, located in Pisa's Duomo, refers to this convert of 1114, but recent authors adhere to the view that it refers to the wife of Mudjāhid, captured in 1015–16 in Sardinia: G. Scalia, "Epigraphica Pisana: Testi latini sulla spedizione contro le Baleari del 1113–15 e su altre imprese del secolo XI," in *Pubblicazioni dell'Istituto di letteratura spagnola e ispano-americana della Università di Pisa*, Miscellanea di studi ispanici, 6 (Florence, 1963), pp. 273–82; M. Tangheroni, "Pisa, l'Islam, il Mediterraneo, la prima crociata: alcune considerazioni," in *Toscana e Terrasanta nel Medioevo*, ed. F. Cardini (Florence, 1982), p. 44. On the conversion of Muslims after the definite conquest of Valencia in the thirteenth century see chap. 4.

[6] *Vita S. Anastasii auctore Galtero*, in PL 149:429A. On the hermit's relations with Abbot Hugh see Noreen Hunt, *Cluny under Saint Hugh, 1049–1109* (London, 1967), pp. 48, 87, 149.

the contest.)[7] Second, Abbot Hugh's interest in Muslim conversion is corroborated by two other sources. In a little-known letter of 1087 to Bernard of Sédirac, archbishop-elect of newly reconquered Toledo, Hugh emphatically urges him to preach the word of God incessantly and to lead an exemplary life, and so bring about the conversion of the infidels.[8] And Hugh's contemporary biographer Gilo relates that during his visit to Spain the abbot assisted at the conversion of a Moor who later attempted to escape with the abbot's gold on the return trip to Cluny. (Unfortunately, Gilo does not spell out the fate of the Moor after his capture.)[9] Finally, Gregory VII's letters suggest that the possibility of Saracen conversion had crossed his mind.[10]

Pope Urban II certainly advocated the conversion of those Spanish Muslims who had come under Spanish Christian rule. Conferring the pallium on Bernard of Sédirac in 1088, the pope exhorted him not to give offense to Christians and Saracens, "and to endeavor by word and example to convert, with God's grace, the infidels to the faith."[11] The

---

[7] *Crónica Najerense*, III, 49, ed. A. Ubieto Arteta, Textos Medievales, 15 (Valencia, 1966), p. 116. Cf. *Annales Compostellani*, in *España sagrada* (chap. 1, n. 19), 23:321.

[8] M. Férotin, "Une lettre inédite de Saint Hugues, abbé de Cluny, à Bernard d'Agen, archevêque de Tolède (1087)," *Bibliothèque de l'Ecole des Chartes* 61 (1900): 343–45; idem, "Complément de la lettre de Saint Hugues," ibid. 63 (1902): 684–85. The author is identified only as "fr. H. peccator," but Férotin convincingly argues that the letter was written by Hugh of Cluny. It was utilized by J. Fechter in *Cluny, Adel und Volk: Studien über das Verhältnis des Klosters zu den Ständen, 910–1156* (Stuttgart, 1966), pp. 11–12.

On Bernard of Sédirac, his purported attempt to join the First Crusade, and his participation in the siege of Alcala, see M. Defourneaux, *Les Français en Espagne aux XIe et XIIe siècles* (Paris, 1949), pp. 32–43.

[9] Gilo, *Vita Sancti Hugonis*, ed. A. L'Huillier, in *Vie de Saint Hugues, abbé de Cluny, 1024–1109* (Paris, 1888), p. 585. Gilo wrote between 1109 and 1114 (pp. 569–71). The story is repeated by Hildebert of Lavardin: PL 159:867AB. Only one Spanish journey of Hugh—to Burgos in 1090—is documented: H. Diener, "Das Itinerar des Abtes Hugo von Cluny," in *Neue Forschungen über Cluny und die Cluniacenser*, ed. G. Tellenbach (Freiburg, 1959), p. 369.

[10] See nn. 42–44 below.

[11] D. Mansilla, ed., *La documentación pontificia hasta Inocencio III (965–1216)*, Monumenta Hispaniae Vaticana, Registros 1 (Rome, 1955), doc. 27, p. 44. Interestingly enough both Urban II and Hugh of Cluny were concerned lest Bernard's personal behavior undermine his position. The pope urged him to be worthy of his office and not to become an offense; the abbot warned him to lead an exemplary life, so that his deeds might not invalidate his teachings. These hints can hardly refer to Bernard's purported seizure of the Grand Mosque of Toledo, as suggested by A. Cutler ("The First Crusade and the Idea of Conversion," *Muslim World* 58 [1968]: 58, n. 7), since this seizure is legendary: cf. Férotin, "Une lettre," p. 340, n. 3. Abbot Hugh's admonition to Bernard starts with the call that he should be *studio castitatis mundus*—perhaps it was in this sphere that Bernard's record had caused concern.

exhortation forms part of later papal confirmations of Toledan arch-bishops.[12] It indicates that the papacy regarded the Christianization of infidels a duty of the archbishop of Toledo, the primate of all Spain. In a similar vein, the rule of the Spanish military order of Santiago—written in the 1170s by Cardinal Alberto de Morra, the future Pope Gregory VIII—calls upon the brethren of the order to abstain from robbery and cruelty, and to regard the defense of Christians against Saracen attacks *and the inducing of Saracens to practice the Christian faith* as the objectives of their activities.[13] The same idea appears in the bull of July 5, 1175, drafted by Alberto de Morra, by which Pope Alexander III gave approval to the new order and received it under papal protection: Here the order is called upon to urge the brethren at the annual general chapters to wage war, not for the sake of glory, bloodshed, or cupidity, but to protect Christians and induce Saracens to practice Christianity.[14] Since the primitive rule of the order, presum-

[12] Mansilla, *La documentación*, docs. 45 (a. 1101), 101 (a. 1156), pp. 65, 121.

[13] *"Quod intentio fratrum sit una in defensione christianorum non crudelitatis et rapinae.* Verum cum uniuersorum specialis unica intentio sit, ecclesiam Dei pro viribus defendere, pro exaltatione nominis Christi animas ponere sarracenorum crudelitati iugiter obuiare, ita tamen quod causa rapinae uel crudelitatis, eorum terram non predentur, vel quicquid contra eos fecerint pro exaltatione nominis Christi faciatur, vel ut christianos ab eorum impugnatione defendant, vel ad culturam christianae fidei ualeant prouocare." *The Rule of the Spanish Military Order of St. James, 1170–1493*, ed. and trans. E. Gallego Blanco (Leiden, 1971), p. 110. Alberto de Morra's authorship is expressly mentioned in the rule (p. 146). For a Castilian version of this clause of the rule see D. W. Lomax, *La Orden de Santiago, 1170–1275* (Madrid, 1965), pp. 225–26.

[14] ". . . ubi praecipue ad defensionem Christianorum intendere moneantur, et districte precipiatur, ut in Saracenos non mundane laudis amore, non desiderio sanguinis effundendi, non terrenarum rerum cupiditate bellum tractent, sed in tantum in pugna sua intendant, ut vel christiani ab eorum tueantur incursu, vel ipsos ad culturam possint christianae fidei provocare." *Bullarium Equestris Ordinis S. Jacobi de Spatha*, ed. J. López Agurleta (Madrid, 1719), p. 15. On Alberto de Morra's authorship of this bull see A. Ferrari, "Alberto de Morra, postulador de la Orden de Santiago y su primer cronista," *Boletín de la Real Academia de la Historia* 146 (1960): 63–64, 117. The bull was repeatedly confirmed by later popes: *Bullarium*, pp. 30–31 (Lucius III = Mansilla, doc. 124, pp. 145–51), 51–52 (Innocent III, 1205), 57–58 (Innocent III, 1210), 79–81 (Honorius III), 173–74 (Innocent IV). In two recent works the bull is ascribed to Innocent III: L. Oliger, *Sancti Francisci Regula Anni 1223* (Rome, 1950), p. 31, note to lines 2–3; H. Roscher, *Papst Innocenz III und die Kreuzzüge* (Göttingen, 1969), pp. 174, 286. This false ascription caused some difficulty of interpretation in the second work. The snag goes back to Migne, who does not seem to have noticed that Innocent III merely reissued the bull of Alexander III: see PL 200:1027–28; 216:209. Robert I. Burns ascribes the bull to Lucius III: "Christian-Islamic Confrontation in the West: The Thirteenth-Century Dream of Conversion," *American Historical Review* 76 (1971): 1389–90, quoting Mansilla, doc. 124. But Mansilla points out in his preface (p. 145) that Lucius III merely reissued the bull of Alexander III. A perception of the objectives of

ably written in Spain, had not mentioned conversion at all and merely called members to defend the Church and assail the Saracens, it is plausible to assume that it was Alberto de Morra who introduced Saracen conversion among the order's goals.[15]

But even as Saracen conversion was being advocated by papal bulls and urged at chapters of the Order of Santiago, mundane considerations militated against it. Since, as it will be shown, baptism entailed a limitation on the economic exploitation of a Muslim slave and, in some regions, paved the way for the slave's liberation, some Christian masters strove to prevent the conversion of their Muslim slaves. Surprisingly enough, the earliest piece of evidence about such endeavors relates to monastic masters. A clause in the Cistercian statutes of 1152 states that "the ancient rule about the Saracens should be observed, namely, that they should not be bought or prohibited from being baptized."[16] Evidently the Cistercians, who founded their first Spanish houses in the 1130s, must have faced the problem before 1152, possibly in some of their southern French monasteries.[17] Since the clause recurs in the statutes of 1157, 1175, and 1215, the question undoubtedly remained acute.[18] And if members of the Cistercian Order, which in that period played so prominent a role in the missionizing of the Slavs, had to be enjoined time and again not to hinder the baptism of their Saracen slaves, it is hardly astonishing that some secular masters did so. In Barcelona some Jewish and Christian masters, "fearing to lose a worldly advantage," endeavored to prevent the conversion of their Saracens, demanding that the church of Barcelona compensate them for the loss incurred through the slaves' baptism—a state of affairs Innocent III attempted to end in 1206.[19]

Christian fighting in Spain similar to that of Alberto de Morra emerges from the complaint of William of Newburgh that the rulers of Europe shrink from waging war there "pro fidei christianae vel propagatione vel defensione." William of Newburgh, *Historia rerum Anglicarum*, V, 13, ed. R. Howlett, Rolls Series, 82 (London, 1884–85), 2:445–46.

[15] "Tota sit omnium intentio ecclesiam Dei defendere, Sarracenos inpugnare." Text edited by J. Leclercq, "La vie et la prière des chevaliers de Santiago d'après leur règle primitive," *Litúrgica* 2 (1958): 354.

[16] "De Saracenis antiqua sententia teneatur, scilicet ut nec emantur, nec baptizari prohibeantur." *Statuta Capitulorum Generalium Ordinis Cisterciensis, 1116–1786*, ed. J.-M. Canivez, 8 vols. (Louvain, 1933–41), 1:49.

[17] On the first Spanish houses see M. Defourneaux, *Les Français*, pp. 49–55.

[18] *Statuta Capitulorum*, ed. Canivez, 1:66, 83, 436. In 1218 a Spanish abbot received permission to baptize Saracens according to the license of his bishop. In 1246 the Cistercians were prohibited from buying Saracen concubines for their Saracen slaves, as three southern French abbots had done, evidently for breeding purposes (1:490; 2:303, 308).

[19] Mansilla, *La documentación*, doc. 352, pp. 375–76. Cf. *Las siete partidas del Rey don Alfonso el Sabio*, 3 vols. (Madrid, 1807), 3:120–21.

A milder compromise between the claims of Christianity and Mammon may be discerned in the late-eleventh-century *fuero* of Medinaceli, Castile, later granted also to three Navarrese localities, which is extant in two diverging versions of about 1130 and about 1198, respectively. The first states that the possessions of a converted *captivo* are to be inherited by his Christian master, or his successor; the other that the master inherits the property of his converted Moors if they die childless. Similarly, the *fuero* granted to Teruel, Aragon, in about 1176, stipulates that the possessions of converted Moors who die childless devolve to their master or, should that one have died, to his heirs.[20] All three texts, undoubtedly referring to converted and manumitted slaves, awarded the master a considerably greater right over the possessions of his converted Moors than did the pertinent stipulation of Roman law, incorporated into some contemporary legal collections, which declared that the master inherits the effects of his freedman only if the latter dies *childless and intestate*.[21]

The Norman conquest of Sicily (1060–91) also entailed some Muslim conversions, some of which occurred during the island's reduction.

---

[20] Version written down about 1130: "Et homes de Carocastello qui suo captivo tornaverit xristiano hereditet illo in vita é in morte." T. Muñoz y Romero, *Colección de fueros municipales y cartas-pueblas de los reinos de Castilla, León, Corona de Aragón y Navarra*, vol. 1 (Madrid, 1847), p. 471. (I take *in vita é in morte* to mean during the lifetime of the master or after his death, an intepretation supported by the parallel clause of the *fuero* of Teruel, quoted below.) Version written down about 1198: "Qui su moro, ó su mora tornaren é christiano, herede su señor, si filos non oviere" (p. 443). See Verlinden, *L'esclavage*, 1:157. On the complicated history of this *fuero* see A. García-Gallo, "Los fueros de Medinaceli," *Anuario de historia del derecho español* 31 (1961): 9–16; for the dates of the two versions see A. Ubieto Arteta, *El 'Cantar de mio Cid' y algunos problemas históricos* (Valencia, 1973), pp. 153–55. Fuero of Teruel, ca. 1176: "De eo qui maurum suum fecerit cristianum. Item mando quod si quis uirum suos mauros[*sic*] cristianos fecerit. et ipsi sine filiis obierint. dominus eorum hereditet sua bona. Si forte dominus illorum proselitorum uiuus non fuerit. filii domini uel heredes hereditent bona superius iam predicta." *Forum Turolii*, c. 313, ed. F. Aznar y Navarro (Saragossa, 1905), p. 179. Cf. Verlinden, 1:162.

[21] §3. *Inst.* de succ. lib. III, 7; *Lo Codi: Eine Summa Codicis in provenzalischer Sprache aus dem XII. Jahrhundert. Die provenzalische Fassung der Handschrift A (Sorbonne 632)*, VI, 21, ed. F. Derrer (Zurich, 1974), p. 138–39; *Lo Codi in der lateinischen Übersetzung des Ricardus Pisanus*, VI, 20, ed. H. Fitting (Halle, 1906), p. 192; *Livre des Assises des Bourgeois*, ed. A. A. Beugnot, in RHC. Lois 2:204. While the crusader *assise* speaks of a slave who has been "made Christian," its apparent model, the Provençal *Lo Codi*, speaks of a *libertinus*; cf. n. 98 below. The connection between the two collections was established by J. Prawer, "Etude préliminaire sur les sources et la composition du *Livre des Assises des Bourgeois*," *Revue historique de droit français et étranger* 32 (1954): 198–227, 358–82; idem, *Crusader Institutions* (Oxford, 1980), pp. 358–411. See also the pertinent stipulation in the 1272 Code of Tortosa, quoted in Verlinden, *L'esclavage*, 1:302, n. 209.

Count Roger, the builder of Norman Sicily, hardly considered it his objective "to extend the worship of the Christian name among the pagans" (i.e., the Muslims), as Pope Gregory VII once had demanded of him.[22] But on occasion he did use conversion to further his aims. In 1087, after some difficulty in reducing Castrogiovanni, the last Muslim castle on the island, he offered its lord, *Chamut* (al-Qāsim b. Ḥammūd), whose wife and children he had taken captive a few days earlier, the chance to surrender the castle and become Christian. The Muslim, who allegedly had already considered conversion, complied on condition that upon conversion he might retain his wife even though she was related to him in a degree forbidden among Christians. (The condition suggests, incidentally, that the lord of Castrogiovanni had been aware of a precedent in which the consanguinity of a converted Muslim couple had formed an obstacle.) Count Roger gave his consent—one is left to wonder on the basis of which canonistic reasoning—and thus the castle was taken, and Chamut, his wife, and children baptized and given land in Calabria, far from their former subjects and coreligionists. (The royal justiciary Rogerius Hamutus, who appears in acts of 1189 and 1193, might have been one of Chamut's descendants.)[23] Chamut's reluctance to stay at Castrogiovanni is understandable in the light of an earlier Muslim conversion. Elias *Cartomensis*, a convert who had fought on the Norman side with some distinction and, sometime after 1082, had fallen into the hands of the Muslims of Castrogiovanni, was promptly put to death when he refused to revert to Islam.[24] Another Muslim, Aḥmad, was Count Roger's godson and was accordingly named Roger Aḥmad; the count gave Roger Aḥmad three villages in the neighborhood of Girgenti, Sicily, which

[22] ". . . et christiani nominis culturam inter paganos amplificare studeat." *Das Register Gregors VII*, ed. E. Caspar (1920), in MGH Epp. sel. 2, 1:272. The letter is from 1076. On the basis of its style, Blaul could not decide whether it was written in its entirety by the pope or not: O. Blaul, "Studien zum Register Gregors VII," *Archiv für Urkundenforschung* 4 (1912): 168.

[23] The source for Chamut's conversion is Gaufredus Malaterra, *De rebus gestis Rogerii Calabriae et Siciliae comitis et Roberti Guiscardi ducis fratris ejus*, IV, 5–6, ed. E. Pontieri (1925–28), in RIS 5, 1:87–88. Malaterra's date was corrected by Amari, *Storia*, 3, 1:177, n. 1. On Chamut's role in the events leading to the Norman occupation of Sicily see U. Rizzitano, "Ruggero il Gran Conte e gli Arabi di Sicilia," in *Ruggero il Gran Conte e l'inizio dello stato normanno: Relazioni e comunicazioni nelle Seconde Giornate normanno-sveve (Bari, maggio 1975)* (Rome, 1977), pp. 205–8. Rizzitano doubts Chamut's conversion, but the reason given is not cogent. On Rogerius Hamutus see L. White, Jr., *Latin Monasticism* (chap. 1, n. 86 above), pp. 201, 282–83.

[24] Malaterra, III, 30, p. 75; see also III, 18, p. 67. A still earlier convert is the baker *genere Sarracenus* who married a prior's sister and in 1081 allegedly poisoned Robert of Grandmesnil, abbot of the Calabrian monastery of St. Eufemia: *The Ecclesiastical History of Orderic Vitalis*, ed. and trans. Marjorie Chibnall, vol. 4 (Oxford, 1973), pp. 22–23.

he later donated to the archbishop of Palermo, in 1141.[25] But Count Roger's support of Muslim conversion had its limits. Eadmer, the biographer of Anselm of Canterbury, relates that when Anselm stayed in 1098 with the Norman army that besieged Capua, many of Roger's Saracen soldiers were so impressed by him that they would have converted to Christianity had they not feared the wrath of their count, for he would not allow them to be baptized with impunity. Evidently, though Eadmer does not say so, the count preferred to have at his disposal a Muslim contingent that could be set in the field against any Christian enemy, the pope included.[26]

During the twelfth century the conversion of Sicilian Muslims gathered momentum. The great majority of the forty-seven "names of the Christians of [the village of] Corleone" that appear in a list of 1178 are typically Arabic and some are typically Islamic; it stands to reason that many of their bearers, all serfs of the abbey of Monreale, were converts to Christianity. Baptism probably did not alter the social status of such converts, for other documents show that Christian serfs were transferred, along with unconverted Muslim serfs, from one owner to another. A document drawn up in 1117 at the monastery of St. Bartholomew of Lipari mentions "the monk Philip the Arab," possibly a convert from Islam.[27] Certainly many of King Roger II's courtiers were converted Muslims. The most conspicuous of those was Philip

[25] E. Caspar, *Roger II (1101–1154) und die Gründung der normannisch-sicilischen Monarchie*, regest 137 (Innsbruck, 1904), p. 543. Caspar considered Roger Aḥmad to have been identical with Chamut; but the three *casalia* Count Roger gave him were in the vicinity of Girgenti (R. Pirro, *Sicilia Sacra* [Palermo, 1733], col. 86), that is, exactly in the area that Chamut had formerly ruled and decided to leave after his conversion.

Another Muslim convert might have been *Sataymamon* (Sitt, or Lady, Maymūnah) of Castrogiovanni, the founder of St. Mary of Bethlehem: Pirro, col. 584; Amari, *Storia*, 3:542.

[26] *The Life of St. Anselm, Archbishop of Canterbury, by Eadmer*, ed. and trans. R. W. Southern (London, 1962), pp. 110–12. Amari's doubts (*Storia*, 3:191, 309, n. 2) seem to be unfounded.

[27] For the list of 1178 see S. Cusa, ed., *I diplomi greci ed arabi di Sicilia*, 2 vols. (Palermo, 1868–82), 1, 1:145–46; for documents of 1136 and 1183 listing other Christian serfs who bear Arabic names see C. A. Garufi, ed., *I documenti inediti dell'epoca normanna in Sicilia*, vol. 1 (Palermo, 1889), pp. 25–26, 187. With regard to the status of converted serfs I follow the conclusion of Dietlind Schack, *Die Araber im Reich Rogers II* (Berlin, 1969), pp. 36–37. For a detailed study of a segment of the rural Muslim population under Norman rule see H. Berchier, Annie Courteaux, and J. Mouton, "Une abbaye latine dans la société musulmane: Monreale au XIIᵉ siècle," *Annales E.S.C.* 34 (1979): 525–47. For the monk Philip see Cusa, *I diplomi*, 1, 2:512, and White, *Latin Monasticism*, p. 59. In the thirteenth century, Muslims of Lucera improved their economic situation by converting to Christianity: see the letter of Frederick II to Gregory IX in *Historia Diplomatica Friderici Secundi*, ed. J.L.A. Huillard-Bréholles, vol. 4, 2 (Paris, 1855), p. 831.

of al-Mahdiyya, the chamberlain and admiral who in 1153 fell from grace and, accused of secretly remaining faithful to his old religion and sending offerings to the tomb of Magumeth, was sentenced to die at the stake. His associates were executed as well.[28] According to a contemporary, the well-informed Archbishop Romuald of Salerno, Roger II endeavored at the end of his life to convert Jews and Saracens "by all methods," showering the converts with presents. Anti-Muslim pogroms, like that which erupted in Palermo in 1160, probably also induced some Muslims to save themselves by becoming Christian. And when the Muslim pilgrim from Granada, Ibn Djubayr, passed through Sicily in the winter of 1184–85, he heard of the ostensible conversions of Muslim courtiers and harem girls, the pressuring of a Muslim jurist into conversion, the flight to baptism of Muslims who had quarreled with their next of kin, and the king's efforts that occasionally led to the apostasy of Muslim women and children. He relates also that he met Muslims who expressed their fear that all of Sicily's Muslims, like those of Crete before them, might gradually become Christian. Ibn Djubayr's last story is the most telling: As he was about to leave Sicily, he heard of a Muslim father who attempted to marry his young daughter to a passenger leaving for a Muslim country and so spare her the temptation of apostasy.[29]

Besides the Muslims who became Christian in the newly conquered parts of Spain and in Sicily, there were others who, upon being reduced to slavery in the wake of campaigns of the Spanish reconquest and of piracy in the Mediterranean, were carried off to the Catholic mainland and there converted to Christianity. The acts of Genoese notaries, which allow glimpses of such Muslim slaves from 1156 on-

---

[28] *Romualdi Salernitani Chronicon*, ed. C. A. Garufi (1914–35), in RIS 7, 1:234–36. The passage, an interpolation, is adjudged contemporaneous and as containing parts of the original sentence against Philip: Amari, *Storia*, 3:443, 445, n. 2; Schack, *Die Araber*, p. 145, n. 597. The main points are corroborated by Ibn al-Athīr: M. Amari, *Biblioteca Arabo-Sicula*, vol. 1 (Turin and Rome, 1880), pp. 479–80. On the precarious position of Muslim officials, opposed by aristocracy and clergy alike, see the perceptive remarks of F. Gabrieli, "La politique arabe des Normands de Sicile," *Studia islamica* 9 (1958): 92–93. On Roger II's legislation on apostasy see Schack, *Die Araber*, p. 149. In 1199 Innocent III called on the bishop of Syracuse to take measures against baptized Saracens who reverted to their old religion: PL 214:471–72.

[29] On Roger's attempts at Christianization see *Romualdi Salernitani Chronicon*, p. 236; for his possible motives see Amari, *Storia*, 3:446–47, and Schack, *Die Araber*, pp. 142–50. For Ibn Djubayr's account see his *Travels*, trans. R.J.C. Broadhurst (London, 1952), pp. 338–60, especially pp. 357–60. It is noteworthy that a few years before Ibn Djubayr heard that the Norman king occasionally induced Muslim women and children to convert, Pope Alexander III had written to the archbishop of Palermo that he had heard that in his archbishopric "Sarraceni mulieres Christianas et pueros rapiunt, et eis abuti praesumunt, et quosdam etiam . . . interdum occidere non veruntur." X 5.17.4.

ward, suggest that only a minority accepted baptism. Of the fifteen Saracen slaves mentioned in the acts drawn up by the notary Guglielmo Cassinese between February 1191 and April 1192, only five may be regarded as baptized; of the twelve referred to in the extant acts of the years 1198 to 1213, four may be considered so; and of the 196 slaves of the extant acts of 1239 to 1274 who are described as Saracens or whose ethnic origin is not specified, 65 bear names that indicate that they underwent baptism.[30] The acts reveal that many converted Muslim slaves were sold by one Christian master to another; incidentally, one baptized Muslim slave girl was bought by a Cistercian monk from Poblet, Catalonia.[31] Evidently baptism did not automatically entail, in Genoa, the manumission of the converted—a state of affairs that will be expressly sanctioned by the canon lawyers of the thirteenth century.[32] On the other hand, since almost all manumitted Muslim slaves had been previously baptized, one may conclude that baptism was normally a prerequisite of manumission.[33] Indeed this is expressly spelled out in a testament of 1192, in which the Genoese Pietro da Croce stipulates that his Saracen slave Oliverio be manumitted on the condition that he first undergo baptism. Similarly Doña Leocadia of Toledo, in an Arabic-written will of 1180, stipulates that the female slave ʿĀisha, coowned by the testator and her husband, Don García, may become Christian should she wish to do so, and then pay half of her price to Don García and become free.[34]

Little can be said about the absorption of these early converts into Christian society. The genealogical list of the Saracen slaves owned by the Galician monastery of Sobrado reveals that the slave Lupi, named Martin Porra after conversion, managed to marry a free Christian woman; eleven sons and daughters of other converted slaves married

[30] For 1191–92 and 1198–1213, see Verlinden, *L'esclavage*, 2:437, 445; for 1239–74, M. Balard, "Remarques sur les esclaves à Gênes dans la seconde moitié du XIIIᵉ siècle," *Mélanges d'archéologie et d'histoire publiés par l'Ecole Française de Rome* 80 (1968): 645, 648. (Balard does not specify how many of the 151 slaves who are described as Saracens bear Christian names.) For an even lower proportion of converts among the Muslim slaves of Sicily in the late thirteenth century see Verlinden, 2:151, 154.

[31] Verlinden, 2:456.

[32] See chap. 4 below and my "Muslim Conversion in Canon Law," *Proceedings of the Sixth International Congress of Medieval Canon Law* (in press).

[33] For cases in which baptism precedes manumission see Balard, pp. 648, 675. In twelfth-century Catalonia, baptism gradually became a prerequisite for manumission: Verlinden, *L'esclavage*, 1:173. For the unusal case of a Muslim from Tunis who was first manumitted and then baptized, see Verlinden, 2:439–40.

[34] A. Haverkamp, "Zur Sklaverei in Genua während des 12. Jahrhunderts," in *Geschichte in der Gesellschaft: Festschrift für Karl Bosl*, ed. F. Prinz et al. (Stuttgart, 1974), p. 209; A. González Palencia, *Los mozárabes de Toledo en los siglos XII y XIII*, vol. 3 (Madrid, 1928), doc. 1018, pp. 388–89; Verlinden, *L'esclavage*, 1:155; 2:437.

servile Christians or entered into liaisons with them; and nine converts, or converts' descendants, married other converts. But the *Genealogia sarracenorum Sancte Marie Superaddi* is a unique document, and there is no way to tell whether so high a rate of intermarriage was common among converted slaves elsewhere. The integration of more highly placed converts, who were fewer in number, appears to have been more difficult: Certainly the converted courtiers of the Norman kings of Sicily aroused antagonism among the Christian populace. Perhaps the smoothest transition befell the few Muslims who, genuinely attracted to Christianity, chose to enter a monastic community. Thus Constantine the African (d. ca. 1087), a Muslim merchant and physician from Tunis who came to Italy of his free will, joined the monastery of Monte Cassino, and was engaged there in translating Arabic medical tracts into Latin. His disciple Johannes Afflacius was another convert from Islam who became a monk and was engaged in translation.[35] But such careers were exceptional.

The new power balance with the world of Islam, which paved the way for a considerable number of Muslim conversions in the recently reconquered territories, also emboldened some Catholic Europeans to consider the conversion of Muslims who had not yet come under Christian rule. According to an Arabic work from Spain, a monk of France (*rāhib min Ifransa*) wrote twice to al-Muqtadir b. Hūd, ruler of Saragossa from 1046 to 1081, calling upon him to convert, and even sent messengers to persuade him of the truth of Christianity. The Arabic work purports to contain the *rāhib*'s second appeal and the reply of Abu 'l-Walīd Sulaymān al-Bādjī, the prominent Spanish theologian who had studied for many years in the Muslim Orient.[36] Even

---

[35] For the *Genealogia sarracenorum* see n. 4 above; Constantine and Johannes Afflacius are dealt with by R. Creutz in four articles: "Der Arzt Constantinus Africanus von Montekassino: Sein Leben, sein Werk und seine Bedeutung für die mittelalterliche medizinische Wissenschaft," *Studien und Mitteilungen zur Geschichte des Benediktiner-Ordens und seiner Zweige* 47 (1929): 1–44; idem, "Der Cassinese Johannes Afflacius Saracenus, ein Arzt aus 'Hochsalerno,'" ibid. 48 (1930): 301–24; idem, "Die Ehrenrettung Konstantins von Afrika," ibid. 49 (1931): 25–44; idem, "Additamenta zu Konstantinus Africanus und seinen Schülern Johannes und Atto," ibid. 50 (1932): 420–42.

On the harassment of converts to Christianity see *Usatges de Barcelona*, c. 75, ed. R. d'Abadal i Vinyals and F. Valls Taberner, Textes de dret català 1 (Barcelona, 1913), p. 32; J. Boswell, *The Royal Treasure. Muslim Communities under the Crown of Aragon in the Fourteenth Century* (New Haven and London, 1977), pp. 378-79.

[36] English translation and Arabic text: D. M. Dunlop, "A Christian Mission to Muslim Spain in the Eleventh Century," *al-Andalus* 17 (1952): 259–310. Arabic text and French translation: Abdelmagid Turki, "La lettre du 'Moine de France' à al-Muqtadir billāh, roi de Saragosse, et la réponse d'al-Bāŷī, le faqīh andalou," *al-Andalus* 31 (1966): 73–153.

though the *rāhib*'s letter shows signs of Muslim redaction, the episto-
lary exchange in its entirety rings authentic.[37] The repeated but oblique
references to the actions of the *rāhib*'s messengers and their interpreter
would have been out of place had the exchange been merely a Muslim
literary exercise. Al-Bādjī's condescension toward the *rāhib*'s ineptitude
at rational reasoning and his allusion to the *rāhib*'s unfamiliarity with
earlier Muslim-Christian polemics also increase the probability that this
is a genuine reply to an appeal by an eleventh-century French monk.[38]
It is true that the single anti-Islamic argument attributed to the *rāhib*—
namely, that the Devil, unable to lead mankind back to idolatry, "used
imposture against the children of Ishmael in the matter of the Envoy
in whose prophecy they believed"—closely parallels the account of the
rise of Mohomat in the Spanish Christian Passion of Nunilón and
Alodia.[39] But since numerous Frenchmen took part in the early stages
of the Spanish reconquest, popular Spanish Christian notions about
the rise of Islam might have filtered into France by the second half of
the eleventh century.

The name of the French *rāhib* is not mentioned in the letters. It has
been suggested that he was no other than Abbot Hugh of Cluny, and
that one of the messengers mentioned in the correspondence was the
hermit Anastasius, sent by Gregory VII and Abbot Hugh to preach
the Gospel to the Saracens of Spain.[40] In any case, the crucial fact is

[37] The Muslim influence is convincingly demonstrated by Turki, pp. 75–80.

[38] References to messengers: Dunlop, pp. 267, 271–72, Turki, pp. 123, 130–31;
condescendence: e.g., Dunlop, pp. 272–73, 276, Turki, pp. 132, 137; unfamiliarity
with Muslim polemics: Dunlop, p. 277, Turki, p. 139.

[39] "Dum hec itaque ageretur, anno ferme sexcentesimo post Domini ad celos ascen-
sionem, uidens antiquissimus serpens diabolus iam pene per omnem mundum Xpi
Euangelium intonare et in fines orbis terre resonare, timens miser ne omnes gentes ipse
penitus perderet, ad pristinam se artem conuertit et transformans se in angelum lucis ad
quendam Arabicum et uersutissimum hominem, nomine Mohomat, in Gabrielum se
angelum mentitus accessit. . . . Per hanc ergo callidam artem gens Arabica male decepta
usque hodie a fide Xpi aliena et exclusa perdurat." J. Gil, ed., "En torno a las Santas
Nunilón y Alodia," pp. 114–15.

"And the accursed Devil . . . tried to change this holy religion after the coming of the
Apostles, who had shown the right way to the people of the earth by their preaching.
. . . So the Devil was incapable of bringing the people of the world to fall, and to lead
them back to their ancient errors of worshiping the idols; so he used imposture against
the children of Ishmael in the matter of the Envoy in whose prophecy they believed,
and in that way he directed many souls to the punishment of hell." Turki, p. 86. (I
would like to thank Professor Eliyahu Ashtor for translating this passage into English.)

[40] A. Cutler, "Who Was the 'Monk of France' and When Did He Write?" *al-Andalus*
28 (1963): 249–69. Cutler's main conjecture may be now supported by Hugh of Cluny's letter to Bernard of Sédirac and Gilo's story about Hugh's assistance at the baptism
of a Spanish Moor. Cutler errs, however, in assuming that the extant Latin translation

that in this Arabic work a Catholic European is reported to have made, on his own initiative, an unequivocal offer of conversion to a Muslim ruler. This unprecedented incident points to the emergence of a new venturesome stance toward the world of Islam, a reflection on the intellectual plane of the Catholic European military counteroffensive.

Traces of this new stance may also be discerned in the outlook of Christians elsewhere. It might have been already adopted by Richard, abbot of St. Vanne, who in 1026–27, while on pilgrimage to Jerusalem, "preached Christ Jesus" to the Saracens he encountered on his way from Antioch southward. "With joy he announced to them, through an interpreter, the things pertaining to Jesus," relates the chronicler Hugh of Flavigny, "and stated that they should refrain from injuring the servants of God."[41] This is the first time a pilgrim is reported to have attempted to preach Christianity while crossing Saracen lands on his way to Jerusalem.

The new stance is more clearly evident in letters Gregory VII sent in the 1070s to North African addressees. When he lauds in 1073 the steadfastness of the bishop of Carthage who did not acquiesce to an uncanonical ordination though he was tortured by the Saracens and then adds, in an outburst of Hildebrandine charity, that the bishop would have done even better had he exposed the Saracens' error, preached the Christian religion, and thus attained death, the pope discloses not only that he, too, knew that the Saracens punished with death attacks against their religion but also that he considered an attempt at converting the Saracens in their own countries most commendable.[42] In 1076, Gregory exhorts the Christian community of the newly founded town of Bidjāya (Bougie) to lead an exemplary life so

---

of the Byzantine Epistle to ʿUmar may antedate Abbot Hugh (p. 267, n. 83); this work was translated from the Syriac at the turn of the fifteenth century by Symphorien Champère. Cf. PG 107:315; F. I. Schwarz, *Super epistola Leonis Sap. Graecorum Imperat. ad Omarum Saracenorum Principem* (Leipzig, 1783), pp. iii–iv.

[41] "Et cum appropinquaret civitatibus eorum, praedicabat omnibus Christum Iesum . . . Pagani autem . . . veniebant ad eum, quibus ipse per interpretem quae de Iesu erant gratanter annunciabat, et ut ab iniuria servorum Dei manus cohiberent praedicabat." *Chronicon Hugonis monachi Virdunensis et Divionensis, abbatis Flaviniacensis*, ed. G. H. Pertz (1848), in MGH SS 8:394–95. For the date of the pilgrimage see chap. 1, n. 86 above.

[42] "Sed quanto pretiosius esset religionis tue confessio, si post verbera, que tunc sustinuisti, errorem eorum ostendendo et Christianam religionem predicando usque ad effusionem ipsius anime pervenisses." *Das Register Gregors VII*, I, 23, p. 39. On Gregory's certain authorship of this letter, see Blaul, "Studien," p. 137. The phrase "ad effusionem ipsius anime" must refer to the bishop's recommended death; cf. *Amalarii episcopi Opera liturgica omnia*, ed. J. M. Hanssens, vol. 2, Studi e Testi, 139 (Città del Vaticano, 1948), p. 93.

that their Saracen neighbors may be induced to emulate the Christian faith rather than hold it in contempt.[43] And his famous letter of the same year to the Berber ruler al-Nāṣir b. ʿAlannās—that masterful exercise in ambiguity in which Christians and Saracens are portrayed as believing in the same God, though in different manners—ends with a valediction that, seen through Christian eyes, conveys the pope's wish for al-Nāṣir's ultimate conversion.[44] (Gregory's conciliatory words about the beliefs of the Saracens should be understood in their context: When the pope writes to Christian addressees, he refers to the Saracens as "pagans" and "impious ones.")[45]

SARACEN CONVERSION: AN AIM OF THE CRUSADES?

To what extent was Muslim conversion furthered by the easternmost prong of the Catholic European counteroffensive, the crusade? As is well known, the text of Urban's Clermont Address of 1095, which triggered the First Crusade, has not survived; nevertheless, none of the chroniclers purporting to report that speech mentions Saracen conversion as an express objective. The passage in Guibert of Nogent's version of the Clermont Address—written about 1108—in which the crusaders are exhorted to go to Jerusalem so that the Christian name may be propagated through them and the Christian empire in the East renewed seems at first glance to connote infidel conversion. In reality Guibert's argument is coined in purely eschatological terms: A Christian presence is needed in Jerusalem so that Antichrist may there find adversaries; this presence cannot be secured through infidel conversion, since the infidels abstain from it, embodying as they do the re-

---

[43] *Das Register Gregors VII*, III, 20, p. 286; for Gregory's authorship see Blaul, pp. 169–70.

[44] "Scit enim Deus, quia pure ad honorem Dei te diligimus et salutem et honorem tuum in presenti et in futura vita desideramus atque, ut ipse Deus in sinum beatitudinis sanctissimi patriarche Abrahe post longa huius vite spatia te perducat, corde et ore rogamus." *Das Register Gregors VII*, III, 21, p. 288; Blaul, pp. 170–71. On Gregory's hope for Muslim conversion as one of his motives in writing the letter see also Ch. Courtois, "Grégoire VII et l'Afrique du Nord: Remarques sur les communautés chrétiennes d'Afrique au XIᵉ siècle," *Revue historique* 195 (1945): 212–13. On the commercial angle of Gregory's initiative see R. S. Lopez, "A propos d'une virgule: Le facteur économique dans la politique africaine des papes," *Revue historique* 198 (1947): 178–85.

[45] *Das Register Gregors VII*, I, 7, pp. 11–12; I, 49, p. 75; II, 3, p. 128; II, 31, p. 166; VI, 16, p. 421. Cf. the remark of C. Cahen in *Settimane di studio del Centro italiano di studi sull'alto medioevo*, vol. 12 (Spoleto, 1965), pp. 369–70; Schwinges, *Kreuzzugsideologie*, p. 135.

bellion that must precede the coming of Antichrist (the allusion, as in the Revelation of Pseudo-Methodius, is to 2 Thessalonians 2:3), and therefore the crusaders are called upon to leave for Jerusalem and supply there the required Christian presence.[46] Robert the Monk, who wrote his version of the Clermont Address about 1122, may be implying that Urban envisaged the possibility of Saracen conversion when he lets the pope urge his listeners to be inspired by the prowess of Charlemagne, Louis the Pious, and other Frankish kings "who destroyed the kingdoms of the pagans and dilated the boundaries of Holy Church into them."[47] But even Robert does not make Urban present Saracen conversion as an explicit goal.

Nor is Saracen conversion mentioned or alluded to in Urban's extant letters from the years 1095 to 1099 in which he refers to the crusade: The expedition's aim is presented as the liberation of the churches and the Christians ravaged and oppressed in the Orient, especially in Jerusalem, by the barbarous Saracens.[48] It is as if to the pope the Saracens were an extraneous force that had recently invaded Christian lands and must be militarily defeated and repulsed. Such a perception would have been realistic enough as far as the Seljuk invasion of Byzantine Asia Minor was concerned, but entirely amiss for the native Muslim population of Syria and Palestine, which, as the German chronicler Ekkehard of Aura was to learn in Jerusalem in 1101, suffered under the Seljuk conquerors no less than the Christians.[49]

Statements made by Urban's humbler contemporaries during the

---

[46] Guibert of Nogent, *Gesta Dei per Francos*, in RHC. HOcc. 4:139. For an interpretation of this passage as alluding to Urban's hope for Saracen conversion see Marianne Plocher, "Studien zum Kreuzzugsgedanken im 12. und 13. Jahrhundert" (Ph.D. diss., University of Freiburg, 1950); see also Cutler, "The First Crusade," p. 59.

[47] Robertus Monachus, *Historia Iherosolimitana*, in RHC. HOcc. 3:728. Cf. J.S.C. Riley-Smith, *What Were the Crusades?* (London, 1977), p. 18.

[48] For Urban's letters see H. Hagenmeyer, *Die Kreuzzugsbriefe aus den Jahren 1088–1100: Eine Quellensammlung zur Geschichte des Ersten Kreuzzuges* (Innsbruck, 1901), pp. 136–38; P. Kehr, *Papsturkunden in Italien: Reiseberichte zur Italia Pontificia*, vol. 3 (Città del Vaticano, 1977), p. 216; idem, *Papsturkunden in Spanien: Vorarbeiten zur Hispania Pontificia*, vol. 1 (Berlin, 1926), pp. 287–88. It is noteworthy that Urban does not refer to the Turks in any of these letters, while in two of them he mentions the Saracens. Only in a letter of 1098 (PL 151:504), written about a year after the crusaders had crossed into Asia Minor, does Urban refer to the Turkish enemy.

[49] *Frutolfi et Ekkehardi Chronica necnon Anonymi Chronica Imperatorum*, ed. and trans. F.-J. Schmale and Irene Schmale-Ott, Ausgewählte Quellen zur deutschen Geschichte des Mittelalters, 15 (Darmstadt, 1972), p. 134. On the suffering of the inhabitants of Jerusalem see J. H. Greenstone, ed. and trans., "The Turkoman Defeat at Cairo, by Solomon ben Joseph ha-Kohen," *American Journal of Semitic Languages and Literatures* 22 (1906): 161, 165; cf. S. D. Goitein, "al-Quds," in *Encyclopaedia of Islam*, 2d ed.

hectic months that preceded the crusade's departure for the East envisage the aims of the projected expedition in well-nigh the same manner. On April 12, 1096, the knight Achard of Montmerle, planning to take part in "this pilgrimage to Jerusalem" and possibly to stay in the lands of the East, enters into an agreement with Abbot Hugh of Cluny and his monks, according to which he will receive from the monastery two thousand sous Lyonnais and four she-mules against the collateral of his possessions. In this agreement, drawn up by Hugh's medic and probably reflecting his thinking, Achard expresses his wish to join, under arms, "the great and extremely numerous summons or expedition of the Christian people endeavoring to go to Jerusalem to wage war, on God's behalf, against the pagans and the Saracens." (We do not know how far east the four mules of Cluny did get; their new owner, Achard, was killed during the siege of Jerusalem in the summer of 1099 while in the vicinity of Ramla.) Sometime in 1096, Count Raymond of St. Gilles, a future leader of the crusade, refers in a grant to the church of Puy to the men setting out "for the liberation of the Lord's sepulcher." And on August 24, 1096, the brothers Gaufredus and Guiogo sell a manse to the abbey of St. Victor of Marseilles, because they intend to go to Jerusalem "both for the sake of pilgrimage and, with God's protection, to quench the accursed madness of the pagans, which rushed out at innumerous Christian peoples, oppressing, capturing, and killing them with a barbarous furor," a formulation that recalls Urban's reference in a letter of 1095 to "the barbarous madness" devastating the churches of the East.[50]

[50] *Recueil des chartes de l'abbaye de Cluny*, ed. A. Bernard and A. Bruel, vol. 5 (Paris, 1894), p. 51; *Cartulaire de l'abbaye de Saint-Victor de Marseille*, ed. B. Guérard, vol. 1 (Paris, 1857), p. 167; C. Devic and J. Vaissete, *Histoire générale de Languedoc*, vol. 5 (Toulouse, 1875), p. 748. The importance of these texts was first pointed out by H.E.J. Cowdrey, "Pope Urban II's Preaching of the First Crusade," *History* 55 (1970): 181–83, and R. Sommerville, "The Council of Clermont and the First Crusade," *Studia Gratiana* 20 (1976): 326, n. 9. For Achard's death see *Le "Liber" de Raymond d'Aguilers*, c. 18, ed. J. H. Hill and Laurita L. Hill (Paris, 1969), p. 141; Albert of Aix, *Liber christianae expeditionis pro ereptione, emundatione et restitutione sanctae Hierosolymitanae ecclesie*, VI, 4, in RHC. HOcc. 4:468.

Another future leader of the crusade, Robert II of Flanders, writes in a grant of 1096 that he is leaving for Jerusalem "ad liberandam Dei ecclesiam diu a feris nationibus conculcatam": *Actes des comtes de Flandre, 1071-1128*, ed. F. Vercauteren, Recueil des actes des princes belges, 2 (Brussels, 1938), p. 63. See also the statement in a contemporary grant to Sauxillanges by one Rotgerius and his son Rotbertus: "Cum ad libertatem orientalis ecclesiae devastandam barbarica persecutio inhorresceret, exhortans decretum a summo pontifice, processit ut omnis occidentalium nationum virtus ac fides in auxilium destructe religionis festinaret." *Cartulaire de Sauxillanges*, ed. H. Doniol (Clermont-Ferrand and Paris, 1864), doc. 697, pp. 502-03. The financial aspect of these

None of the extant papal summons to later crusading expeditions, which call for the defense or recovery of Jerusalem and the Crusading Kingdom, presents Saracen conversion as a goal of the crusade.[51] Neither does any of the extant papal letters to the prelates of the Crusading Kingdom dictate the conversion of the infidel as one of their main duties, as do the exhortations of Urban II, Paschal II, and Hadrian IV to the archbishops of Toledo. Nor does any rule of the military orders established in the Crusading Kingdom contain a clause similar to that of the Spanish Order of Santiago that prompts the brethren to lead the Saracens to the practice of Christianity.

Bernard of Clairvaux, the authoritative leader who wholeheartedly supported the Jerusalemite Order of the Temple, wrote about 1130 in an exhortation to the knights of the new order that "it would not be fitting to kill the pagans [= the Muslims] if by some other means they could be restrained from extremely harassing and oppressing the faithful. Now, however, it is better that they be killed than to let them remain a rod of sinners [hovering] over the fate of the just, lest perchance the just [also] extend their hands toward iniquity."[52] Evidently Bernard could only conceive of force as an effective means to counter the Muslim threat to the Crusading Kingdom, implicitly ruling out Christianization as a viable mode of coping with it. In 1146, when Bernard calls for the Second Crusade, he alludes to Saracen conversion as a merely hypothetical possibility. In a passage whose wording varies in the manuscript tradition, Bernard states that if the Saracens were subjugated to Christian rule as the Jews are, the Christians would await their conversion as they await that of the Jews; but at the present the Saracens attack the Christians and therefore must be repulsed. The crusade is thus presented as a defensive war, with Bernard employing

---

grants has been discussed by G. Constable, "The Financing of the Crusades in the Twelfth Century," in *Outremer. Studies in the History of the Crusading Kingdom of Jerusalem presented to Joshua Prawer*, ed. B. Z. Kedar, H. E. Mayer, and R. C. Smail (Jerusalem, 1982), p. 83.

[51] For an analysis of the papal appeals see Ursula Schwerin, *Die Aufrufe der Päpste zur Befreiung des Heiligen Landes von den Anfängen bis zum Ausgang Innozenz IV: Ein Beitrag zur Geschichte der kurialen Kreuzzugspropaganda und der päpstlichen Epistolographie* (Berlin, 1937); on the absence of conversion as an aim, see p. 41.

[52] See Appendix 4/b. Jean Richard and Jean Leclercq present Bernard's view as somewhat milder than it is in fact: Richard writes that Bernard "déplore qu'il faille mettre les infidèles à mort" (*L'esprit de la croisade* [Paris, 1969], p. 28), and Leclercq writes that, according to Bernard, "the Templars did not have the right to kill pagans unless it was impossible to do otherwise" ("Saint Bernard's Attitude toward War," in *Studies in Medieval Cistercian History*, ed. J. R. Sommerfeldt, vol. 2 [Kalamazoo, Mich., 1976], p. 23). The extremeness of Bernard's position in *De laude novae militiae* can be better appreciated when compared with Alberto de Morra's stance.

the Roman legal maxim *vim vi repellere*, which justifies the use of force in self-defense.[53]

In 1152, toward the end of his life, Bernard came to espouse rather forcefully the peaceful conversion of the Gentiles. In his tractate *De consideratione*, he deplores the absence of missionary work among the Gentiles and emphatically calls on Pope Eugene III to send preachers to them. "Are we waiting for faith to descend on them?" asks Bernard. "Who [ever] came to believe through chance? How are they to believe without being preached to?"[54] But Bernard does not spell out the relationship between this presentation of universal missionizing as one of the pope's duties—a presentation that does not mention the Saracens by name—and his previous statements that implicitly or explicitly precluded the conversion of the Saracens who were facing the Crusading Kingdom. His insistence on preaching does not imply a repudiation of crusading; the lengthy disquisition on the Second Crusade, in the same tractate, contains no reference that may be interpreted as a rejection of the idea of crusading itself. At any rate, Bernard's advocacy of preaching Christianity to the Gentiles had no impact on later papal calls for crusades, in which the defense, or recovery, of the Holy Land continued to be the aim of the projected expeditions.

Though the official appeals did not mention Saracen conversion as

[53] See Appendix 4/c. For the consecutive stages of the critical edition of this passage see J. Leclercq, ed., "L'encyclique de Saint Bernard en faveur de la croisade," *Revue Bénédictine* 81 (1971), 299; idem, "A propos de l'encyclique de Saint Bernard sur la croisade," ibid. 82 (1972): 312. For earlier editions based on single manuscripts see P. Rassow, "Die Kanzlei St. Bernhards von Clairvaux," *Studien und Mitteilungen zur Geschichte des Benediktiner-Ordens und seiner Zweige* 34 (1913): 293; L. Grill, "Die Kreuzzugsepistel St. Bernhards: Ad Peregrinantes Jerusalem," ibid. 67 (1956): 253; J. Greven, "Die Kölnfahrt Bernhards von Clairvaux," *Annalen des historischen Vereins für den Niederrhein* 120 (1932): 47. See also J. Leclercq, "Pour l'histoire de l'encyclique de Saint Bernard sur la croisade," in *Etudes de civilisation médiévale: Mélanges offerts à E.-R. Labande* (Poitiers, 1974), pp. 479–90. Bernard's reasoning partly resembles a passage of Alexander II incorporated into Gratian's *Decreta* (C.23 q.8 c.11), and even more so the comment of the *glossa ordinaria* on this passage that "si sarraceni non persequuntur christianos, quod non possumus inpetere eos" (Clm 14005, fol. 235ra).

[54] *De consideratione*, III, 1, 3–4, in *S. Bernardi opera*, ed. J. Leclercq and H. M. Rochais, 8 vols. to date (Rome, 1957–), 3: 433. See also P. Dérumeaux, "Saint Bernard et les Infidèles," in *Mélanges St. Bernard: XXIVᵉ Congrès de l'Association bourguignonne des sociétés savantes* (Dijon, 1953), pp. 77–79. On the basis of the above passage in the *De consideratione*, Robert I. Burns writes that Bernard "had urged that energy be channeled into converting Muslims and 'masses of pagans' ": "Christian-Islamic Confrontation," p. 1390. Bernard, however, did not explicitly mention the Saracens. Still less founded is the assertion of Norman Daniel (presumably based on Epp. 457–58, and the above passage) that Bernard "envisaged *only the conversion or the extermination* of the Muslims" of the Holy Land: *Islam and the West*, p. 109 (my emphasis).

a goal of the crusades, conversions did occur in their course. In 1098 the commander of the citadel of Antioch, after having held his own for more than three weeks, agreed to surrender to Bohemond, the Norman leader from southern Italy, and to convert to Christianity with those of his men who chose to do so; this is reminiscent of the agreement Bohemond's uncle, Count Roger of Sicily, made eleven years before with Chamut of Castrogiovanni.[55] Somewhat earlier Bohemond had given his name to a multilingual Turk whom he received at the baptismal font, as his uncle Roger before him had bestowed his name on Roger Aḥmad.[56] The choice between conversion and death, which the crusaders forced upon the Jews of northern France and Germany, was in the East occasionally given by victor to vanquished: by the Turks to the remnants of the Peasant's Crusade, and by Raymond Pilet to the Muslim peasants around Tel-Mannas in northern Syria.[57] In addition, some Muslims, fearing for their lives, asked the crusaders for baptism.[58] And in 1100 the crusaders offered the besieged Jews and Muslims of Haifa the opportunity to accept Christianity.[59]

The conversion motif is especially salient in the chronicle written by Albert of Aachen about 1130. Albert, who had not been to the East but had probably relied on a no-longer-extant account by a Lotharingian crusader, deals with conversion more frequently than any other chronicler either because the source on which he relies did so, or because of his own sensitivity to the subject. He alone is critical of the murder and enforced conversion of Jews by bands of the Peasants' Crusade, so much so that he considers their subsequent destruction in Hungary God's just punishment for these deeds.[60] Later in his chron-

---

[55] Hagenmeyer, *Kreuzzugsbriefe*, p. 164; *Gesta Francorum et aliorum Hierosolimitanorum*, IX, 29, ed. and trans. K. Mynors and Rosalind Hill (London, 1962), p. 71.

[56] *Le "Liber" de Raymond d'Aguilers*, c. 18, p. 159. According to Albert of Aachen (III, 61, and IV, 15–16, in RHC. HOcc. 4:381–82, 399–400), the Turk Bohemond converted before the conquest of Antioch and played an important role in its reduction. A comparison between the descriptions of Raymond and Albert leaves little doubt that both chronicles refer to the same man. But he cannot be identical with Firuz Bohemond, the betrayer of Seljuk Antioch mentioned by Guibert of Nogent and in a variant version of Baudri of Dol (RHC. HOcc. 4:212, and 79, n. 11), because Raymond, an eyewitness of the events, does not identify his Turkish Bohemond with the betrayer of Antioch, whom he mentions earlier in his account.

[57] *Gesta Francorum*, I, 2, and X, 30, pp. 4, 73.

[58] *Le "Liber" de Raymond d'Aguilers*, c. 17, p. 112.

[59] *Monachi Littorensis Historia de Translatione S. Nicolai*, in RHC. HOcc. 5:276; for the identity of the defenders see Albert of Aachen, VII, 22–25, in RHC. HOcc. 4:521–23.

[60] Albert of Aachen, I, 29, in RHC. HOcc. 4:295. It is symptomatic that on the basis

icle a captured Turkish messenger asks for baptism "more out of fear than love for the Catholic faith"; a Turk falls in love with a nun and promises to convert; negotiations are scheduled to determine whether the inhabitants of Tarsus should remain pagan or convert to Christianity; Egyptian envoys offer to discuss with the crusaders "the profession of the Christian faith," after which they would decide on conversion; and fugitives from besieged Antioch ask for baptism.[61] According to Albert, Peter the Hermit offered Kerbogha, the ruler of Mosul, a chance to convert or join battle with the crusaders. (Peter may have done so in response to the offer to convert to Islam that Kerbogha, in conformity with Islamic usage, had extended to the crusaders.)[62] Baldwin of Bourg and other leaders of the crusade offered baptism to a noble Saracen warrior captured during the siege of Jerusalem in 1099. They often engaged in inquiring and disputing (*inquirentes et disputantes*) with their captive about his life and customs, but failed to persuade him to convert, whereupon Baldwin of Bourg's esquire decapitated him in front of the Muslim-held Tower of David, Jerusalem's citadel.[63] Again, Albert is the only one to relate that when the erstwhile Saracen ruler of the Palestinian town of Ramla accompanied his crusader allies to the battle of Ascalon in August 1099, Godfrey of Bouillon succeeded in persuading him to accept Christianity. (Albert's remark that he is not certain whether baptism took place before or after the battle lends some credibility to the story, though not to the speech he lets Godfrey address to the Saracen chieftain.)[64] Finally, only

---

of this single statement, Sir Steven Runciman writes that "to most good Christians [the rout of the Peasants] appeared as a punishment meted out from on high to the murderers of the Jews." *A History* (chap. 1, n. 56), 1:141.

[61] Albert of Aachen, II, 26; II, 37; III, 11; III, 59; III, 66, in RHC. HOcc. 4:319, 327–28, 346, 380, 386.

[62] Albert of Aachen, IV, 44–45, in RHC. HOcc. 4:420–21. Cf. Baudri of Dol, *Historia Jerosolimitana*, III, 15, in RHC. HOcc. 4:74–75. The words that the author of the anonymous *Gesta Francorum* (IX, 28, p. 66) lets Peter say to Kerbogha cannot be construed as hinting at a conversion offer, as proposed by Cutler, "The First Crusade," p. 66; for a partial rebuttal see J. Waltz, "Historical Perspectives on 'Early Missions' to Muslims," *Muslim World* 61 (1971): 184, n. 74.

For Kerbogha's offer to convert to Islam see the letter of Anselm of Ribemont written in Antioch in July 1098: Hagenmeyer, *Die Kreuzzugsbriefe*, p. 160. See also Caffaro, *De liberatione civitatum Orientis*, ed. L. T. Belgrano, in *Annali Genovesi di Caffaro e de'suoi continuatori*, vol. 1 (Rome, 1890), p. 107, where the offer is made by Turkish soldiers.

[63] Albert of Aachen, VI, 5, p. 469. It is strange, in view of this and the above-mentioned episodes, that a leading historian of the crusades writes: "le baptême forcé ne se rencontre pas dans les textes relatifs aux croisades." Richard, *L'esprit*, p. 28.

[64] Albert of Aachen, VI, 42–44, pp. 491–93. A twelfth-century adaptor of the chronicle of Baudri of Dol, using the same expression as Alberto de Morra, writes that in

Albert relates that Tancred, the Norman prince of Galilee, in 1100 sent six knights to Duqāq of Damascus to demand that he surrender the city and become Christian. (The Turk executed five knights; the sixth preferred to become Muslim.)[65]

The account about the readiness of the Egyptian envoys to accept Christianity must obviously be due to a misunderstanding by Albert or his source, but other episodes, which at first glance seem to be far-fetched, should not be quickly dismissed. The scene of crusading leaders disputing during the siege of Jerusalem with a noble Muslim in an attempt to persuade him to convert hardly conforms to the customary notion about the First Crusade, but fragments of a letter found in the Cairo Geniza lend the scene considerable credibility. In the letter, written about a year after the crusader conquest of Jerusalem in July 1099, the leaders of the Karaite Jewish community of Ascalon report that the crusaders had urged a captured Jerusalemite Jew, a member of the prominent Tustarī family, "to embrace the Christian faith of his free will, and promised to treat him well; but he told them, how could he become a Christian priest [kohen naṣrānī] and be left in peace by them [the Jews], who had disbursed on his behalf a great sum." The letter reports, though, that other captured Jerusalemite Jews did become Christian.[66]

Did the leaders of the First Crusade consider Muslim conversion an explicit aim? A passage in their letter to the pope, written in Septem-

---

1099 the crusaders asked the first Frankish bishop of Ramla "de plebe ad fidem catholicam provocanda": RHC. HOcc. 4:96, n. 7. (Other MSS have "convocanda" or "convertenda" instead of "provocanda.")

[65] Ibid., VII, 17, p. 518. Most of these episodes have been noted by Peter Knoch, who considered them additions by Albert to the chronicle of the Lotharingian crusader: P. Knoch, *Studien zu Albert von Aachen: Der erste Kreuzzug in der deutschen Chronistik* (Stuttgart, 1966), pp. 75–77; but see the observation of Schwinges, *Kreuzzugsideologie*, p. 276. Knoch does not seem to have been aware that many of these episodes appear solely in Albert's chronicle. On Albert's relative matter-of-factness, and even empathy, with the Saracens, see H. Szklenar, *Studien zum Bild des Orients in vorhöfischen deutschen Epen* (Göttingen, 1966), pp. 193–96.

[66] The letter, mostly in Arabic but in Hebrew characters, was edited by S. D. Goitein in *Zion* 17 (1952): 129–47; the passage quoted appears on p. 137. For an English translation see S. D. Goitein, "Contemporary Letters on the Capture of Jerusalem by the Crusaders," *Journal of Jewish Studies* 3 (1952): 172. For further details see S. D. Goitein, *Palestinian Jewry in Early Islamic and Crusader Times in the Light of the Geniza Documents* (Jerusalem, 1980), pp. 231–58 (in Hebrew). For a Geniza fragment that suggests that a crusader was curious about the contents of a Hebrew book and a Palestinian Jew enlightened him about them, see my "A Commentary on the Book of Isaiah Ransomed from the Crusaders," in *Jerusalem in the Middle Ages: Selected Papers*, ed. B. Z. Kedar (Jerusalem, 1979), pp. 107–111 (in Hebrew, with English summary).

ber 1099, has been interpreted as confirming that aim: Before joining forces with the Egyptians at Ascalon one month earlier—so write Daimbert of Pisa, Godfrey of Bouillon, and Raymond of St. Gilles— the crusaders prayed that in the forthcoming battle God would, "by shattering the might of the Saracens and the devil, dilate the kingdom of Christ and the Church everywhere from sea to sea."[67] Phrases like "to dilate the name of Christ" or "to dilate the Kingdom of Christianity" were used by Pope Gregory I in the sixth century, Alcuin in the ninth, Archbishop Hatto of Mainz in the tenth, and Robert the Monk in the twelfth, in a context in which the *dilatatio* led to, or coincided with, the Christianization of newly conquered territories.[68] But conversion is not the only possible connotation of the term *dilatatio*; it may also be understood in the strictly territorial sense, with the infidel inhabitants of the conquered territories being annihilated or expelled. Precisely in this sense is the term used by a contemporary of Daimbert, Godfrey, and Raymond, the anonymous annalist from Augsburg who succinctly summarizes the First Crusade: "1099. Jerusalem was captured by Duke Godfrey and his followers; the Christian religion was dilated through the provinces; all the barbarians were either killed or put to flight."[69]

In later years conversion was repeatedly and ever more unequivocally presented as an aim of the crusade. An anonymous chronicler writing in Trier around the year 1130 describes the participants of the First Crusade as desiring "either to undergo death themselves, or sub-

[67] "ut . . . confractis viribus Saracenorum et diaboli, regnum Christi et ecclesiae a mari ad mare usquequaque dilataret." Hagenmeyer, *Die Kreuzzugsbriefe*, pp. 171–72. The rapid diffusion of the letter is attested by the fact that it is quoted by Frutolf of Michelsberg, who died in January 1103: *Frutolfi et Ekkehardi Chronica*, s.a. 1098, p. 116. For the view that in this passage Saracen conversion is presented as an aim of the crusaders see Plocher, "Studien zum Kreuzzugsgedanken," p. 58; P. Rousset, "L'idée de croisade chez les chroniqueurs d'Occident," in *Relazioni del X Congresso internazionale di scienze storiche*, vol. 3 (Florence, 1955), pp. 550–51.

[68] *Gregorii I papae Registrum epistolarum*, ed. P. Ewald and L. M. Hartmann (1887– 91), in MGH Epist. 1:93–94 (= C.23 q.4 c.49); *Alcuini Epistolae*, in MGH Epist. 4:157; cf. Margret Bünding-Naujoks, "Das Imperium Christianum und die deutschen Ostkriege vom zehnten bis zum zwölften Jahrhundert," in *Heidenmission und Kreuzzugsgedanke*, pp. 70–71, 92. (The article was originally published in 1940.) For Robert the Monk see n. 47 above.

[69] "1099: Hierosolima a duce Gotefrido et sequacibus est capta; religio christiana per provintias dilatatur; barbari omnes aut extincti aut fugati sunt." *Annales Augustani*, ed. G. H. Pertz (1839), in MGH SS 3:135. Similarly Fulk of Chartres writes that at Clermont Urban "paganos de terris Christianorum instinctu vivaci effugare conatus est." *Fulcherii Carnotensis Historia Hierosolymitana*, I, 4, 6, ed. H. Hagenmeyer (Heidelberg, 1913), p. 143.

jugate the necks of the unbelieving to the faith."[70] Leaders of the French army participating in the Second Crusade declared in October 1147 in Constantinople that their aim was "to visit the Holy Sepulcher and, by the command of the Supreme Pontiff, wipe out our sins with the blood or conversion of the pagans": thus reports Eudes of Deuil, the chaplain who accompanied King Louis VII of France on that ill-starred expedition.[71] Two months later, Gerhoch of Reichersberg concluded his Christmas sermon with the prayer that the expedition launched by Eugene III and Bernard of Clairvaux, then on its way to Jerusalem, might succeed and that the hitherto unconverted nations attain salvation.[72] And the north German priest Helmold of Bosau, summing up in the 1160s the exploits of the Second Crusade, asserts that Bernard of Clairvaux had exhorted the faithful "to set out for

[70] *Gesta Treverorum*, ed. G. Waitz (1848), in MGH SS 8:190. The north European chronicler probably perceived subjugation as a step leading to conversion.

[71] "Visitare sepulcrum Domini cognovimus nos et ipse et nostra crimina, praecepto summi pontificis, paganorum sanguine vel conversione delere." Odo de Deogilo, *De profectione Ludovici VII in Orientem*, ed. and trans. Virginia G. Berry (New York, 1948), pp. 70–71. Schwinges (*Kreuzzugsideologie*, p. 272, n. 14) misunderstood the passage. In reality French knights went over to the Turks during the Second Crusade: Odo de Deogilo, p. 140.

[72] "(hortatu Eugenii papae III et venerabilis viri Bernhardi abbatis Clarevallensis) re-pentina mutacione signaculo sancte crucis communiti arma contra inimicas Christi et civitatis Iherusalem gentes corripiunt et pro Christo mori aut vincere (parati) ad bella proficiscuntur, tanta multitudine de universis terminis ecclesie simul properante, quanta nunquam super terram visa legitur. Ut igitur ille bellorum motus ad laudem et benedic-tionem Dei maximam proveniat atque ut gentium que adhuc supersunt reliquie salve fiant (et) in filios benedictionis commutate in vallem benedictionis ad laudandum Deum nobiscum occurrant, ubi benedicamus manentem nobiscum Deum Emmanuel in eter-num, prestet ipse Dominus noster Ihesus Christus." Edited from Cod. Vind. 1558, fol. 50r, by P. Classen, *Gerhoch von Reichersberg: Eine Biographie* (Wiesbaden, 1960), p. 132, n. 19. The words in parentheses were added in the margins of the manuscript, probably by Gerhoch himself. Classen (pp. 132–33) interprets this passage to mean that Gerhoch considered pagan conversion, not Christian military victory, the crusade's objective. This may be far-fetched; but Gerhoch evidently regarded Christianization a crusading goal. For further evidence on this point see his *De investigatione Antichristi*, ed. E. Sackur (1897), in MGH Libelli de lite 3:375, lines 18–21. On Gerhoch's subsequent criticism of the Second Crusade, see Classen, pp. 133–34; also J. Prawer, *Histoire du royaume latin de Jérusalem*, 2 vols. (Paris, 1969–70), 1:391–92.

Saracen conversion also figures in an account of the Catholic conquest of Lisbon in 1147, albeit not as an explicit aim of that campaign. The anonymous author lets the archbishop of Braga begin his speech to the beleaguered Saracens by expressing his desire for their conversion; later he makes the archbishop promise that upon surrender-ing the city the Saracens may live there according to their customs, unless some volun-tarily choose to convert: *De expugnatione Lyxbonensi*, ed. C. W. David (New York, 1936), pp. 114–18. Cf. N. Daniel, *The Arabs*, p. 87.

Jerusalem in order to repress and bring under Christian laws the barbarous nations of the Orient, saying that the time draws near in which the fullness of nations ought to enter, and thus all Israel will be saved."[73] Thus, although neither Eugene III nor Bernard mentioned Saracen conversion in his call for the Second Crusade, both men were presented as having done so. Evidently, Christianizing the Saracen became an obvious goal of the crusade for many a Catholic European of the mid-twelfth century.

This is not to say that every Muslim offering to convert during hostilities was indeed spared and baptized; revenge and battle brutality took their toll too. Thus when starving Muslims sneaked out of besieged Lisbon and crossed into the Christian camp in 1147, some were baptized, others beheaded, and still others sent back with their hands cut off, to be stoned to death by their fellow citizens.[74] But battlefield practice rarely mirrors the proclaimed ethic of a society, and by 1147 the ethic of Catholic Europe certainly called for the sparing of a baptism-seeking Saracen. It is significant, from this point of view, that the *Chronica regia Coloniensis*, which copies word for word the notice about the baptism granted to the starving fugitives from Lisbon, suppresses altogether the subsequent sentence about the beheading and mutilation.[75]

The reasons behind the evolution of Saracen conversion into a crusading goal lie close at hand. By the mid-twelfth century, war waged with the intent of bringing Christianity to vanquished infidels, or even

[73] *Helmoldi Cronica Slavorum*, ed. B. Schmeidler (1937), in MGH Scr. rer. Germ. 32:114–15. Bernard's call for a crusade against the Wends, which includes the statement "Sed aliud damnum veretur longe amplius de conversione gentium, cum audivit plenitudinem eorum introituram, et omnem quoque Israel fore salvandum" (PL 182:651C), might have been at the root of the eschatological argument Helmold attributes to him, although Rom. 11:25 is used quite differently in Bernard's call and in Helmold's purported paraphrase. The same is true of Bernard's use of Rom. 11:25 in his letter to the Germans in 1146 (PL 182:567C).

In his exhortation of 1152 to Eugene III to engage in missionizing among the pagans, Bernard's use of Rom. 11:25 is close to that of the statement Helmold ascribes to him: *De consideratione*, III, 4 in *S. Bernardi opera*, 3:433. Did Helmold know this work of Bernard? Or had Bernard used the eschatological argument for conversion in an exhortation for the crusades no longer extant?

[74] *Dudechini epistola*, in *Annales Sancti Disibodi*, a. 1147, ed. G. Waitz (1861), in MGH SS 17:27–28; *Arnulfi epistola*, in RHGF 14:326C; *Annales Magdeburgenses*, a. 1147, ed. G. H. Pertz (1859), in MGH SS 16:189, lines 38–40. On this "Teutonic source" on the conquest of Lisbon see G. Constable, "The Second Crusade as Seen by Contemporaries," *Traditio* 9 (1953): 221.

[75] *Chronica regia Coloniensis*, a. 1147, ed. G. Waitz (1880), in MGH Scr. rer. Germ. 18:85 (both recensions).

of forcing them to convert, had a long tradition in Catholic Europe. Gregory I had lauded the African exarch Gennadius for seeking wars that made possible the preaching of Christianity to the subjugated pagans; Charlemagne's wars against the Saxons were aimed at their forcible conversion—"preaching [the faith] with an iron tongue," to use the words of a ninth-century writer. In 892, King Eudes of France forced a defeated Viking chieftain to choose between baptism and death. The military campaigns against the heathen Slavs, pursued from the tenth century onward, paved the way for their conversion, and Brun of Querfurt, a prominent missionary in that area, openly called in 1008 on Henry II of Germany to consider it his duty to compel the pagans to accept Christianity.[76] In the opening stages of the First Crusade, the Jews of northern France and Germany were repeatedly faced with a choice between baptism and death, and in the great vernacular work of that age, the *Chanson de Roland*, Charlemagne, in the midst of battle, offers conversion to the Saracen leader and, once victorious, has the vanquished Saracens driven to the baptistery and forced to become true Christians (*veir chrestien*): "Should someone defy Charles, he orders to seize or burn or kill him."[77] (Only the captive Saracen queen

[76] For Gregory I see n. 68 above. *Annales regni Francorum*, ed. F. Kurze (1895), in MGH Scr. rer. Germ. 6:41; for the quotation on the Saxons see *Translatio S. Liborii*, ed. G. H. Pertz (1841), in MGH SS 4:151, lines 21–22; cf. Bünding-Naujoks, "Imperium Christianum," pp. 70–86; Beumann, "Kreuzzugsgedanke und Ostpolitik im hohen Mittelalter," in *Heidenmission und Kreuzzugsgedanke*, pp. 127–29. (The article was originally published in 1953.) For Eudes of France see Richer, *Histoire de France (888–995)*, I, 10, ed. R. Latouche, 2d. ed. (Paris, 1967), p. 26. For Brun's call see *Epistola Brunonis ad Henricum regem*, ed. Jadwiga Karwasińska, Monumenta Poloniae Historica NS 4 (Warsaw, 1973), 3:104; *S. Adalberti Pragensis episcopi et martyris Vita altera*, ed. J. Karwasińska, ibid. (Warsaw, 1969), 2:9–10. H. D. Kahl and R. Wenskus argue that Brun's call for a king "qui ecclesiam intrare compellat paganum" refers only to the Liuticians, who had been Christianized but had reverted to paganism and were considered apostates. Brun therefore justified the use of force to bring them back into the fold, as Augustine had done for the correction of heretics: H.-D. Kahl, "Compellere intrare: Die Wendenpolitik Bruns von Querfurt im Lichte hochmittelalterlichen Missions- und Völkerrechts," in *Heidenmission und Kreuzzugsgedanke*, pp. 177–274; R. Wenskus, *Studien zur historisch-politischen Gendankenwelt Bruns von Querfurt* (Münster and Cologne, 1956), pp. 143–53. In only one of the relevant texts, however, in Brun's letter to King Henry II, does *compellere intrare* refer exclusively to the Liuticians; in the other, *Saracen pagans* are mentioned immediately before Brun's call for compulsory conversion (a fact Kahl and Wenskus did not take into account).

[77]   Meinent paien entesqu'al baptisterie:
              S'or i ad cel qui Carle contredie,
              Il le fait prendre o ardeir ou ocire.

La Chanson de Roland, ed. and modern French trans. J. Bédier, 56th ed. (Paris, 1924), laisse 266, lines 3668–70. For parallels in later *chansons* see, for instance, P. Rousset, *Les origines et les caractères de la première croisade* (Neuchâtel, 1945), pp. 127–28.

is not forcibly baptized, because Charlemagne wants her to convert "par amur," and therefore takes her to France. Having heard many "sermuns e essamples," she asks to become Christian and is baptized in the baths of Aachen.)[78] Thus forcible baptism of Saracens is extolled in a work that probably shaped the ethic of the crusading stratum par excellence—the knighthood—more decisively than many an encyclical or learned treatise. In the *Historia Karoli Magni et Rotholandi*, a Latin adaptation of the *Chanson* written about 1130—and utilized by no less a man than Rolando Bandinelli, the future Pope Alexander III, as a trustworthy factual account!—forced conversion of Saracens is even more prominent.[79] In the Middle High German *Rolandslied* of the Pfaffe Konrad (ca. 1170) the very objective of Charlemagne's expedition to Spain is to convert the idolatrous Saracens.[80]

Besides the motif of conversion offered to the Saracens before or during battle and of baptism enforced upon victory, there appears in the first half of the twelfth century the theme of the alluring Saracen princess who falls in love with a captured Christian knight, helps him to regain his liberty, and ultimately accepts baptism for his sake. Bohemond of Antioch was the first real-life crusader about whom such a story was woven, possibly not without his active assistance.[81] In the realm of fiction such liaisons between a brave Christian knight and a sensuous Saracen maiden will recur time and again, with the knight

[78] *La Chanson de Roland*, laisse 266, lines 3673–74; laisse 290, lines 3975–87.

[79] *Historia Karoli Magni et Rotholandi; ou, Chronique du Pseudo-Turpin*, ed. C. Meredith-Jones (Paris, 1936), pp. 92–95, 128–39, 168–69; see also *Vita Karoli Magni*, ed. G. Rauscher, in *Die Legenden Karls des Grossen im 11. und 12 Jahrhundert* (Leipzig, 1890), pp. 69–70. For the utilization by Rolando Bandinelli see *Die Summa magistri Rolandi*, to C.23 q.8, ed. F. Thaner (Innsbruck, 1874), pp. 96–97: "Ad cuius instar archiepiscopum Turpinum, prout Francorum habet historia, materiali gladio Sarracenos impugnasse non dubitamus." See also Humbertus de Romanis, *Opusculum tripartitum*, I, 20, in E. Brown, *Appendix ad fasciculum rerum expetendarum et fugiendarum sive tomus secundus* (London, 1690), p. 200.

[80] *Das Rolandslied des Pfaffen Konrad*, ed. and modern German trans. D. Kartschoke, vol. 1 (Munich, 1971), especially verses 30–64, 80–86, 351–70, 8620–33. For the date see D. Kartschoke. *Die Datierung des deutschen Rolandsliedes* (Stuttgart, 1965).

[81] The story of Bohemond appears in *The Ecclesiastical History of Orderic Vitalis*, ed. and trans. Marjorie Chibnall, vol. 5 (Oxford, 1975), pp. 358–78; for a similar account about Baldwin II, see *Orderici Vitalis Historiae Ecclesiasticae libri tredecim*, ed. A. Le Prévost, vol. 4 (Paris, 1852; reprint, New York, 1965), pp. 252–55. Cf. F. M. Warren, "The Enamoured Moslem Princess in Orderic Vital and the French Epic," *Publications of the Modern Language Association of America* 29 (1914): 341–58. Orderic's account should also be compared with the Byzantine epic in which the daughter of a Saracen amir falls in love with a captive Greek warrior, delivers him from prison, is baptized for his sake, and then flees with him to Romania: *Digenes Akrites*, ed. and trans. J. Mavrogordato (Oxford, 1956), pp. 144–59.

sometimes refusing to kiss the maiden on her lips as long as she remains unbaptized.[82] Rumors about prospective Christian-Muslim liaisons also appear in late-twelfth-century chronicles.[83] Thus Saracen conversion became entwined with two essential components of the chivalrous culture: the good fight and the pursuit of ladies.

Even as the *Chanson de Roland* and its derivatives made current the notion of baptism under the threat of death, one of the most influential leaders of Catholic Europe in that age held the view that the aims of a projected military expedition should be the extermination or Christianization of the enemy. This was Bernard of Clairvaux, who issued a letter in 1147 in support of the German expedition against the Wends—the northeastern counterpart of Louis VII's and Conrad III's expedition to the Levant—calling on the Christians to take the cross in order to "utterly annihilate or surely convert" the pagan enemy and not desist from fighting "until, God helping, either that rite itself or that nation be annihilated."[84] In the same year Pope Eugene III

[82] C. Meredith-Jones, "The Conventional Saracen of the Songs of Geste," *Speculum* 17 (1942): 221; A. R. Harden, "The Element of Love in the *Chansons de Geste,*" *Duquesne Studies: Annuale Medievale* 5 (1964): 73–74.

The literary motif of love (and marriage) between Christians and Muslims deserves a cross-European comparative study. In addition to the studies quoted in this and the previous note, see, for England, Metlitzki, *The Matter of Araby,* pp. 136–77; for Germany, S. Stein, *Die Ungläubigen in der mittelhochdeutschen Literatur von 1050 bis 1250* (1933; reprint, Darmstadt, 1963); F. W. Wentzlaff-Eggebert, *Kreuzzugsdichtung des Mittelalters: Studien zu ihrer geschichtlichen und dichterischen Wirklichkeit* (Berlin, 1960), especially pp. 98–111. And see also *Os Livros de Linhagens do Conde D. Pedro,* ed. A. Herculano (Lisbon, 1856), in *Portugalliae Monumenta Historica: Scriptores,* 1:274–77.

[83] Two German chronicles assert that the legates of Saladin or of the sultan of Iconium proposed to Frederick Barbarossa, in 1173 or 1179, that he give his daughter in marriage to Saladin's son (or to the sultan of Iconium himself), and in return these Saracen kingdoms would convert to Christianity: *Chronica regia Coloniensis,* in MGH Scr. rer. Germ. 18:124; *Ottonis Frisigensis continuatio Sanblasiana,* ed. R. Wilmans (1868), in MGH SS 20:317. Roger Howden relates that in the 1190s an African princess was so eager to marry Sancho VII of Navarre (the brother of Berengaria, Richard Lion-Heart's wife) that she offered to convert. Her father was willing to give her for dowry all *Hispania saracenica: Chronica magistri Rogeri de Houedene,* ed. W. Stubbs, 4 vols., Rolls Series, 51 (London, 1868–71), 3:90–92. Richard Lion-Heart's offer that his sister marry Saladin's brother is well known.

[84] "denuntiamus armari christianorum robur adversus illos, et ad delendas penitus, aut certe convertendas nationes illas signum salutare suscipere . . . [they should go on fighting] donec, auxiliante Deo, aut ritus ipse, aut natio deleatur." Ep. 457, in *S. Bernardi opera,* 8:433. J. Leclercq suggests translating *aut certe* as or preferably: "Saint Bernard's Attitude toward War," p. 21. But see Bernard's use of *certe* in *De laude novae militiae,* III, 4, in *S. Bernardi opera,* 3:217. Moreover, in his attempt to prove that Bernard did not aim at the forced conversion of the Wends, Leclercq writes, "In the light of what

exhorted the crusaders to subjugate the Wends "to the Christian religion," and sternly warned them against permitting these pagans to remain in their "perfidy"—that is, in their old beliefs—in return for bribes.[85] Bernard and Eugene unequivocally referred to the Wends, but their words might have been misunderstood—as was probably the case with the country priest Helmold—to apply to the Saracens as well.

Against this background, it is hardly surprising that by 1147 Saracen conversion had become a major objective of the Oriental crusade not only for the leading French knights Eudes of Deuil mentions but also for Gerhoch, the learned provost of Reichersberg. The tendency must have been gaining momentum, for seventy years later, at the time of the Fifth Crusade, Saracen conversion is reported to have been pre-

we know of his reaction in other conflicts, it seems just to adopt the opinion of one of the foremost specialists on the subject of this Crusade: 'We believe that we can class this appeal as a part of a strictly missionary concept.' " "Saint Bernard's Attitude toward War," p. 22. That specialist is Hans-Dietrich Kahl; but what Kahl really writes in parentheses, at the spot referred to by Leclercq, is: "(sofern wir Bernhards Aufruf wirklich unter die Missionsanschauungen im strengen Sinn einreihen dürfen)": H.-D. Kahl, "Zum Ergebnis des Wendenkreuzzugs von 1147," in *Heidenmission und Kreuzzugsgedanke*, p. 282. For Kahl's real opinion on Bernard's call see Kahl, "Compellere intrare," pp. 227–28.

More recently, Friedrich Lotter has argued that by the words *natio deleatur* Bernard referred to the pagans' loss of ethnic identity, not to their physical destruction: F. Lotter, *Die Konzeption des Wendenkreuzzugs: Ideengeschichtliche, kirchenrechtliche und historisch-politische Voraussetzungen der Missionierung von Elb- und Ostseeslawen um die Mitte des 12. Jahrhunderts*, Vorträge und Forschungen, Sonderband 23 (Sigmaringen, 1977), especially pp. 41, 68–69; for a more moderate formulation see his "Die Vorstellungen von Heidenkrieg und Wendenmission bei Heinrich dem Löwen," in W.-D. Mohrmann, ed., *Heinrich der Löwe* (Göttingen, 1980), pp. 11–12. For a critique of this view see E. D. Hehl, *Kirche und Krieg im 12. Jahrhundert: Studien zu kanonischem Recht und politischer Wirklichkeit*, Monographien zur Geschichte des Mittelalters, 19 (Stuttgart, 1980), p. 134, n. 573.

Hehl has ingeniously suggested that the statement in Ep. 457 that the Devil fears a *conversio gentium* refers to the *gentes* of the Orient rather than to those of northeastern Europe; hence Bernard implies that the Oriental crusade provides an opportunity for missionizing: Hehl, *Kirche*, pp. 133, n. 571; 135, n. 573. But if this identification of *gentes* and the subsequent reasoning are correct, how should we explain the fact that in his call for the Oriental crusade Bernard refrains altogether from presenting Saracen conversion as a goal? (It is possible, however, that Helmold understood the passage of Ep. 457 in the manner suggested by Hehl.)

[85] PL 180:1203BC; cf. Hehl, *Kirche*, p. 135. For an interpretation of Eugene's call that allows for its reconciliation with contemporary canon law, see Lotter, *Konzeption*, p. 18. For a formulation more outspoken than that of Eugene, see the letter Innocent III sent in 1209 to Valdemar II of Denmark; here the pope calls for a crusade to extirpate the error of paganism and compel the infidel to enter: PL 216:116–17. Cf. Riley-Smith, *What Were the Crusades?* p. 19.

sented as the primary goal on the battlefield itself. The anonymous author of the *Gesta Obsidionis Damiate*, an eyewitness who probably wrote his account before the crusade ended in defeat, reports that the papal legate, the Spaniard Pelagius, led the crusading army into battle on October 26, 1218, with an invocation to God to help the Christians "so that we may be able to convert the perfidious and worthless people, so that they ought duly to believe with us in the Holy Trinity and in Your Nativity and in Your Passion and death and resurrection, so that Your name be invoked throughout the world and be blessed in all eternity." Five years later, Pope Honorius III lamented that after the crusader conquest of Damietta, the Christian warriors had fallen into sin, and so "the Faith was slandered at the place where the infidels were to be converted." And the chronicle of San Juan de la Peña presents Saracen conversion as the aim of the campaigns of Jaume I of Aragon against Majorca and Valencia; in fact, while Jaume and his men were besieging Valencia, two Muslims were publicly baptized in a church just outside the walls of the beleaguered city.[86]

THE IDEA of enforced Saracen conversion also made a solitary inroad into the realm of canon law. Commenting on Gratian's *Decreta* about 1210, the eminent canonist Alanus Anglicus voices the opinion that infidels, like the Saracens, who obstinately resist the Christians may be compelled to accept the Christian faith by removal of their property and "by corporeal scourges short of death" (*citra mortem*).[87] Alanus is aware that his opinion was not customary among canonists, for he immediately adds that "others, however, say that we should only defend ourselves against them and not go on the attack." The majority view is expressed by the author of the *Summa Parisiensis* of about 1160, who lays down that it is unlawful to scourge men into accepting the Christian faith; Saracens and Jews ought to be persecuted as long as they are rebellious, but once subjugated they ought not to be killed or forced to convert.[88]

[86] *Gesta Obsidionis Damiate*, ed. R. Röhricht, in *Quinti belli sacri scriptores minores* (Geneva, 1879), p. 78; see also pp. 81–82. Letter of Honorius III: Pressutti no. 4388; Ch. L. Hugo, *Sacrae antiquitatis monumenta*, 2 vols. (Etival, 1725), 1:122 ("detrahe-batur fidei, ubi convertendi fuerant infideles"). *Crónica de San Juan de la Peña*, ed. A. Ubieto Arteta, Textos Medievales, 4 (Valencia, 1961), pp. 148–49 (the Latin text of the chronicle dates from 1369 to 1372); cf. Burns, "Christian-Islamic Confrontation," p. 1394.

[87] Alanus, *Apparatus*: 'Ius Naturale,' to C.23 q.4 d.p.c.36, v. *rationabiliter*, BN lat. 15393, fol. 186va. A part of this gloss was quoted by F. H. Russell, *The Just War in the Middle Ages* (Cambridge, 1975), p. 197, n. 194; for a fuller quotation see Kedar, "Muslim Conversion in Canon Law." See also Hehl, *Kirche*, p. 239.

[88] *Summa Parisiensis*, to D.45 c.1: "Quidam quosdam flagellis ad fidem cogunt, quod

But while canonists regarded enforced baptism as unlawful, they considered valid and binding most acts of baptism so performed. The decision made in 633 at the Fourth Council of Toledo that Jews should not be forced to convert, but once baptized against their will must remain Christian, was incorporated by Gratian into his *Decreta* and served as a point of departure for a discussion among decretists about the validity of forcible baptism in general. Finally, in 1201 Innocent III ruled that if an infidel was physically forced to undergo baptism even as he continued to profess his unwillingness (a case of *coactio absoluta*), the act of baptism was neither valid nor binding; but if the infidel agreed to baptism after having been violently constrained by terror and pain and hence wishing to spare himself further harm (a case of *coactio conditionalis*), the act of baptism was valid and binding, and the baptized had to be compelled to observe the Christian religion.[89] Innocent's ruling, later incorporated in the Decretals, rendered binding the vast majority of enforced baptisms; cases like the one in which one Christian held the infidel bound and another poured water on him—a vivid example of *coactio absoluta* given by Innocent's teacher, Huguccio—must have been quite rare.[90]

Although enforced baptism continued to be considered unlawful, the reluctance of canonists to condone the use of harsh means in the process of furthering infidel conversion was perceptibly diminishing. In his *Decreta* of about 1140, Gratian included Gregory I's declaration of 602 that Christians should strive to lead the infidels to the faith by

---

non licet." To D.45 c.3: "Peccant enim qui in Sarracenis armantur? Ad quod dicimus, debemus persequi quia nos et nostra invadere enituntur, sed Judaeos nequaquam, quia parati sunt servire. Ut generaliter dicamus, quoniam sive sunt Saraceni sive Judaei, dum rebelles fuerint, debemus eos persequi. Postquam vero eos subjugaverimus, neque interficere, nec ad fidem cogere debemus." *The Summa Parisiensis on the Decretum Gratiani*, ed. T. P. McLaughlin (Toronto, 1952), p. 40.

[89] Mansi, *Concilia*, 10:633; Gratian, D.45 c.4; Innocent III in X 3.42.3. For a detailed discussion of the treatment of this problem from Gratian to Innocent see M. Condorelli, *I fondamenti giuridici della tolleranza religiosa nell'elaborazione canonistica dei secoli XII–XIV: Contributo storico-dogmatico* (Milan, 1960), pp. 31–105. For a lucid definition of *coactio absoluta* and *coactio conditionalis* in general, see S. Kuttner, *Kanonistische Schuldlehre von Gratian bis auf die Dekretalen Gregors IX*, Studi e Testi, 64 (Città del Vaticano, 1935), pp. 301–7.

[90] "Si absoluta coactione quis baptizetur, puta unus tenet eum ligatum et alius superfundit aquam. . . ." Huguccio, to D.45 c.5, v. *adsotiatos, unctos, corporis domini*. Quoted by F. Gillmann, *Die Notwendigkeit der Intention auf Seiten des Spenders und des Empfängers der Sakramente nach der Anschauung der Frühscholastik* (Mainz, 1916), p. 16, n. 1. See also Condorelli, p. 55. Kenneth Pennington has recently challenged the accepted opinion that Innocent III studied law under Huguccio: "The Legal Education of Innocent III," *Bulletin of Medieval Canon Law* NS 4 (1974): 70–77. The argument hinges on the questionable assumption that the testimony of Joannes Andreae to the contrary is a corrupted version of a gloss by Hostiensis.

blandishments, not asperities (*blandimentis debent, non asperitatibus studere*). But in the 1190s Bernard of Pavia, in his influential *Summa Decretalium*, asserted that Jews and Saracens should be invited to the Christian faith by the recourse to authorities, reasonings, and blandishments rather than by asperities (*auctoritatibus rationibus et blandimentis potius quam asperitatibus*): The recourse to asperities, though not recommended, was no longer ruled out. Bernard's formulation was taken over verbatim into the *Summa de casibus poenitentiae* of Ramon of Penyaforte and the *Summa super titulis decretalium* of Goffredus of Trani.[91] Again, Gregory I's call of 594 to impose heavy taxes on Sardinian rustics unwilling "to come to the Lord" and thereby compel them to hasten in the right direction, a call that allowed Gratian to maintain that the bad ought be compelled toward the good and Bernard of Pavia to state that Christians may burden with taxes the Jews and Saracens living in their midst, became with Ramon of Penyaforte the basis for still another constraint to pressure these infidels into the faith. Referring to Gregory's letter as quoted by Gratian, Ramon writes that a Christian may draw such as these to the faith by promises and gifts, and also by a more severe exaction of taxes.[92]

MUSLIM CONVERSION IN THE CRUSADING KINGDOM OF JERUSALEM

Latin chronicle accounts of the early days of the kingdom mention a few Saracen converts in the entourage of Godfrey of Bouillon and Baldwin I, the first two rulers of crusader Jerusalem. Albert of Aachen, as mentioned above, reports the conversion of a Saracen ally of Godfrey in August 1099. In November 1100, when Baldwin I of Jerusalem plans an expedition to the Dead Sea and beyond, he is advised by

[91] *Gregorii I papae Registrum epistolarum*, ed. L. M. Hartmann (1899), in MGH Epist. 2:383; Gratian, D.45 c.3; *Bernardi Papiensis Faventini episcopi Summa Decretalium*, 5.5.3, ed. E.A.D. Laspeyres (Regensburg, 1860; reprint, Graz, 1956), pp. 210–11; Goffredus Tranensis, *Summa super titulis decretalium*, 5.5.4 (Lyons, 1519), fol. 205b; Ramon of Penyaforte, *Summa de casibus poenitentiae*, 1.4.2 (Rome, 1603), pp. 32–33. Norman Daniel's statements (on the basis of the above passage of the *Summa de casibus* as printed on p. 24 of the Verona 1744 edition) that Ramon insisted that "Jews and Muslims must be converted, not by harshness, but by reason and kindness—*coacta servicia non placent Deo*"—and that he taught that "Jews and Muslims ought to be 'stimulated to the Christian faith by authorities, by reasons and by kindnesses, and ought not to be forced'" obviously go beyond the text. N. Daniel, *Islam and the West*, pp. 116, 253.

[92] *Gregorii I papae Registrum epistolarum*, in MGH Epist. 1:261; Gratian, C.23 q.6 d.p.c.4; *Bernardi Papiensis Summa Decretalium*, 5.5.4, p. 211; Ramon of Penyaforte, *Summa de casibus poenitentiae*, 1.4.3, p. 34b.

"natives of the country who had been formerly Saracens but recently had become Christian": so relates Fulk of Chartres, the chaplain of Baldwin I. And William of Tyre, the well-known chronicler of the Crusading Kingdom, writes that Baldwin I raised a Saracen from the font, gave him his name, and received him among his domestics, so that ultimately he becomes "almost a chamberlain." But this converted Baldwin, like the Moor baptized with the assistance of Hugh of Cluny, disappointed his patron: In 1110 he conspired with the Saracens of Sidon to assassinate his royal godfather, was apprehended, and hanged.[93] Again, an anonymous account not devoid of legendary overtones mentions a man whose proper name the author does not know but who, "for an unknown reason," was surnamed Machomus. Captured by crusaders in his youth and baptized, he rose in the royal service and, in 1112, was left in charge of the affairs of Baldwin I in Jerusalem while the king led an expedition into the desert. His story is recorded because his fluency in Arabic purportedly enabled him to expose a Saracen plot to conquer the city. It is tempting to identify the convert surnamed Machomus in this anonymous account with *Walterus cognomine Mahumeth*, who witnessed royal charters from 1104 to 1115 and became the lord of Hebron sometime after 1107. Like Roger Aḥmad in Sicily, he might have received the name Walterus from his crusader godfather.[94] It is noteworthy that the presence of these Muslim converts in the entourage of Baldwin I can be ascertained solely because of the roles they played in the king's exploits; the act of conversion as such was not deemed worthy of mention. In other words, it is possible that in the early years of the kingdom there were other Muslim converts in royal or seigniorial service.[95]

[93] For Albert see n. 64 above; Fulk of Chartres (n. 69 above), II, 4, 4, pp. 374–75; William of Tyre, *Historia rerum in partibus transmarinis gestarum* XI, 14, in RHC. HOcc. 1:477.

[94] The anonymous account is printed in RHC. HOcc. 4:262. On *Walterus cognomine Mahumeth* see Albert of Aachen, X, 33, and XI, 40, in RHC. HOcc. 4:646, 683; R. Röhricht, comp., *Regesta regni Hierosolymitani, 1097–1291* (Innsbruck, 1893–1904; hereafter cited as *RRH*), nos. 43, 52, 76b, 79, 80, 134. See also *Les Familles d'Outre-Mer de DuCange*, ed. E.-G. Rey (Paris, 1869), p. 424.

[95] Muisse Arrabit (Arrabi), a vassal of Hugh of Ibelin, who appears in documents of 1158 and 1160 (*Cartulaire de l'église du Saint-Sépulcre de Jérusalem*, ed. E. de Rozière [Paris, 1849], docs. 57, 60, 63, pp. 113, 121, 128–29), may have been of Muslim origin. The evidence about Muisse, his son George, and four grandchildren was first assembled by J. Richard, *Le royaume latin de Jérusalem* (Paris, 1953), p. 130 [= *The Latin Kingdom of Jerusalem*, trans. Janet Shirley (Amsterdam, 1979), p. 141]; see also J.S.C. Riley-Smith, *The Feudal Nobility and the Kingdom of Jerusalem* (London, 1973), p. 10. The statement that Muisse had a brother named Baldwin seems to depend on an erroneous summary of an act of 1158 by Röhricht: *RRH* no. 332.

Converts from Islam certainly played some role in the crusader army. It has been suggested that there were numerous converts among the light cavalry, or Turkopoles, since two short lists of such soldiers contain the names Petrus Baptizatus and Gaifredus Baptizatus. The chronicler Abū Shāma reports that after the Muslim victory at Jacob's Ford in 1179, Saladin ordered the execution of the captured apostates from Islam and the archers.[96] Again, during Saladin's siege of Tyre in 1187, an amir's son, angry with his father, left the Muslim camp for the beleaguered city, promptly converted to Christianity, became Conrad of Montferrat's valet, and helped him to trap five of Saladin's galleys.[97] Unlike the practice in Norman Sicily, however, converted (or unconverted) Muslims at no time played a major role in the political, military, or administrative history of the kingdom. On the other hand, crusader Jerusalem never witnessed anything like Philip of al-Mahdiyya's auto-da-fé of 1153 in Palermo, or outbursts of violence like those against the Sicilian officials of Muslim descent. Obscurity evidently had its benefits.

At the other end of the social scale there must have been conversions of Muslim slaves, since several chapters of the crusader *Assises de la Cour des Bourgeois* deal with converts of this class. "The freedman," expound the *Assises*, "is that one who had been a Saracen slave and became Christian." On three occasions the term *libertins* ("freedman") of the Provençal *Lo Codi*, the apparent model of the crusader *Assises*, appears in the *Assises* as *batié* ("baptized"). Obviously "freedman" and "baptized Saracen slave" had become equivalent in the Crusading Kingdom.[98] But was baptism merely a prerequisite for manumission,

---

It should be noted, however, that one *Simeon f. Benedicti Arrabiti* appears in 1139 as the owner of a vineyard in Barletta, and that *Maio miles f. Arrabiti* appears in acts drawn up in the Apulian town of Canne in 1179, 1182, 1197, and about 1200: *Codice diplomatico Barese*, vol. 8, *Le pergamene di Barletta, archivio capitolare (897–1285)*, ed. F. Nitti di Vito (Bari, 1914), docs. 45, 135, 137, 176, 181, pp. 75, 179, 181, 224, 232. On southern Italians in the entourage of the early Ibelins see W. H. Rüdt de Collenberg, "Les premiers Ibelins," *Le Moyen Age* 71 (1965): 473–74.

[96] On converts among the Turkopoles see Richard, *The Latin Kingdom*, p. 140, on the basis of two lists of 1163 and 1180 (*RRH* nos. 389, 594). Abū Shāma, *Kitāb al-rawḍatayn*, in RHC. HOr. 4:205. But it would seem far-fetched to regard all Turkopoles converts (Richard, *La papauté*, p. 7, and n. 19 *in fine*). An episode described by Ambroise suggests that normally—but not always—Turkopoles were Arabic-speaking natives: cf. J. Prawer, *The Latin Kingdom of Jerusalem: European Colonialism in the Middle Ages* (London, 1972), p. 341. Of course, Arabic-speaking natives must not have been converted Muslims.

[97] Margaret R. Morgan, ed., *La Continuation de Guillaume de Tyr (1184–1197)*, Documents relatifs à l'histoire des croisades, 14 (Paris, 1982), pp. 77–78.

[98] *Assises de la Cour des Bourgeois*, chap. 16, in RHC. Lois 2: 29. *libertins* (Prov.),

as in Genoa and elsewhere, or did it actually bestow free status on a servile convert? The pompous statement of the *Assises* that "the land of the Christians is the land of the Franks, and for this reason Christians ought to enjoy there all liberties" may be a later addition, but a papal letter of 1237 states explicitly that the customary law of the Crusading Kingdom (*consuetudo terre*) grants freedom to a converted slave.[99]

The origins of this law remain unknown. Did the early crusaders, few as they were amid a hostile population, endeavor to bolster their native support by offering freedom to enslaved Muslims who were willing to accept Christianity? Or was a Catholic, or Catholicized, slave simply inconceivable in that new society polarized between a few Catholic conquerors and a mass of non-Catholic subjects? It is also possible that these circumstances were less decisive, for Christian slavery was unknown also in Catalonia, a country of a distinctly different ethnic composition. Because of a *consuetudo bona*, remarks Ramon of Penyaforte, Christian slaves were unheard of in Catalonia, the implication being that converted slaves were set free there.[100] And the Cistercian statutes suggest that the basic norm of the order called for some amelioration in the status of a converted Muslim slave, possibly even for his manumission. (In Castile the situation must have been different: Since the *fuero* of Lara, confirmed in 1135 by Alfonso VII,

---

libertinus (Lat.) = *batié: Lo Codi*, VI.20.1, VI.21.1, VI.25.1–3, ed. Derrer (n. 21 above), pp. 138–40; *Lo Codi*, VI.19.1, VI.20.1, VI.24.1–3, ed. Fitting (n. 21 above), pp. 191–93; *Assises*, chaps. 203–5, pp. 137–39. While a rubric of a chapter of the *Assises* mentions "celui qui l'a fait faire crestien," the chapter itself deals with "celuy qui l'avoit franchi": chap. 204, p. 138. See also the rubric of chap. 203 (p. 137): "celui ou cele qui le franchi, ce est qui le fist faire Crestien," and chap. 211 (p. 143), where "et il est puis devenus frans" in the rubric equals "et puis il devint Crestien" in the text. See, however, Verlinden, *L'esclavage*, 2:969, n. 15, for a case in 1138 in which baptism might not have led to the slave's manumission.

[99] *Assises*, chap. 255, p. 191. See also Verlinden, 2:965; Prawer, "Serfs, Slaves, and Bedouin," in *Crusader Institutions*, p. 209. Jonathan Riley-Smith (*The Feudal Nobility*, p. 258, n. 10) has suggested that this passage may be a later addition. For the papal letter see Appendix 2/a.

[100] After stating that masters must not prevent the conversion of their slaves and that the act of conversion should not alter the slave's status vis-à-vis his master, Ramon adds: "Ubi tamen de consuetudine bona non essent Christiani servi, ut in Cathalonia, consulerem quod dominus in remissionem peccatorum suorum manumitteret [Clm 6040, fol. 7vb: remitteret] eum; vel saltem, ne dominus damnificaretur nimis, ostiatim peteret eleemosynas." *Summa de casibus poenitentiae*, 1.4.7, p. 37. (Ramon wrote his *Summa* between 1222 and 1235.) On Ramon and the situation in conquered Valencia see R. I. Burns, "Journey from Islam: Incipient Cultural Transition in the Conquered Kingdom of Valencia (1240–1280)," *Speculum* 35 (1960): 344–45 (reprinted in his *Moors and Crusaders in Mediterranean Spain: Collected Essays* [London, 1978], XII:344–45).

stipulates that a converted slave willing to settle in that place should be granted freedom, it follows that mere conversion would not have led to the slave's manumission.)[101] Perhaps the crusader and Catalan *consuetudines*, as well as the Cistercian norm, arose when voluntary Muslim conversion was so rare that Catholics were ready to sustain some material losses in return for an uncommon testimony to the attractiveness of their religion. In any case one may surmise that clerics intent on furthering Christianization played some role in the genesis of these usages. Two capitals of the crusader Church of the Annunciation, depicting the apocryphal missions of the apostles Bartholomew and Matthew to the pagans of India and Ethiopia, suggest the presence of such clerics in twelfth-century Nazareth.

Whatever the origins of the crusader *consuetudo terre*, it soon came about that more Muslim slaves asked for baptism than the crusader lords were willing to free. An *assise* lays down that a slave who flees his master and is baptized elsewhere in the Crusading Kingdom must be returned to his former state of servitude, since he sought baptism in ill faith *por estre delivres dou servage* (to be freed from servitude). The fugitive evidently knew that his master would not let him be baptized (and thus become free), and therefore single-handedly sought his salvation elsewhere, a deduction corroborated by a letter of Jacques of Vitry, bishop of Acre between 1216 and 1228. Jacques thunders against crusader masters who refused their Saracens baptism "although these earnestly and tearfully requested it." The masters, relates Jacques, rejoined that had the Saracens converted, they would not have been able to oppress them at will. Similarly Guillaume of Rennes, commenting sometime between 1240 and 1245 on Ramon of Penyaforte's mention of the Catalan *consuetudo bona*, complains that because of such usage, masters do not let their slaves accept Christianity.[102]

[101] "Tornadizo qui in Lara populaverit, ingenuus fiat." L. Serrano, ed., *Cartulario de San Pedro de Arlanza* (Madrid, 1925), p. 179. Cf. Verlinden, *L'esclavage*, 1:254.

According to González Palencia's summary of an act of manumission, written in Arabic and drawn up in Toledo in 1163, a Muslim female slave was manumitted *because* of her baptism; *Los mozárabes* (n. 34 above), doc. 785. The summary was used by Verlinden, *L'esclavage*, 1:155. The Arabic text does not mention at all a causal relationship between baptism and liberation.

[102] *Assises*, chap. 255, p. 191. The *assise* also states that a fugitive who escapes *en Paienime*—to the realm of Islam—subsequently returns to the Crusading Kingdom, and asks for baptism proves thereby the sincerity of his intentions and obtains free status. Adolf Waas, who first drew attention to this *assise* (*Geschichte der Kreuzzüge*, 2 vols. [Freiburg i/Br., 1956], 2:187), exaggerated in his claim that a Muslim slave had to flee in order to obtain baptism. *Lettres de Jacques de Vitry, évêque de Saint-Jean d'Acre*, II, lines 205–10, ed. R.B.C. Huygens (Leiden, 1960), pp. 87–88. (This part of Letter II

The conversion of several free but inconspicuous Muslims is also mentioned in the sources. In his oft-quoted description of the new society the crusaders established in the Holy Land, Fulk of Chartres mentions Franks who took for wives "a Syrian, an Armenian, or even a baptized Saracen." *Aluis baptizata*, mentioned in an inventory of Hospitaller property in Jerusalem as the wife of the Frank Robert, was probably such a convert from Islam.[103] Usāma b. Munqidh (1095–1188), a Syrian noble who repeatedly fought the crusaders yet frequently visited their kingdom, tells of a Frank named Raoul who, captured by the men of Shaizar, converted to Islam and learned the craft of marble carving. He seemed so sincere in his prayers and fasting that the ruler of Shaizar, Usāma's father, married him to the daughter of a pious family; she bore him two sons. When the boys were five or six years old, Raoul fled with his Muslim family to Apamea, in the crusader principality of Antioch, where he reverted to Christianity together with his children. (Usāma does not indicate whether the wife also became Christian.) Elsewhere, Usāma writes of a man he had met in Nablus whose Muslim mother killed the Frank to whom she had

---

was written in the winter of 1216–17.) Guillaume of Rennes: "Cum alicubi propter consuetudinem huiusmodi non permittunt domini servos suos baptizari, et credo, quod male faciunt omnes tales." Commentary on Ramon's *Summa*, 1.4.7, p. 47. On Teutonic knights who prohibited Prussian catechumens from receiving baptism, arguing—quite like Jacques's crusader masters—"quod fortiores, quam Deo credentium, esse possent domini paganorum," see the letter of Gregory IX of April 11, 1240, to the bishop of Meissen: R. Philippi, ed., *Preussisches Urkundenbuch*, Politische Abtheilung, 1, 1 (Königsberg, 1882), no. 134, p. 101. Cf. F. Blanke, "Die Entscheidungsjahre der Preussenmission (1206–1274)," in *Heidenmission und Kreuzzugsgedanke*, pp. 408–9. See also A. Stroick, ed., "Collectio de scandalis ecclesie," *Archivum Franciscanum Historicum* 24 (1931): 39: "Quidam converti non permittuntur a suis dominis, ne perdant in eis consuetas operas servitutis."

[103] Fulk of Chartres (n. 69 above), III, 37, 4, p. 748; S. Pauli, ed., *Codice diplomatico del sacro militare ordine gerosolimitano*, vol. 1 (Lucca, 1733), doc. 190, p. 236: "due volte que fuerunt Roberti mariti Aluis baptizatae."

There were also illicit liaisons with unconverted Muslim women. Patriarch Arnulf of Jerusalem (1112–18) was accused of maintaining relations with "the wife of Girard, and a Saracen, who did bear him a son": PL 163:410. In 1120 the Council of Nablus decreed that a Christian who had sexual relations with a Saracen woman, whether of her own free will or not, should be castrated; the same punishment was to be meted out to a Saracen who had relations with a Christian woman: Mansi, *Concilia*, 21:264. Verlinden (*L'esclavage*, 2:968) drew attention to the fact that these decisions were not incorporated into the *Assises*. For the pertinent Castilian legislation see *Las siete partidas* (n. 19 above), VII, 25, 10, 3:681.

A Willelmus Baptizatus of Blanche Garde, who buys two houses in Jerusalem, and Uldricus Baptizatus *de curia Jerusalem* appear in two acts of 1178: J. Delaville le Roulx, ed., *Cartulaire général de l'Ordre des Hospitaliers de S.-Jean de Jérusalem, 1100–1310*, 4 vols. (Paris, 1894–1906), docs. 537–38, 1:366–67.

been married.[104] And Ibn Djubayr, who passed through Galilee in 1184 on his return voyage from Mecca, mentions a Maghrebi Muslim ransomed from Christian captivity who joined a merchant caravan going from Damascus to Acre, mixed there with Christians, and came under their influence until—to use the words of Ibn Djubayr—"he had been baptized and become unclean, and had put on the girdle of a monk, thereby hastening for himself the flames of hell, verifying the threats of torture, and exposing himself to a grievous account and a long-distant return [from hell]."[105] In other words, his was a genuine conversion.

Important evidence of Muslim conversion in the Crusading Kingdom at the close of the twelfth and the beginning of the thirteenth centuries is found also in two decretals that have been hitherto unnoticed, probably because they survive only in canon law tradition. The first decretal, sent early in 1193 by Pope Celestine III to Theobald, bishop of Acre, answers inter alia three difficult questions about Saracen conversion.[106] May a Saracen captive who killed his Christian captor with the wife's connivance and then converted to Christianity legally marry the slain captor's widow? No, answers the pope, the Church does not want to compensate so great a loss with such a gain. Bishop Theobald's question seems to smack of fiction—until one recalls that only two decades later another bishop of Acre, Jacques of Vitry, will lament the poisonous machinations to which the ladies of the Crusading Kingdom had recourse in order to dispose of their husbands and be free to marry others.[107] The second question also deals with a problem that pertains to the warrior class. May a Saracen who killed a Christian in battle and then converted to Christianity marry the dead man's widow? And may a Christian marry the converted widow of a Saracen he slew? Yes, answers Celestine, these widows had no part in the deaths of their husbands; their second marriages are binding; if they should demand divorce upon discovering that the second husband killed the first, their requests must be rejected. These suspiciously symmetrical liaisons between slayers and widows sound

---

[104] *An Arab Syrian Gentleman and Warrior in the Period of the Crusades: Memoirs of Usāmah ibn-Munqidh*, trans. P. K. Hitti (New York, 1929), pp. 160, 168.

[105] *The Travels of Ibn Jubayr* (n. 29 above), p. 323. The case resembles that of the fugitive who escapes to *Paienime*, then returns, and asks for baptism (see n. 102 above).

[106] The pertinent part of the decretal appears in X 3.33.1. For the identification of its recipient see W. Holtzmann, "Die Benutzung Gratians in der päpstlichen Kanzlei im 12. Jahrhundert," *Studia Gratiana* 1 (1933): 339; idem, "La 'Collectio seguntina' et les décrétales de Clément III et de Célestin III," *Revue d'histoire ecclésiastique* 50 (1955): 443–44; Kedar, "Muslim Conversion in Canon Law."

[107] *Lettres de Jacques de Vitry*, II, lines 192–94, p. 87.

rather hypothetical. Not so the next case, which deals with a Christian who left his faith and wife and, according to Gentile rites, took a pagan woman for wife, who in due time bore him a number of sons.[108] (In twelfth-century Palestine, the pagan woman married according to Gentile rites could only have been a Muslim.) What should be done, asks Theobald in one of his queries on this case, if the renegade, after the death of his Christian wife, decides to return to Christianity and marry the pagan wife "who because of him converted to our faith together with her children"? (This is a close parallel to the case of the craftsman Raoul mentioned by Usāma.) The pope rules that revert and convert may marry and their children be considered legitimate.

The second decretal was sent by Pope Innocent III, in 1201, to the bishop of Tiberias—this must have been a titular bishop, for Tiberias had been in Muslim hands since 1187.[109] The pope is delighted at learning that recently God "had inspired the hearts of many pagans to come to the Christian faith," and goes on to answer questions that arose in connection with these conversions. Since some of these pagans were related to their spouses in degrees prohibited by canon law, the bishop asked whether upon conversion they might remain married. (This was the problem that had vexed the Sicilian Chamut of Castrogiovanni back in 1087, and had arisen also in Spain, according to a decretal of Clement III sent to Ciudad Rodrigo.)[110] Like Clement III before him, Innocent ruled that such marriages between consanguineous converts were valid, and their offspring legitimate. Then Innocent III raised the question of polygamous converts and ruled that despite Biblical precedents, polygamy is inadmissible after conversion. Although he did not state so explicitly, the context suggests that he meant that the convert was to stay with the wife he had married first,

[108] On the similar case of Christians who settled in Saracen lands and renounced their Christian faith, see the recently published letter of Alexander III to an archbishop of Tyre, possibly the chronicler William: *Decretales ineditae saeculi XII*, ed. S. Chodorow and C. Duggan, Monumenta Iuris Canonici, Series B, vol. 4 (Città del Vaticano, 1982), doc. 94, pp. 166–67. The letter should be compared with the crusader *Livre au Roi*, chap. 23 (RHC. Lois 1:622), and *Abrégé du Livre des Assises de la Cour des Bourgeois*, chap. 24 (RHC. Lois 2:325).

[109] X 4.19.8. For the decretal's date see Kedar, "Muslim Conversion in Canon Law." In the late 1190s a bishop of Tiberias attempted to extract from the Templars a sum his predecessor had deposited with them: PL 214:816–18; cf. J.S.C. Riley-Smith, "Latin Titular Bishops in Palestine and Syria, 1137–1291," *Catholic Historical Review* 64 (1978): 9.

[110] 2 Comp. 3.20.1; for the address, see Holtzmann, "Die Benutzung," p. 333. A similar decretal, sent in 1198 to Tyre (X 4.14.4), clearly refers to converts from Judaism, but the decretalists interpret it as applying to Jews or Saracens.

and thus was the ruling interpreted by the decretalists.[111] Finally, the pope declared that divorce according to non-Christian rites is not valid, and a divorced convert should, under normal circumstances, return to his first wife if she has become Christian too. In setting down his decision on consanguinity, Innocent implied that it would further conversion; he should have been aware that his decisions on polygamy and divorce would have a contrary effect.

Evidently Muslim conversion was not a mass phenomenon in the Crusading Kingdom. Ibn Djubayr, who quotes Sicilian Muslims' fears that Islam might disappear from the island, reports nothing of the kind about the Muslims of the Crusading Kingdom. Lack of enthusiasm for Muslim conversion was exhibited, in the twelfth century, not only by crusader lords but also by the Knights Templar. William of Tyre relates that in 1154 a fugitive son of an Egyptian vizier fell into Templar captivity, expressed his wish to convert to Christianity, and even learned to read Latin, but the Knights Templar preferred to hand him over to the Egyptians in return for sixty thousand pieces of gold. According to William, the Templars also thwarted the overtures of the Syrian Assassins to become Christian in 1172. (These stories about the Templars soon came to be known in Europe: Walter Map, the acerbic courtier of Henry II of England, puts them to use in the framework of his attack on the Templars, relating them in the same order as they appear in William's chronicle, and Guido of Bazoches, who died as cantor of St. Etienne of Châlons in 1203, repeats them as well, evidently summarizing William's account.)[112] As for William himself, it has been recently pointed out that he did not reproduce in his chronicle episodes of Muslim conversion he must have encountered in the sources he used, probably because on principle he opposed enforced conver-

[111] Ramon of Penyaforte, *Summa de casibus poenitentiae*, 4.10.3, p. 548b; Hostiensis, *Commentaria*, to X 4.19.8, v. *non ad imparia iudicentur*, no. 10 (Venice, 1581), fol. 46ra; Joannes Andreae, *Commentaria*, to X 4.19.7, v. *iudicentur*, no. 10 (Venice, 1581), fol. 67va. See also A. Esmein, *Le mariage en droit canonique*, 2d ed. (Paris, 1929), pp. 254–55.

[112] William of Tyre (n. 93 above), XVIII, 9, XXI, 29–30, pp. 833–34, 995–99. Walter Map, *De nugis curialium*, I, 21–22, ed. M. R. James (Oxford, 1914), pp. 31–33. Guido de Bazoches, *Apologia contra maledicos*, BN lat. 4998, fol. 63rb, 63va; the second passage is quoted, with insignificant variations, by Albericus Trium Fontium, *Chronica*, ed. P. Scheffer-Boichorst (1874), in MGH SS 23:859. On the capture of the vizier's son see Runciman, *History*, 2:365–66; on the possible reasons for William's belief that the Assassins were ready to convert see J. Hauziński, "O domniemanych próbach konwersji asasynów na chrześcijaństwo w świetle relacji Wilhelma z Tyru," *Przegląd historyczny* 64 (1973): 243–53.

sion; nor did he speak out on the issue of peaceful conversion.[113] And some crusaders came to realize that the baptizing of defeated Saracens could be of little value indeed: When upon the conquest of Acre in 1191 the kings of England and France ordered the release of Saracens willing to receive baptism, and the neophytes hastened to flee to Saladin's camp, the kings promptly prohibited further baptisms of this kind.[114] Nevertheless, the evidence of the Latin and Arabic narrative sources, as well as of the *Assises des Bourgeois* and canon law, leaves no doubt that in the twelfth-century kingdom of Jerusalem the dividing line between Islam and Christendom was crossed on numerous occasions.[115]

THUS, on all three fronts of the Catholic counteroffensive against Islam, the new imbalance between Catholic conqueror and subjugated Muslim paved the way for some coerced or voluntary conversions to Christianity, a phenomenon previously almost unknown. The data are far too scanty to allow for an estimate, however tentative, of the rate of conversion. They do suggest that most of the early converts originated in either the uppermost or the lowest stratum of Muslim society, with former members of the ruling class, as well as warriors, largely maintaining their old status, and slaves and serfs aspiring to ameliorate their situation.[116] The emotional and social context of the formal act of conversion surely varied from case to case, but baptism motivated by genuine interest or attraction appears to have been quite rare. It is

[113] Schwinges, *Kreuzzugsideologie*, pp. 275–81. But the suggestion that William believed in "passive" missionizing seems conjectural.

[114] *Chronica magistri Rogeri de Houedene* (n. 83 above), 3:121; *Gesta regis Henrici II et Ricardi I*, ed. W. Stubbs, 2 vols., Rolls Series, 49 (London, 1867), 2:179; *Continuatio Guilelmi Tyrii*, III, 23, ed. Marianne Salloch (Berlin, 1934), p. 141. Saladin was said to have observed that a bad Christian never becomes a good Muslim, nor a bad Muslim a good Christian: Jean, sire de Joinville, *Histoire de Saint Louis*, §331, ed. N. de Wailly (Paris, 1874), p. 180.

Crossing the battle lines in order to convert to the opponents' faith must have been quite common. When a Muslim warrior drew near to the Franks during the desultory fighting that took place in the Jezreel Valley in 1183, the Franks initially assumed that he intended to convert; likewise, when Francis of Assisi crossed into the Egyptian camp in 1219, he was asked if he came to convert: *Chronique d'Ernoul et de Bernard le Trésorier*, ed. L. de Mas Matrie (Paris, 1871), pp. 101, 432.

[115] For the conversion of crusaders to Islam see, in addition to n. 108 above, the occasionally uncritical survey of T. W. Arnold, *The Preaching of Islam: A History of the Propagation of the Muslim Faith*, 2d ed. (London, 1913), pp. 88–95.

[116] On the similar social origins of early converts to Islam see R. W. Bulliet, *Conversion to Islam in the Medieval Period: An Essay in Quantitative History* (Cambridge, Mass., and London, 1979), p. 42.

noteworthy, from this point of view, that while fragments of an account of conversion by a twelfth-century Christian who became a Jew (the south Italian Norman cleric Johannes, later 'Obadyah the Proselyte) and a full-fledged report by a twelfth-century Jew who became a Christian (Judah b. David of Cologne, later Hermann, Premonstratensian prior of Scheda) are extant, no contemporary record of a Muslim's conversion to Catholicism has ever come to light.

In all three areas of Catholic reconquest, Muslim conversions gave rise to very similar problems: The validity of Muslim consanguineous marriages contracted before baptism is a source of concern in Castrogiovanni, Sicily, in Ciudad Rodrigo, Spain, and in crusader Palestine, while the reluctance of Catholic masters to allow the baptism of their Muslim soldiers, slaves, or serfs manifests itself in Capua, Barcelona, Acre, Palermo, and even some Cistercian monasteries. At the same time, forcing baptism on the defeated Saracen warrior and carrying off to the lands of Christendom the sensuous Saracen maiden must have come to play a considerable role in the dream life of many a European knight.

Still, no sustained efforts at preaching to the Muslims were being attempted. The dispatch of the hermit Anastasius to the Saracens of Spain, engineered by Pope Gregory VII and Abbot Hugh of Cluny, remained a fruitless, isolated episode. In later decades, a few hermits occasionally endeavored to stimulate Muslim conversion on their own. It has already been seen that according to Albert of Aachen, Peter the Hermit offered the ruler of Mosul the choice of converting or engaging in battle with the crusaders. Elias of Palmaria, a grammarian from the region of Narbonne who first became a hermit and then an abbot of a Galilean monastery, once intended to go to Spain and preach Christianity to the Saracens, but was dissuaded from doing so. In 1123 or 1124, Bernard of Blois, leader of an eremitical community on the Black Mountain near Antioch, visited King Baldwin II in his captivity and preached the Christian faith to his Turkish captor; when the Turk became incensed with ire, Bernard reportedly told him that even a lance thrust through his heart would not prevent him from declaring the truth. (The scene, which anticipates to some extent Francis of Assisi's famous encounter with al-Malik al-Kāmil of Egypt about a century later, is described in a little-known tract by Gerard of Nazareth.) But these efforts, reminiscent of contemporary eremitical preaching to the pagans of northeastern Europe, were sporadic and, with Peter the Hermit and Bernard of Blois, merely incidental to the main purpose. Similarly incidental was the preaching of the Carthusian monk Einard, who, probably in the 1160s, reportedly "attacked the blindness of the

Agarens [of Africa] with so much freedom and vigor, and had made known to them with so much faith and conviction the light of Christian truth, that none of them dared to mock him." For Einard went to Africa, not to convert Muslims, but to rescue two Spanish hermits who had been abducted by Muslim raiders.[117] Neither did the papacy promote missionary work in the realm of Islam. When Celestine III asked the archbishop of Toledo in 1192 to send an Arabic-speaking priest to "Morocco, Seville, and other cities of the Saracens," he made clear that it was among the Christians of these places, who had asked for instruction, that the priest was to work; the possibility of preaching to the Saracens is not even hinted at.[118]

PERCEPTIONS OF ISLAM IN THE AGE OF RECONQUEST

As Muslim conversion became an element of European reality and, perhaps even more so, of European imagination, the beliefs of the Muslims became better known. Accounts of two early episodes of the Catholic counteroffensive testify to an awareness of Muhammad's existence. Describing Abbot Maieul's captivity, which triggered the reduction of Muslim Fraxinetum, Raoul Glaber (d. ca. 1050) remarks that the Saracens read the Hebrew and the Christian prophets and believe that whatever the prophets foretold of Christ was fulfilled in one of their own, "whom they call Mahomed."[119] The anonymous Pisan poet who celebrates the victory in 1087 of his fellow citizens over the North African city of al-Mahdiyya has the enemy invoke Machumat, whose perfidy threw the entire world into disorder: A heresiarch mightier than Arius, he did not believe in the Trinity or in Jesus

---

[117] On Anastasius and Peter the Hermit see nn. 6 and 62 above; Gerard of Nazareth's description of Elias of Palmaria and Bernard of Blois is reproduced and discussed in B. Z. Kedar, "Gerard of Nazareth, a Neglected Twelfth-Century Writer in the Crusader East: A Contribution to the Intellectual and Monastic History of the Crusader States," *Dumbarton Oaks Papers* 37 (1983): 55–77. Einard's preaching is described by Adam of Eynsham, *Magna Vita Sancti Hugonis*, ed. and trans. Decima L. Douie and H. Farmer, 2 vols. (London, 1961–62), 2:65.

[118] The letter, of June 4, 1192, was edited by Fidel Fita in "Noticias," *Boletín de la Real Academia de la Historia* 11 (1887): 456. Robert Burns writes ("Christian-Islamic Confrontation," p. 1390) that "presumably such a missioner also served the dreams of conversion," but nothing in the text supports this assumption. The dispatch of the priest was certainly a novel step: In the early twelfth century Mozarabs complained that no Catholic teachers came to instruct them; see chap. 1, n. 22 above.

[119] Raoul Glaber, *Les cinq livres* (n. 3 above), I, 4, 9, pp. 11–12.

being the Word of God.[120] About the same time the narrative of Theophanes, as reproduced in the works of Anastasius the Librarian and Landulf Sagax, came to be known north of the Alps, and thus several northern chroniclers had easy access for the first time to a written account of the rise of Muhammad and the history of the caliphate in the first 150 years of its existence.

Let us peer over the shoulders of these chroniclers as they confront the new information about the teachings of Muhammad contained in the Anastasian-Landulfian account, and let us observe how they put it to use.[121] These teachings were, as mentioned above, that (1) he who kills the enemy or falls in battle against him will enter Paradise; (2) Paradise is full of carnal delights; and (3) men should show compassion to one another and help the suffering. Frutolf of Michelsberg (d. 1103), who spells the name of the Prophet "Muhammad" and reveals thereby that he drew on Landulf, not Anastasius, remains closest to his prototype, though he shortens the description of the sexual delights of Paradise. But he skips altogether the reference to compassion and help, of which a Christian reader might have approved, and inserts instead the remark that Muhammad's teachings seemed delectable to fools and therefore worthy of their belief. Sigebert of Gembloux (d. 1112), who also drew on the work of Landulf, faithfully reproduces the references to Holy War and Paradise, suppresses, like Frutolf, the reference to compassion and help, and then adds on his own "This is Muhammad to whom the Gentiles hitherto offer the worship of a deity." Evidently Sigebert is insensitive to the discrepancy between his intelligently rearranged summary of Landulf's account, in which Muhammad is presented as a pseudoprophet, and his subsequent restatement of the popular notion that the Saracens worship Muhammad as God.[122] Hugh of Flavigny, whose chronicle reaches to 1102, must have known Anastasius's *Chronographia Tripertita*, to which he explicitly refers as the source for his description of Church-State relationships in sixth-century Alexandria.[123] But when he comes to deal with

---

[120] *Carmen in victoriam Pisanorum*, cc. 32, 52, ed. H.E.J. Cowdrey, in "The Mahdia Campaign of 1087," *English Historical Review* 92 (1977): 26–27. Cf. Manuella Allegretto and G. Lachin, "Epica latina medioevale ed escatologia cristiana: il 'Carmen in victoriam Pisanorum,' " *Atti dell'Istituto Veneto di scienze, lettere ed arti, Classe di scienze morali, lettere ed arti* 131 (1972–73): 213–14, 223. For references in a somewhat later Pisan poem to *Rasulla*, and to *Machomatus ebrius*, who proclaimed the Saracens' worthless faith, see *Liber Maiolichinus de gestis Pisanorum illustribus*, ed. C. Calisse (Rome, 1904), lines 19, 1088, 2510, 3362, pp. 6, 47, 97, 126.

[121] The texts compared below are reproduced in Appendixes 1/b-d.

[122] Cf. Schwinges, *Kreuzzugsideologie*, p. 104.

[123] *Chronicon Hugonis abbatis Flaviniacensis*, in MGH SS 8:320; Anastasius

the Prophet, he dispenses with Anastasius and presents a succinct account, evidently influenced by the Spanish Note on Mahmeth, in which the Devil, claiming to be the archangel Gabriel, sends Mahamet to preach to the Arabs what he had heard in the schools of the Christians, and to call for the worship of one God and the abandonment of the idols.

In the first redaction of the *Historia ecclesiastica* Hugh of Fleury presents a short account, in 1109, about the rise of Muameth that is undoubtedly derived from Anastasius, although Hugh does not seem to be aware of the fact. This account—the first to place Muameth in the province of *Corozania*—mentions the teachings on Paradise and Holy War, but not on compassion and help. In the second redaction of the chronicle, written in 1110, things take an unexpected turn. In one of the prologues Hugh joyfully remarks that Anastasius's work had recently come into his hands, but he found there only little about "the pseudoprophet Muhamet."[124] Yet when he comes to describe Muhamet's rise, he transcribes the short account from the first redaction, dispensing altogether with Anastasius's fuller narration! Indeed, Hugh not only refrains from copying from Anastasius the reference to the teaching on compassion and help, but skips the teachings he had mentioned in the first redaction, stating only that Muhamet adduced proofs from both Testaments for the new laws he invented. One is left with the impression that Hugh's curiosity about the details of Muhamet's creed definitely diminished over the years.

These responses to the Anastasian stimulus demonstrate that confrontation with relatively accurate information did not necessarily lead to its absorption. Time and again, the new data failed to modify the writers' preconceptions; on the contrary, the preconceptions dictated the extent to which the data were absorbed. Nor did the availability of correct information guarantee its acceptance by all the learned, to say nothing of the unlearned, of that time. Saracen monotheism, for example, was noted by a number of important writers: Guibert of Nogent wrote that the Saracens do not consider Mathomus God, "as some people hold," but as a just man through whom the divine laws were transmitted; William of Malmesbury, about 1127, claims that the Saracens worship Muameth not as a God, "as some people think," but as the prophet of God the Highest; later, about 1136, William goes so far as to describe the Christians, the Jews, and the Saracens as sects

---

Bibliothecarius, *Chronographia Tripertita* (chap. 1, n. 1), ed. de Boor, p. 129.

[124] *Ex Hugonis Floriacensis Historia ecclesiastica, Editio altera*, ed. G. Waitz (1851), in MGH SS 9:357. Hugh believed that Anastasius lived in the days of Charlemagne.

(*secte*) that differ with regard to the Son, but worship God the Father and Creator; Otto of Freising, in the 1150s, doubts the veracity of an account in which Saracens attempted to force a captive crusader to worship their idols, because he knows that all Saracens worship a single God.[125] But the dissemination of correct information reflected by these statements did not prevent a learned man like Gerhoch of Reichersberg, in 1147, from making a defeated Egyptian ruler blaspheme "his God Machmoth" in a manner reminiscent of the vanquished Saracens of the *chansons de geste*.[126] Moreover, the Saracens were squarely presented as idolaters in widely read and studied texts. Azo (ca. 1150– ca. 1230), the prominent Bolognese professor of civil law, writes in his extensively used commentary on the Code of Justinian that "the pagans, that is, the Saracens, worship innumerable gods, goddesses, and indeed demons." Hostiensis (1200–1270), one of the most important commentators on the Decretals, defines the Saracens in his *Summa Aurea*—obviously under the influence of Azo—as "those who worship innumerous gods, goddesses, and demons, and accept neither the New nor the Old Testament." Evidently, awareness of Islam's monotheism must have been unevenly distributed among the learned of Catholic Europe if two such central works could so unequivocally define the Saracens as idolaters.[127] Small wonder that in the 1270s the

---

[125] Guibert of Nogent, *Gesta Dei per Francos*, I, 3, in RHC. HOcc. 4:130; William of Malmesbury, *Digest of Aimoin*, excerpt edited in R. M. Thomson, "William of Malmesbury and Some Other Western Writers on Islam," *Medievalia et Humanistica* NS 6 (1975): 181–82 (the approximate date is 1127, not 1137); Thomson also quotes from William's *Commentary on Lamentations* (p. 180). See also William's *Gesta regum Anglorum*, ed. W. Stubbs, 2 vols., Rolls Series, 90 (London, 1887–89), 1:230; *Ottonis episcopi Frisingensis Chronica sive Historia de duabus civitatibus*, VII, 7, ed. A. Hofmeister (1912), in MGH Scr. rer. Germ. 45:317.

[126] *Gerhohi praepositi Reichersbergensis Opera inedita*, vol. 2, *Expositionis psalmorum pars tertia et nona*, ed. D. van den Eynde, O. van den Eynde, and A. Rijmersdael (Rome, 1956), p. 262. On the date of Gerhoch's commentary on Psalm 33 in which this passage occurs, see Gerhoch of Reichersberg, *Letter to Pope Hadrian about the Novelties of the Day*, ed. N. M. Häring (Toronto, 1974), p. 18. Walter Map believed that the Egyptians of his day worshiped "the Gods of their fathers": *De nugis curialium* (n. 112 above), I, 21, p. 32; see also IV, 14.

[127] "Dictum est infra de Iudaeis: modo ponit de paganis, id est de sarracenis qui deos innumeros, deasque, imo daemones colunt, et adorant." Azo, *Summa Aurea*, to Cod. 1.11 (Lyons, 1557), col. 7a; cf. Russell, *The Just War*, p. 51. Hostiensis, *Summa Aurea*, to 5.5. (Venice, 1574), col. 1523. The latter part of Hostiensis obviously depends on the statement by Bernard of Pavia that "Sarraceni vero dicuntur, qui nec vetus nec novum recipiunt testamentum" (*Summa Decretalium*, to 5.5.2, p. 210), a statement taken over by Goffredus of Trani, Ramon of Penyaforte, and *Las siete partidas*.

Even if Azo and Hostiensis merely attempted to create a legal fiction about the Saracens, their readers might have taken it for a statement of fact. In any case, Norman

Dominican Humbert of Romans wrote that many Christians, not only laymen but clerics as well, believe that the Saracens consider Mahumet their God, "which, however, is false."[128]

How did physical proximity to the Muslims affect the extent of knowledge about their beliefs? William of Tyre, who was born in Jerusalem about 1130, studied in Europe, and became the chancellor of the Crusading Kingdom, never used in his chronicle the term "pagans" in reference to the Saracens, and was able to portray Nūr al-Dīn, an archenemy of the Crusading Kingdom, as a man who feared God "according to the superstitious traditions of that people."[129] But William should not be considered representative of the Westerners who settled, or were born, in the Crusading Kingdom. Fulk of Chartres, who took part in the First Crusade and lived in Jerusalem for more than a quarter of a century, relates that in the Dome of the Rock in Jerusalem the Saracens used to pray to an idol made in the name of Mahumet; he later squarely denounces the law of the Saracens as idolatry.[130] The anonymous author of a detailed description of crusader Edessa, probably writing in 1145, remarks that "in Mecca Mahumet, the apostate Nicholas, is worshiped"—an early occurrence of that variant of the legend of Baḥīrā-Sergius in which Muhammad and the apostate Christian monk, or cardinal, merge into one person.[131] (It is noteworthy that about the same time Peter of Cluny, who never lived among Muslims, rejected the identification of Nicholas with Mahumet, basing himself on the chronicle of Anastasius.)[132] In an official report sent

---

Daniel's conclusion that "no serious writer doubted that Islam proclaims the one God" (*Islam and the West*, p. 313) must be significantly modified.

[128] "Sunt enim multi non solum laici, sed etiam clerici, qui nesciunt neque de Mahumeto neque de Saracenis quasi aliquid: nisi quod audiunt quod sunt quidam infideles non credentes in Christum, et putant quod isti Saraceni reputent Mahumetum Deum suum, quod tamen falsum est." Humbertus de Romanis, *Opusculum tripartitum* (n. 79 above), I, 27, p. 205.

[129] William of Tyre, XVI, 7, and XX, 31, pp. 714, 1000. For a discussion see Schwinges, *Kreuzzugsideologie*, pp. 187–99. Burchard of Strasbourg, whom Frederick I sent in 1175 on an embassy to Saladin, speaks of the careful ablutions of the Saracens who are *religiosi*. Later he remarks that some are "adeo religiosi quod non nisi unam habent uxorem": *Arnoldi abbatis Lubecensis Cronica*, ed. M. Lappenberg (1869), in MGH SS 21:241.

[130] *Fulcherii Carnotensis Historia Hierosolymitana*, I, 26, 9, and 28, 3, pp. 290, 303. On the other hand, the tenets of Islam appear in a remarkably accurate way in the account of the anonymous, probably Anglo-Norman participant in the conquest of Lisbon in 1147: *De expugnatione Lyxbonensi* (n. 72 above), pp. 130, 132.

[131] "Ibi est mecha in qua colitur mahumet apostata nikolaus." The description of Edessa is edited by R. Röhricht, "Studien zur mittelalterlichen Geographie und Topographie Syriens," *Zeitschrift des Deutschen Palästina-Vereins* 10 (1887): 298.

[132] Petrus Venerabilis, *Summa totius haeresis Saracenorum*, ed. J. Kritzeck, in *Peter the*

from Acre to Innocent III in 1204, the patriarch of Jerusalem and the grand masters of the Knights Hospitaller and Templar assert that the Saracens daily visit and adore their "God Magometh, just as the Christians worship Christ in their churches."[133] And Jacques of Vitry, bishop of crusader Acre, believed that Mahometus considered Mecca and Jerusalem the cities of God, Antioch and Rome the cities of the Devil.[134] (A similar view will be held, more than a century later, by Francesco Petrarca.)[135] Proximity to the Muslims evidently did not guarantee an accurate perception of their beliefs; the writer's preexisting notions and possibly his exposure to Oriental Christian views about Islam must have been more decisive factors than the opportunity for direct contacts with the Muslims themselves.

But even though knowledge about Islam did not spread evenly among the learned of Catholic Europe and proximity to Muslims did not preclude misconceptions, the total amount of interest in, and knowledge about, the Saracens was undoubtedly larger in the twelfth than in any preceding century. Catholic Europeans also came to know and appreciate some of the secular literature created in the Muslim realm. Numerous scientific tracts originating in the land of Islam were translated into Latin in the twelfth century, particularly by translators of the school of Toledo, and some of the stories circulating in the Muslim world became for the first time accessible to readers of Latin through the *Disciplina Clericalis* of Pedro Alfonsi, a Spanish Jew who converted to Christianity in 1106. It is symptomatic that the translators of the scientific tracts repeatedly present their material as Arabic, not Saracen: It is to the opinions of the Arabs, Arabic teachers, the treasures of the Arabs, that they refer.[136] The distinction is best exemplified in an

---

Venerable and Islam (Princeton, 1964), p. 205. See also Marie-Thérèse d'Alverny, "Pierre le Vénérable et la légende de Mahomet," in *A Cluny: Congrès scientifique, 9–11 juillet 1949* (Dijon, 1950), pp. 161–70. Peter's monastery, Cluny, owned a copy of Anastasius's chronicle in the mid-twelfth century: L. Delisle, *Inventaire des manuscrits de la Bibliothèque Nationale: Fonds de Cluni* (Paris, 1884), p. 338, no. 18.

[133] *Ryccardi de S. Germano Chronica*, ed. C. A. Garufi (1936–38), in RIS 7, 2:57. Old French version in C. Hopf, ed., *Chroniques gréco-romanes inédites ou peu connues* (Berlin, 1873), p. 31n, where other versions are enumerated too. For a discussion of the report and its date see P. A. Throop, *Criticism of the Crusade: A Study of Public Opinion and Crusade Propaganda* (Amsterdam, 1940; reprint, Philadelphia, 1975), pp. 8–10.

[134] *Jacobi de Vitriaco Historia Orientalis*, ed. F. Moschus (Douai, 1597; reprint, Westmead, 1971), p. 30.

[135] *De vita solitaria*, II, 9, ed. G. Martelotti, in *Francesco Petrarca: Prose*, La letteratura italiana, Storia e Testi, (Milan and Naples, 1955), p. 496.

[136] For examples see Metlitzki, *The Matter of Araby*, pp. 29, 49, 54, 259, n. 100, and 260, n. 134; C.S.F. Burnett, "A Group of Arabic-Latin Translators Working in Northern Spain in the Mid-Twelfth Century," *Journal of the Royal Asiatic Society*, 1977: 90. It is symptomatic, from this point of view, that the earliest translator from Arabic into

imaginary dialogue between Adelard of Bath, the translator of al-Khwārizmī's tables, and his nephew: The nephew attacks the opinions of the Saracens, while Adelard pleads the case of the Arabs.[137] In the same vein, Alfonsi consistently presents his heroes as Arabs. The reason is obvious: "Arab" designates an ethnic or linguistic entity, "Saracen," the rival religion. "To become Saracen" meant "to become Muslim": In a decretal issued by Innocent III in 1203, Agnes, a Christian woman from the archbishopric of Tarragona, furious with her husband for breaking their agreement to forgo sexual relations, affirms that she would sooner become Saracen (*prius se faceret Saracenam*) and lose her soul than return to her fickle husband.[138] Yet the more intelligent reader of Alfonsi's stories must have understood that his Arab fathers and sons, his merchants of Egypt and Baghdad, or pilgrims going to Mecca were in reality Saracens. Consequently it is plausible to assume that Alfonsi's immensely popular collection—there are four manuscripts of the twelfth, twenty-three of the thirteenth, and twenty-nine of the fourteenth centuries extant, as well as several translations into the vernacular—played a role in undemonizing and humanizing the Saracen.[139] When in the same collection of stories some men make a pilgrimage to Rome and others to Mecca (and Alfonsi uses the same word, *oratio*, to denote the aim of both kinds of pilgrims),[140] when an Arab father's counsel to his son is presented for the edification of Christian readers, the chasm between Christian and Saracen narrows by necessity.[141]

Latin, Constantine the African, admits that he rendered into Latin the work of Isaac Judaeus, but suppresses the names of the Muslim authors whose works he translated: R. Creutz, "Die Ehrenrettung," pp. 43–44; K. Sudhoff, "Constantin, der erste Vermittler muslimischer Wissenschaft ins Abendland und die beiden Salernitaner Frühscholastiker Maurus and Urso, als Exponenten dieser Vermittlung," *Archeion* 14 (1932): 362.

[137] *Die Quaestiones Naturales des Adelardus von Bath*, ed. M. Müller (Münster, 1934), pp. 4–5, 9. The editor argues that the *Quaestiones* were written between 1111 and 1116 (p. 77). On Adelard see Metlitzki, pp. 26–30.

[138] X 2.24.24. In the Latin translation of the Letter of al-Kindi, too, *sarracenus* means Muslim: Muñoz Sendino, "Al-Kindi" (chap. 1, n. 37), pp. 395, 416, 419.

[139] For the Latin manuscripts see Díaz y Díaz, *Index* (n. 4 above), no. 892, 1:201–2. For the translations into the vernacular see A. Hilka and W. Söderhjelm, *Die Disciplina Clericalis des Petrus Alfonsi* (Heidelberg, 1911), pp. xii–xv.

[140] *Petri Alfonsi Disciplina Clericalis*, ed. A. Hilka and W. Söderhjelm, Acta societatis scientiarum fennicae, 38, 4 (Helsinki, 1911), pp. 17, 27.

[141] A similar function may be ascribed to the vernacular epics in which the Saracen adversary came to be depicted ever more favorably. See H. Naumann, "Der wilde und der edle Heide," in *Vom Werden des deutschen Geistes: Festgabe Gustav Ehrismann*, ed. P. Merker and W. Stammler (Berlin and Leipzig, 1925), pp. 80–101. This is the classical study of this trend; for later literature see Schwinges, *Kreuzzugsideologie*, p. 13, n. 36.

Pedro Alfonsi also wrote the first Latin tract explicitly attempting to refute Islam, proving thereby that it was possible to undemonize the Saracen and yet assail his religion. In a chapter of his Dialogue between Peter the Christian and Moses the Jew—an altercation between his new Christian and old Jewish egos—Alfonsi describes the tenets and rites of Islam (*Musulmitica religio*) in unprecedented detail and then, probably under the influence of the Letter of al-Kindi, engages in polemics against it. Alfonsi's tractate enjoyed wide diffusion (though, to judge by the extant manuscripts, less than his *Disciplina Clericalis*) and probably served as the single most important source of information about Islam.[142] A far more ambitious attempt at polemics against Islam was made by Peter of Cluny (d. 1156), who had the Koran, the Letter of al-Kindi, and other, shorter writings rendered into Latin by translators of the school of Toledo; he then utilized the translations to write a summary of Islamic beliefs and a polemical tract against Islam.[143] Since there is only one extant manuscript of the tract, one may assume that its impact was quite limited. A lesser effort at anti-Islamic polemics was made by the theologian Alain of Lille (d. 1202), who in his tractate against the heretics included a chapter entitled Against the Pagans or Mahometans.[144] Some oral discussions with Muslims also took place. The captured Saracen with whom, according to Albert of Aachen, the crusader leaders disputed at the siege of Jerusalem has already been mentioned. Another German chronicler,

[142] For the chapter of the *Dialogus* dealing with Islam see PL 157:597–606. Eleven manuscripts of the twelfth, sixteen of the thirteenth, and nine of the fourteenth century are listed by Díaz y Díaz, *Index*, 1:202, and Cutler, "Peter the Venerable and Islam," p. 185, n. 5. Alfonsi's dependence on the Letter of al-Kindi is especially evident in his description of Muhammad's career; cf. PL 157:599D–600A, and Muñoz Sendino, "Al-Kindi," p. 400, line 40 to p. 401, line 13.

[143] On Peter's project see Marie-Thérèse d'Alverny, "Deux traductions latines du Coran au moyen âge," *Archives d'histoire doctrinale et littéraire du moyen âge* 22–23 (1947–48): 69–113; Kritzeck, *Peter the Venerable and Islam.*

[144] PL 210:421–29. For a short discussion see Alain de Lille, *Textes inédits*, ed. Marie-Thérèse d'Alverny (Paris, 1965), pp. 161–62.

It has been suggested that the pagans in *Cur Deus homo*, by Anselm of Canterbury, and the philosopher of Abelard's *Dialogus* are Muslims: R. Roques, *Structures théologiques de la gnose à Richard de Saint-Victor: Essais et analyses critiques* (Paris, 1962), pp. 258–72; J. Jolivet, "Abélard et le Philosophe (Occident et Islam au XIIᵉ siècle)," *Revue de l'histoire des religions* 164 (1963): 181–89; and three articles by Julia Gauss: "Anselm von Canterbury und die Islamfrage" (chap. 1, n. 59); "Anselm von Canterbury: Zur Begegnung und Auseinandersetzung der Religionen," *Saeculum* 17 (1966): 277–363; and "Das Religionsgespräch von Abaelard," *Theologische Zeitschrift* 27 (1971): 30–36. But see the remarks of Marie-Thérèse d'Alverny in discussion at the Spoleto *Settimane*, vol. 12 (Spoleto, 1965), pp. 792–93.

Arnold of Lübeck, reports that in 1172 Henry the Lion, then on his way home from the Holy Land, reproved a friendly Turkish sultan for adhering to the errors of the heathen and revealed to him the tenets of Christianity. To imagine the aggressive duke of Saxony and Bavaria trying to persuade a Turkish sultan to convert may be somewhat taxing, but the scene is not altogether implausible, since the sultan in question was probably the ruler of Iconium who reputedly had asked Alexander III for instruction in the Christian faith.[145]

Thus, in the era of the Catholic counteroffensive, whose beginning roughly coincides with the onset of the cultural unfolding commonly known as the Renaissance of the Twelfth Century, the stance toward the world of Islam is distinctly different from that of the preceding period. The difference, however, is less dramatic when compared with the relevant developments in the other Christendom that waged a counteroffensive against the Muslims, namely, Byzantium.

The Byzantine reconquest of Muslim territories, which reached its height in the middle of the tenth century, was, like the later, Catholic reconquest, occasionally accompanied by enforced baptism. When the conquest of Melitene in 934 brought a large Muslim town under Byzantine rule for the first time, the inhabitants were given the choice between conversion and exile.[146] But forcible conversion was the exception. Byzantine policy was to warmly receive Muslim refugees coming from the lands of the caliphate and to absorb them in the empire. Besides individual refugees, on two different occasions (once in the 830s and again in the 940s) several thousand Muslim warriors decided to cross the border into Byzantium, and there converted to Christianity. The Byzantines also endeavored to induce Muslim prisoners of war to convert and settle in the empire. The remuneration such converts were to receive was specified in written instructions: three nomismata upon baptism, six nomismata for their ploughing oxen, and

[145] *Arnoldi abbatis Lubecensis Cronica* (n. 129 above), p. 122; also *Annales Colonienses maximi*, ed. K. Pertz (1861), in MGH SS 17:786. Cf. E. Joranson, "The Palestine Pilgrimage of Henry the Lion," in *Medieval and Historiographical Essays in Honor of J. W. Thompson*, ed. J. L. Cate and E. N. Anderson (Chicago, 1938), pp. 199–202. The *Instructio fidei catholicae ab Alexandro III pontifice romano ad soldanum Iconii* is printed in PL 207:1069–78. And see also J. Rousset de Pina, "L'entrevue du Pape Alexandre III et d'un prince sarrasin à Montpellier, le 11 avril 1162: Notes sur les relations islamo-chrétiennes à la fin du XIIᶜ siècle," in *Etudes médiévales offertes à A. Fliche*, Publications de la Faculté des Lettres de l' Université de Montpellier, 4 (Montpellier, 1953), pp. 161–85.

[146] A. A. Vasiliev, *Byzance et les Arabes*, vol. 2, 2 (Brussels, 1950), p. 154. The source is the late but dependable Ibn al-Athīr. See also Jenkins and Westerink, *Nicholas I, Patriarch of Constantinople: Letters* (chap. 1, n. 43), no. 102, pp. 380–81.

fifty-four measures of grain for seed corn. Christian families who gave their daughters in marriage to baptized Muslims were exempt from the produce tax and the hearth tax for three years.[147] And while Byzantine officials were instructed to offer material incentives to would-be converts, Byzantine clerics evolved a specific ritual for the abjuration of Islam.[148] This conscious policy of furthering Muslim conversion met with some success. For instance, when Crete was captured in 961, the son of the last Muslim ruler converted to Christianity, served with distinction in the imperial army, and fell, in 972, in battle against the Russians. And Taticius, the Byzantine general who accompanied the First Crusade to Antioch, was the son of a Muslim prisoner of war. (One is left wondering whether the crusaders were aware of the fact.)[149]

The propagation of Christianity among the Muslims was sometimes explicitly mentioned as an imperial goal. In the Arabic-written poem sent to Caliph al-Muṭīʿ of Baghdad about 966, Emperor Nicephorus Phocas threatens to conquer the caliph's lands and there spread the Christian religion. Alexius I Comnenus (1081–1118), so relates his daughter Anna, was "eager to convert to Christ not only the nomad Scyths, but also the whole of Persia and all the barbarians who dwell in Egypt or Libya and worship Moámed with mystic rites."[150] Byzantine emperors initiated, or even took part in, polemics with Islam: To Leo III (717–40) is attributed an answer to Caliph ʿUmar II (717–20); Michael III (842–67) directed Nicetas of Byzantium to reply to two tracts he received from the Saracens; Romanus Lecapenus (919–44) is said to have ordered an answer be sent to an amir of Damascus; Alexius Comnenus entrusted the monk Euthymius Zigabenus with composing a refutation of heresies that includes a lengthy chapter on

[147] Canard, "Quelques 'à-côté,' " pp. 106–9; and "Les relations politiques," pp. 42–43; A. Toynbee, *Constantine Porphyrogenitus and His World* (London, 1973), pp. 82–85, 382–85; the instructions appear in translation on pp. 82–83.

[148] Khoury, *Théologiens*, pp. 187–94. No Catholic ritual of this kind has come to light. In a twelfth-century Arabic formulary from Spain there appears a formula for Christian or Jewish converts to Islam: E. Lévi-Provençal, *Histoire de l'Espagne musulmane*, 3 vols. (Paris, 1950–53), 3:458. There existed also a formula for Muslims who had converted to Christianity and then wished to revert to Islam. Christians who had converted to Islam and wished to revert to Christianity formed the subject of consultations (ibid., n. 1).

[149] G. Schlumberger, *Un empereur byzantin au dixième siècle: Nicéphore Phocas* (Paris, 1880), p. 112; *The Alexiad of Anna Comnena*, 4, iv, trans. E.R.A. Sewter (Harmondsworth, 1969), p. 141.

[150] G. von Grünebaum, "Eine poetische Polemik" (chap. 1, n. 38), pp. 49, line 51, and 58, line 51; see also 62, line 88; *The Alexiad*, 6, xiii, p. 212.

the beliefs of the Saracens.[151] And in the closing days of Manuel Comnenus (1143–80), a major clash between the emperor and the high clergy erupted over the sentence in the ritual for the abjuration of Islam, which, under the obvious influence of Nicetas of Byzantium, anathematized "the God of Moámet about whom he says: 'He is God alone, a God of hammer-beaten metal.'" Manuel attempted to delete this anathema, claiming that would-be converts—and he himself—considered it a damnation of God. Manuel's opponents adhered to the traditional formula, asserting that it did not refer to the true God, the creator of earth and heaven, but to the God of hammer-beaten metal invented by Muhammad. In other words, Manuel regarded the God of Muhammad and the God he believed in as one and the same; the church leaders insisted that Christians and Saracens did not believe in the same God. At one point Manuel, who defended his position in a tract, threatened to bring the question before the Roman pontiff—and one is left to wonder how Alexander III would have reacted to the question and how a papal ruling would have affected Catholic thinking about Islam. But the pope was not asked for his opinion, for emperor and clergy reached a compromise: Converts were to direct their anathema "to Moámet, to all his teaching and all his inheritance."[152]

The difference between the Byzantine and Catholic European approaches to Islam during their respective ages of reconquest are striking indeed. The Byzantines, eager to populate the newly reconquered lands of Asia Minor, enticed Muslims to convert and settle the land; the Catholics, whose reconquest coincided with a marked increase in the European population, either settled the conquered lands with surplus people from the Catholic heartland or created, in the Crusading Kingdom, a dual, protocolonial society divided into Catholic, exploiting conquerors and non-Catholic, exploited subjects, with some of the subjects attempting to assimilate to the conquerors.[153] The case of the Castilian Lara, where converted Muslim slaves were promised freedom

---

[151] Khoury, *Théologiens*, chaps. 5, 9–11. For the involvement of later Byzantine emperors in anti-Islamic polemics see S. Vryonis, Jr., "Byzantine Attitudes toward Islam during the Later Middle Ages," *Greek, Roman and Byzantine Studies* 12 (1971): 270–71.

[152] The clash is vividly described by the contemporary chronicler Nicetas Choniates, *Historia*, VII, 6, ed. I. Bekker, in *Corpus Scriptorum Historiae Byzantinae*, vol. 21 (Bonn, 1835), pp. 278–84. German translation by F. Grabler, *Die Krone der Komnenen: Die Regierungszeit der Kaiser Johannes und Manuel Komnenos (1118–1180) aus dem Geschichtswerk des Niketas Choniates* (Graz and Vienna, 1958), pp. 263–68. Cf. Meyendorff, "Byzantine Views of Islam," pp. 124–25.

[153] For this view of the society of crusader Palestine see Prawer, *The Latin Kingdom*, pp. 504–10.

in return for settling the area, seems to have been quite exceptional. (But by the time of the conquest of the Balearic Islands and of Valencia, when Christian settlers were no longer available in large numbers, the kings of Aragon had to import Muslim ones.)[154] The intellectual altercation with Islam in Byzantium preceded or coincided with the reconquest; in the previously disinterested West it started when the reconquest was already well underway, and the Catholic polemical efforts never enjoyed a sponsorship comparable to that of the Byzantine emperors. Nor did the normative attitude toward Islam ever become in Catholic Europe a major issue as it did in Byzantium under Manuel.

But Catholic Europe developed an activity never attempted by the Byzantines: the organized dispatch of missionaries to the realm of Islam. The time has come to examine the origins of this exclusively Western phenomenon, and its relation to the criticism of the crusades.

[154] R. I. Burns, "Immigrants from Islam: The Crusaders' Use of Muslims as Settlers in Thirteenth-Century Spain," *American Historical Review* 80 (1975): 21–42; for some twelfth-century precedents, possibly internal transfers, see pp. 24–25.

THREE

The Espousal of Mission: A Criticism
of the Crusade?

CRITICISM of the crusade on moral grounds is almost as old as the crusade itself. During the siege of Caesarea in the spring of 1101, two envoys of the beleaguered Muslim town reproached the patriarch of Jerusalem and the papal legate for having called on the crusaders to slay the Saracens and take their land, thereby contravening the Christian injunctions against murder and robbery. So reports the Genoese chronicler Caffaro, an eyewitness to that siege, who also relates that the patriarch brushed aside this criticism by telling the envoys that Caesarea, the city of Peter, belongs to the Christians by right, and those who impugn God's laws ought to be slain.[1]

It is possible that the Muslim envoys did indeed censure the crusaders for violating basic Christian precepts. As far back as the mid-ninth century, Constantine-Cyril's Muslim adversaries challenged him to explain why the Christians violate Christ's precepts by fighting those who assail them rather than turning the other cheek. Nicetas Choniates (ca. 1138–ca. 1214) writes that the Agarens accused the Christians of transgressing Christ's commandments by returning evil with evil. A Franciscan tradition of the mid-thirteenth century has the Egyptian sultan al-Kāmil tell Francis of Assisi that surely the Chris-

---

[1] Caffaro, *Annales Ianuenses*, ed. L. T. Belgrano, in *Annali Genovesi di Caffaro e de' suoi continuatori*, vol. 1 (Rome, 1890), pp. 9–10. Cf. Prawer, *The Latin Kingdom*, pp. 474–75, who considers the exchange an imaginary one. But as Norman Daniel remarked, "It would be an even more remarkable conversation if the speech of the Muslims had been solely the invention of the Christian conscience": *The Arabs*, p. 116. A close parallel to the patriarch's argument concerning Caesarea may be found in the appeal the archbishop of Braga is said to have made in 1147 to the Muslims of Lisbon, shortly before the conquest of that city: *De expugnatione Lyxbonensi* (chap. 2, n. 72 above), pp. 114–16.

In the *Historia Karoli Magni et Rotholandi*, written about 1130, Charlemagne gives a quite different reason for his claim on Spain when his Saracen adversary accuses him of taking by force a land that did not belong to him by hereditary right: "Ideo, inquit Karolus, quod Dominus noster Iesus Christus . . . gentem nostram, scilicet Christianam, prae omnibus gentibus elegit, et super omnes gentes tocius mundi eam dominari instituit, tuam gentem sarracenicam legi nostrae in quantum potui converti." *Historia Karoli Magni et Rotholandi* (chap. 2, n. 79 above), pp. 130–31.

tians, who had been taught by their God not to render evil for evil, should abstain from invading the lands of the Saracens. And the Muslim polemicist al-Qarāfī (d. 1285), demonstrating a lucid perception of the crusaders' motivation, rebukes them for engaging in acts of violence they consider their foremost duty and the surest guarantee of their salvation even though the Gospel forbids such deeds and prescribes peacefulness; he also observes that such violent conduct befits rather the Muslims, whose Holy Book enjoins them to fight the enemies of God.[2] In view of these parallels, the censure of the crusade by the envoys of Caesarea as reported by Caffaro may be regarded as yet another instance of an oft-repeated Muslim argument. On the other hand, it is also conceivable that in his chronicle Caffaro chose to have the Saracens voice objections to the crusade that in reality he had heard from Christians. In any case, he considered the censure of the crusade, and its rebuttal, so noteworthy that he accorded it considerable space.

Whereas in Caffaro's account a patriarch of Jerusalem rejects the charge that the slaying of Saracens runs counter to Christian teaching, later in the twelfth century another patriarch of Jerusalem is depicted as having qualms about whether the slaying of Saracens is in keeping with Christian morality. In the beginning of a short tract by the French theologian Peter Comestor (ca. 1100–ca. 1179), a patriarch of Jerusalem asks "whether Christians are permitted to wage war against the pagans and kill them, as the Lord says in the Law, 'Thou shalt not kill,' and in the Gospel, 'For all they that take the sword shall perish with the sword.' "[3] The name of the soul-searching patriarch is not given, but if Peter Comestor really did receive such a query, the sender might well have been Amaury of Nesle, the patriarch of Jerusalem in 1157–80 whom William of Tyre was to characterize as "well learned,

---

[2] *Constantinus et Methodius Thessalonicenses: Fontes* (chap. 1, n. 101 above), VI, 33–35, pp. 104–5, 181; Nicetas Choniates, *De superstitione Agarenorum,* in PG 140:121–122AB; Khoury, *Théologiens,* p. 257; L. Oliger, ed., "Liber exemplorum fratrum minorum saeculi XIII," *Antonianum* 2 (1927): 251. For the quotation from al-Qarāfī see E. Fritsch, *Islam und Christentum im Mittelalter: Beiträge zur Geschichte der muslimischen Polemik gegen das Christentum in arabischer Sprache* (Breslau, 1930), p. 149. For a close parallel to al-Qarāfī's argument see R. Sugranyes de Franch, "Un texte de Ramón Lull sur la croisade et les missions," *Nova et Vetera* 21 (1946): 106.

[3] The text has been edited by J. Leclercq, "Gratien, Pierre de Troyes et la seconde croisade," *Studia Gratiana* 2 (1954): 589–93. Since Peter's tract is preserved in a Troyes manuscript of the twelfth century, Leclercq surmises that he wrote it while he was the dean of Troyes (ca. 1145–67). For biographical details see Saralyn R. Daly, "Peter Comestor: Master of Histories," *Speculum* 32 (1957): 62–73. For critics of anti-Saracen warfare who maintained on the eve of the Third Crusade that "qui infideles occidit, homicida est," see PL 207:532D.

but very simple and nearly useless."[4] At any rate, Peter sternly rebuked his questioner for his "irresolution," which might undermine the morale of his countrymen, and called upon him to "act in a manly way, be composed, and shed the blood of Christ's enemies."[5] The tenor of Peter's answer, bolstered by numerous quotations from Gratian's *Causa* 23, is predictable; it is the query that is surprising, for it presents the head of the ecclesiastical hierarchy in the Crusading Kingdom as harboring doubts about the moral defensibility of warfare against the Saracens.

THE CONVERSION MOTIF AND THE CRITICS OF THE CRUSADE

To what extent is the questioning of the morality of crusading related to the espousal of the idea of mission? Sword and word are first presented as two distinct approaches to the Saracens by Peter of Cluny at the beginning of his Book against the Abominable Heresy or Sect of the Saracens, a polemical tractate he wrote in 1143 or 1144.[6] "I approach you," Peter addresses the Arabs of the East and south, "not, as our men often do, with arms, but with words; not with force but with reason; not in hatred but in love."[7] Thus Peter forcefully emphasizes the difference between peaceful persuasion, the approach he adopts in his tractate, and the usual Catholic recourse to violence. Moreover, as he goes on to explain that the love he feels toward his distant readers is the love that ought to exist between Christians and unbelievers, according to divine precept, and must prevail between all members of the human species, according to the call of nature and reason, he implies that his approach of words and love is superior, from the viewpoint of Christian morality, to the approach of force and hatred.

Yet the same man who wrote the oft-quoted words "I love you; loving you I write you, writing you I invite you to salvation" in the

[4] William of Tyre (chap. 2, n. 93 above), XVIII, 20, p. 854.

[5] Leclercq, "Gratien," p. 592. For a detailed discussion of Peter's tract see Hehl, *Kirche*, pp. 154–58.

[6] The tractate has been edited by James Kritzeck in *Peter the Venerable and Islam*, pp. 220–91. For the tractate's full title see p. 231.

[7] Ibid., p. 231. An earlier abbot of Cluny, Odilo (994–1048), has been presented as maintaining that the barbarity of the heathens would be overcome through the efforts of humble preachers: Delaruelle, "The Crusading Idea," (chap. 2, n. 3 above), p. 208. Delaruelle's statement becomes even more extreme in the paraphrase of H.E.J. Cowdrey, "Cluny and the First Crusade," *Revue Bénédictine* 83 (1973): 288. But the relevant passage by Odilo (PL 142:945) does not warrant either of these interpretations.

aforementioned appeal to the Saracens[8] professes, in a letter to the grand master of the Templars, his perpetual love for that order, and lauds it for its incessant and assiduous fight against the Saracens. In a letter to an unnamed crusader king of Jerusalem, Peter writes that since he cannot join him, sword in hand, in smashing the enemies of Christ, he attempts to help him with his prayers as much as he can. Similarly, in a letter written to King Louis VII sometime before the departure of the Second Crusade, Peter states that although he is unable personally to accompany the expedition, he desires to follow it to the best of his ability by devotion, prayer, aid, and counsel, and expresses the hope that King Louis will destroy the Saracens as Moses and Joshua had destroyed the Amorites and Canaanites of old.[9] And after the failure of the Second Crusade, Peter will support the efforts to organize yet another military expedition to the East.[10]

Since Peter never comments on the relationship between his support of the armed crusade against the Saracens and his attempt to persuade them peacefully of the truth of Christianity, the field is open to conjecture. One recent writer, who believes that the espousal of Saracen conversion was Peter's basic attitude, goes so far as to suggest that in taking part in the preparations for the Second Crusade and later in lending a hand in the attempts at another expedition, Peter "was willing to allow for the manias of his friends," hoping that Saracen conversion would become the crusade's main objective.[11] But this interpretation cannot be reconciled with Peter's letters in which he fully identifies with the crusade, hopes for the destruction of the Saracens, and makes no mention whatsoever of the possibility of their conversion.[12] Another recent writer has suggested that Peter was attracted

[8] *Adversus . . . sectam Sarracenorum*, ed. Kritzeck (n. 6 above), p. 232. In a number of recent works these quoted words of Peter's are cited immediately after his earlier statement that he approaches his Saracen readers not in hatred but in love: e.g., J. Kritzeck, "Jews, Christians, and Moslems," *The Bridge: A Yearbook of Judaeo-Christian Studies* 3 (1958): 115; idem, "Moslem-Christian Understanding in Mediaeval Times," *Comparative Studies in Society and History* 4 (1961–62): 395; Southern, *Western Views*, p. 39. Since the intervening passage in which Peter explains the motives for his love is omitted (and since the omission is not always indicated by ellipses), the conflation acquires an emotional quality that does not exist in the full text.

[9] *The Letters of Peter the Venerable*, ed. G. Constable, vol. 1 (Cambridge, 1967), Letter 172, pp. 407–8; Letter 82, p. 219; Letter 130, p. 327.

[10] Ibid., Letters 162, 164, 166, pp. 394–400. For a detailed description of Peter's continuous support of the crusades see Virginia Berry, "Peter the Venerable and the Crusades," in *Petrus Venerabilis (1156–1956): Studies and Texts Commemorating the Eighth Centenary of His Death*, ed. G. Constable and J. Kritzeck (Rome, 1956), pp. 141–62.

[11] Kritzeck, *Peter the Venerable and Islam*, p. 23.

[12] The phrases that Kritzeck adduces from Peter's letters as evidence of a call for

by the crusade because it was a defensive war that provided an opportunity for the salvation of Christian sinners and, in the formulations of Eugene III and Bernard of Clairvaux, also allowed for infidel conversion.[13] Yet on one occasion Peter approvingly referred to the campaign waged by Roger II of Sicily against the Saracens of North Africa, a campaign that could hardly have been considered defensive.[14] Moreover, as was shown above, the appeals of Eugene and Bernard for a crusade against the Saracens—just like Peter's crusading letter to King Louis—did not mention the possibility of Saracen conversion.[15]

Perhaps the simpler solution would be to regard Peter's passage on love and persuasion, contrasting as it does with his other references to the Saracens, as a rhetorical formulation considered appropriate for an appeal that might one day be translated into Arabic. After all, Patriarch Nicholas of Constantinople in the tenth century and Pope Gregory VII in the eleventh used quite different language when addressing the Saracens directly or writing letters intended for Christian eyes. It is also possible that, in drafting his call to the Saracens of the east and south, Peter was to some extent influenced by the appeal of the fictional Muslim correspondent of the Christian al-Kindi; in this appeal the Muslim professes his love for al-Kindi and points out that in so doing he is following the example of Mahumet himself.[16] A Latin translation of the Muslim's appeal as well as of al-Kindi's lengthy reply, which Peter commissioned during a visit to Christian Spain, was available to him at the time he set out to compose his call to the Saracens.

Muslim conversion (Kritzeck, pp. 21–22) are read out of context; indeed Kritzeck himself admits that his argument is "thin" (p. 21, n. 57), Incidentally, when Peter claims, with regard to Saracen captives, "et sola ad proprium solum redeundi facultate subtracta, linguae libertatem non adimunt" (p. 244), he does not mean that " 'the one faculty for returning to the only right,' freedom of speech and decision, is not taken from them" (p. 172), but rather that "having only taken away from them the possibility to return to their own country, they [the Christians] do not deprive them of the freedom of speech."

[13] Berry, "Peter the Venerable and the Crusades," p. 146.

[14] *The Letters of Peter the Venerable*, ed. Constable, Letter 162, pp. 394–95.

[15] Virginia Berry (see n. 13) quotes the French crusaders who said that the pope ordered them to wipe out their sins with the blood or the conversion of the infidels, and the letter in which Bernard writes that the Wendish expedition aims at destroying or converting the pagans. But the French crusaders *attribute* this aim to Eugene, and Bernard speaks of Wends, not Saracens.

[16] "Deinde compulsus ea, quam erga te habeo, dilectione, imo cum dominus meus meusque propheta Mahumet—oracio dei super illum et salus—dixerit: 'Amor Arabum credulitas et fides'; ego vero parens nuncio dei—super quo salus—fideliter amo te." Muñoz Sendino, "Al-Kindi," p. 378; for the date of the Latin translation, see pp. 368–75, and d'Alverny, "Deux traductions," pp. 95–96.

Perhaps, then, it is no mere coincidence that Peter, like the fictional Muslim, opens his invitation to conversion with a profession of love for the would-be convert, and goes on to emphasize that this love stems from the precepts of his religion. And while Peter's words on love have sometimes been likened to Francis of Assisi's approach less than a century later, they may also be considered in conjunction with a gloss-ordinary on Gratian's *Decreta*, also from Francis's day. Commenting on the injunction by Julianus Pomerius that we should love our neighbors because they share with us the same nature (an idea very close to Peter's explanation of the reasons for his love for the Saracens), the glossator wryly remarks, possibly under the influence of Peter Lombard, that "the Jews and the Saracens are our neighbors and ought to be loved by us as we love ourselves; nevertheless, all works of love ought to be employed according to each man's condition."[17] Evidently, the glow of such a love was not always bright.

Peter, like other Catholics before him, was well aware of the Saracens' violent reaction to attacks upon their religion,[18] and seems to have entertained little hope that a written refutation of Islam would bring about their conversion. Indeed, in a letter urging Bernard of Clairvaux to undertake such a refutation, Peter voices the opinion that such a work will be of no use to "those lost ones," namely the Saracens, but may be helpful to weak Christians who are apt to be seduced by evil.[19] Peter dwells on this theme in more detail in the prologue to his polemical tractate. Defending the tractate's usefulness, he argues that it may be translated into Arabic or used to bolster at least the Christian spiritual armory; it may also counteract the secret opinions of Christians "who think that there is some piety among those impious [that is, the Saracens] and believe that there is some truth among the

---

[17] Gl. *participes* to D.2 c.5, *de poenit.*, Bamberg Can. 13 [P.I.16], fol. 221va: "Ergo iudei et sarraceni proximi nostri sunt. et diligendi et a nobis ut nos. verumtamen omnia opera dilectionis inpendere debemus secundum uniuscuiusque condictionem. lxxxvi. di. pasche etc. non satis." This is a gloss of Johannes Teutonicus; its reading in Bamberg Can. 13 is preferable to that of Clm. 14005, fol. 294va: "Et diligendi a nobis ut nos et verum est. verumtamen etc." It might have been influenced by Peter Lombard's discussion of the order of loving: *Sententiae*, IV, 29–30, in PL 192:816–19, recently summarized by J.S.C. Riley-Smith, "Crusading as an Act of Love," *History* 65 (1980): 185.

This important gloss was first quoted in the little-known article by E. Bussi, "La condizione giuridica dei musulmani nel diritto canonico," *Rivista di storia del diritto italiano* 8 (1935): 489; see also J. Brundage, "Holy War and the Medieval Lawyers," in *The Holy War*, ed. T. P. Murphy (Columbus, 1976), p. 121.

[18] *Adversus . . . sectam Sarracenorum*, ed. Kritzeck, pp. 233, 244.

[19] *The Letters of Peter the Venerable*, ed. Constable, Letter 111, p. 298. Cf. Lamma, *Momenti*, p. 137; see also Cutler, "Peter the Venerable and Islam," p. 189.

servants of falsehood."[20] Peter was evidently aware of Christian views of Islam resembling those held by the Nestorian patriarch Timothy and the Spanish Christian opponents of Eulogius, and endeavored to thwart them, as well as to strengthen wavering Christians in their faith. In fact, in the twelfth century and later, the sight of Christians converting to Islam must have been more common than is generally realized. On a number of occasions, some crusaders were coerced or chose to become Muslim. A law of the kingdom of Jerusalem deals with a Catholic knight who "se renoie de la lei de Ihesu Crist por cele de Mahoumet." A Spanish Muslim formulary of the twelfth century contains a ritual for conversion from Christianity to Islam, possibly going back to the tenth century but not necessarily a dead letter by the twelfth, for Caffaro, the Genoese chronicler, writes that before the Catholic conquest of Almeria, Spain, in 1147, many of the Christians who had been captured by the Saracens of that city "left the law of God and invoked, out of fear of torture, Machomet's diabolical name."[21] And there seems to have existed also some genuine Christian-Muslim syncretism: Writing in Barcelona in the 1220s, Ramon of Penyaforte mentions Christians living under Saracen rule who consider Machomet a messenger of God and venerate him as a saint, or who show their reverence at the tomb of "Almaedi."[22]

A humbler contemporary of Peter, the anonymous, probably Anglo-Norman author of the account of the Christian conquest of Lisbon in 1147, makes a more impassioned plea for Muslim conversion. Unlike

[20] *Adversus . . . sectam Sarracenorum*, pp. 229–30, and Kritzeck's introduction, pp. 158–59. For the view that Christian anti-Islamic polemic in general aimed at a Christian audience see N. Daniel, *Islam and the West*, pp. 262–65.

[21] On conversions to Islam during the crusades see Arnold, *The Preaching of Islam*, pp. 88–92; Waas, *Geschichte der Kreuzzüge*, 2:240–41; N. Daniel, *The Arabs*, pp. 196–98. For the law of the Crusading Kingdom see *Le livre au Roi*, c. 23, in RHC. Lois 1:622; also *Abrégé du livre des assises de la cour des bourgeois*, c. 24, in RHC. Lois 2:325. For other cases of conversion to Islam in the Crusading Kingdom see chap. 2, nn. 104, 108.

For the Spanish Muslim formula see Lévi-Provençal, *Histoire de l'Espagne musulmane*, 3:458. For Caffaro's statement see his *Ystoria captionis Almerie et Turtuose*, in *Annali Genovesi* (n. 1 above), 1:79.

[22] Ramon of Penyaforte, *Summa de casibus poenitentiae*, 1.7.7 (Rome, 1603), p. 49. Ramon especially mentions the veneration of Machomet among the Christians called *Atrones*. Clm 6040, fol. 11ra, has *arromi*; this manuscript contains the first recension of Ramon's work. Cf. K. Pennington, "A 'Consilium' of Johannes Teutonicus," *Traditio* 26 (1970): 438. On the date of the first recension see S. Kuttner, "Zur Entstehungsgeschichte der Summa de casibus poenitentiae des hl. Raymund von Penyafort," *Zeitschrift der Savigny-Stiftung für Rechtsgeschichte, Kanonistische Abteilung* 39 (1953): 421, 433.

Peter, he actively participates in a crusade, but he is an uncommon crusader indeed. First he reports with a remarkable accuracy the objections against Christianity made by the Muslim defenders of Lisbon; then he expresses empathy with the vanquished, pestilence-stricken enemy, and refuses to explain the crusader triumph as God's recompense for Christian righteousness and Saracen iniquity.[23] Shocked by the Saracens' plight, he concludes his account by calling upon God to stop chastising the vanquished and let them see the light of Christianity: "Spare now, Lord, spare the work of Your hands," he writes, "Lord, let the works of Your wrath be still. Lord, 'stay now Your hand, it is enough' [1 Chronicles 21:15]. It is indeed enough that You had fought for us thus far against them. But rather, if it be possible, let their sorrow be turned into joy, 'in order that they may know You, the only living and true God, and Jesus Christ, whom You had sent' [John 17:3], Your son, who lives and reigns for ever and ever. Amen."[24] This thinly veiled disapproval of the Lord's doings at Lisbon is audacious indeed, with the anonymous crusader half-beseeching, half-enjoining the Lord with the same words, from the First Book of Chronicles, the Lord uses to command his angel who brought pestilence upon Israel. Small wonder that the crusader confesses that it was "with fear and anguish of spirit" that he brought himself to make this bold appeal.

While Peter of Cluny, in his appeal to the Saracens, opposed words to force, and while the anonymous participant in the conquest of Lisbon preferred the crusade to end with the Saracens' conversion rather than their extinction, three other twelfth-century men went beyond juxtaposition or preference, explicitly objecting to the use of violence and espousing the preaching of the faith as the true Christian approach. It is noteworthy that all three were Englishmen who spent considerable time in France. The earliest of them was Isaac, the Cistercian philosopher and theologian who about 1147 became the abbot of the small monastery of L'Etoile in the vicinity of Poitiers.[25] In a sermon in which he attempts to inculcate in his monks a wariness toward novelties, Isaac refers specifically to two phenomena: innovations in theology and the emergence of a new military order. This order, which is left unnamed, forces unbelievers into the Christian faith by means of lances and clubs, despoils and kills those who are

[23] *De expugnatione Lyxbonensi* (chap. 2, n. 72 above), pp. 130–32, 182–85.
[24] Ibid., pp. 184–85.
[25] The latest appraisal is that of G. Raciti, "Isaac de L'Etoile," *Dictionnaire de Spiritualité*, vol. 7, 2 (Paris, 1971), pp. 2011–38. See also L. Boyer, *La spiritualité de Cîteaux* (Paris, 1955), chap. 7.

not Christians, and regards as martyrs those members of the order who fall during this campaign of depopulation. Do not these knights, asks Isaac, supply the justification for Antichrist's future cruelty against the Christians? "How will it be possible to set against him Christ's clemency, patience, and manner of preaching?"[26]

It is difficult to ascertain the identity of this military order, which Isaac considers a *monstrum novum*, a "new monstrosity." On the one hand, he calls it *nova militia*, a term that evokes the title of Bernard of Clairvaux's tractate in support of the Templars, *De laude novae militiae*; Isaac's acid remark that the order "despoils licitly and murders religiously" looks as if it were written in rebuttal of the assertion that the Templars "do not wrongfully hate when they kill, and do not unjustly covet when they despoil."[27] On the other hand, the Templars are not known to have engaged in forcible conversion, or to have favored infidel conversion in general. Therefore, it is possible that Isaac was thinking of the new military orders springing up in Spain in his time. As has been shown, in 1175 Alexander III called on the new Order of Santiago to avoid pillage and cruelty, and aim instead at attracting the Saracens to the Christian faith—in other words, Alexander mentions, albeit from a different point of view, the very same issues that Isaac discusses in his sermon.[28] But whatever the identity of the *monstrum novum*, Isaac's attitude is clear: Forcing unbelievers into the faith at the point of the lance, plundering and murdering them, are activities that do not conform to the true teachings of Christianity. Isaac approvingly quotes an unnamed contemporary who referred to the new order as the Order of the Fifth Gospel, implying that it did not follow

[26] *Sermo* 48, critically edited by G. Raciti, "Isaac de l'Etoile et son siècle: Texte et commentaire historique du sermon XLVIII," *Cîteaux: Commentarii Cistercienses* 12 (1961): 290. The sermon will appear in the third volume of Isaac's *Sermones*, to be published in the *Sources chrétiennes* series. See also PL 194:1854BC.

[27] "licenter expoliet et religiose trucidet." *Sermo* 48, ed. Raciti, p. 290. ". . . quia occidendo non inique oditis, et spoliando non iniuste concupiscitis." J. Leclercq, "Un document sur les débuts des Templiers," *Revue d'histoire ecclésiastique* 52 (1957): 87. F. Lotter has convincingly shown that the passage justifying Templar warfare alludes to a canon of the Synod of Worms, 868, which made its way into the collections of Burchard and Ivo: Lotter, *Konzeption*, pp. 21–22. On the problem of the authorship of the pro-Templar tract edited by Leclercq, see J. Fleckenstein, "Die Rechtfertigung der geistlichen Ritterorden nach der Schrift 'De laude novae militiae' Bernhards von Clairvaux," in *Die geistlichen Ritterorden Europas*, Vorträge und Forschungen, 26 (Sigmaringen, 1980), pp. 9–10; for a discussion of the tract see Hehl, *Kirche*, pp. 109–11.

[28] Raciti is certain that Isaac refers to the Order of Calatrava (*Cîteaux* 13 [1962]: 20–21), but his reasons are not cogent. Jean Leclercq tends to think that Isaac is speaking of the Templars: "Saint Bernard's Attitude toward War," pp. 27–29. Both authors do not take into account the forcible Christianization that Isaac attributes to the new order.

the original four. And yet Isaac stops short of an outright condemnation of the new order or the innovators in theology, observing that their deeds are not altogether evil but may become the causes of evil, just as in general almost all evils develop from good beginnings and virtues nourish vices until they are finally swallowed up by them.[29]

Isaac of L'Etoile became known through his Epistle on the Soul, in which he attempted to harmonize Platonic and Aristotelian trains of thought; Walter Map (ca. 1140–1209) authored the aptly titled Courtiers' Trifles, a hodgepodge of witty anecdotes and reflections with many a non sequitur among them. The first writer, a Cistercian abbot, was a friend and supporter of Thomas Becket; the second, an outspoken critic of the Cistercians, was a courtier of Henry II. Yet abbot and courtier share a basically similar outlook on the warfare of the military orders. Speaking of the Templars in a part of his work probably written in the 1180s, Map contrasts the charity and poverty of the early Templars with the opulence and avarice of their successors.[30] Like Isaac, he reflects on virtue giving way to vice in the history of orders in general.[31] His criticism of Templar warfare takes the same direction as Isaac's disapproval of the Order of the Fifth, unevangelical, Gospel, but is far more extreme:

[In Jerusalem the Templars] take up in defense of Christianity the sword that had been denied to Peter in the defense of Christ. Peter had learned there to seek peace by patience; I do not know who taught them to overcome force by violence. "They take up the sword," and "they perish by the sword." They assert, however, [that] "all laws and all rights permit to repulse force by force." Yet He rejected this law when, with Peter striking, He did not command His legions of angels. Moreover, it seems that they [the

---

[29] *Sermo* 48, ed. Raciti, p. 290. In a similar vein, Ivo of Chartres writes to Count Hugh of Troyes, who was to leave in 1104 for Jerusalem to fulfill his crusading vow, that the Devil attempts to deceive some men through vices that resemble virtues: Ep. 245, in PL 162:252. Yet Ivo is not branding the crusade one of these vices—although some of his readers might have thought so—but is calling on Hugh to ensure that the implementation of the crusading vow not cause him to neglect his conjugal duty. Cf. R. Sprandel. *Ivo von Chartres und seine Stellung in der Kirchengeschichte* (Stuttgart, 1962), p. 140; Sprandel's paraphrase of the letter presents it as more reserved toward the crusade than it really is (see also Hehl, *Kirche*, p. 11).

[30] I. Hinton dated the entire part to 1182: "Walter Map's *De Nugis Curialium*: Its Plan and Composition," *Publications of the Modern Language Association of America* 32 (1917): 121. F. Seibt, however, has persuasively argued that the passage quoted below is an addition from the years 1187–91: "Über den Plan der Schrift 'De nugis curialium' des Magisters Walter Map," *Archiv für Kulturgeschichte* 37 (1955): 199, and n. 61.

[31] Walter Map, *De nugis curialium* (chap. 2, n. 112 above), I, 18–20, pp. 27–31.

Templars] did not choose the best part, as under their protection our boundaries in those parts are becoming ever narrower, and the enemies' widen; with the word of the Lord, not with the edge of the sword, had the Apostles conquered Damascus, Alexandria, and a great part of the world, which the sword did lose.[32]

Thus Map, who had earlier approved of the first Templars for defending the Christians and repulsing Saracen attacks, now censures the Templars for engaging even in defensive warfare.[33] Bernard of Clairvaux, the patron of the Templars, justified warfare against the Saracens on the basis of the Roman legal maxim that permits the use of force in self-defense.[34] By contrast, Map—a bitter opponent of the Cistercians who relates many a derogatory, even risqué, story about Bernard—maintains that this maxim was abrogated once and for all by Jesus himself.[35] The extremeness of Map's position stands out when it is compared with those of the canon lawyers and theologians of his day who attempted to harmonize the Roman maxim on self-defense with the teachings of the Gospel. The most radical of these attempts was that of the Bolognese decretist Huguccio—a contemporary of Map—who determined that self-defense is legitimate only as long as the assaulted fends off his assailant by passive means and does not actively strike back at him.[36] Map goes still further and, without any attempt at harmonization, considers the Roman maxim void. Like the patriarch of Jerusalem in his query to Peter Comestor, Map refers to Jesus' words on the fate of those who take up the sword; but whereas the patriarch is depicted as posing questions about the lawfulness of

---

[32] Ibid., I, 20, p. 30. In part, Map's attitude resembles the critics of the Templars who claimed that the knights' battling with the Saracens was illicit: Leclercq, "Un document sur les débuts des Templiers," p. 87.

Adolf Waas seems to be the only historian of the crusades to have taken notice of Map's attitude, but his references to the text are perfunctory: Waas, *Geschichte der Kreuzzüge*, 2:72, 272.

[33] For his earlier approval, see *De nugis curialium*, I, 18, p. 27. F. Seibt suggests that Map's shift of attitude with regard to the Templars was occasioned by the worsening political situation in the Crusading Kingdom: F. Seibt, "Die Schrift De nugis curialium: Studien zum Weltbild und zur geistigen Persönlichkeit Walter Maps" (Ph.D. diss., Munich University, 1952), pp. 36–37.

[34] See chap. 2, n. 53 above.

[35] *De nugis curialium*, I, 24–25, p. 35ff.

[36] For a discussion of the various attempts at harmonization see Kuttner, *Kanonistische Schuldlehre*, pp. 349–54. See also Russell, *The Just War*, pp. 94–95.

It is noteworthy that the Waldensians adopted a more aggressive stance than Huguccio, interpreting the Roman maxim as allowing for the capture or repulsion of the enemy, though not for his killing: Alanus de Insulis, *Contra hereticos*, in PL 210:396A.

anti-Saracen warfare, the mind of the English courtier is set. His are answers, not queries.

Unlike Isaac of L'Etoile in his broadside against the unnamed *nova militia*, Map does not claim that the Templars attempted to force Christianity on their foes. But the issue of conversion, nevertheless, figures in his attack on the Templars. First, Map juxtaposes the meager results of Templar warfare in his day with the past successes of apostolic preaching in the same geographical region, thus pointing up the superiority of the apostolic word over the Templar sword. (One is left to wonder whether he knew that a chronicler of the First Crusade presented the crusaders as the "sons of the Apostles" [*filii apostolorum*], who conquered Jerusalem on the very day of the year on which the Apostles had been ejected from it.)[37] Later Map insinuates that the Templars' infatuation with the sword made them uninterested in conversion, which would have brought about peace, and goes on to tell about two Saracen attempts at conversion that were foiled by the Templars (the stories of the Egyptian prince and of the Order of the Assassins, which are also told by William of Tyre).[38] But only rarely is Map consistent, and so it happens that elsewhere in his book he tells the story of Salius, the son of an amir, who became Christian and joined the Templars.[39] There can be no doubt, however, that Map—again like Isaac of L'Etoile—opposed enforced conversion, since in his diatribe against the Cistercians he casually remarks that "it is not permitted to do violence to the heathen, or to force them into the faith."[40]

After the fall of the Crusading Kingdom of Jerusalem in 1187, Map shows no enthusiasm for a new crusade. He laments the fall of Jerusalem (incidentally referring to it only on this one occasion as *sancta civitas*), terms the Christian dead martyrs, grieves that the Holy Sepulcher and the Holy Cross have become "the spoil of dogs," and expresses his confidence that should Christ wish it, Jerusalem might once more be liberated, though at present the case seems lost. But then he pungently adds that heavenly Jerusalem, not the earthly one, should be the Christian goal.[41]

The third Englishman to disapprove of the use of violence was the

---

[37] *Le "Liber" de Raymond d'Aguilers* (chap. 2, n. 50 above), c. 18, p. 151. See also the thesis of A. Katzenellenbogen, "The Central Tympanum at Vézelay: Its Encyclopedic Meaning and Its Relation to the First Crusade," *Art Bulletin* 26 (1944): 141–51.

[38] *De nugis curialium*, I, 20–22, pp. 30–34.

[39] Ibid., IV, 14.

[40] Ibid., I, 25: "Cum ergo non liceat ethnicis inferre violentiam, vel etiam ad fidem cogere, quomodo quos Deus suscipit spernendi sunt et spoliandi?"

[41] Ibid., I, 15, pp. 21–23.

Biblical commentator and chronicler Ralph Niger (ca. 1140–ca. 1199). Like Walter Map, he studied in Paris; like Isaac of L'Etoile, he supported Thomas Becket in his struggle with Henry II, and therefore had to live in French exile until Henry's death in 1189.[42] In a tractate he wrote shortly upon Saladin's conquest of Jerusalem in October 1187, and dedicated to Philip II Augustus of France, Niger cautiously attempts to dissuade the king from taking the cross, at least at that juncture, and discusses at great length the crusading idea itself. Not unlike Peter Comestor's patriarch of Jerusalem, he poses the question whether the Saracens may be slaughtered, and answers that "undoubtedly they may be repulsed and expelled from our territory, because 'all rights permit to repulse force by force'; however, [this should be done] 'within the bounds of a blameless act of defense,' lest the medicine exceed the due measure. Undoubtedly they are to be smitten with the sword of God's word, so that they may come to the faith of their own will and not by coercion, for God hates forced services. Therefore, whosoever seeks to spread the faith by violence transgresses the teachings of the faith."[43] This emphatic rejection of the admissibility of enforced Saracen conversion appearing in the framework of a discussion of the justifiability of crusading warfare is remarkable. Enforced Saracen baptism never figured among the declared aims of the crusade: why, then, this vehement denunciation? Could it be that, in the reality of the twelfth century, forcible conversion became so salient a part of the image of the crusade that it warranted this emphatic criticism? Or did Niger attack it so forcefully because it was rather an unintentional, popularly conceived outgrowth of the original, papally conceived crusading idea, and therefore presented a relatively safe target? In any case, like Isaac of L'Etoile and Walter Map, Niger opposed enforced baptism and regarded preaching as the proper mode of propagating Christianity. In fact, all three adopted a stance that closely resembled that of the Oriental Christians who, in their polemics against Islam, repeatedly contrasted the peaceful spread of Christianity with the purportedly forcible imposition of Islam.[44] While Isaac, Map, and Niger were certainly unaware of this resemblance, they might have been in-

---

[42] G. B. Flahiff, "Ralph Niger: An Introduction to His Life and Works," *Mediaeval Studies* 2 (1940): 104–26; Radulfus Niger, *De re militari et triplici via peregrinationis Ierosolimitane*, ed. L. Schmugge, Beiträge zur Geschichte und Quellenkunde des Mittelalters, 6 (Berlin and New York, 1977), pp. 3–10. See also L. Schmugge, "Thomas Becket und König Heinrich II in der Sicht des Radulfus Niger," *Deutsches Archiv* 32 (1976): 572–79.

[43] Niger, *De re militari*, III, 90, p. 196.

[44] See chap. 1, nn. 53, 55 above.

fluenced by the arguments against papally initiated Christian warfare that Egilbert of Trier, the antipope Wibert, and others employed in the late eleventh century in their struggle against Gregory VII and his adherents. The similar objections of a leading spokesman of the reform party, Peter Damiani, also might have been influential.[45]

The similarity between the arguments of Map, the courtier of Henry II, and of Niger, the supporter of Becket, is striking: The one opposes word to sword, the other calls for the employment of "the sword of God's word," and both refer to the Roman legal maxim *vim vi repellere*. Over the last point, however, the two diverge. While Map takes the extreme view that Jesus had abrogated the right to oppose one's assailant, Niger adheres to the teachings of the canon and civil lawyers of his day who, on the basis of the Roman maxim, permit the repulsion of an attack, but insist on a number of limitations, one of which demands—again on the basis of the Roman law—that the act of repulsion remain within the bounds of true defense.[46] In Niger's interpretation, this means that the Saracens who invade Christian territory may be repulsed and expelled, but not slaughtered or forced to become Christian.

Niger repeatedly voices his opposition to enforced conversion, both in his tractate on the crusading idea and in his Biblical commentaries.[47] But Niger is not consistent in his opposition. In his Longer Chronicle, written in England in the 1190s, he presents King Valdemar I of

---

[45] For a summary of the views of Peter Damiani, Egilbert of Trier, Wibert of Ravenna, and the monk of Hersfeld, see C. Erdmann, *The Origin of the Idea of Crusade*, trans. M. W. Baldwin and W. Goffart (Princeton, 1977), pp. 144–45, 231, 256–58, 260–61.

[46] The words of Niger, "vim vi repellere omnia iura permittunt, verumtamen cum moderamine inculpate tutele" (p. 196)—as Lugwig Schmugge, Niger's recent editor, has noticed—echo the formulation of Niger's exact contemporary, the decretist Stephanus Tornacensis (1135–1203): "vim enim vi repellere omnes leges et omnia iura permittunt cum moderamine tamen inculpate tutelae." J. F. v. Schulte, ed., *Die Summa des Stephanus Tornacensis über das Decretum Gratiani*, to D.1 c.7 (Giessen, 1891), p. 10. For a detailed discussion of the canonists' views on this issue see Kuttner, *Kanonistische Schuldlehre*, pp. 336–43; it is noteworthy that Alanus Anglicus, who advocates the enforced conversion of Saracens (chap. 2, n. 87 above), permits the killing of the assailant if he cannot otherwise be fended off: Kuttner, p. 342, n. 2. Among civilists, the issue is discussed from Irnerius onward: "permittitur enim recte possidenti cum inculpate tutele moderatione vim illatam propulsare: eum enim qui cum armis venit possumus armis repellere." H. Fitting, ed., *Summa Codicis des Irnerius*, VIII, 4, 6 (Berlin, 1894), p. 267; for later writers, see Russell, *The Just War,* pp. 41–44. William of Tyre uses the expression *vim vi repellere* twice (XIII, 6, p. 564, and XVII, 14, p. 783)—yet another proof of his legal training.

[47] The relevant passages are quoted by Schmugge in his introduction to Niger's *De re militari*, p. 65, n. 292.

Denmark as "a good propagator of the faith" for having forced the Slavic Rugians to accept Christianity in 1168.[48] Later in the chronicle, when Niger comes to describe Frederick Barbarossa's march through Asia Minor during the Third Crusade, he expresses his dismay that Frederick did not make use of his conquest of Iconium to bring about the conversion of its people.[49] Niger does not spell out which method of propagating the faith he would have preferred Frederick to have employed at Iconium; but he must have known that, under the circumstances, it must have been closer to the action of King Valdemar than to the acts of the Apostles. Again, there is nothing in Niger's two chronicles to indicate criticism of the three crusades he discusses in the course of his narrative. Quite the contrary, on one occasion Niger goes so far as to refer to Renaud of Châtillon, the adventurous and aggressive lord of crusader Oultrejourdain, as *beatus Reinaldus*, the "blessed Renaud," and to claim that after his capture by Saladin, he was not ready to surrender even one foot of the Holy Land in return for his life.[50] Perhaps a study of all of Niger's works, most of which remain unedited, will provide an explanation of the obvious discrepancy between the views expressed in his tractate on the crusade and elsewhere, and the statements made in his chronicle.

How influential was the criticism voiced by Isaac of L'Etoile, Walter Map, and Ralph Niger? None of the three was a leading figure of his age. The sermon in which Isaac refers to the Order of the Fifth Gospel survives in a unique manuscript; the same is true of Map's *Courtiers' Trifles*; and Niger's tractate on the crusade survives in only two manuscripts.[51] On the other hand, the contemporary *Historia Karoli Magni et Rotholandi*, which relates that Charlemagne left alive the defeated

---

[48] E. *Radulfi Nigri Chronica Universali*, ed. R. Pauli (1885), in MGH SS 27:335, lines 1–3. On Valdemar's campaign see *Helmoldi Cronica Slavorum*, in MGH Scr. rer. Germ. 32:211–14. (For Niger's use of *adigere* in the sense of "to force" see MGH SS 27:338, line 26.)

[49] MGH SS 27:338, lines 31–33. A little earlier (lines 23–28), Niger rebukes Frederick for not having purged Constantinople of the Turks whom the Byzantines had admitted into the city.

[50] MGH SS 27:336, lines 32–34. Peter of Blois, who wrote a veritable Passion of the Blessed Renaud, has Saladin call upon Renaud to abjure Christ and Renaud invite Saladin to the Christian faith: *Passio Reginaldi principis olim Antiocheni*, in PL 207:969BC. For a recent discussion see B. Hamilton, "The Elephant of Christ: Reynald of Châtillon," *Studies in Church History* 15 (1978): 97–108.

Norman Daniel is patently wrong when he writes (*The Arabs*, p. 187) that Renaud's execution by Saladin "seems to have had general European approval." This is one of many factual errors that mar Daniel's stimulating book.

[51] Peter of Cluny's polemic tract, too, probably survives in a single manuscript: Kritzeck, *Peter the Venerable and Islam*, p. 155.

Saracens who were willing to convert and killed those who refused to do so, is extant in nine manuscripts of the twelfth and twenty-three manuscripts of the thirteenth century.[52] And there is no way of telling how many men and women of that age heard the *Chanson de Roland*; a recent study found that by the second half of the twelfth century the Song had attracted audiences even in German lands.[53] Against this background, it is safe to assume that the writings of Isaac, Map, and Niger had only a limited impact on their contemporaries. And yet that basically similar ideas were expressed by three men who occupied quite different positions in the Anglo-French world of the twelfth century, and that two of these men, Map and Niger, demonstrated a remarkable affinity in their expressions, suggests that the relationship between fighting the Saracens and preaching Christianity to them was discussed in some learned circles.[54]

JOACHIM OF FIORE ON CRUSADE AND PREACHING

The possibility of preaching to the Saracens rather than waging war against them was also contemplated by a far better known figure of that age: Joachim of Fiore (ca. 1135–1202), the Calabrian abbot whom many contemporaries considered a prophet, and whose vision of a peaceful, sabbath Age of the Holy Spirit had a profound impact on later generations. Joachim was relatively well informed about Islam, a fact that is not surprising in a learned southern Italian of his age. He knew that the Saracens believed in one God and considered Mahometh God's great prophet and herald, and demonstrated some knowledge of the extent of their conquests; like many of his contemporaries, he regarded Mahometh's teachings as a heresy advocating lust as the greatest joy and blessing.[55] But he was not interested, like Peter of Cluny, in arguing against Islam; nor was he troubled, like Map and Niger, about the defensibility of Christian warfare against the Saracens. Joachim

---

[52] Cf. chap. 2, n. 79 above. The count of manuscripts is based on *Historia Karoli Magni et Rotholandi*, ed. Meredith-Jones (chap. 2, n. 79 above), pp. 5–17, and *Turpini Historia Karoli Magni et Rotholandi*, ed. F. Castets (Montpellier and Paris, 1880), pp. vi–vii.

[53] P. Geary, "Songs of Roland in Twelfth-Century Germany," *Zeitschrift für deutsches Altertum und deutsche Literatur* 105 (1976): 112–15.

[54] For evidence that the related issue of the admissibility of enforced Saracen conversion was touched upon in the schools see chap. 2, nn. 87–88 above, and Russell, *The Just War*, p. 197.

[55] For Joachim's knowledge of Islam see E. Bonaiuti, ed., *Tractatus super Quatuor Evangelia di Gioacchino da Fiore* (Rome, 1930), p. 262; Joachim of Fiore, *Expositio in Apocalypsim* (Venice, 1527; reprint, Frankfurt/M, 1964), pp. 10d, 130a, 163c, 167d.

dealt with the Saracens, past, present, and future, within the framework of his eschatological view of history, and endeavored to locate them at the appropriate junctures of his idiosyncratic grid. For him, they were the Beast of the Sea of the Apocalypse and the Fourth Beast of Daniel; Mahometh was the fourth head of the seven-headed Dragon of the Apocalypse, and Saladin was the sixth (or, in another formulation, the "beginning" of the sixth). Under Mahometh the Saracens persecuted the Church in its fourth age; later they were defeated by the Christians and almost came to nought, but in the imminent sixth age of turmoil, which must precede the sabbath Age of the Holy Spirit, the Saracens were to resurge and menace the Church once more (according to a formulation of 1196, in alliance with the heretic Patarines, the Beast from the Land).[56]

How was Christendom to overcome this renewed Saracen threat, which, according to Joachim, began with Saladin?[57] On the eve of the Third Crusade, Joachim believed in a Christian military victory. When Richard I of England, then on his way to the Levant, consulted him at Messina in December 1190, Joachim unequivocally identified Saladin with the sixth head of the Dragon, and prophesied that if Richard should persevere, he would gain a decisive victory over Saladin. So

---

[56] *Expositio in Apocalypsim*, pp. 10bc. 116c, 134b–35a, 162d–65a, 196a–97a; *Enchiridion in Apocalypsim*, ed. J. C. Huck, in *Joachim von Floris und die joachitische Literatur* (Freiburg, 1938), p. 295; *De titulo libri Apochalipsis*, ed. J. C. Huck, ibid., pp. 297, 301–2; C. Baraut, ed., "Un tratado inédito de Joaquín de Fiore: De Vita S. Benedicti et de Officio divino secundum eius doctrinam," cc. 24, 27, 28, 41, *Analecta Sacra Tarraconensia* 24 (1951): 84–85, 91–92, 111; L. Tondelli, Marjorie Reeves, and Beatrice Hirsch-Reich, eds., *Il Libro delle Figure dell'abate Gioacchino da Fiore*, vol. 2, 2d ed. (Turin, 1953), tav. XIV. Cf. Marjorie Reeves and Beatrice Hirsch-Reich, *The Figurae of Joachim of Fiore* (Oxford, 1972), pp. 146–52. There are differences between the various references to the Saracens, but as most are undated, it is difficult to follow the development of Joachim's views on the subject. The passage from 1196 on the Saracen-Patarine alliance (*Expositio*, p. 134bc) was recently utilized by R. Manselli, "Testimonianze minori sulle eresie: Gioacchino da Fiore di fronte a Catari e Valdesi," *Studi Medievali* 18, 2 (1977): 14–15.

In a crusade appeal of 1213, Innocent III refers to Machometus and his followers as the Beast of the Apocalypse whose days are numbered: PL 216:818B. Allan Cutler considers this passage of crucial importance to the understanding of Innocent's attitude toward Islam: "Innocent III and the Distinctive Clothing of Jews and Muslims," in *Studies in Medieval Culture*, ed. J. R. Sommerfeldt, vol. 3 (Kalamazoo, Mich., 1970), pp. 92–96. But Paul Alphandéry already argued persuasively that this assimilation of Muhammad to Antichrist should be regarded as an isolated piece of pious rhetoric: "Mahomet-Antichrist dans le Moyen Age latin," in *Mélanges Hartwig Derenbourg* (Paris, 1909), pp. 263–65.

[57] *Expositio*, pp. 10b, 197a; *Il Libro delle Figure*, tav. XIV.

reports Roger Howden, who accompanied Richard on his crusade.[58] But after that expedition ended in failure, Joachim asked himself, in a little-noticed passage of his Commentary on the Apocalypse, why, despite their zeal to avenge the capture of the Holy Cross and the profanation of the Holy Temple, the crusaders did not achieve their purpose. His answer is coined, rather unexpectedly, in traditional, moralistic terms: The crusaders lacked the proper disposition and offended God. In the future, they should first wage an internal battle and overcome their sins, and then "should it still be necessary," they should proceed to wage war with God as their leader.[59]

Thus, even after the failure of the Third Crusade Joachim did not discard the possibility of a future military expedition to Jerusalem. Indeed, since Innocent III in 1198 recommended the bishop of Lydda, then on his way to Sicily to preach a crusade for the liberation of Jerusalem, to Joachim, and also instructed Joachim to relieve would-be crusaders of excommunication incurred for assaults on clerics, it is certain that he was not then known as an outright critic of the crusade.[60] And yet, as has been shown, Joachim about the same time expressed the doubt that a military expedition to Jerusalem would still

[58] "Benedict of Peterborough" (= Roger Howden), *Gesta regis Henrici II et Ricardi I*, ed. Stubbs (chap. 2, n. 114), 2:151–55. On the authenticity of this account of Joachim's prophecy, which differs from accounts written after the failure of the Third Crusade, see H. Grundmann, *Ausgewählte Aufsätze*, pt. 2, *Joachim von Fiore*, Schriften der MGH, 25, 2 (Stuttgart, 1977), pp. 82–84, 316; Marjorie Reeves, *The Influence of Prophecy in the Later Middle Ages: A Study in Joachimism* (Oxford, 1969), pp. 6–9.

[59] For the text see Appendix 5/c below (= *Expositio*, p. 192b). This passage, which has already been noted by Huck (*Joachim von Floris*, p. 153), necessitates a revision of E. R. Daniel's conclusion that Joachim believed that crusades could no longer lead to victory: E. R. Daniel, "Apocalyptic Conversion: The Joachite Alternative to the Crusades," *Traditio* 25 (1969): 135–39; idem, *The Franciscan Concept of Mission in the High Middle Ages* (Lexington, Ky., 1975), pp. 18–20.

In another passage (Appendix 5/a below = *Expositio*, p. 134d), Joachim writes that the fate of the large army that accompanied Frederick Barbarossa on the Third Crusade should teach the Church that victory is not given to the numerous, "sed reliquiis fidelis populi qui contendunt in fide." Daniel interpreted this passage to mean that Joachim considered further crusading futile: "Apocalyptic Conversion," pp. 135–36; *The Franciscan Concept*, p. 20. But the passage should be rather understood as a positive formulation of Joachim's above-mentioned statement that the Third Crusade failed because the participants lacked the proper disposition.

[60] *Die Register Innocenz' III*, ed. O. Hageneder and A. Haidacher, vol. 1 (Graz and Cologne, 1964), nos. 343–44, pp. 512–14 (which replace PL 214:317–18); cf. L. Schmugge, "Zisterzienser, Kreuzzug und Heidenkrieg," in *Die Zisterzienser: Ordensleben zwischen Ideal und Wirklichkeit*, ed. K. Elm et al. (Aachen, 1980), p. 64. It is also possible that Joachim was one of the recipients of Innocent's call to preach the crusade: PL 214:263–66.

be needed. This doubt should probably be understood against the background of one of his speculations about the beast head of Apocalypse 13:3 that seemed to have been almost dead, and then recovered. Joachim identifies the Saracens with this beast head, and asks whether the Christians will overcome it in the future "by preaching more than by waging war."[61] For Christian victories had prostrated the beast head: The exhortation of Pope Urban led to the liberation of the Sepulcher; the Saracens of Egypt had to pay tribute to the Crusading Kingdom, and those of Asia Minor, to Byzantium; the king of Sicily captured the coast of North Africa and settled Christian colonists there; and the kings of Spain repeatedly triumphed over their Saracen foes. Yet the beast head, which seemed to have been defunct, has now recovered its old vigor, ready once again to cut to pieces, kill, and devour, all according to God's foreknowledge.[62] It is possible, however, to bring this beast head speedily to its end "by another and more solemn order." In Joachim's vocabulary, this probably means that the Order (or Orders) of Spiritual Men, whom he expected to appear in the near future, preach the faith, convert the Jews and most Gentiles, and usher in the Age of the Holy Spirit, were also to convert the Saracens.[63] A further crusade would indeed be redundant should this conversion occur before the Christians become worthy of God's help in battle, or so one should understand Joachim's above-mentioned doubt about whether it would still be necessary to recover Jerusalem by force of arms.

In sum, Joachim did not reject the crusades altogether. The First Crusade certainly played a role in God's plan as he understood it, since it contributed to the fulfillment of the prophecy about the beast head that seemed to have been mortally wounded. Joachim also believed

[61] "predicando magis quam preliando:" Appendix 5/b below. It should be noted that the MS of the Ambrosiana differs at this juncture from the MSS of Todi and the Biblioteca Casanatense, which give a less coherent reading. (The version of the printed edition of 1527 [*Expositio*, p. 164d] is almost identical with that of these two MSS.) But the reading of the Ambrosiana MS, too, is problematic. The context and a comparison with Baraut, "Un tratado inédito," c. 24, p. 53, allow for the conjecture that the original had something like: "Forte futurum est ut capud illud christiani [superent] et predicando magis quam preliando; [nam preliando] usque pene etc."

[62] Appendix 5/b below. Cf. Baraut, "Un tratado inédito," c. 24, p. 53; *De titulo libri Apochalipsis*, ed. Huck, p. 302. Ibn al–Athīr, a younger contemporary of Joachim, shares this panoramic view of the Catholic counteroffensive: Ibn al–Athīr, *Al-Kāmil fī'l-ta'rikh*, in RHC. HOr. 1:189, discussed by Lewis, *The Muslim Discovery*, p. 23.

[63] "alio et sollempniori ordine": Appendix 5/b below (= *Expositio*, p. 165a). On the preaching of the Spiritual Men, see *Expositio*, pp. 137b, 147b, 175c, 176a; Baraut, "Un tratado inédito," c. 43, p. 114; cf. E. R. Daniel, "Apocalyptic Conversion," pp. 138–39; *The Franciscan Concept*, pp. 19–20.

that a future crusade might enjoy divine support if the participants were to conquer their sins first. But he seems to have expected that spiritual action would once and for all eliminate the Saracen danger the crusade had only temporarily checked.

When did these views of Joachim begin to be influential? In his lifetime, and in the first decades after his death in 1202, Joachim was known mainly as a prophet who foretold the imminent advent of Antichrist and the End of the World, and not as the author of a revolutionary eschatological program centering on the Age of the Holy Spirit.[64] In his Longer Chronicle Ralph Niger exhibits such limited knowledge of Joachim's views, adding that he regards the Commentary on the Apocalypse by Geoffrey of Auxerre, the erstwhile secretary of Bernard of Clairvaux, as "more outstanding" than that of Joachim. But the English chronicler Ralph of Coggeshall (d. 1228), who, like Niger, betrays no knowledge of Joachim's views on the Age of the Holy Spirit, relates that Joachim foretold that the sixth age, the age of Antichrist's rise and fall, would begin in 1199, and that before the advent of Antichrist the Gospel of Christ would be preached everywhere and the Church spread to all pagan nations. Evidently Joachim's views on the imminence of universal evangelization reached an audience unfamiliar with his genuine writings. Moreover, the French cleric Guillaume of Auvergne (d. 1249) refers to Joachim's Commentary on the Apocalypse as a well-known work.[65] It is possible, therefore, that Joachim's vision of a spiritual answer to the Saracen menace did reach a considerable public already in the first half of the thirteenth century. And yet there is no evidence that these Joachite ideas did influence the early efforts at systematic preaching to the Muslims, or that they were known at all to the men who were to initiate these efforts in the second decade of the thirteenth century.[66]

JACQUES OF VITRY AND FRANCIS OF ASSISI: MOTIVES FOR PREACHING TO SARACENS

The two men who pioneered sustained missionizing among the Saracens were Jacques of Vitry and Francis of Assisi.

Jacques of Vitry began to preach to Muslims a short time after his arrival at crusader Acre, his new bishopric, in November 1216. It was

---

[64] Grundmann, *Ausgewählte Aufsätze*, p. 199; Reeves, *The Influence*, pp. 37–44.

[65] MGH SS 27:338, lines 3–8; *Radulphi de Coggeshall Chronicon Anglicanum*, ed. J. Stevenson, Rolls Series, 66 (London, 1875), p. 68; Reeves, *The Influence*, p. 42.

[66] In 1289, however, some missionaries imbued with Joachite ideas left for Armenia: E. R. Daniel, *The Franciscan Concept*, pp. 87, 98.

a novel departure, quite unlike the sporadic, incidental attempts of Richard of St. Vanne, Peter the Hermit, or Bernard of Blois. But for Jacques recurrent preaching was nothing new. Five years earlier, at the very beginning of a long ecclesiastical career, he came under the influence of Marie d'Oignies, a central figure in the northern feminine movement that endeavored to realize the precepts of the Gospel.[67] There are many indications that the encounter with Marie's ecstatic religiosity was the formative experience of Jacques's life, and it was certainly Marie who launched him on a lifelong career as a preacher. Unable to preach herself, so relates Jacques in his *Vita Marie Oigniacensis*, she often prayed to God to send her a preacher. Thus when Jacques came under her influence, she considered him the answer to her prayers and "compelled him" (the words are those of the Dominican Thomas of Cantimpré) "to preach to the people."[68] So it came about that under Marie's tutelage, Jacques, the learned cleric from Paris, began to call upon uneducated laymen to embrace the true Christian life. His lively style and liberal use of down-to-earth anecdotes soon attracted large crowds, and his fame as a preacher first caused a papal legate to entrust him in 1213 with preaching the cross against the Albigensians, and then led the canons of Acre to elect him as their bishop in 1216.[69]

Even after his election to the episcopate there remained in Jacques more than an inkling of the itinerant preacher. On the way to his consecration at the Curia, he preached against the local heretics in Milan; at the Curia he obtained a papal preaching license for all regions of the Orient and Occident (as well as a permit for the pious women of Liège, France, and Germany to form independent congregations); before embarking from Genoa, he preached the cross, first to the women, then to their men.[70] Upon his arrival in Acre, Jacques entered the church of the Jacobites and preached there through a translator; in like manner he later preached to the Syrians; and when

---

[67] On Jacques's relationship with this movement see P. Funk, *Jakob von Vitry: Leben und Werke* (Leipzig and Berlin, 1909), pp. 15–28, 113–30; H. Grundmann, *Religiöse Bewegungen im Mittelalter*, 2d ed. (Darmstadt, 1961), chap. 4; E. W. McDonnell, *The Beguines and Beghards in Medieval Culture, with special emphasis on the Belgian Scene* (New Brunswick, N.J., 1954), especially pp. 3–39. On the problem of Jacques's social origins see J. F. Benton, "Qui étaient les parents de Jacques de Vitry?" *Moyen Age* 70 (1964): 39–47.

[68] AA. SS. Jun. V, pp. 562F, 573D.

[69] *Petri Vallium Sarnaii Hystoria Albigensis*, ed. P. Guébin and E. Lyon, vol. 1 (Paris, 1926), pp. 281–83; *Chronique d'Ernoul* (chap. 2, n. 114 above), p. 410. Cf. Funk, pp. 31–37.

[70] *Lettres de Jacques de Vitry* (chap. 2, n. 102 above), pp. 72, 74, 77.

the members of the Italian colonies at Acre refused to come to his sermons, he did not delay in going to preach in their own quarters. Soon he could report to his friends in Europe that his sermons were so well attended that he had to deliver them in an open space outside the town.[71] In the spring of 1217 Jacques was asked to undertake a preaching tour of the cities of the Syrian littoral, which were then under crusader rule, and proceeding from town to castle, he preached the cross and strengthened in their faith Christians who vacillated between Christianity and Islam. It was in the course of this tour that Jacques made his first two Saracen converts and baptized them in the church of Tortosa. He wished to extend his activities to the adjacent Muslim-ruled territory, but unable to do so, he preached in the Christian-Muslim borderland whenever possible and, in addition, sent letters in Arabic to the Muslims beyond the border.[72]

These attempts at converting the Saracens were an obvious extension of Jacques's efforts to evangelize his fellow Christians, first in Europe and then in the Levant. It is revealing that at the end of the letter in which he describes his preaching activities among the Christians and Saracens of the Crusading Kingdom, and expresses the opinion that preaching may cause the conversion of many Oriental heretics and Saracens, he quotes Paul's words to Timothy that God wants all men to attain the recognition of truth.[73] The preaching mission on which Jacques had embarked under the prodding of Marie d'Oignies—whose finger, encased in a silver casket, must have dangled from his neck throughout his sojourn in the Orient[74]—evidently did not stop at the boundaries of Christendom.

In the autumn of 1217, after the arrival of the Fifth Crusade in Acre, Jacques's efforts at converting the Saracens took a new direction. When the crusaders returned from their expeditions to Bethsan and Mount Tabor with a large number of Muslim captives, Jacques obtained—"by payment or by entreaty"—the children who were among them, baptized them, and distributed them among the nuns of Acre to ensure their Christian education.[75] And when the crusaders conquered the Egyptian town of Damietta on November 5, 1219, Jacques

---

[71] Ibid., pp. 83, 85–86.

[72] Ibid., pp. 91–94, 96.

[73] Ibid., p. 97.

[74] Thomas de Cantimpré, *Vita S. Lutgardis*, in AA. SS. Jun. IV, p. 209; idem, Supplement to Jacques de Vitry's *Vita B. Marie Oigniacensis*, in AA. SS. Jun. V, p. 578B.

[75] Oliver of Cologne, *Historia Damiatina*, c. 3, in H. Hoogeweg, ed., *Die Schriften des Kölner Domscholasters Oliverus* (Tübingen, 1894), p. 167; *Relatio magistri Oliveri scholastici de expeditione Jherosolimitana*, ibid., p. 289.

prevented the captured Muslim children from being sold into slavery, and baptized them. More than five hundred of these young captives died soon after baptism—a belated toll of the desperate conditions in Muslim Damietta, under siege for five months—the rest were retained by Jacques or sent to his friends to be raised as Christians.[76] ("A nice trait of Jacques," remarks his early twentieth-century biographer.)[77]

The career of Francis of Assisi is too well known to require retelling. Important in the present context is that Francis's two unsuccessful attempts, in 1212 and 1213, to go to the lands of the Saracens, his actual crossing of the Christian-Muslim lines near Damietta in 1219, and his subsequent meeting with Sultan al-Kāmil of Egypt took place amid, and against the background of, his efforts at evangelizing his fellow Christians. For Francis perceived his mission, and that of his friars, as truly universal. In the early rule he wrote for his order, the so-called *Regula non bullata*, which did not receive papal approval and so may be considered an unadulterated expression of his thought, he appeals to "all peoples, races, tribes, and tongues, all nations and all men of all countries, who are and who shall be," that together with the Friars Minor they persevere in true faith and penance.[78] With Francis of Assisi, as with Jacques of Vitry, the desire to preach to the Saracens was part of the deeper urge to convert all human beings to what he perceived as the true profession of Christianity.[79]

These two pioneer preachers to the Muslims pursued different careers and had a quite dissimilar impact on posterity, yet both were bent on a return to evangelical life, and participated in the current of intense religiosity that spread through Europe beginning in the eleventh century: Francis as the prime mover behind one of the most influential orders to which this current gave rise, Jacques as the mouthpiece of Marie d'Oignies, as spokesman at the papal court for the feminine religious movement of the north (which exhibited numerous similarities with the Humiliati and Franciscans of Lombardy and Um-

[76] *Lettres de Jacques de Vitry*, pp. 127–28. Cf. Roger de Wendower, *Flores Historiarum*, ed. H. G. Howlett, 3 vols., Rolls Series, 84 (London, 1886–89), 2:250: "Episcopus Achonensis parvulos omnes, qui in urbe reperti sunt vivi, baptizavit." See also p. 249.

[77] "Ein schöner Zug an Jacob." Funk, p. 46.

[78] D. E. Flood, ed., *Die Regula non bullata der Minderbrüder*, c. XXIII, 7 (Werl/ Westf., 1967), p. 73; see also the comment on pp. 134–35. For an earlier edition see H. Boehmer, ed., *Analekten zur Geschichte des Franciscus von Assisi*, 3d ed. (Tübingen, 1961), p. 17.

[79] For similar appraisals of Francis see, for instance, E. R. Daniel, *The Franciscan Concept*, pp. 37–38; K. Elm, "Franz von Assisi: Busspredigt oder Heidenmission?" in *Espansione del Francescanesimo*, pp. 72–80.

bria), and as the sympathetic recorder of various manifestations of the desire to emulate the ways of the primitive Church.[80]

Jacques and Francis were the first of this current to actually include the Muslims in their wide-ranging attempts at evangelization, but earlier exponents of the new, intense religiosity preceded them in extending their activities beyond the frontiers of Christendom, and even in preaching to some Muslims or in contemplating sustained activity among them. The Premonstratensians, and later the Cistercians, played an important role in the Christianization of the pagan Slavs.[81] Numerous hermits were similarly active in Europe's northeast, and a handful of them, as has been seen, made sporadic attempts with regard to Saracens. Diego of Osma (d. 1207), the Spanish bishop under whom Dominic served as subprior, and who may be considered the initiator of the Dominican method of preaching in humility in imitation of Jesus and the Apostles—and, more immediately, in imitation of the Albigensian heretics—attempted in 1206 to resign his office so that he might be free to preach the Gospel to the Saracens. But Innocent III turned down his offer of resignation and did not even permit him to undertake missions to the Saracens while retaining his episcopal responsibilities.[82] As for Dominic himself, the early biographer Pedro Ferrando maintains that Dominic planned to go to the lands of the Saracens and preach the faith to them, and to this end he let his beard grow for some time. At Dominic's process of canonization held at

[80] In addition to Jacques's *Vita* of Marie d'Oignies (AA. SS. Jun. V, pp. 547–72) and the references to the Humiliati and Friars Minor in his letters, (*Lettres*, pp. 72–73, 131–33), see also J. F. Hinnebusch, ed., *The Historia Occidentalis of Jacques de Vitry: A critical edition* (Fribourg, 1972), especially chaps. 11–32. On Jacques's involvement with the circle of Oignies as explaining his interest in the Franciscans and in related groups, see also Pia Gemelli, "Giacomo da Vitry e le origini del movimento francescano," *Aevum* 39 (1965): 474–86.

[81] F. Winter, *Die Prämonstratenser des zwölften Jahrhunderts und ihre Bedeutung für das nordöstliche Deutschland: Ein Beitrag zur Geschichte der Christianisirung und Germanisirung des Wendenlands* (Berlin, 1865); idem, *Die Cistercienser des nordöstlichen Deutschlands bis zum Auftreten der Bettelorden* (Gotha, 1868), chap. 5. And see chap. 4, nn. 12–14, 16 below.

[82] *Petri Vallium Sarnaii Hystoria Albigensis*, 1:21–24; Iordanus de Saxonia, *Libellus de principiis ordinis praedicatorum*, ed. H. C. Scheeben, Monumenta Ordinis Fratrum Praedicatorum Historica 16 (Rome, 1935), pp. 34–37. Scheeben's preference for the reading *Saracenorum* rather than *Cumanorum* may be substantiated by the argument that Diego might have hoped to persuade Innocent of the feasibility of conducting missionary expeditions to the Saracens while remaining bishop of Osma; he could hardly have proposed to retain his bishopric while going to preach to the Cumans. For a reconstruction of the events and an appraisal of Diego's role in the evolution of the Dominican method, see H. C. Scheeben, "Dominikaner oder Innozentianer," *Archivum Fratrum Praedicatorum* 9 (1939): 237–68; Grundmann, *Religiöse Bewegungen*, pp. 100–105, 507.

Bologna in 1233, one of his companions testified that "he was zealous not only for the salvation of Christians but also of Saracens and other infidels, and exhorted the friars to that purpose."[83] The same could also have been said of Francis or Jacques.

A similar tendency may also be encountered beyond the limits of Catholic Europe. The tenth-century Byzantine monk Nikon *Metanoeite* ("Do Penance"), who preached Christianity to the Muslim, or Islam-ized, inhabitants of Crete shortly after its reconquest in 961, had al-ready preached repentance to the Christians of Asia Minor and went on to preach to the Christians of the Peloponnesus after the comple-tion of his Cretan mission.[84] With Nikon, too, preaching Christianity to Muslims was an extension of preaching a more intense religiosity to his fellow Christians.

Francis's dramatic crossing of the crusader-Egyptian lines captured the imagination of many generations, and his encounter with the sul-tan is, owing to Giotto and many other artists, one of the most fre-quently depicted scenes of medieval history. But seen against its im-mediate background, Francis's journey to the sultan loses some of its extraordinariness. For in the crusader camp at Damietta the issue of conversion probably engaged the minds more intensely than on pre-vious crusading expeditions. It has already been noted that an eye-witness reports that when the papal legate Pelagius led the crusaders into battle on October 26, 1218, he presented Saracen conversion as the objective of the Christian fighting.[85] Moreover, much is told dur-ing this expedition about Saracens crossing the Christian lines and receiving baptism—the mention of the converts' subsequent dissatis-faction with the austerity of Christian life lends credibility to these accounts as do, in a different way, the reports about Christians cross-ing the Saracen lines and becoming Muslims.[86] (In the Old French

---

[83] *Legenda S. Dominici auctore Petro Ferrandi*, c. 32, ed. M.-H. Laurent, Monumenta Ordinis Fratrum Praedicatorum Historica, 16 (Rome, 1935), p. 232, cf. pp. 305, 393; *Actus canonizationis S. Dominici*, c. 47, ed. A. Walz, ibid., pp. 165–66.

M.-H. Vicaire recently drew attention to the fact that Dominic never preached the cross against the Albigensians, although he was in the critical area after 1206: "Les clercs de la croisade: L'absence de Dominique," *Cahiers de Fanjeaux*, vol. 4 (Toulouse, 1969), reprinted in M.-H. Vicaire, *Dominique et ses prêcheurs* (Paris, 1977), p. 34.

[84] *Vita S. Niconis Metanoitae monachi*, Latin trans. J. Sirmond, in E. Martène and U. Durand, *Veterum Scriptorum . . . amplissima collectio*, vol. 6 (Paris, 1729), pp. 851–60. On the Christianization of Crete see also the remark quoted by Ibn Djubayr (chap. 2, n. 29.)

[85] See chap. 2, n. 86 above.

[86] *Lettres de Jacques de Vitry*, pp. 108, 137–38; *Relatio magistri Oliveri* (n. 75 above), p. 289; *Alberti Milioli notarii Regini Liber de temporibus*, ed. O. Holder-Egger (1903), in MGH SS 31:484.

crusader chronicle named after its reputed author Ernoul, the sultan asks Francis and his companion whether they come as messengers or as petitioners for conversion to Islam. The question not only implies that such bids for conversion must have been common, but also suggests that Francis made his trip during a lull in the fighting while the sultan awaited a crusader reply to his proposals.)[87] Furthermore, an important member of the crusading army—Jacques of Vitry—had preached to the Muslims, baptized some, and sent to others a written refutation of Islam. And among the many German-speaking crusaders in camp, some might have heard or read the *Rolandslied des Pfaffen Konrad*, a German adaptation of the *Chanson de Roland* written about 1170. This work relates that after Naimes of Bavaria has proposed to Charlemagne to go on the attack, eject Machmet and Apollo, and honorably receive the Saracens willing to convert (that is, the usual sequence of Christian warfare leading to Saracen conversion), the bishop of St. Johannes rises to suggest quite a different course of action: He asks Charlemagne for permission to go to Spain, cross the Guadalquivir into Saracen Almeria, and proclaim the word of God. It is significant that St. Johannes adds that he does not fear the Saracens' threats of death; evidently the author of the *Rolandslied* was also aware of the Muslim prohibition against Christian proselytizing.[88] Later on in the poem, Archbishop Turpin makes a similar offer:

> I tell them [the Saracens] the prophets,
> What they taught us about God.
> I proclaim them the Holy Christ,
> —Perhaps it may be of use?—
> The Holy Gospel.
> What can you do better?
> If somebody taught them,
> Maybe they would convert?[89]

Francis's great originality consisted in actually carrying out what the bishops of the German poem merely proposed to do. Nothing certain

---

[87] *Chronique d'Ernoul* (n. 69 above), p. 432. The text also shows an awareness of the Islamic prohibition of Christian preaching. For an attempt to clarify the nature of this chronicle see M. R. Morgan, *The Chronicle of Ernoul and the Continuations of William of Tyre* (London, 1973).

[88] *Das Rolandslied des Pfaffen Konrad* (chap. 2, n. 80 above), vv. 1054–89.

[89] Ibid., vv. 1336–43. This and the preceding passage have no counterparts in the original French version. Cf. H. Richter, *Kommentar zum Rolandslied des Pfaffen Konrad*, vol. 1 (Bern and Frankfurt/M, 1972), pp. 225–29, 238–39.

can be said about the encounter between Francis and Sultan al–Kāmil. Given the fact—hitherto unnoticed in this context—that at a somewhat later date the sultan did attend a religious disputation between some learned Muslims and the Coptic patriarch of Alexandria, it is conceivable that he did indeed allow Francis to speak out in his presence on matters of religion.[90] In any case, it is certain that Francis crossed the lines with the intention of preaching to the sultan, then returned unharmed to the crusader camp. It is also clear that immediate observers were less impressed than were future generations. Of the many contemporary sources describing the Fifth Crusade, only two mention Francis's feat: the crusader chronicle attributed to Ernoul and a letter by Jacques of Vitry. And one may surmise that Jacques did not consider the event very important at the time, because he mentions it only in an appendix to a version of his letter sent to pious friends in the diocese of Liège, not in the version addressed to Pope Honorius III.[91] It would seem that if Francis had been a private man rather than the founder of an important order, his attempt at preaching to the sultan might have left as modest a mark as Jacques's more persistent though less-courageous endeavors to convert the Saracens.[92]

But Francis was not a private man, and so his feat was described and eulogized time and again in the writings of his followers. Moreover, on the matter of Saracen conversion, Francis took a truly far-

[90] For the sources on Francis's journey see L. Lemmens, "De sancto Francisco Christum praedicante coram sultano Aegypti," *Archivum Franciscanum Historicum* 19 (1926): 559–78. On the religious disputation with the Coptic patriarch see Graf, *Geschichte der christlichen arabischen Literatur*, 2:357, 365. It is notable that in 1221 Emperor Theodore I Lascaris of Nicaea sent a religious tract to Sultan al-Kāmil: Fritsch, *Islam*, p. 17. A disputation between a Maronite abbot and three Muslim sages purportedly took place in 1215–16 in Aleppo, in the presence of az̧-Z̧āhir, a son of Saladin who ruled that city: E.A.M. Le Grand, trans., *Controverse sur la religion chrétienne et celle des mahométans, entre trois docteurs musulmans et un religieux de la nation maronite* (Paris, 1767).

[91] *Lettres de Jacques de Vitry*, pp. 131–33. Cf. R.B.C. Huygens, "Les passages des lettres de Jacques de Vitry relatifs à Saint François d'Assise et à ses premiers disciples," in *Hommages à Léon Herrmann*, Collection Latomus, 44 (Brussels, 1960), p. 450. Later, in his *Historia Occidentalis*, Jacques dwelt on Francis's encounter in more detail: Hinnebusch, ed., *The Historia Occidentalis* (n. 80 above), pp. 161–62.

[92] Incidentally, Jacques also went to the sultan, but did so (in July 1221) to settle the terms of capitulation of the encircled crusader army, and then to serve as one of the hostages: *Chronique d'Ernoul*, pp. 444–46; *Chronique rimée de Philippe Mouskes*, ed. de Reiffenberg, vol. 2 (Brussels, 1838), vv. 22919–20. Funk, who doubts that Jacques played a role in these events, assumed that Mousket got his information from Ernoul: *Jakob von Vitry*, p. 49. But Mousket, a burgher of Tournai, seems to be exceptionally well acquainted with Jacques's career: see vv. 23465, 26867, 27817–24, more readily accessible in MGH SS 26:767, 791, 795. (The reference on p. 791, which escaped Funk's notice, may necessitate a slight revision of Jacques's itinerary.)

reaching step by including in the Rule of the Friars Minor a chapter dealing specifically with missionary work among the Saracens and other infidels.[93] Henceforth Saracen conversion was no longer a private notion, inducing one man to attempt a written refutation of Islam and another to preach on the crusader-Muslim frontier, but the recognized objective of an important order. There is a significant difference between Francis's own version of rule, the *Regula non bullata*, and the later version approved by Honorius III. The first calls on the ministers, or superiors, of the order to permit friars to go to the lands of the Saracens if they consider themselves suitable for the task, while the second calls on the ministers not to license any but those whom they consider suitable, thereby placing the emphasis on the ministers' authority rather than on the friars' right.[94] Still, both versions present the friars' desire to work among the Saracens as legitimate, and efforts at Saracen conversion as laudable.

Francis's ability to elevate his own urge to preach to the Saracens into a recognized aim of his order is one of the differences between him and Jacques of Vitry; the link between that urge to preach and the attitude toward martyrdom is another. Jacques shows no desire whatever for martyrdom: During his preaching tour along the Syrian littoral he always made sure, "out of fear of the pagans," to obtain armed escorts for the various stages of his journey. True, in Damietta he once rode unarmed into battle in the company of Pelagius and the patriarch of Jerusalem, and later wrote in a letter that he returned unharmed, since God did not wish him to become one of his martyrs, but there is nothing to suggest that this is more than a turn of speech.[95]

Francis, on the other hand, in the chapter of the *Regula non bullata* dealing with the evangelization of Saracens, concludes with a string of Gospel quotations on the prize due to those who suffer for Christ even unto death, and elsewhere exhorts his friars to love those who unjustly inflict upon them torments, martyrdom, and death, because eternal life

[93] Flood, ed., *Regula non bullata* (n. 78 above), c. 16, pp. 64–65; Boehmer, ed., *Analekten*, (n. 78 above), pp. 10–11. For the parallel clause (c. 12) in the *Regula bullata*, see Boehmer, p. 24.

On the other hand, the Dominican regulations on preaching do not specifically mention work among the Saracens: H. Denifle, "Die Constitutionen des Prediger-Ordens vom Jahre 1228," *Archiv für Litteratur- und Kirchengeschichte des Mittelalters* 1 (1885): 219; R. Greytens, "Les constitutions des Frères Prêcheurs dans la rédaction de s. Raymond de Peñafort (1241)," *Archivum Fratrum Praedicatorum* 18 (1948): 64.

[94] The difference was noted by O. van der Vat, *Die Anfänge der Franziskanermissionen und ihre Weiterentwicklung im nahen Orient und in den mohammedanischen Ländern während des 13. Jahrhunderts* (Werl/Westf., 1934), p. 26.

[95] *Lettres de Jacques de Vitry*, pp. 91–94, 130.

will be the reward of these tribulations.[96] Francis's Franciscan biographers—though not the non–Franciscan Jacques and Ernoul—insist that the desire for martyrdom was the underlying motive behind his attempts to go to the lands of the Saracens and preach there, while several Franciscan commentators upon the *Regula bullata* present that desire as one of the reasons that may impel a friar to go among Saracens and other infidels.[97]

The relationship between preaching and martyrdom was not devoid of tension. On the abstract level, it was easy to present martyrdom as the ultimate completion of preaching, the exemplary imitation of the suffering Christ. But the individual missionary leaving for the lands of Islam had to make up his mind whether his foremost aim was to persuade the infidels of Christianity's truth, or to attain self-fulfillment by suffering death at their hands. In his commentary on the *Regula*, Hugh of Digne (d. ca. 1255), well aware of this dual pull, emphatically counsels restraint. "Because of the desire for martyrdom," he writes, "one should not act precipitously but in fact prudently. For we should strive for the death for Christ and [yet] flee in an ordinate manner."[98] With some friars, however, the quest for martyrdom clearly outweighed the desire to convert Saracens, and led them, not unlike the ninth-century enthusiasts of Cordova, to publicly assail Islam and thus bring death upon themselves. This is true of the five friars who attacked Islam in 1219–20 first in Muslim Seville and then in Morocco, the four friars who did the same in 1391 before the cadi of Jerusalem, and several others.[99] This aggressive stance starkly contrasts with Francis's meas-

[96] Flood, ed., *Regula non bullata*, cc. 16, 23, pp. 65, 69; Boehmer, ed., *Analekten*, pp. 11–13.

[97] For Francis's *Lives* see, for example, Thomas de Celano, *Vita prima*, n. 55, in *Analecta Franciscana*, vol. 10 (Quaracchi, 1926–41), p. 42; idem, *Vita secunda*, n. 30, ibid., p. 149; Johannes de Spira, *Vita S. Francisci*, n. 36, ibid., p. 352. On the commentaries see the overview of van der Vat, *Die Anfänge*, pp. 34–38; E. R. Daniel, "The Desire for Martyrdom: A *Leitmotiv* of St. Bonaventure," *Franciscan Studies* 32 (1972): 74–87. On the Franciscan view of martyrdom in general, see E. R. Daniel, *The Franciscan Concept*, especially pp. 40–49.

[98] "Nec desiderio martirii praecipitanter agendum est sed prudenter. Mortem enim pro Christo appetere debemus et fugere ordinate." D. Flood, ed., *Hugh of Digne's Rule Commentary*, Spicilegium Bonaventurianum, 14 (Grottaferrata, 1979), p. 192. Somewhat earlier (p. 191) Hugh speaks of would-be missionaries "ad conversionem gentium vel martirium anhelantes." On the tension between self-centered martyrdom and other-centered preaching, see also the perceptive discussion in Elm, "Franz von Assisi," pp. 84–86.

[99] *Passio sanctorum martyrum . . . in Marochio martyrizatorum*, in *Analecta Franciscana*, vol. 3 (Quaracchi, 1897), pp. 584–90; *Chronica 24 Generalium*, ibid., pp. 15–19; P. Durrieu, "Procès-verbal du martyre de quatre frères mineurs, 1391," *Archives de l'Ori-

ured injunctions in his *Regula non bullata* to friars intent on going among the Saracens. It should be noted, however, that at a very early stage of Franciscan history Francis came to be portrayed as advocating such militant behavior: The account about the five friars who went to Seville and Morocco includes Francis instructing them "to preach and confess Christ's faith and assail the religion of Machomet."[100]

Moreover, it is plausible to assume that among the friars who adopted this stance there were some who, not unlike Alvar of Cordova, believed that by openly attacking the religion of the Saracens and calling upon them to convert, they would ensure eternal punishment for their unrepentant listeners. Indeed, the seven Tuscan Franciscans who in 1227 attempted to preach Christianity in the streets of Ceuta wrote in their letter from prison that "the death and damnation of the infidels" was one of the objectives toward which Christ had directed them.[101] Their train of thought is made amply clear through their earlier quotation of Jesus' evangelization charge according to the lesser-known version in Mark 16:15–16: "Go, and preach the Gospel to every creature."[102] For Jesus there goes on to say, "He that believeth and is baptized shall be saved, but he that believeth not shall be damned." Similarly, the four friars who attacked Islam in 1391 in Jerusalem quoted Mark 16:16 in their speech before the cadi.[103] Evidently martyrdom could also harbor a malevolent intent.

JACQUES OF VITRY AND FRANCIS OF ASSISI: ATTITUDES TOWARD CRUSADING

Jacques of Vitry was a fervent supporter of the crusades throughout his career. He preached the crusade both before and during his ministry in Acre, was one of the first participants in the Fifth Crusade to land in Egypt, and again preached the crusade after his return to Eu-

---

ent latin 1 (1881): 539–46. On this type see N. Daniel, *Islam and the West*, pp. 121–22; E. R. Daniel, *The Franciscan Concept*, pp. 42–45, 53.

[100] ". . . ad predicandum et confitendum eius [= Christi] fidem et legem Machometicam impugnandum." *Passio sanctorum martyrum*, p. 581.

[101] "Dominus Iesus Christus . . . direxit vias nostras in semitis suis ad laudem eius et salutem fidelium et honorem Christianorum et ad mortem et damnationem infidelium." *Passio sanctorum fratrum Danielis, Agnelli, Samuelis, Donnuli, Leonis, Nicolai, Hugolini ordinis fratrum minorum*, in *Analecta Franciscana*, vol. 3 (Quaracchi, 1897), p. 615.

[102] Ibid., p. 614. Subsequently (p. 615) the friars quote the words of Jesus according to John 15:22: "Nam si non venissem, ait Christus, et locutus eis non fuissem, peccatum non haberent; nunc autem excusationem non habent de peccato."

[103] Durrieu, "Procès-verbal," p. 543.

rope in 1225. Four of his crusading sermons are extant.[104] Jacques was well aware that Catholic, or at least Templar, fighting against the Saracens was regarded by some of his contemporaries as a violation of Christian morality, but he resolutely rejected this criticism. In a sermon to the Knights Templar that contains a warning against putting trust in "false Christians, Saracens, and Beduins" (a possible indication that it was delivered in the Crusading Kingdom), Jacques mentions that the heretics maintain that the Templars should not wage warfare for any cause whatsoever, and that they quote in support of their position a number of New Testament injunctions, one of which is, "He who shall take the sword, will perish by it."[105] This is the same anti-Templar argument, making use of the same verse of the Gospel according to Matthew, that Walter Map had advanced about twenty-five years earlier; still earlier, that verse had figured in the query of the Jerusalemite patriarch to Peter Comestor.[106] Possibly for tactical reasons, Jacques attributes this critique solely to the heretics, then marshals his considerable rhetorical powers to rebut it. He first brands the heretics' New Testament quotations as an abuse of Scripture, apt to lead astray the simple-minded, and then goes on to explain that the New Testament injunctions in question should be related to the inward readying of the heart (*preparatio cordis*) rather than to overt activity (*ostentatio corporis*). (It is noteworthy that though this reasoning closely depends on a dictum of Gratian and on a passage of Augustine as quoted by Gratian, Jacques acknowledges his debt solely to Augustine.)[107] Jacques concludes his rebuttal by pointing out that had the Christians not resisted their enemies, the Saracens and the heretics

---

[104] On Jacques's landing in Egypt see his *Lettres*, p. 103. The four sermons appear in BN lat. 17509, fol. 93r–102r. The first two were partially printed in J.-B. Pitra, *Analecta novissima Spicilegii Solesmensis altera continuatio*, vol. 2 (Tusculum, 1888), pp. 421–30; for excerpts see T. F. Crane, ed., *The Exempla or Illustrative Stories from the "Sermones Vulgares" of Jacques de Vitry* (London, 1890), pp. 54–59. For summaries of all four sermons see R. Röhricht, "Die Kreuzpredigten gegen den Islam: Ein Beitrag zur Geschichte der christlichen Predigt im 12. und 13. Jahrhundert," *Zeitschrift für Kirchengeschichte* 6 (1883–84): 562–72.

[105] Jacques of Vitry, *Alius sermo ad fratres milicie*, BN lat. 17509, fol. 74v; Pitra, *Analecta*, p. 419 (where *Praedicti enim patientiae praecepta* should be corrected to *Predicta* etc.).

[106] The other New Testament injunctions the heretics are said to quote appear also at the beginning of Gratian's discussion of the legitimacy of warfare in his *Causa* 23.

[107] Cf. Gratian, C.23, q.1, d.p.c.1, and C.23, q.1, c.2; *S. Aureli Augustini Hipponiensis episcopi epistulae*, vol. 2, 3, ed. A. Goldbacher, Corpus Scriptorum Ecclesiasticorum Latinorum, 44 (Vienna and Leipzig, 1904), Ep. 138, lines 12–14, pp. 138–40. Cf. Kuttner, *Kanonistische Schuldlehre*, pp. 349–51.

would already have destroyed the entire Church.[108] In other words, the crusade is a defensive, and hence just, act of warfare.

Jacques nowhere remarks explicitly on the relationship between his attempts at converting the Saracens and his support for the crusade against them, but his writings do contain several remarks that bear on the issue. In the letter written in Acre to his friends in Europe in the spring of 1217 Jacques reports on his missionary activities among the Saracens, relating with approval that many Saracens requested baptism after Christ or the Virgin appeared in their dreams and warned them that unless they did so, the participants of the Fifth Crusade would slaughter them upon their arrival at Acre. A few lines later, Jacques gives his opinion that once the crusaders arrive, Saracens who had hitherto feared the vengeance of their brethren would dare to convert to Christianity.[109] Thus it is evident that Jacques considers the crusade an efficient means for the furthering of Saracen conversion. At this stage he is optimistic about the prospects of evangelizing the Saracens, and concludes his letter with the observation that the Oriental heretics and Saracens may "easily" (*facile*) convert once they hear the tenets of Christianity.[110] Perhaps the effect of the personal encounter with Muslims, the fact that it had been possible to communicate with them, and the satisfaction derived from the two baptisms performed at Tortosa encouraged Jacques to entertain these unrealistic hopes.

But this initial optimism did not last long. In the prologue to his *Historia Hierosolimitana*, probably written in 1220, Jacques expresses the hope that he will be able to finish his work with a description of "the recovery of the Holy Land, the conversion or destruction of the Saracens (*Sarracenorum conversione vel destructione*), and the repair of the Oriental Church": Evidently he is no longer sure that conversion will be so easily attained. Later in the book Jacques remarks that some of the more thoughtful Saracens, convinced of the erroneousness of Machomet's law after reading the ancient philosophers and the Gospel, frequently asked for baptism, and many others would have followed them but for their attraction to the worldly delights offered by their

---

[108] This view may be compared with Joachim's warning about an impending alliance between the Saracens and the heretics (n. 56 above). Ralph Niger, on the other hand, considered heresy the far graver danger: *De re militari*, ed. Schmugge, III, 66 and 82, pp. 187–88, 193.

Already the anonymous author of the *Summa: 'Elegantius in Iure Divino'* asserted that contemporary imitation of evangelical perfection and martyrlike patience would be tantamount to the Church's submission to pagan rule: Russell, *The Just War*, p. 94 and n. 19.

[109] *Lettres de Jacques de Vitry*, pp. 88–89; see also p. 95.

[110] Ibid., p. 97.

religion and their fear of the stringencies of Christian morality.[111] Thus, after a few years in the Levant, Jacques became aware, however distortedly, of Islam's hold over its practitioners, and took into account the possibility that conversion would not be feasible in all cases and that at least some of the Saracens would have to be destroyed. His early belief in the efficacy of mere preaching must have been shattered when, as he describes in his *Historia Occidentalis*, the early Franciscans were scourged and driven out of the cities of the Saracens whenever they stopped exposing the tenets of Christianity and began to attack Machomet.[112]

These shifts in his views on the prospects of Saracen conversion were only secondary to Jacques's steadfast and continuous support of the crusade, a support that found expression in his writings and his preaching alike. As he formulated it in one of his sermons, the "material sword" was the Church's answer to pagan and Saracen violence.[113] Therefore, at no time did he present the attempts at Saracen conversion as surrogates for the crusade, the lifting of the material sword against what he considered Saracen aggression. Even in his early days in Acre, while still optimistic about Saracen conversion, he frequently gazed out to the sea, "expecting with tears in [his] eyes and a great longing the arrival of the crusaders."[114]

Francis's attitude to the armed struggle against the Muslims must remain a moot point, since none of his scanty writings bears on the issue. Nevertheless, some modern historians have argued that Francis's very attempts to preach to the Saracens implied his disapproval of the

---

[111] *Historia Hierosolimitana*, in J. Bongars, *Gesta Dei per Francos*, vol. 1 (Hanau, 1611), pp. 1048, 1058; ed. F. Moschus (Douai, 1597; reprint, Farnborough, 1971), pp. 24–25. (The first passage referred to appears in the prologue to the work, which was not reproduced by Moschus.) Cf. *Lettres*, p. 137.

[112] Hinnebusch, ed., *The Historia Occidentalis*, p. 162.

[113] *Sermo ad fratres ordinis milicie*, BN lat. 17509, fol. 72ra: "Contra iudeos et hereticos opponit doctores sanctos, aperiens eis sensum ut intelligant scripturas. contra scismaticos sanctorum communionem, regimen prelatorum, et obedientiam subditorum. contra paganorum et sarracenorum violentiam gladium materialem. contra tyrannos et falsos fratres gladium spiritualem qui etiam contra hereticos et scismaticos exercetur ut compellantur intrare et ad ecclesiam redire." Cf. Pitra, *Analecta*, p. 405.

[114] *Lettres de Jacques de Vitry*, p. 95. Jacques's preaching Christianity to Muslims and participating in a crusade against them, though unprecedented in the crusader East, has parallels in Europe's northeast. For instance, Bishop Henry of Moravia, who in 1141 obtained Innocent II's permission to preach Christianity to the pagan Prussians, in 1147 took the cross against the Wends: *Preussisches Urkundenbuch* (chap. 2, n. 102 above), docs. 2–3, 1, 1:1–2; *Annales Magdeburgenses*, in MGH SS 16: 188. (The annalist mentions Henry as one of the bishops who joined the Christian host that descended on the pagans "ut eos aut christiane religioni subderet, aut Deo auxiliante omnino deleret.")

crusade. They also point out that while at the camp near Damietta, he attempted to dissuade the crusaders from launching an attack against the Saracens.[115] But none of the sources attributes to Francis any remarks that may be interpreted as critical of the crusades, and Thomas of Celano, the biographer who relates that Francis objected to a Christian attack, leaves no doubt that Francis was attempting to dissuade the Christians from joining battle on a certain day (*tali die*) on which, as God told him, they were bound to lose.[116] Significantly, the same biographer relates that after the attack ended in a Christian defeat, Francis particularly mourned the Spanish crusaders who had been decimated because of their outstandingly daring feats on the battlefield.[117] And another early Franciscan source depicts Francis as still more appreciative of Christians who fell in battle against the Saracens. This is the story reported by the three companions Leo, Rufino, and Angelo in which Francis tells a novice, "The Emperor Charles, Roland and Oliver, and all the paladins and strong men mighty in battle, pursuing the infidel with much sweat and toil even unto death, gained over them a glorious and memorable victory; and in the end these holy martyrs died in battle for the faith of Christ."[118] Here speaks a Francis who admires the heroes of Roncevalles, approves of warfare against the infidels, and regards as martyrs the Christians who fall in battle against them.[119] If this story does indeed reflect Francis's atti-

---

[115] See for instance Waas, *Geschichte der Kreuzzüge*, 1:40, 2:298; L. Bréhier, *L'église et l'Orient au moyen-âge: les croisades*, 2d ed. (Paris, 1928), p. 213; P. Rousset, *Histoire des croisades* (Paris, 1957), p. 238; E. Buonaiuti, "Origini cristiane e movimento francescano," in *Saggi di storia del cristianesimo*, ed. A Donini and M. Niccoli (Vicenza, 1957), p. 396 (the article originally appeared in 1925); K. Esser, "Das missionarische Anliegen des heiligen Franziskus," *Wissenschaft und Weisheit* 35 (1972): 14–15. See also the remarks of Giovanni Gonnet and Marco Bartoli in the discussion printed in *Espansione del Francescanesimo*, pp. 17, 20. (For a more exact, though still ambiguous, formulation, see A. Rotzetter, "Kreuzzugskritik und Ablehnung der Feudalordnung in der Gefolgschaft des Franziskus von Assisi," *Wissenschaft und Weisheit* 35 [1972]: 128.)

[116] Thomas de Celano, *Vita secunda* (n. 97 above), n. 30, p. 149. For the same interpretation of this passage see Throop, *Criticism of the Crusade*, p. 128, n. 64; N. Daniel, *Islam and the West*, p. 118; F. Cardini, " 'Nella presenza del Soldan superba': Bernardo, Francesco, Bonaventura e il superamento dell'idea di crociata," *Studi Francescani* 71 (1974): 235.

[117] "Verum praecipue Hispanos plangebat, quorum promptiorem in armis audaciam cernebat pauculos reliquisse." Thomas de Celano, *Vita secunda*, p. 149.

[118] *Scripta Leonis, Rufini et Angeli Sociorum S. Francisci*, ed. and trans. Rosalind B. Brooke (Oxford, 1970), pp. 214–15; cf. p. 208, n. e.

[119] On this and other evidence of the impact of chivalry on Francis see the provocative though one-sided article by P. Rajna, "San Francesco d'Assisi e gli spiriti cavallereschi," *Nuova Antologia: Rivista di Lettere, Scienze ed Arti* 327 (1926): 385–95. For a Franciscan source of the later thirteenth century that depicts Francis as an outright apologist for

tude toward the armed struggle against the Saracens, one may well conjecture that he regarded his own attempts at preaching as a supplementary rather than a contradictory alternative to the crusade, with both options imbued with the values of chivalry and demanding a willingness to undergo martyrdom.[120]

OLIVER OF COLOGNE AND THE EARLIEST CONVERGENCE OF CRUSADE AND MISSION

While the views of Jacques and Francis on the relationship between mission and crusade may be circumscribed by deduction and conjecture, respectively, there exists an explicit, strictly contemporary comment on that relationship by a man who, like Jacques and Francis, stayed in the crusader camp near Damietta. This man was Oliver, head of the cathedral school of Cologne, who played a major role in the preaching of the Fifth Crusade and in the subsequent attack on Egypt. The comment appears in the letter of September 1221 in which Oliver invited Sultan al–Kāmil to convert to Christianity.[121]

Oliver's was not the first Catholic written appeal for Muslim conversion. Gregory VII hinted at conversion in his letter to al-Nāṣir of Bidjāya; the *rāhib* of France is said to have sent two appeals to al-Muqtadir of Saragossa; Peter of Cluny addressed his *Liber adversus nefandam heresim sive sectam Sarracenorum* to the Saracens of the East and the south; Alexander III sent an *Instructio fidei* to the sultan of Iconium; and in two letters on current issues, sent in 1199 and 1211 to the rulers of Aleppo and Morocco, Innocent III also expressed the hope for the conversion of his addressees. (Writing to the ruler of Morocco, Innocent—quite unlike Gregory VII—refers to the Saracens as pagans—a reference that, if brought to the attention of the Almohad ruler, would hardly have made him receptive to the pope's wishes.)[122] But these appeals were written from a position of relative

---

the crusade see Oliger, ed., "Liber exemplorum" (n. 2 above), p. 251 (= Appendix 4/g).

[120] This conjecture has been proposed in a rather too forceful formulation by F. Cardini, " 'Nella presenza,' " p. 250.

[121] For biographical data see the introduction of H. Hoogeweg, ed., *Die Schriften* (n. 75 above), pp. ix–lii; on Oliver's preaching of the Fifth Crusade see P. B. Pixton, "Die Anwerbung des Heeres Christi: Prediger des Fünften Kreuzzuges in Deutschland," *Deutsches Archiv* 34 (1978): 166–91. The letter to al-Kāmil is edited in Hoogeweg, ed., *Die Schriften*, pp. 296–307; it is followed by a letter to the *doctores* of Egypt (pp. 307–14).

[122] For Innocent's letters see PL 214:544–45 (a. 1199), 216:434 (a. 1211). The letter of 1199 has been newly edited by J. Borrego, *La regla de Orden de la Santissima Trinidad: Contexto histórico* (Rome, 1973), doc. 12, p. 260. Innocent III showed no interest

strength and addressed to distant rulers, whereas Oliver was writing to a man whose acts he was able to observe at close range, and whose lenient behavior toward the defeated crusaders evoked his gratitude and admiration. Hence his letter stands out for its warmth and immediacy. This warmth, though, is not always present. In his *Historia Damiatina* Oliver remarks that since many Oriental Christians live among the Saracens, the latter will not be able to excuse themselves through ignorance; in other words, like Alvar of Cordova, Oliver expects the Saracens to suffer damnation because they had the opportunity to accept Christianity but refused to do so.[123] Evidently Oliver, like Nicholas of Constantinople and Gregory VII before him, employs different modes of expression in writing to Christian and Muslim addressees.

In the letter to the sultan, Oliver displays some knowledge of Islam and Muslim history and, like so many Christians before him, contrasts Jesus' teaching of love and the Apostles' preaching to all people with Mahumeth's resort to the sword.[124] Then, as if to anticipate the sultan's inevitable question as to why the followers of Jesus and the Apostles chose to invade his country sword in hand, Oliver goes on to say,

> If your people had publicly granted admittance to the teaching of Christ and his preachers, God's church would gladly have sent them the sword of God's word, and joyfully invited them to the community of the Catholic faith. But because it does not find any other remedy against the Saracen might, the law of the Catholic princes licitly makes use of the material sword for the defense of Christianity and the recovery of its right. For assuredly all laws and all rights permit the repulsion of force by force.[125]

---

in furthering missions to the Saracens. The one letter that has been adduced as displaying a missionary motive (PL 216:209A; cf. Roscher, *Papst Innocenz III*, pp. 174, 186) is nothing but a routine reissue of Alexander III's bull for the Order of Santiago. See chap. 2, n. 14 above.

[123] "Hee Christianorum diversitates per totam Asiam Sarracenis sunt permixte, ne gens illa perfida per ignorantiam se valeat excusare." *Historia Damiatina*, in Hoogeweg, ed., *Die Schriften*, pp. 266–67.

[124] On the sources of Oliver's knowledge of Islam see R. Röhricht, "Die Briefe des Kölner Scholasticus Oliver," *Westdeutsche Zeitschrift für Geschichte und Kunst* 10 (1891):165–68; J. Schäfers, "Olivers, des Bischofs von Paderborn und Kardinalbischofs von S. Sabina († 1227), Kenntnis des Mohammedanismus," *Theologie und Glaube: Zeitschrift für den katholischen Klerus* 4 (1912): 535–44. Cf. Hoogeweg, ed., *Die Schriften*, pp. 121–23, 203–5.

[125] See Appendix 4/d.

In this short passage Oliver presents a bundle of arguments in favor of the crusade. The legitimacy of defensive warfare, based once again on the Roman maxim, and the historic right of Christendom to the Holy Land—a theme that Oliver later expands—are arguments that had been voiced before. But Oliver also presents a new justification of Christian warfare, a justification in which mission and crusade converge for the first time: Since the Saracens do not allow access to Christian preachers, the Christians have no choice but to confront Saracen might, arms in hand, and so defend themselves and attempt to recover their right. Components of this argument had appeared before: In the ninth century, Ermold the Black had Louis the Pious say that since the Saracens are not willing to convert, the Franks must wage war against them; some three centuries later, Bernard of Clairvaux maintained that it would not have been lawful to kill the Saracens if it were possible to prevent them by some other means from attacking the Christians. But it is only with Oliver that mission and crusade are explicitly brought into a causal relationship, with the Saracen prohibition of missionizing making the crusade inevitable. True, the causal link between the two is still encumbered by other, traditional elements. But less than a generation later the link was to become disentangled and precise.

MISSIONARY preaching to the Muslims did not evolve out of criticism of the crusades. To be sure, in twelfth-century Europe a few critics of crusading presented preaching as the true Christian method of expansion. But it was not the position of these critics that caused the first Catholic preachers to leave for the lands of Islam. Significantly, Jacques of Vitry, the first Catholic in the crusader era to earnestly endeavor to preach to the Muslims of the Levant, forcefully objected to such criticism of the crusade. The undoubted spread of information about Islam—factual or distorted—during the twelfth century probably aided the early missionaries. Jacques was well informed enough to compose a written refutation of "Saracen errors" a few months after his arrival at Acre, and the early Franciscans were able, in their sermons to the Muslims, to denounce Machomet as a liar and a scoundrel.[126] But the moving force behind the emergence of sustained preaching to the Muslims was the urge to bring the Gospel to all men, an urge characteristic of the keen new religiosity focusing on the imitation of the

[126] *Lettres de Jacques de Vitry*, p. 96; Hinnebusch, ed., *The Historia Occidentalis*, p. 162.

133

Apostles. The mission to the Muslims should thus be considered the outgrowth of an internal Catholic European development that spilled over the boundaries of Catholic Christendom: Preaching to the Muslims was an extension of preaching to the Christians.

Why did not earlier waves of the new religiosity wash over the Catholic-Muslim frontier, and why did merely a handful of hermits make a few, mostly incidental attempts in that direction? Why, for instance, did not that great wandering preacher and exponent of apostolic life, Norbert of Xanten (d. 1134), attempt to preach also to the Muslims?[127] As with all questions about an event that might have happened but did not, the answer is not an easy one, and the factor of chance—like the election of the preacher of Marie d'Oignies to the bishopric of Acre—should not be ruled out. But it is possible that by the time of Jacques and Francis, the tales about the crusades and the prominence of the Saracens in the *chansons* made people more acutely aware of the existence of a Saracen realm. The progressive undemonizing and humanizing of the Saracen in vernacular literature, as well as the fact that by the beginning of the thirteenth century Saracen conversion had become a phenomenon familiar to many a Catholic European—from the Genoese who rubbed shoulders with baptized Saracens in the narrow lanes of his own city to the canon lawyer who perused papal decisions on the validity of consanguineous marriages among Saracen converts—helped to render the Saracen a major target for a preacher intent on bringing the Gospel to all men.

In the annals of the Catholic reconquest, the emergence of preachers to the Muslims certainly signals the beginning of a new stage. But its groundwork was laid much earlier. It has been shown that from the very beginning of the Catholic counteroffensive, Muslim conversion occurred on all three of its fronts and was often presented (and not only in popular works) as one of the objectives of Christian fighting. Exhortations to work for the conversion of the Saracens of reconquered Spain recurred from the late eleventh century onward. The appearance of missionaries willing to preach to the Saracens of the reconquered areas thus meant, first, that there were men available to

---

[127] According to a late tradition, in 1131 Innocent II sent the Premonstratensian Amalric of Floreffe to preach to the Christians and the pagans of the Holy Land. Several recent writers have accepted this tradition as fact: F. Petit, *La spiritualité des Prémontrés aux XII⁰ et XIII⁰ siècles* (Paris, 1947), p. 81; N. Backmund, *Monasticon Praemonstratense*, vol. 1 (Straubing, 1949), pp. 397, 404; B. Hamilton, *The Latin Church in the Crusader States: The Secular Church* (London, 1980), p. 101. This tradition, however, is unfounded: W. M. Grauwen, *Norbertus, aartsbisschop van Maagdenburg (1126–1134)* (Brussels, 1978), pp. 481–82.

carry out a scheme that, at least with regard to Spain, had been repeatedly suggested decades earlier, and, second, that these men could
steer the hitherto spontaneous religious drift toward the religion of
the conquerors. Moreover, the Franciscan emphasis on martyrdom
emboldened many a friar to overcome the paralyzing effect of the Muslim
prohibition against Christian proselytizing, and to attempt the preaching of Christianity in the lands of Islam proper.

FOUR

The Mendicants: Preaching the Gospel
to Saracens, Preaching the Cross
to Christians

IN THE early years of their existence, the Franciscan and Dominican orders dedicated considerable energy to the furthering of Saracen conversion. The memory of Francis's attempts to go to the Saracens and of Dominic's plan to do so was still fresh. The Aragonese conquest of Majorca (1229–35) and the kingdom of Valencia (1229–45) and the Castilian push to Cordova (1236) and Seville (1248) made large Muslim populations accessible to Catholic missionizing, while the spectacle of an erstwhile ruler of Muslim Valencia becoming Catholic and assisting the crusaders of Jaume I of Aragon in the conquest of his former possessions boded well for further conversions. The fact that the ruler, Abū Zayd, converted to Christianity not long after ordering the execution of two Italian Franciscans who had attempted to assail Islam publicly in Valencia city must have fortified Franciscan enthusiasts in their belief in the efficacy of the practice of preaching even unto martyrdom. Further, recurring prophecies of the impending end of Islam—like the one about the speedy destruction of Mecca and Baghdad, the spread of doubt and uncertainty among the Saracens, and the abandonment of their mosques, which was attributed to Master John of Toledo and widely diffused after 1229—might have beguiled some Mendicants into seriously underestimating the durability of Muslim resistance to Christianization.[1]

Against this background, several Franciscan and Dominican houses were established in Catholic countries with Muslim populations, namely in the kingdoms of Spain and the crusader-ruled littoral of the eastern Mediterranean, and footholds were gained in Tunis and Morocco. The

[1] For the career of Abū Zayd, see R. I. Burns, *Islam under the Crusaders: Colonial Survival in the Thirteenth-Century Kingdom of Valencia* (Princeton, 1973), pp. 32–37, 286–87, 301–4, 355–59; on his execution of two Italian Franciscans in 1231 see *Analecta Franciscana*, vol. 3 (Quaracchi, 1897), p. 186. For the prophecies about the impending end of Islam see H. Grauert, "Meister Johann von Toledo," *Sitzungsberichte der Bayerischen Akademie der Wissenschaften, philos.-philol. u. hist. Kl.*, 1901, fascicle 2, pp. 165–73; N. Daniel, *The Arabs*, p. 159.

Dominican Order devoted much thought to the adequate preparation of would-be missionaries for their task. In 1237 Philip, the prior of the Dominicans in the Holy Land, informed Pope Gregory IX that he had ordered the study of Oriental languages in the convents of his province, and that his friars were already capable of conversing and preaching in the newly acquired languages, "and especially in Arabic, which is the more common among the people." Besides reporting to the pope on activities among Oriental Christians, Philip writes that he sent three friars to preach to the Saracens who had witnessed the miracles that occurred near the spot where the Dominican master general, Jordan of Saxony, had drowned a short time before.[2] In the western Mediterranean, the Dominicans, under the leadership of Ramon of Penyaforte, established schools where friars were trained to engage in polemics with Muslims. The first of these schools was set up in Tunis in the early 1240s; others soon followed in Muslim cities recently conquered by the Aragonese and Castilians.[3]

These Mendicant efforts enjoyed wide support. Canon lawyers from Tancredus onward exempted missionaries from the prohibition against sharing roof and table with Saracens and Jews.[4] Popes Gregory IX and Innocent IV wrote to several Muslim rulers recommending Franciscan and Dominican friars to them, in some cases openly expressing the wish that the friars might bring about their conversion. In 1233 Gregory IX secured Frederick II's good will toward the Dominicans who intended to preach in Lucera, the colony of Sicilian Muslims the emperor had established on south Italian soil. In 1242, probably at the instigation of Ramon of Penyaforte, Jaume I of Aragon coerced the Jews and Saracens of his kingdom into attending sermons delivered by bishops or Dominican and Franciscan friars. And if one may believe Ibn Abī Zar', the Moroccan chronicler who died sometime between 1310 and 1320, one Christian ruler succeeded in obtaining the Mus-

---

[2] For Philip's letter see Matthew Paris, *Chronica Majora*, ed. H. R. Luard, Rolls Series, 57 (London, 1876), 3:498–99; *Chronica Alberici monachi Trium-Fontium*, ed. F. Scheffer-Boichorst (1874), in MGH SS 35:942.

[3] For a succinct and critical survey of the literature on these schools see Burns, "Christian-Islamic Confrontation," pp. 1402–8.

[4] Cf. P. Herde, "Christians, and Saracens at the Time of the Crusades: Some Comments of Contemporary Medieval Canonists," *Studia Gratiana* 12 (1967): 369. To the sources adduced there, one may add Ramon of Penyaforte, *Summa de casibus poenitentiae*, 1.4.3, p. 33. Missionaries did not always avail themselves of this exemption: In the account about his stay among the Saracens, Ricoldo da Monte Croce observes that "unum eciam valde grauiter ferebant, quod nolebamus cum eis comedere." *Liber Peregrinacionis*, in J.C.M. Laurent, ed., *Peregrinatores medii aevi quatuor* (Leipzig, 1864), p. 134.

lim concession the friars must have coveted most: the permission for Muslim subjects of a Muslim ruler to convert openly to Christianity. Ferdinand III of Castile extracted this concession in 1228 (or 1229) from al-Ma'mūn, the Almohad ruler then desperately in need of Castilian help. The concession, as well as the commitment to build a church in Marrakech and let its bells ring and to prohibit Christian conversion to Islam, must have been short-lived, for some time before al-Ma'mūn's death in 1231–32 the church at Marrakech was demolished by a rival.[5]

Even as some Dominicans and Franciscans attempted to preach Christianity to the Muslims, other members of their orders preached the crusade against them. Occasionally the same friar engaged in both activities: Ramon of Penyaforte, who was to rise to fame as the great *zelator fidei propagandae inter Sarracenos*, in 1229 was authorized by Pope Gregory IX to preach the crusade against Saracen Majorca.[6] From the 1220s onward, the papacy relied increasingly on the Mendicants to drum up support for the crusading expeditions it attempted to launch.[7]

[5] The best general accounts of Dominican and Franciscan missionary efforts among the Muslims are B. Altaner, *Die Dominikanermissionen des 13. Jahrhunderts: Forschungen zur Geschichte der kirchlichen Unionen und der Mohammedaner-und Heidenmission des Mittelaters* (Habelschwerdt, 1924), pp. 72–114; van der Vat, Die Anfänge, pp. 60–123. See also E. R. Daniel, *The Franciscan Concept*, esp. chaps. 3, 6. The letters of Gregory IX and Innocent IV to various Muslim rulers, as well as the rulers' Latin replies, have been reedited by K.-E. Lupprian, *Die Beziehungen der Päpste zu islamischen und mongolischen Herrschern im 13. Jahrhundert anhand ihres Briefwechsels*, Studi e Testi, 291 (Città del Vaticano, 1981). The reply of an Almohad ruler, extant in its Arabic original, was edited and translated by E. Tisserant and G. Wiet, "Une lettre de l'almohade Murtaḍā au pape Innocent IV," *Hespéris* 6 (1926): 27–53 (translation reproduced in Lupprian, *Die Beziehungen*, pp. 199–203). For the correspondence concerning Lucera see *Historia Diplomatica* (chap. 2, n. 27 above), ed. J.L.A. Huillard-Bréholles, vol. 4, 1 (Paris, 1854), pp. 452, 457–58; cf. Altaner, *Dominikanermissionen*, p. 113. On al-Ma'mūn's concessions see Ibn Abī Zar', *Annales regum Mauritanie*, ed. and Latin trans. C. J. Tornberg, 2 vols. (Uppsala, 1843–46), 1:167 (text), 2:219; for the background, see Ch.-E. Dufourcq, "Les relations du Maroc et de la Castille pendant la première moitié du XIIIᵉ siècle," *Revue d'histoire et de civilisation du Maghreb* 5 (juillet 1968): 42–53. Another short-lived hope for unhampered missionizing among North African Muslims arose in 1245, when the ruler of Sale was believed to wish to convert: Lopez, "A propos d'une virgule," pp. 187–88; J. Muldoon, *Popes, Lawyers, and Infidels: The Church and the Non-Christian World, 1250–1550* (Philadelphia, 1979), p. 40.

[6] *Raymundiana*, ed. F. Balme, C. Paban, and J. Collomb, Monumenta Ordinis Fratrum Praedicatorum Historica, 6 (Rome and Stuttgart, 1898–1901), 1:3, 2:12–13; see also 1:7.

[7] See for instance P. Gratien, *Histoire de la fondation et de l'évolution de l'Ordre des Frères Mineurs au XIIIᵉ siècle* (Paris, 1928), pp. 642–49; Cardini, " 'Nella presenza,' " pp. 236–37. It is Cardini's impression that in promoting the crusade the Franciscans acted more out of obedience to the popes than out of the sense of a calling; but his

Some Mendicant preachers of the crusade even accompanied the crusading armies. Thus, the Franciscan Guillaume of Cordelle, who preached the crusade in France from 1235 on, joined Thibaud IV of Champagne's expedition to the Holy Land and delivered numerous sermons before the crusaders.[8] Fortunately, the sources allow us a glimpse of Guillaume's efforts on behalf of the crusade in Europe as well as in Palestine. A collection of Franciscan *exempla* preserves a description of one of his attempts at recruiting crusaders. At a tournament, the assembled knights prevented him from preaching the cross; whether they were unwilling to have their games spoiled by a sermon, or their objection was more deeply motivated, the *exemplum* does not reveal. But Guillaume was not to be put off. "He said to them," relates the anonymous Franciscan author, " 'Would you allow me at least to say a few other words without preaching?' They gave him permission. Ascending a wagon he said, 'Does Count So-and-so have any knight here?' And many rose saying they were the knights of that count. Then he asked about another count, then about a third and a fourth and so on, whether they had any knight there. And many rose professing to be their knights. Finally he asked whether Christ had any knight there, and all fell silent. Then be began to pull his hair and to exclaim, 'Oh me! All the barons have their knights here, and Christ, the lord of all, has none!' Then arose one of the more important [of the assembled] and went up to him and was signed with the cross, and after him went all the others and accepted the cross."[9] His effective if roundabout chiding of the knights' indifference in France was paralleled in Pales-

---

impression remains unsubstantiated. For a list of Dominicans who preached the crusade see Altaner, *Dominikanermissionen*, pp. 114–16; also H. Finke, *Ungedruckte Dominikanerbriefe des 13. Jahrhunderts* (Paderborn, 1891), nos. 21, 36, pp. 64, 73–74. For Franciscans see F. Delorme, "De praedicatione cruciatae saec. XIII per Fratres Minores," *Archivum Franciscanum Historicum* 9 (1916): 99–117; F. Cardini, "Gilberto di Tournai: Un francescano predicatore della crociata," *Studi Francescani* 72 (1975): 31–48. Gilbert's remarks in the tractate *Eruditio regum et principum*, addressed to Louis IX, should not be considered critical of the crusades in general. When he writes, "Non reducet ergo rex populum in Egiptum, equitatus numero sublevatus, quia non in multitudine armatorum, nec in virtute pugnantium datur victoria Christi militibus. Sed in Domino virtutum vincit et vincet si Christo inhaeserit exercitus christianus" (Guibert de Tournai, *Le traité Eruditio regum et principum*, ed. A. de Poorter [Louvain, 1914], p. 16), he repeats an idea that goes back to Bernard of Clairvaux, namely, that only a pious crusading army will be granted victory. See also Joachim of Fiore, Appendix 5/c below.

[8] A. van den Wyngaert, "Frère Guillaume de Cordelle, O.F.M.," *La France Franciscaine* 4 (1921): 52–71. For later examples see G. Golubovich, *Biblioteca bio-bibliografica della Terra Santa e dell'Oriente francescano*, 1st ser., 5 vols. (Quaracchi, 1906–27), 1:228, 271–75, 281.

[9] *Analecta Franciscana*, vol. 1 (Quaracchi, 1885), p. 416.

tine by an equally oblique but unmistakable thrust at the crusading leaders. As recorded by a continuator of William of Tyre's chronicle, Guillaume repeatedly concluded his sermons to the crusading host with the following exhortation: "For God's sake, good people, pray to Our Lord that He restore the hearts of the great men of this army! You may be sure that they lost them because of their sins, for so large a body of Christians as there is here should have been able to beat the infidels roundly if God had taken up their cause with favor."[10] Whether Guillaume should really be regarded as "un des plus nobles fils du Poverello d'Assisi"—the words are those of his twentieth-century Franciscan biographer—depends on one's perception of Francis.[11] But there remains little doubt that contemporaries were impressed with Guillaume's exercises in indirect denunciation.

In their simultaneous espousal of mission and crusade, the Mendicants resembled the Cistercians who labored from the late twelfth century onward for the conversion of the pagans of northeastern Europe while supporting crusades against them.[12] Some Cistercians personally engaged in both activities. Theoderich of Treyden, for instance, who began to preach to the Livonians sometime before 1191, led an armed expedition against a pagan stronghold in 1208 and ceased hostilities only after the defenders consented to receive baptism; in 1213 Theoderich asked for additional missionaries from the West, persuaded King Valdemar II of Denmark to lead an expedition against the pagan Estonians in 1218, and finally, one year later, joined the king's expedition, during which he met his death.[13] But Mendicant activity differed from that of the Cistercians in two main respects. First, while the Franciscans and Dominicans considered missionizing among the infidels one of their principal objectives, the Cistercian Order took a con-

[10] *Continuation de Guillaume de Tyr dite du manuscrit de Rothelin*, in RHC. HOcc. 2:550–51.

[11] Wyngaert, "Frère Guillaume," p. 64.

[12] For a short summary see A. Schneider, "Kolonisation und Mission im Osten," in A. Schneider et al., eds., *Die Cistercienser: Geschichte, Geist, Kunst* (Cologne, 1974), pp. 74–106. Later in the thirteenth century, the Mendicants took upon themselves the promotion of mission and crusade in northeastern Europe: see for example L. Pellegrini, "Le missioni francescane sotto Alessandro IV (1254–1261)," *Studi Francesani* 64 (1967): 93–102.

[13] *Heinrici Chronicon Livoniae*, XI, 6, XXII, 1, XXIII, 2, ed. and German trans. A. Bauer (Würzburg, 1959), pp. 76–78, 218–20, 231–33; English trans. J. Brundage (Madison, Wis., 1961), pp. 73–74, 166, 173–74; *Liv-, Est-und Curländisches Urkundenbuch*, ed. F. G. von Bunge, vol. 1, 2 (Reval, 1853; reprint Aalen, 1967), doc. 34, cols. 40–41. Cf. T. Grentrup, "Der Zisterzienser Dietrich in der altlivländischen Mission," *Zeitschrift für Missionswissenschaft* 40 (1956): 265–81. See also Roscher, *Papst Innocenz III*, pp. 198–207.

siderably more reserved stand; indeed, in 1212 Innocent III felt constrained to order the Cistercian chapter general to stop hindering the
White Monks the archbishop of Gnezno had found fit to preach the
Gospel to the Prussians.[14] Second, the Mendicant orders never advocated the forcible baptism of infidels. True, in 1233 Pierre de Sézanne,
a Dominican legate in Constantinople, ordered the imprisonment of a
Saracen who had denied Jesus' divinity. Pierre reasoned that since the
Saracens decapitate Christians who dare blaspheme Machomet, Christians ought by rights to punish Saracen blasphemers of God. After
two days of voluntary fasting in jail, the Saracen had a vision, which
Pierre promptly interpreted as proving the superiority of Christianity;
the Saracen was released from prison and subsequently asked for baptism.[15] But this isolated case of indirect and probably unwitting coercion at the hands of Mendicants starkly contrasts with the overt and
large-scale compulsion practiced by Cistercians like Berno, bishop of
Schwerin in the years 1160–90, who, unable to persuade the pagan
Rugians to convert, urged Christianized Slavic chieftains to impose on
them baptism by force of arms.[16]

It is noteworthy that the simultaneous upholding of mission and
crusade by the Mendicants was never criticized either from within the
orders or from without. A letter by the influential English Franciscan
Adam Marsh (d. 1258) suggests how the Mendicants might have perceived their concomitant espousal of these two approaches to the Saracens. In his letter Marsh pleads with the pope to support the plan of
Henry III of England to lead a crusade for the liberation of the Holy
Land, the exaltation of the Catholic faith, and the spread of the Chris-

---

[14] PL 216:668–70. The chapter general responded by empowering the abbot of
Morimond to act in a manner that would "both keep the supreme pontiff satisfied, and
yet not debilitate the rigor of our order": Philippi, *Preussisches Urkundenbuch* (chap. 2,
n. 102 above), no. 8, p. 6; *Statuta Capitulorum* (chap. 2, n. 16 above), c. 52, ed.
Canivez, 1:414. See also c. 22, 1:373.

[15] Gerardus de Fracheto, *Vitae fratrum ordinis praedicatorum*, ed. B. M. Reichert,
Monumenta Ordinis Fratrum Praedicatorum Historica, 1 (Rome and Stuttgart, 1897),
pp. 218–20; cf. N. Daniel, *Islam and the West*, p. 350, n. 19.

[16] Frederick I, who relates these facts while confirming in 1170 the boundaries of the
bishopric of Schwerin, adds that after the forcible baptism Berno "visited in a spirit of
lenience those who had been terrified by the rod." Significantly, Alexander III, confirming the boundaries eight years later, totally ignores the forced baptisms and mentions
only Berno's preaching: *Meklenburgisches Urkundenbuch*, vol. 1 (Schwerin, 1863), nos.
91, 124, pp. 85–87, 120–21; cf. *Helmoldi Cronica Slavorum*, in MGH Scr. rer. Germ.
32:212. The text of Frederick's confirmation is a forgery of about 1225–30, based on
an authentic original: H. Jordan, *Die Bistumsgründungen Heinrichs des Löwen*, Schriften
der MGH, 3 (Stuttgart, 1939), pp. 55–59. Helmold's account substantiates the relevant
passage of Frederick's confirmation.

tian religion. At the same time Marsh sternly warns against a suspension of missionary activity and an exclusive reliance on warfare, and quotes at length from Bernard of Clairvaux's *De consideratione* on the papal duty to further preaching to the infidels. The possibility of the preachers' death at the hands of the infidels should not deter Christians from assuming this mission, for from its very beginnings the Church has grown through crucifixion and martyrdom. Upon quoting once more from Bernard, Marsh concludes that the Church should wield its spiritual sword directly and its material one indirectly.[17] Utilizing the age-old simile of the two swords, Marsh thus portrays crusade and mission as two aspects of the same effort, and thereby supplies an explicit rationale for the Mendicant involvement in both. A few years earlier, in a bull of March 4, 1238, issued to the Franciscans and Dominicans, Gregory IX had declared that "it is no less commendable in the eyes of the Redeemer to convert the infidels to the faith by preaching the divine word than it is to subdue by arms the perfidy of the Saracens," and therefore went on to grant the friars who engaged in missionary work among the pagans of the Holy Land (that is, the Muslims) the same indulgence that the Fourth Lateran Council had given the crusaders.[18] Thus, just two decades after the pioneering endeavors of Jacques and Francis, missionary efforts among the Saracens of the Holy Land were accorded the same importance as the military attempts to wrest the country from them by military means. Adam Marsh went one step further, pointing out that these two activities were indispensable and complementary as well.

[17] Adam de Marisco, *Epistolae*, in *Monumenta Franciscana*, ed. J. S. Brewer, Rolls Series, 4, 1 (London, 1858), pp. 416, 431, 434, 436–37. The influence of *De consideratione*, III, 1, 3–4, IV, 3, 6–7, on Marsh seems to have escaped the notice of recent writers like L. Gatto, "I problemi della guerra e della pace nel pensiero politico di Pierre Dubois," *Bullettino dell'Istituto Italiano per il Medio Evo e Archivio Muratoriano* 71 (1959): 156–57; A. Rotzetter, "Kreuzzugskritik," p. 130; D. Bigalli, "Giudizio escatologico e tecnica di missione nei pensatori francescani: Ruggero Bacone," in *Espansione del Francescanesimo*, pp. 161–62. Interestingly enough, while Rotzetter presents Marsh as an indirect critic of the crusade, Norman Daniel (*Islam and the West*, p. 117) believes, on the basis of the same letter, that he "felt some need to apologise for the use of the material sword." Both interpretations seem to go beyond the text.

For Adam Marsh's biography see A. G. Little, "The Franciscan School at Oxford in the Thirteenth Century," *Archivum Franciscanum Historicum* 19 (1926): 831–37; D. A. Callus, "Robert Grosseteste as Scholar," in *Robert Grosseteste, Scholar and Bishop*, ed. D. A. Callus (Oxford, 1955), pp. 41–42; E. R. Daniel, *The Franciscan Concept*, pp. 56–57, with a short appraisal of his view on mission and crusade on p. 59. For a similar appraisal see Schwinges, *Kreuzzugsideologie*, p. 273.

[18] See Appendix 2/b.

Preferred Directions of Missionary Activity

In simultaneously preaching the crusade and working for Muslim conversion, the Mendicants followed in the footsteps of Jacques of Vitry rather than in those of Francis. Most of the Mendicant missionary efforts also resemble those of Jacques rather than those of Francis, since the majority of such activities among the Muslims were carried out in countries subjected to Catholic rule. Evidently the orders soon realized that the prospects of winning converts in Muslim-ruled countries were slight. Jacques himself reports that the Franciscans who attempted to preach in Saracen cities were given a hearing only as long as they expounded the tenets of Christianity; the moment they started to attack Machomet they were seized, flogged, and expelled.[19] Under the umbrella of Catholic rule, on the other hand, the friars could engage in missionary work without jeopardizing their safety. An anonymous account of the erection of the crusader castle at Safed in Upper Galilee in 1240 clearly expresses the awareness that Catholic military presence was the prerequisite for missionary activity among the Muslims. The author of this account, written between 1261 and 1266, exults that after the construction of the stronghold, it was possible to preach the Christian faith freely and publicly attack the blasphemy of Machomet throughout the entire district, "which was not feasible before the construction of Safed"; neither do the Saracens dare any longer to proclaim publicly the blasphemies of Machomet against the faith of Christ.[20]

In the western Mediterranean the friars fared no differently. Initial high hopes for success in the lands of Islam dwindled within a few decades. In 1225, Pope Honorius III authorized the Dominicans and Franciscans working in North Africa to preach the faith, convert infidels, and reconcile apostate Christians. Some thirty years later, in a six-point survey of Dominican work in Africa and Spain, Ramon of Pen-

---

[19] Hinnebusch, ed., *The Historia Occidentalis* (chap. 3, n. 80 above), p. 162. Martiniano Roncaglia believes that this Muslim reaction took place in crusader-ruled territory: M. Roncaglia, *St. Francis of Assisi and the Middle East*, trans. S. A. Janto, 3d ed. (Cairo, 1957), p. 73. But it is hardly conceivable that Catholic rulers would allow their Muslim subjects to treat the friars in this manner.

[20] R.B.C. Huygens, "Un nouveau texte du traité "De constructione castri Saphet," *Studi Medievali* 6.1 (1965): 386, idem, *De constructione castri Saphet: Construction et fonctions d'un chateau fort franc en Terre Sainte*, Koninklijke Nederlandse Akademie van Wetenschapen, Afdeling Letterkunde, Verhandelingen Nieuwe Reeks 111 (Amsterdam, 1981), p. 43. For the castle's importance after 1240 in general see Marie-Luise Favreau-Lilie, "Landesausbau und Burg während der Kreuzfahrerzeit: Ṣafad in Obergalilaea," *Zeitschrift des Deutschen Palästina-Vereins* 96 (1980): 82–87.

yaforte listed the friars' endeavors in reverse order, mentioning first their efforts among Christian mercenaries, apostates, and slaves living in Saracen lands, and only at the very end relating that leading Saracens, including the king of Tunis himself, were leaning toward Christianity, while many others, "especially in [Christian-ruled] Murcia," have already clandestinely or overtly converted. And out of the thirty-six answers on canon law issues that Ramon of Penyaforte sent to the Dominicans and Franciscans of Tunis, only one pertains to the Christianization of Saracens: It deals, significantly enough, with Christian captives clandestinely baptizing little Saracen infants.[21]

Reports of real or purported offers by North African rulers or their sons to convert to Christianity repeatedly stirred the imagination of thirteenth-century Catholics, but even the few actual cases of such conversion remained isolated acts.[22] "Vertical mission"—the Christianization of a tribe or a people that follows upon the conversion of the ruler—was simply not feasible in the realm of Islam. On the other hand, in the lands of Valencia and Murcia, brought under Catholic rule in the very years in which the Mendicant orders grew into major organizations, the friars soon engaged in missionary work among the subjected Muslims and succeeded in making numerous converts. Thus, despite the example of Francis and the willingness of some Mendicants—as well as Trinitarians and Mercedarians—to preach by word and martyrdom in the lands of Islam, the basic paradigm remained unaltered in East and West: The effectiveness of the Christian word remained almost exclusively limited to countries that had been conquered by the Christian sword.[23]

For the more venturesome Mendicants of the age, preaching to Muslims subjected to Catholic rule could hardly have competed with

[21] The bull of Honorius III is printed in *Bullarium Ordinis Fratrum Praedicatorum*, ed. T. Ripoll and A. Bremond, 8 vols. (Rome, 1729–49), 1:16. For Ramon of Penyaforte's six-point survey see Gerardus de Fracheto (n. 15 above), pp. 309–10; cf. J. M. Coll, "San Raymundo de Peñafort y las Misiones del Norte Africano en la Edad Media," *Missionalia Hispanica* 5 (1948): 424–26; N. Daniel, *Islam and the West*, p. 119. Ramon's thirty-six answers are printed in *Raymundiana* (n. 6 above), 2:29–37. Similarly, Jean Richard believes that the Franciscan activity in the crusader East was mainly directed at Christians: Richard, *La papauté*, p. 38.

[22] For a discussion of these offers to convert see Burns, "Christian-Islamic Confrontation," pp. 1391–94.

[23] The conversion of Valencia's Muslims has been the subject of several studies by Robert I. Burns; see especially his "Journey from Islam." For a succinct account of Trinitarian and Mercedarian activities in North Africa see R. Brunschvig, *La Berbérie orientale sous les Ḥafsides: Des origines à la fin du XVᵉ siècle*, vol. 1 (Paris, 1940), pp. 465–69.

missionary activity in the vast, recently established Mongol Empire: Here one could preach freely to large numbers of pagans and hope with some reason for the conversion of their rulers. It is symptomatic, from this point of view, that the Franciscan Giovanni of Montecorvino, who traveled all the way to Khanbaliq, the capital of Mongol China, in 1293, and spent some thirty years attempting to convert the infidel of the Far East, is not known ever to have approached the Muslim infidels of Lucera, who lived about sixty miles from his native Salerno. No other missionaries are known to have been active in Lucera; and it was not conversion to Christianity but the dispersal and enslavement ordered in 1300 by Charles II of Anjou that put an end to the existence of this last Muslim community on Italian soil.[24]

MISSION AND CONVERSION IN THE CRUSADING KINGDOM OF ACRE

Because of the direction of Mendicant evangelizing activities toward Muslims, Jews, and pagans of numerous countries, only a minority of the friars interested in missionary work made their way to the Syro-Palestinian littoral. For the missionary, as for the thirteenth-century crusader, the Holy Land was merely one of many potential areas of activity; but while the crusade to Jerusalem enjoyed at least chronological and legal precedence, the evangelizing activities of the Mendicants were from the very beginning aimed at all men. The number of Mendicants active in the Crusading Kingdom is unknown, but it is significant that at the 1279 election of the prior of the Dominican convent at Acre—probably the largest Dominican establishment in the crusader East—only thirteen friars cast their votes.[25] None of the friars who made their abode in the Crusading Kingdom produced anti-Islamic tracts of the kind written by the Spaniards Ramon Martí, Ra-

[24] On Giovanni of Montecorvino's origin from the province of Salerno see Richard, *La papauté*, p. 145. In 1233, Frederick II permitted the Dominicans to preach in Lucera; on whether they actually preached there, and on Ramon Llull's attempt to go there in 1294, see P. Egidi, *La colonia saracena di Lucera e la sua distruzione* (Naples, 1912), pp. 37, 134–35; idem, *Codice diplomatico dei Saraceni di Lucera* (Naples, 1917), docs. 98, 100, pp. 32–33.

[25] F. Balme, "La province dominicaine de Terre-Sainte de janvier 1277 à octobre 1280," *Revue de l'Orient latin* 1 (1893): 531–34, doc. 2. Only eight friars participated in the 1280 election of the prior of another Dominican convent, probably that of Tripoli (pp. 534–36, doc. 3). On the Dominican convent at Acre see F.-M. Abel, "Le couvent des Frères Prêcheurs à Saint-Jean d'Acre," *Revue biblique* 43 (1934): 265–84. On the history of the Dominican province of the Holy Land in general see Altaner, *Dominikanermissionen*, pp. 19–41.

mon Llull, or Pedro Pascual. The one polemical tractate expressly composed for the benefit of the Latins living in the crusader East was the *De rationibus fidei*, which Thomas Aquinas wrote, sometime between 1264 and 1268, at the request of a cantor of Antioch.[26] William of Tripoli, Dominican of the convent of Acre, wrote an account of Islam in 1273, but it was addressed to Latin Europeans, not to Saracens, and its purpose was informative rather than polemical.[27] And when in the early fourteenth century some Cypriots—possibly Mendicants—attempted to initiate a religious disputation with leading Muslim scholars of Syria, they resorted to plagiarizing an Arabic tract by a Melkite bishop of Sidon, a tract apparently so well known that their Muslim opponents immediately identified its true author.[28]

Since the laws of the Crusading Kingdom stipulated that the baptism of a Muslim slave entailed his liberation, crusader lords hampered Mendicant efforts at converting their servile Muslims. A similar situation obtained in Catalonia.[29] Ramon of Penyaforte—a Catalan and a great proponent of infidel conversion—was the first canon lawyer to come to grips with this problem; he laid down that baptism does not as a rule bestow free status, since slavery is manifestly legal. He recommended, however, that in countries where Christian slavery was unknown, masters should, "in remission of their sins," manumit their slaves or allow them to redeem themselves.[30] Thus he advocated a de facto preservation of the custom of freeing converted slaves even while

[26] *De rationibus fidei ad Cantorem Antiochenum*, in *Sancti Thomae de Aquino Opera omnia*, vol. 40, B (Rome, 1968). For a discussion, see M. Grabmann, "Die Schrift: De rationibus fidei contra Saracenos Graecos et Armenos ad Cantorem Antiochenum des heiligen Thomas von Aqui," *Scholastik: Vierteljahresschrift für Theologie und Philosophie* 17 (1942): 187–216. According to Grabmann (p. 188) Aquinas wrote this tractate after completing the *Summa contra Gentiles* before October 1264; on the other hand, Antioch was conquered by Sultan Baybars in 1268. See also J. Waltz, "Muḥammad and the Muslims in St. Thomas Aquinas," *Muslim World* 66 (1976): 81–95.

[27] William of Tripoli, *De statu Saracenorum et de Mahomete pseudopropheta*, in H. Prutz, *Kulturgeschichte der Kreuzzüge* (Berlin, 1883), pp. 575–98.

[28] The tract was sent to Muḥammad Ibn-abī-Ṭālib (d. 1327) and Abu'l ʿAbbās Aḥmad Ibn Taymīyya (d. 1328): Fritsch, *Islam*, pp. 28–34. Paul Khoury claims that the Melkite bishop, Paul of Antioch, lived in the twelfth century: P. Khoury, *Paul d'Antioche, évêque melkite de Sidon (XIIᵉ s.)* (Beirut, 1964). But, it is hardly probable that the tract was written in that century: A bishop of crusader-ruled Sidon would not need to travel to Europe to learn what the Franks thought of Islam.

[29] See chap. 2 above.

[30] Ramon of Penyaforte, *Summa de casibus poenitentiae*, 1.4.7 (Rome, 1603), p. 37; and see chap. 2, n. 100, 102 above. On the centrality and diffusion of Ramon's work see A. Teetaert, "La 'Summa de poenitentia' de S. Raymond de Penyafort," *Ephemerides theologicae Lovanienses* 5 (1928): 58; K. Pennington, "Summae on Raymond de Pennafort's 'Summa de casibus' in the Bayerische Staatsbibliothek, Munich," *Traditio* 27

he refused to consider it legally binding. Pope Gregory IX adopted a much more radical and unequivocal solution. Probably alerted by the Mendicants of the Holy Land,[31] he first came to deal with the issue in a letter sent on July 28, 1237, to Patriarch Gerold of Jerusalem and to the masters of the Hospitallers, the Templars, and the Teutonic Knights. It came to his attention, the pope writes, that very frequently "slaves" (*sclavi*) accept baptism with the sole intention of obtaining the status of freemen according to the custom of the land, only to later revert to their old unbelief. Because of such deceivers, slaves humbly asking for baptism have been refused. In addition, some masters, monastic masters included, prohibit their slaves from converting simply because they do not want to lose them. (It should be noted that, in this letter, Gregory's presentation of the masters' prohibition is milder than that of Jacques of Vitry. The basic objection to conversion Gregory quotes is the insincerity of the would-be converts; only then does he mention the masters' reluctance to lose their slaves, whereas Jacques presented this as their only reason.) To Gregory, denial of baptism to sincere petitioners was unthinkable; he therefore ruled that slaves who genuinely wish to be baptized must be allowed to do so. But he was evidently realistic enough to understand that as long as baptism were to entail liberation, masters would attempt to thwart his ruling. Hence he took the bold step of explicitly overruling the *consuetudo terre*, the custom of the land: Henceforth baptized slaves should remain in their servile status. Gregory demanded that converted slaves be allowed to attend church and receive the sacraments, and proposed that they be treated humanely, but basically he left their legal standing unaltered.[32] One may say that he knowingly sacrificed the amelioration of their temporal status as promised by local law in order to overcome the masters' opposition to the amelioration he considered paramount, namely, baptism.

Gregory's ruling went unheeded, and thus within less than a year he was constrained to write once more to the patriarch of Jerusalem. This time he dealt with the issue in more detail and with considerably more urgency. In the kingdom of Jerusalem, writes Gregory, several masters prohibit their slaves from listening to sermons and receiving baptism, "for they love possessions more than souls." (Jacques's old accusation is thus bluntly repeated, and nothing is said this time about

---

(1971): 471–80. On the dates of the work's two recensions see Kuttner, "Zur Entstehungsgeschichte" (chap. 3, n. 22 above), pp. 419–34.

[31] Cf. *Bullarium*, ed. Ripoll and Bremond (n. 21 above), 7:15.

[32] See Appendix 2/a.

the insincere motivation of prospective converts.) The pope remarks acidly that the patriarch took no action at all upon receipt of the former letter, and then expressly orders him and his suffragans to compel the masters to permit their slaves to attend sermons at least once a month as well as on the main holidays, and to receive baptism. He reiterates that the converts will not lose their servile status, and adds that the masters should permit them to attend confession and Divine Office on the principal holidays and Sundays, but significantly refrains from repeating the recommendation that they treat the converts humanely. Gregory concludes his letter with a stern call to implement his order in a manner that will confirm the patriarch and his suffragans as zealous seekers of souls and relieve the pope of the necessity of writing again on the matter.[33]

It is noteworthy that in his second letter Gregory mentions not only the prohibition of baptism but also that of attending sermons: Evidently the nature of the masters' doings had been brought to his attention in some detail. The date of the second letter, March 9, 1238, provides a clue to the identity of the pope's informants. Five days earlier, on March 4, Gregory had granted the crusader indulgence to the Franciscan and Dominican missionaries working for the conversion of the Saracens of the Holy Land.[34] Thus it is plausible to assume that the same friars who prompted the pope to express his appreciation of their missionary work in the Crusading Kingdom on March 4, also informed him of the persistence of the masters' opposition to their missionary work among the servile Muslim population, and requested him to intervene once more with the patriarch of Jerusalem. In any case, in his letter of March 9, Gregory took care not to antagonize the crusader lords excessively, and so limited his demands to what he must have considered the absolute minimum. This conclusion is borne out by a comparison of Gregory's letter to the patriarch, his legate in the Holy Land, and his letter to William of Modena, his legate in Livonia, which bears the same date, March 9, 1238, and prescribes the treatment of converted Livonian slaves.[35] The basic approach is the same: Whether in the eastern Mediterranean or along the Baltic, a slave who converts to Christianity remains in servitude. But while Gregory instructs his legate in Livonia to make the masters alleviate somewhat

---

[33] See Appendix 2/c.

[34] See Appendix 2/b.

[35] See Appendix 2/d. Cf. Blanke, "Die Entscheidungsjahre," p. 395. A day earlier the pope instructs his legate in Livonia to defend free neophytes from Teutonic Knights and other Christians who attempt to force them into servitude: *Liv-, Est- und Curländisches Urkundenbuch* (n. 13 above), doc. 158, cols. 203–4.

the burden of the converted slaves, he writes nothing of the kind to the patriarch; and while the converted slaves of Livonia were to be given *libera facultas* to go to church and hear Divine Office, their counterparts in the Holy Land were merely to be permitted to attend Divine Office on the main holidays and Sundays. Evidently at the Curia the Palestinian masters were considered more intractable.

Gregory's abrogation of the crusader *consuetudo* on the liberation of converted Muslim slaves was probably welcomed by Catalonian masters, who had to contend with a similar custom. In 1240 Christian masters of the recently conquered island of Majorca petitioned Gregory to permit Christians to continue to own their Saracen slaves even after these had been baptized, for it turned out that many slaves chose baptism with the intent of escaping slavery and later returned to their old ways, "not without grave damage to the believers."[36] One almost suspects that the Majorcan petitioners were aware of Gregory's first letter to the patriarch of Jerusalem and formulated their plea accordingly. In his reply of January 26, 1240, Gregory empowered the bishop of Majorca to decide in the matter according to his appraisal of the situation; three months later, on April 24, 1240, Gregory took a further step, authorizing the bishop to permit the masters to sell their baptized slaves.[37] It would not be surprising to learn that Gregory had sent a similar instruction to Catalonia proper, but no such directive has been uncovered to date. There can be little doubt, however, that at both ends of the Mediterranean, old local custom or law gave way to the new papal ruling. Writing from Cyprus to Pope Innocent IV in 1249, the papal legate Odo of Châteauroux reports that on Cyprus he had catechized fifty-seven captured Saracens who asked for baptism even though they were "expressly told" that the sacrament would not entail their liberation.[38] In 1272, the laws of Tortosa, Catalonia, stipulated that if a Saracen slave proved the sincerity of his intentions by staying in a church for three days, he must be baptized even if his

---

[36] See Appendix 2/e. Cf. Burns, "Journey from Islam," p. 342.

[37] See Appendix 2/f. Consequently, converted slaves had to redeem themselves in order to attain free status. The earliest deed of redemption dates from April 29, 1241: Elena Lourie, "Free Moslems in the Balearics under Christian Rule in the Thirteenth Century," *Speculum* 45 (1970): 648, n. 96.

[38] "die vero Epiphanie catechizavi quinquaginta VII saracenos captivos qui licet deberent nullam libertatem assequi, prout illis expresse dictum est, tamen instanter petebant fidei sacramentum. Et postquam ex illis triginta manu propria baptizavi. . . ." L. d'Achéry, *Spicilegium sive collectio veterum aliquot scriptorum*, ed. E. Baluze, vol. 3 (Paris, 1723), p. 627. Comte Beugnot, quoting this passage in a note to his edition of the crusader laws (RHC. Lois 2:138, n. b), omitted the word "captivos," thereby causing some difficulty to later writers on the subject.

master had not given his consent; the act of baptism did not, however, alter the neophyte's servile condition.[39] Notarial acts drawn up in Barcelona and elsewhere in Catalonia from the latter part of the thirteenth century onward leave no doubt that in practice, too, a slave's conversion no longer automatically brought about liberation.[40]

Issued too late to be included in the Decretals, Gregory's bulls nevertheless seem to have influenced decretalist thinking on the issue. Both Goffredus of Trani and Hostiensis, who quote almost verbatim Ramon of Penyaforte's statement that a converted slave remains in his servile condition, pass over the recommendation to manumit the convert wherever local custom so prescribes.[41] Hostiensis adds, quite in line with Gregory's letter to Acre in 1237 and to Livonia in 1238, that the master should not vent his anger on his converted slave as he had before baptism, but should treat him more mildly and benignly than the non-Christian slaves.[42] Hostiensis' formulation influenced Arnau of Villanova, whose memorandum in turn exerted a decisive influence on Frederick III of Sicily. And so it came about that the laws of Aragonese Sicily, promulgated on November 25, 1310, at Messina, stipulate that a master must permit his Saracen slaves to receive baptism, after which the master should not vent his anger on them but rather punish them "justly, mildly, and benignly."[43] The laws of 1310

[39] Verlinden, L'esclavage, 1:292, n. 170. For a similar formulation see canon 24 of the Council of Tarragona, 1329, in Mansi, Concilia, 25:846. See also Jaume I's 1268 charter for Valencia, discussed by Burns, "Journey from Islam," pp. 339–40.

[40] Verlinden, 1:303, 363–67, 456–58. Charles II of Anjou also seems to have known the papal ruling. Asked in 1301 what should be done with Luceran Saracens who hastened to receive baptism after the destruction of their city but before their arrest, he answered, "Cum baptismi susceptio servo non tribuat libertatem, id de batizatis [sic] ipsis curetis facere quod vobis de aliis est iniunctum." Egidi, Codice diplomatico (n. 24 above), doc. 497 of April 17, 1301, p. 246; cf. doc. 460 of February 11, 1301, p. 217, and Egidi, Colonia, pp. 137–38.

[41] Goffredus Tranensis, Summa super titulis decretalium, 5.5.8 (Lyons, 1519), p. 206c; Hostiensis, Summa Aurea, De servis Iudeorum et Saracenorum, no. 5 (Venice, 1574), col. 1528.

[42] "puto tamen quod non est ita desaeviendum in eo sicut prius immo inter alios servos suos non christianos est tractandus leviter et benigne." (The printed edition has leniter, but Clm 14006, fol. 170vb, and Clm 15707, fol. 240va, both of the fourteenth century, have leviter.)

[43] "nullis licere providimus Christiana mancipia vulneribus aut flagellis afficere . . . aut in ea aliquatenus insevire. . . . Eos tamen a dominis castigari permittimus, cum culpa processerit et christiani sint, iuste, leviter et benigne." H. Finke, Acta Aragonensia, vol. 2 (Berlin, 1908), no. 438, p. 697; Verlinden, 2:194, chap. 62. Sending the constitutions of 1310 to his brother, Jaume II of Aragon, Frederick of Sicily announces that they were taken from a tractate of Arnau of Villanova. Finke (p. 695, n. 1), who was not aware of Hostiensis' influence writes that this tract must have been the one opening

also prescribe the baptism of offspring born to Saracen slaves.[44] Evidently Christianization unprejudicial to property rights was a solution that could become royal policy.

In the crusader East, opposition to the conversion of Muslim slaves did not collapse in the wake of Gregory's ruling. Masters continued to impede the instruction and the baptism of their slaves and captives, and therefore Odo of Châteauroux, the papal legate, saw fit to promulgate in 1253 at Jaffa a statute threatening all offenders with excommunication. At the same time he reiterated that conversion would not affect at all the slave's servile status. Since Odo ordered that the statute be proclaimed in the future twice a year in all the churches of the crusader East as well as in Cyprus, he evidently did not envisage prompt compliance.[45]

In crusader Acre there seems to have prevailed a lukewarm attitude toward the conversion of lower-class Muslims in general. On July 26, 1264, Pope Urban IV wrote the patriarch of Jerusalem, Guillaume of Agen, that it had been brought to his attention that poor Saracens and Jews who come to Acre with the intention of becoming Christian and are unable to support themselves there during their period of instruction in the faith because of their destitution tend to give up their wish to be baptized and revert to their old errors. Though the papal letter does not state so expressly, it is evident that the inhabitants of Acre did not consider it their duty to support such prospective converts. The pope, however, orders the patriarch to impose on the churches and monasteries of Acre the duty of providing sustenance to such catechumens "at least for a few days."[46] Several days may have been regarded as a short period for instruction in Christianity, yet Urban, who had been patriarch of Jerusalem before his election to the papacy, must have known the limits of the charitableness of Acre's clergymen and monks. The fact that two converts from Bethlehem, unable to sustain themselves in the Crusading Kingdom, had to travel all the

---

with the words "Seynor, vos sots tenguts," published by M. Menendez Pelayo, *História de los heterodoxos españoles*, vol. 1 (Madrid, 1880), pp. 745ff. But the relevant passage of that tract (p. 749) does not contain the expressions that appear in Hostiensis and in the constitutions of 1310, and therefore Finke's assumption must be discarded.

[44] Finke, p. 697; Verlinden, 2:194–95, chap. 64. See also the letter of 1327 by Philip of Majorca, which includes an order to all confessors to induce their penitents to baptize the children of their slaves, with the act of baptism not affecting the children's personal status: Verlinden, 1:458.

[45] Mansi, *Concilia*, 26:317–18. As late as 1298 a synod of Nicosia threatened with excommunication "illos omnes, qui non permittunt sclavos, sive sclavas, sine suo prejudicio baptizari volentes": ibid., col. 350.

[46] See Appendix 3.

way to Orvieto to obtain a letter from Urban IV ordering the patriarch
of Jerusalem to make some Palestinian monastery supply the converts'
livelihood also suggests that the clergy of the kingdom was less than
enthusiastic about welcoming destitute converts.[47] Incidentally, Urban
himself exhibits more concern for prominent than for penniless converts from Islam: While he orders that the poor Saracens who come
to Acre be given sustenance "at least for a few days," and the destitute
converts from Bethlehem be provided with the necessaries of life, he
instructs the Benedictine and Cluniac monasteries of the province of
Reims to provide one Petrus Alfonsus, converted son of a sultan of
Iconium, with the considerable sum of one hundred *livres parisis* a year
for the rest of his life.[48]

Nevertheless, Saracen conversion continued to occur at the lower
levels of crusader society. A testament drawn up at Acre on September
16, 1264, affords a unique glimpse of a household in that time.[49] The
testator, Saliba—his name marks him as an Oriental Christian—is a
burgess of Acre and a confrere of the Order of the Hospital; his testament has been preserved in the archive of the order because he bequeathed much of his property to it. In the will he leaves forty besants
to Maria, his *baptizata*, that is, his converted slave. (Saliba must have
been quite fond of her, for he bequeathed his nephews only twenty
besants.) He also manumits his male slave Amet (= Aḥmad) and his
female slave Sofia, and orders them to be Christians.[50] One of the
witnesses to the testament is Marinetus, a *baptizatus* of the testator;
this convert must have been manumitted by Saliba in the past, for
otherwise he would not have been able to act as a witness. In sum,
Saliba is surrounded by two converts and two future converts. One
can only wonder how many other converts may have been mentioned
in the no-longer-extant cartularies of Acre's notaries.

The conversion of a Muslim of more elevated social standing is alluded to in a recently discovered Arabic-French glossary composed in
the Levant toward the end of the thirteenth century. "Mestre Jaques
Sarasin le ypoticaires, noveau crestien," one of the two men who col-

[47] *Reg. Urbain IV*, no. 2518.

[48] Ibid., no. 2706 (July 7, 1264).

[49] Delaville Le Roulx, ed., *Cartulaire général* (chap. 2, n. 103 above), 3:91–92, doc.
3105.

[50] Ibid., p. 92: "et jubeo dictos Ametum et Sofiam Christianos esse." This may be
compared with a 1074 will of Ponce, precentor of the church of Barcelona, which states:
"Et jubeo ut faciant babtizare sarracenum meum et sarracenam meam, propter remedium animae meae." Quoted by Verlinden, 1:133, n. 82. (It is plausible to assume that,
in conformity with Catalonian custom, Ponce's slaves were liberated upon baptism; the
same may be assumed about the *Sarracenae* whose baptism is stipulated in the 1030 will
of a daughter of Borrell II, count of Barcelona: ibid., p. 132, n. 79.)

laborated in writing this glossary, was evidently a converted Muslim; his manner of transliterating the Arabic terms into the Roman alphabet suggests that he was of Egyptian origin.[51] The conversion of married Muslims, which had occupied Innocent III back in 1201, must also have continued. When Cardinal Simon of St. Caecilia, papal legate to the Crusading Kingdom, was about to sail east in 1274, Pope Gregory X empowered him to allow converts to retain the wives they had married before conversion, even though they were related to them in the third degree.[52] The fact that the pope saw fit to invest his legate with this authority suggests that such conversions continued to take place; but the authorization was legally superfluous, since Innocent III, in the 1201 bull that made its way into the Decretals, had already allowed converts to retain wives related to them not only in the third but even in the second degree.

Treaties between the Mamelukes and the crusaders drawn up between 1267 and 1283 reveal a different type of convert: fugitives from the sultanate who became Christians upon reaching the rump kingdom of Acre, or fugitives from the kingdom who became Muslims after arriving in the lands of the sultan.[53] Two of the treaties allow fugitive converted slaves to stay put; another stipulates the return even of those slaves who sought sanctuary in a church. But the fact that the issue is discussed time and again suggests that such conversions were not infrequent. Indeed, the chroniclers Ibn al-Furāt and al-Maqrīzī relate that in A.H. 667 (A.D. 1268–69), four Mamelukes of Sultan Baybars fled to Acre and became Christian. Ibn al-Furāt reports also that a Muslim girl who had been ransomed by her mother from imprisonment in crusader Tyre was seized in the vicinity of Safed by a band of Christians sent after her from Tyre, and then forced to become Christian. "When the sultan heard this story," he writes, "his anger was stirred in the cause of Almighty God and he wrote demanding the girl. The Franks, however, excused themselves (from complying) on the ground that she had become a Christian." Ibn al-Furāt adds that about the

[51] The text has been edited by G. Ineichen, "Il glossario arabo-francese di messer Guglielmo e maestro Giacomo," *Atti dell'Istituto Veneto di scienze, lettere ed arti: Classe di scienze morali, lettere ed arti* 130 (1971–72): 353–407; the names of the authors appear on p. 363.

[52] *Reg. Grégoire X*, no. 565 (September 22, 1274). The various powers invested in Simon permit the reconstruction of the role of a late thirteenth-century legate to the crusader East.

[53] The treatment of fugitives in the treaties is discussed by P. M. Holt, "Qalawūn's Treaty with Acre in 1283," *English Historical Review* 91 (1976): 810–11; see also Prawer, *Crusader Institutions*, p. 206. For the relevant clause of the treaty of 1283—taken from Ibn al-Furāt—see E. Quatremère, *Histoire des sultans mamlouks par Makrizi*, vol. 2, 1 (Paris, 1842), pp. 181–82 (text), 230 (translation).

same time, a Mameluke fled to Tyre, was immediately made to become a Christian, and given protection by the lord of the city.[54] Al-Maqrīzī, who presents a variant version of the story of the abducted Muslim girl, observes that the Franks frequently used to coerce Muslims to convert.[55] The statement does not necessarily conflict with the papal letters mentioning opposition and indifference to Saracen conversion, since al-Maqrīzī apparently refers to the Christianization of relatively prominent Muslims, not of slaves or paupers.

The sources do not specify to what extent these diverse conversions were due to Mendicant efforts. The Dominican William of Tripoli, writing in 1273, states that he baptized more than one thousand Saracens, a declaration usually discounted as an outrageous exaggeration.[56] Yet when the baptism-seeking slaves and paupers of the papal bulls and the fugitives of the crusader-Mameluke treaties are taken into account, William's figure may well fall within the range of the normal medieval unconcern for numerical exactitude.[57] Indeed one might speculate, against the background of the various notices about Muslim conversion, that if the Crusading Kingdom had continued to exist, the number of converts might steadily have mounted and the Muslim population constantly dwindled, as in the other Muslim regions that came under permanent Catholic rule.

DISILLUSION WITH THE PROSPECTS OF MISSIONIZING, GROWING EMPHASIS ON THE CRUSADE

The fact that many Mendicants supported, preached, and participated in the crusades must not have prevented their contemporaries from musing whether Mendicant missionizing might provide the solution

[54] U. Lyons and M. C. Lyons, *Ayyubids, Mamlukes, and Crusaders: Selections from the Tārīkh al-Duwal wa'l-Mulūk of Ibn al-Furāt*, Historical Introduction by J.S.C. Riley-Smith, 2 vols. (Cambridge, 1971), 1:168–69 (text), 2:132–33 (translation); Quatremère, *Histoire*, vol. 1, 2 (Paris, 1840), pp. 68–69.

[55] Observation mentioned by M. H. Chéhab, *Tyr à l'époque des croisades*, vol. 1 (Paris, 1975), p. 536, who refers to a Paris manuscript (BN ar. 1726, p. 177) of al-Maqrīzī's work, in which the observation and the story about the abducted Muslim girl follow the account about the four Mamelukes.

[56] William of Tripoli, *De statu Saracenorum* (n. 27 above), p. 598.

[57] The possibility that William's converts were slaves and prisoners of war has been suggested by J. Henninger, "Sur la contribution des missionnaires à la connaissance de l'Islam, surtout pendant le moyen âge," *Neue Zeitschrift für Missionswissenschaft* 9 (1953): 176. The fourth canon of the Synod of Nicosia, 1298, mentions among other *majora peccata* the cases of "coiens cum Iudea vel Saracena, coiens cum ea quam baptizavit": Mansi, *Concilia*, 26:349. There are indications that the canon reflects legislation passed in the Crusading Kingdom of Jerusalem.

to the Saracen problem and thereby render superfluous the crusades, which in any case repeatedly ended in failure. This might have been the view of Joachite Franciscans, who identified Francis and Dominic with the *viri religiosi* who, according to Joachim, would speedily convert all infidels.[58] The view certainly appealed to those Christians who objected in principle to all bloodshed, and probably also to laymen in search of a high-minded reason for dodging a crusade. Thus it is possible that, for a while, Mendicant missionary activities somewhat diminished the appeal of the crusade.

But since it soon transpired that Mendicant missionizing in Muslim countries was much more conducive to filling heaven with Christian martyrs than the earth with Muslim converts, and that preaching stood a chance of success only among Muslims subjected to Christian rule, practical men could not regard this Mendicant activity as a viable solution to the Muslim threat to the existence of the rump Crusading Kingdom. Leading Mendicants did indeed draw this conclusion, offering the crusade as the only adequate solution. Humbert of Romans, who in 1255 as master general of the Dominican Order had presented Saracen conversion as one of the order's aims and called on the friars to study Arabic and leave for the Dominican province of the Holy Land, some twenty years later urged the launching of a new crusade.[59] With resignation he remarked that Saracens, unlike other persecutors of the Church, have almost never converted to Christianity, "unless perhaps a few captives, and this rarely," while at the same time many Christians have accepted and are accepting the Saracens' religion.[60]

---

[58] See for instance Fiorella Simoni, "Il 'Super Hieremiam' e il gioachimismo francescano," *Bullettino dell'Istituto Storico Italiano per il Medio Evo e Archivio Muratoriano* 82 (1970): 13–46, esp. p. 40; the passage from Olivi's *Lectura super Apocalypsim*, in R. Manselli, "La Terza Età, *Babylon* e l'Anticristo mistico," ibid., pp. 72–74; and, in general, E. R. Daniel, *The Franciscan Concept*, chap. 5.

[59] B. M. Reichert, ed., *Litterae encyclicae magistrorum generalium Ordinis Praedicatorum, 1233–1376*, Monumenta Ordinis Fratrum Praedicatorum Historica, 5 (Rome and Stuttgart, 1900), pp. 18–20; Humbertus de Romanis, *De vita regulari*, ed. J. J. Berthier, vol. 2 (Rome, 1889), pp. 492–93.

[60] Humbertus de Romanis, *Opusculum tripartitum* (chap. 2, n. 79 above), I, 6, p. 188. Humbert, like many before him, believes that it is the undemanding nature of Islam that makes it attractive to Christians. For other references to Christian conversion to Islam see for instance Ch.-E. Dufourcq, *L'Espagne catalane et le Maghrib aux XIIIᵉ et XIVᵉ siècles* (Paris, 1965), p. 108; R. Scholz, ed., *Unbekannte kirchenpolitische Streitschriften aus der Zeit Ludwigs des Bayern (1327–1354): Analysen und Texte*, vol. 2 (Rome, 1914), pp. 493, 510; *Bullarium*, ed. Ripoll and Bremond (n. 21 above), 2:275; Brunschvig, *Berbérie*, 1:469–72. Pedro Pascual, executed by the Muslims of Granada in 1300, wrote his main works with the aim of preventing Christians living under Muslim rule from converting to Islam: *Obras de S. Pedro Pascual, mártir, obispo de Jaen y religioso*

"The Saracens," writes Humbert, "close for themselves the way of preaching, for according to their law they decapitate everybody who wishes to preach anything against the law or sect of Mahumet."[61] (The decapitation of two Dominicans in the Holy Land during the period in which Humbert served as master general, and whom he possibly had sent there as missionaries, must have weighed heavily upon him.)[62] And Fidenzio of Padua, who served as vicar of the Franciscan province of the Holy Land in the 1260s, spent many years in the Levant, and wrote a tract on the recovery of the Holy Land by military means a few months before the fall of Acre in May 1291, observed in words strikingly similar to those of Humbert that the Saracens "had closed off for themselves the way of salvation; they do not want to hear anything that seems to be contrary to the sayings of their prophet Machometh, and should someone say anything contrary, he is killed without mercy."[63] Thus the Dominican Humbert and the Franciscan Fidenzio leave no doubt that it is the Muslim prohibition of Christian preaching that renders their peaceful evangelization impossible. But both of them are also vaguely aware—not unlike Jacques of Vitry two generations earlier—of Islam's positive hold over its believers.[64]

While Mendicant preaching to the unsubjected Muslims bore mea-

---

de la Merced, ed. and Latin trans. P. Armengol Valenzuela, 4 vols. (Rome, 1906–8), 3:91, 4:2–3.

[61] "Sed Saraceni excluserunt a se viam praedicationis, quia secundum legem suam decapitant omnem hominem, qui eis vellet aliquid praedicare contra Mahumeti legem vel sectam." Humbertus de Romanis, Opusculum tripartitum, I, 20, p. 200.

[62] Humbert announced at the general chapter of Paris in 1256 that "duo [fratres] a Saracenis decapitati sunt in Terra Sancta": Reichert, ed., Litterae, p. 42. The circumstances under which these friars found their death remain unknown. In 1257 Alexander IV mentions that several friars who extended spiritual help to the defenders of the Crusading Kingdom were executed by the enemy: Golubovich, Biblioteca, 2:391.

It should be noted that Humbert repeatedly speaks of the "decapitation" of those who dare to attack Mahumet's law. In addition to the passage of the Opusculum tripartitum quoted in the previous note, see also the following two sentences in his De predicatione crucis (Nürnberg, [1490?]; I am using the copy of the Munich Staatsbibliothek): "saraceni vero decapitant omnes qui vellent eos de errore suo dimittendo informare" (c. 8); "ipsi enim saraceni sic zelant pro lege sua quod sine misericordia decapitant omnem hominem ubicunque habent potestatem, qui contra legem suam predicat" (c. 12).

[63] "Stoliditas in hoc in Saracenos esse comprobatur, quia ipsi precluserunt sibi viam salutis. Nichil enim audire volunt, quod dictis prophete sui Machometh videatur esse contrarium, et si quis aliquid contrarium dixerit, sine misericordia occiditur." Fidenzio of Padua, Liber recuperationis Terre Sancte, I, 20, in Golubovich, Biblioteca (n. 8 above), 2:23. Fidenzio also mentions conversions to Islam (cc. 15, 17, pp. 21–22).

[64] Humbertus de Romanis, Opusculum tripartitum, I, 6, p. 188; Fidenzio of Padua, Liber recuperationis Terre Sancte, I, 15–16, 20; II, 47, in Golubovich, Biblioteca, 2:21–23, 41. See also Ricoldo da Monte Croce, Liber Peregrinacionis (n. 4 above), pp. 131–33.

ger results and Mendicant participation in propagating the crusade became ever more noticeable, some friars went so far as to portray Francis of Assisi himself as an ardent and radical supporter of crusading. A Franciscan collection of *exempla* dating from the second half of the thirteenth century includes a story purportedly originating with the friar who accompanied Francis on his way to the sultan and related by a minister general of the Franciscan Order, presumably Bonaventure. According to this story, the sultan asked Francis why the Christians, taught by Christ's Gospel not to render evil by evil, were invading his lands. The question resembles the one posed, according to Caffaro, by the Muslims of Caesarea, which, under a different guise, occurs elsewhere. But it is the answer attributed to Francis that is remarkable. "You do not seem to have read the entire Gospel of Christ our Lord," Francis retorts. "For elsewhere He says, 'If your eye offends you, pluck it out and fling it away from you, etc.,' whereby He wanted to teach us that no man, even if he were so dear to us as the eye in our head, should be so dear or so close to us that we should not sever, cast forth, and utterly root him out if he tries to turn us aside from the faith and love of our God. This is the reason why Christians justly invade you and the land you have occupied, for you blaspheme the name of Christ and turn aside from his worship whomever you can. But if you were willing to recognize, acknowledge, and worship the Creator and Redeemer, the Christians would love you almost as themselves."[65] This is an extreme formulation indeed. Unlike Caffaro's patriarch at Caesarea, Francis is not presented as stressing the Christians' historical right to the Holy Land (although the statement that the Saracens had "occupied" the land vaguely echoes that argument). Unlike Bernard of Clairvaux, Oliver of Cologne, and many others, the Francis of the *exemplum* does not uphold the crusade as an act of legitimate defense. Neither does he underline, as did Oliver of Cologne, the Muslim unwillingness to admit Christian preachers. For him, the crusade is a just act of retribution, deduced from the Gospel itself, for the Saracens' blasphemies against Christ and their efforts to enlarge their numbers at the expense of Christendom. In other words, the very existence of Islam as a religion denying Jesus' divinity and aiming at universal adherence justifies Christian military expeditions against its believers.[66]

[65] See Appendix 4/g. Golubovich (*Biblioteca*, 1:37) rightly deduced from the context that Bonaventure is probably the *generalis minister* who purportedly told the story.

[66] For the Muslim denial of Jesus' divinity being perceived by Christians as blasphemy see, for example, the account about the 1233 clash between Pierre de Sézanne and the Saracen at Constantinople: "cum blasphemasset dominum Ihesum Christum dicens, purum hominem esse, non Deum." Gerardus de Fracheto, *Vitae fratrum* (n. 15 above), p. 218.

The story, surviving in only a single manuscript, does not seem to have reached a wide audience. But that it could have been told at all, and its transmission attributed to a Franciscan minister general, suggests the extent to which unreserved support of the crusade had become normative in the order. It also suggests that if indeed the real-life Francis had ever dissociated himself from the crusades, this dissociation must have been forgotten within a relatively short time.

FIVE

A Contested Linkage: Crusading for the Advancement of Missions

BY 1240 several linkages between crusade and conversion were on record. At one extreme, the enforced Christianization of Saracens was openly presented, for instance, by the French knights at Constantinople in 1147, as a central aim of the crusade. More moderately, Jacques of Vitry hoped at one point that the arrival of the crusader army would permit conversion-minded Saracens to overcome their fears and accept baptism. Oliver of Cologne justified the crusade as an act of legitimate defense, made inevitable by the Saracen prohibition of Christian preaching. Gregory IX, by granting the crusader indulgence to the Mendicant missionaries of the Holy Land, accorded the same importance to crusade and mission, without spelling out his view on the relationship between the two. At the other extreme there were voices, the clearest of which was Ralph Niger's, claiming that the crusade, a justifiable war of defense, must not aim at enforced Christianization.

THE INNOCENTIAN CONCEPTION AND THE CRUSADES OF LOUIS IX

It fell to Pope Innocent IV, the erstwhile canon lawyer Sinibaldo dei Fieschi, to formulate the linkage between Christian warfare and infidel conversion that would become normative. Discussing papal world dominion Innocent argues that the pope as God's vicar on earth has jurisdiction over Christians as well as infidels. Consequently the pope may punish not only a Christian for contravening the law of the Gospel but also a pagan for transgressing the law of nature and a Jew for deviating from the law of Moses or inventing heresies against it.[1] Further, though infidels must not be coerced into accepting the Christian faith, the pope may nevertheless order them to admit preachers of the Gospel into their lands. Should they prohibit the preachers from exercising their office, they ought to be coerced by the secular arm, act-

---

[1] Innocent IV, *Apparatus super quinque libros Decretalium*, to X 3.34.8, par. 5. Passage edited and discussed in my "Canon Law and the Burning of the Talmud," *Bulletin of Medieval Canon Law* NS 9 (1979): 79–82.

ing at the pope's behest.[2] Thus, forcible conversion is inadmissible, but warfare aimed at opening the way for Christian preachers is lawful if papally authorized.[3] Innocent does not spell out whether participants in such warfare are to enjoy the crusader indulgence; indeed, he mentions the granting of indulgences only to Christians fighting for the defense or recovery of the Holy Land.[4] But since by Innocent's day the crusader indulgence had been repeatedly conceded to warriors engaged in various theaters, and even to those who undertook, on papal orders, to fight against heretics or lay opponents of the papacy within Catholic Europe—in 1246 Innocent himself was to grant that indulgence to his supporters in the struggle with Frederick II—it stands to reason that he intended to confer the crusader indulgence on Christians struggling to open infidel countries to Catholic preaching.

Innocent's linkage was foreshadowed by Oliver of Cologne's formulation in the letter to Sultan al-Kāmil (as Oliver's formulation was foreshadowed in turn by those of Ermold the Black in the ninth century and of Bernard of Clairvaux in the twelfth). But while Oliver's reference to the Saracen unwillingness to admit Christian preachers is still intertwined with his arguments about the legitimacy of defensive warfare and the Christians' historic title to the Holy Land, in Innocent's view the infidels' unwillingness to admit preachers becomes an *independent* justification for waging war against them. The struggle for the Holy Land, on the other hand, is justified solely by the Christian right to it. Innocent must have been aware that in a real-life situation these two justifications of Christian warfare could converge: For instance, an attack against Egypt could have constituted both a blow against the sultan's unlawful occupation of a large part of the Holy

[2] See Appendix 4/e. Innocent does not refer to C.23 q.4 c.49, possibly because the otherwise similar warfare praised there by Gregory I was not papally initiated.

[3] In an addition to the *Apparatus* that appears in the Frankfurt 1570 edition but not in Vat. lat. 1443, Clm 6350 and Clm 15704, or in the edition of Lyons 1525, it is argued that the *compelle intrare* of the Gospel should not be interpreted as calling for the forcible Christianization of infidels; consequently one should not wage war against the Saracens with the purpose of Christianizing them ("Ex his ergo apparet Sarracenis, ut fiant Christiani, bellum indicendum non esse"). Nevertheless, war against Saracens who occupy the Holy Land may be waged by the Church or by any Christian prince. *Apparatus*, to X 3.42.4, ad v. *compellantur* (Frankfurt, 1570), p. 456b. In Urb. lat. 157, an important manuscript of the *Apparatus* with additions of Innocent as well as of others in the margins, the beginning of the addition in question appears on fol. 174; the end and presumably the *siglum* too were written on a folio no longer extant. It is to be hoped that Martin Bertram's ongoing research into the manuscript tradition of the *Apparatus* will reveal whether this addition goes back to Innocent himself.

[4] *Apparatus*, to X 3.34.8, par. 1 and 7, pp. 429d and 430b of the Frankfurt 1570 edition.

Land and an act of retaliation against his hindrance of Catholic preaching. But Innocent does not mention this possibility, since his discussion of legitimate Christian warfare against infidels (which includes categories other than the two mentioned above) is evidently aimed at laying bare fundamental distinctions rather than enumerating actual cases.[5]

Innocent's linkage is yet another instance of canonistic harmony arising from dissonance, if one may borrow Stephan Kuttner's apposite phrase. Forcible conversion ran counter to the basic maxim that a man must adopt the Christian faith of his free will; yet warfare aimed at spreading the faith was a part of Christian reality. By unequivocally rejecting forcible conversion while at the same time endorsing the forcible opening of an infidel country to Catholic preachers, Innocent largely reconciled the fundamental principle of free choice with the popularly evolved notion of Christianization as one of the goals of crusading. In formulating his solution, Innocent was also probably reacting to the Muslim prohibition of Christian preaching. Though he speaks of non-admittance of preachers to infidel countries in general, he must have had in mind mainly Saracen infidels, for he goes on to deal with the quite hypothetical question of whether the pope should insist equally on the right of preachers of "the law of Machomet" to enter Christian lands. Innocent's answer is clear-cut, though not exactly compelling from the legal point of view: "No," he writes, "for we must not equate them with us, as they are in error and we on the way of truth."[6] Evidently the campaign he endorses for free speech is a campaign for Christian free speech only.

Did Innocent's notion of warfare waged to force open the way for missionaries exert some influence on subsequent crusading activity? To answer this question, we must consider the two crusades that postdate the publication of Innocent's *Apparatus* shortly after 1245, namely, Louis IX's expeditions to the Orient in 1248–54 and to Tunis in 1270.

Before Louis left for the Orient, an anonymous poet wrote that the king "will be able to conquer Romania easily, baptize the sultan of Turkey, and thereby free the world."[7] After the crusade ended in de-

---

[5] On this discussion about warfare see Condorelli, *I fondamenti*, pp. 121–29; J. Muldoon, "*Extra Ecclesiam non est imperium*: The Canonists and the Legitimacy of Secular Power," *Studia Gratiana* 9 (1966): 572–74; Russell, *The Just War*, pp. 199–201; Brundage, "Holy War," pp. 120–22; and, most recently, Muldoon, *Popes, Lawyers, and Infidels*, pp. 5–15.

[6] See Appendix 4/e.

[7] "Un serventois, plait de deduit, de joie," in J. Bédier and P. Aubry, ed., *Les chansons de croisade avec leur mélodies* (Paris, 1909; reprint, Geneva, 1974), p. 253. (My attention

feat and captivity, Matthew Paris, the contemporary chronicler of St. Albans, has the sultan ask the captive Louis why he looks dejected; the king answers that he is disconsolate because he did not gain what he desired most and what had caused him to leave sweet France behind, namely, the sultan's soul. The sultan then realizes that he and his people had erred in assuming that the crusaders merely coveted their lands, and Louis passionately vows that he will not return to France before making the sultan and his men glorify God. When the sultan interjects that his people hope to attain bliss by following the ordinances of the most benign Machomet, Louis expresses his amazement that men so discerning and circumspect follow that deceiver, whose most foul *Alchoran* he, Louis, has examined. The sultan, not unlike Francis's sultan a generation earlier, is depicted as wavering under the impact of this exhortation, and Matthew concludes his account of the encounter—which the nineteenth-century editor labels an "interview between Louis IX and the Soldan of Egypt"—with the remark that the sultan may yet convert and the report that Louis decided to remain in the East, "fighting in the Holy Land for winning souls."[8] Never before, either in Eudes of Deuil's depiction of the French knights on the Second Crusade or in the anonymous account about Pelagius's battle sermon on the Fifth, was Muslim conversion so openly presented as a crusade's aim.

In a letter sent to Cairo before the commencement of hostilities and preserved in the chronicles of Ibn al-Furāt and al-Maqrīzī, Louis threatens the sultan: "Were you to swear to me by every oath, present yourself to the priests and monks, and obediently carry candles before me to the crosses (good; otherwise) I will come to you and kill you in that part of your lands which is dearest to you."[9] At first glance,

---

was drawn to this poem by Throop, *Criticism of the Crusade*, p. 126, n. 55; but the translation appearing there is not exact.)

[8] Matthew Paris, *Chronica Majora*, ed. H. R. Luard, Rolls Series, 57 (London, 1872–83), 5:309–10. On what Louis and his crusaders might really have known about Islam, see Marie–Thérèse d'Alverny, "La connaissance de l'Islam au temps de Saint Louis," in *Septième centenaire de la mort de Saint Louis: Actes des colloques de Royaumont et de Paris (21-27 mai 1970)* (Paris, 1976), pp. 235–36.

[9] English translation of Ibn al-Furāt's version in Lyons and Lyons, *Ayyubids* (chap. 4, n. 54 above), 2:13; the Arabic text is edited in 1:16. Al-Maqrīzī's version appears in his *Sulūk*, ed. M. M. Ziada and S.A.F. Ashour, 4 vols. (Cairo, 1934–73), 1, 2:334; the literal translation in F. Gabrieli, *Storici arabici delle crociate* (Turin, 1963), p. 295, does not convey the true meaning of the sentence. For a longer version of this letter see *Die Chronik des Ibn ad-Dawādārī*, pt. 7, *Der Bericht über die Ayyubiden*, ed. S. ʿAbd al-Fattāh ʿĀsūr (Freiburg/Br., 1972), pp. 366–67. (I would like to thank my student ʿAmikam Elʿad for translating this version for me.)

this looks like a call for conversion; in reality it is a call for the sultan's submission to Louis in a ceremony resembling the signing of a treaty between Egypt and a European power, at which native Christian clergy used to assist.[10] Louis's aim in attacking Egypt was to conquer the country; his subsequent four-year stay in Palestine was mainly motivated by his hope of taking advantage of the Ayyubid-Mameluke struggle in order to enlarge the rump kingdom of Acre.[11] And yet Matthew Paris's imaginary "interview" was not entirely divorced from reality, as several sources indicate that Saracen conversion was indeed close to Louis's heart. The Dominican friar Geoffroi of Beaulieu, Louis's confessor on both of his crusades, reports that when the king was in Palestine, "many Saracens came to him in order to accept Christianity," and that the king had them baptized, instructed in the faith, and later transported to France, where they and their families were provided for as long as they lived. Geoffroi adds that Louis bought many slaves and Saracens with his own money, and had them baptized and provided for.[12] Matthew Paris adds that some of the Saracens were already baptized when they were sent to France before the king's own departure from Acre, while others still awaited baptism. He also asserts that they decided to convert after having been impressed with Louis's perseverance and zeal and with the expositions of Dominicans and Franciscans on the dangerousness of Machomet's most foul law.[13] Writing in 1303, Guillaume of St. Pathus specifies that the number of Saracens who came to Louis was forty or more, including several amirs; Louis entrusted their instruction to Dominicans and others and, after bringing them to France, made many of them rich and married them to Christian women.[14] Guillaume's figure is probably more realistic than that of Primat, who speaks of five hundred Saracens who, impressed by Louis's courage and firmness, came over to him, were in-

[10] For a parallel see, for example, the Genoese-Mameluke treaty of 1290, edited and translated by M. Amari in "Nuovi ricordi arabici su la storia di Genova," *Atti della Società Ligure di Storia Patria* 5 (1867): 608–12; P. M. Holt, "Qalawūn's Treaty with Genoa in 1290," *Der Islam* 57 (1980): 105–8. I would like to thank Professor E. Ashtor for discussing Louis's letter with me at great length.

[11] Persuasively argued by J. Richard, "La politique orientale de Saint Louis: La croisade de 1248," in *Septième centenaire de la mort de Saint Louis: Actes des colloques de Royaumont et de Paris (21–27 mai 1970)* (Paris, 1976), pp. 205–6.

[12] Gaufridus de Belloloco, *Vita Sancti Ludovici*, in RHGF 20:16–17. See also the account of the anonymous monk of St. Denis, on p. 55D.

[13] Matthew Paris, *Chronica Majora*, 5:425.

[14] H. F. Delaborde, ed., *Vie de Saint Louis par Guillaume de Saint-Pathus* (Paris, 1899), p. 21.

structed by the Mendicants and baptized, then battled the Saracens under a Christian-born commander.[15]

Some documentary evidence for Louis's provisions for his converts after their arrival in France exists in the royal accounts of 1256, where, immediately after the arbalesters and the sergeants, there appear six *bapthisati*; one of them, Droco *baptisatus*, receives from the king ten pounds for his wedding.[16] The integration of these converts into French society must have been a protracted process, for even a century later, in 1350, one *Raymundus Amffocii* of Beaucaire appears in a document as "belonging to the stock of the baptized brought a long time ago from Outremer by our lord Louis of sacred memory, late king of the French."[17] Yet the assertion of the chroniclers that the Saracens decided to convert to Christianity under the impact of Louis's virtues ought to be regarded as part of the veil of saintliness in which Louis's admirers endeavored to enshroud him. But that veil was pierced, probably inadvertently, by the Venetian merchant Marino Sanudo when he wrote to Philip VI of France on October 13, 1334, that during Louis's stay at Acre he turned a great many Saracens toward the faith *by offering them presents*; he also relates that many of these later reverted to their original faith. But even Sanudo knows that Louis was sincerely interested in Saracen conversion, for he adds that when the king was warned and reproved by his men on this account, he answered that he considered it worthwhile to expend all his treasure for the salvation of a single soul.[18]

[15] *Chronique de Primat*, in RHGF 23:14. On a Saracen who joined the crusaders after the conquest of Damietta, fought with them at Mansūra, and was captured and tortured by his former coreligionists, see A. Lecoy de la Marche, ed., *Anecdotes historiques, légendes et apologues tirés du recueil inédit d'Etienne de Bourbon, dominicain du XIIIᵉ siècle* (Paris, 1877), pp. 377–38.

[16] *Tabulae ceratae Johannis Saraceni*, in RHGF 21:365–66. The names of the *bapthisati* are Droco, Bartholomeus (probably identical with *Bertelemi baptisatus*, mentioned on pp. 325E, 326J), Berteran Mareschal, T. clericus (*clericus* might have been a nickname, as in *Theobaldus dictus Clericus, castellanus Senonensis*, p. 539H), as well as two unnamed *baptisati*. On the king's gift on the occasion of the marriage of Droco *baptisatus*, see p. 355D.

[17] "Raymundus Amffocii de Bellicadro, de stipite Baptizatorum, adductorum jam dudum de partibus ultramarinis per sanctae memoriae dominum nostrum Ludovicum, quendam regem Francorum." Quoted from MS by Ducange, *Glossarium mediae et infimae Latinitatis*, s. v. *Baptizati*.

[18] "Nam ut communiter fertur sanctissimus et serenissimus rex Ludovicus dudum Francorum rex . . . dum in Accon ageret pro cursu terrae sanctae, multam Saracenorum congeriem oblatis muneribus declinavit ad fidem, quamvis ex eis plures ad vomitem velut canes redeuntes, apostatantes fidem resumebant priorem. De quo ipse rex reverenter a suis monitus et quodammodo increpatus respondebat, praedicta non posse sine quoquo

Nor should the possibility be ruled out that Louis really did issue orders, as mentioned by Guillaume of St. Pathus, to spare the Saracens' wives and children and lead them toward baptism, as well as to endeavor to take the Saracen men prisoner rather than kill them.[19] It is also plausible to assume that Louis intended the numerous Dominicans who accompanied him on his crusade to work for the conversion of the population to be conquered.[20] Indeed, coins struck at Acre during Louis's sojourn in Outremer bear inscriptions in Arabic that proclaim some of the main tenets of Christianity.[21] But despite the many indications that Louis was interested in Saracen conversion, probably more so than any previous crusading leader, there is nothing to suggest that his campaign aimed at the novel target set by Innocent IV. Louis's Oriental expedition was a traditional crusade of conquest and defense; it was not a campaign to force the Muslim rulers to open their country to Catholic preachers.

To what extent were things different on Louis's second crusade, the Tunisian expedition of 1270?[22] As is well known, contemporaries left

---

beneficio procedere, eo quod saltem salus unius animae totius sui thesauri pretium merebatur." The letter has been edited by F. Kunstmann, *Studien über Marino Sanudo den Älteren, mit einem Anhange seiner ungedruckten Briefe* (Munich, 1855), p. 110 [= *Abhandlungen der k. Bayerischen Akademie der Wissenschaften, Hist. Classe*, vol. 7 (1855), p. 806]. I would like to thank my colleague David Jacoby for having brought this revealing text to my attention.

[19] Delaborde, ed., *Vie de Saint Louis par Guillaume de Saint-Pathus*, p. 151. The anonymous compiler of Louis IX's biography that forms part of the *Grandes Chroniques de France* relates that Louis had many Saracen slaves baptized and freed on Cyprus in 1248–49: *Les Grandes Chroniques de France*, ed. J. Viard, vol. 7 (Paris, 1932), p. 120. The apparent source of the *Grandes Chroniques* at this juncture, the Life of St. Louis by Guillaume of Nangis (who literally copies Vincent of Beauvais), merely mentions that "multi etiam Saraceni qui detinebantur in Cypro captivi, baptismum instanter petentes, insigniti sunt caractere baptismali." Guillaume de Nangis, *Vie de Saint Louis*, in RHGF 20:357-58; Vincent de Beauvais, *Speculum Historiale*, XXXI, 89 (Douai, 1624; reprint, Graz, 1965), p. 1316a. Vincent, in turn, probably depends on the letter of Odo of Châteauroux (see chap. 4, n. 38 above), where it is said that the captive Saracens "instanter petebant fidei sacramentum." Consequently it would seem that the compiler of the *Grandes Chroniques*, who ascribes the deed to Louis and adds the detail that the Saracens were set free, merely embroidered on the facts he found in his source.

[20] On the Dominicans who accompanied Louis see Gerardus de Fracheto, *Vitae fratrum* (chap. 4, n. 15 above), p. 265. On the Franciscans see the data assembled by Gratien, *Histoire* (chap. 4, n. 7 above), p. 648n.

[21] P. Balog and J. Yvon, "Monnaies à légendes arabes de l'Orient latin," *Revue numismatique* 6.1 (1958): 157–62; Prawer, *The Latin Kingdom*, pp. 386–87; W. C. Jordan, *Louis IX and the Challenge of the Crusade: A Study in Rulership* (Princeton, 1979), p. 132.

[22] For two discussions of the Tunis crusade, one in the crusader, the other in the Muslim context, see J. R. Strayer, "The Crusades of Louis IX," in K. M. Setton, ed., *A*

behind widely divergent accounts about the goal of this expedition. On the one hand, Geoffroi of Beaulieu, the king's confessor and counselor who accompanied him on the campaign, presents as the primary objective the conversion of the ruler of Tunis, who had hinted at his readiness to receive baptism should the circumstances permit. According to Geoffroi, Louis hoped that the presence of the French army would enable the ruler of Tunis and like-minded Saracens to convert to Christianity without risking the wrath of the local population, and also lead to the re-Christianization of the province of Africa, the home of Augustine and other doctors of the Church.[23] Indeed Geoffroi depicts Louis on his deathbed in the crusader camp at Carthage musing how the Catholic faith might be preached and implanted in Tunis and who might be suitable to go thither to preach.[24] The official reason for the descent on Tunis must have been quite similar to that given by Geoffroi, for in a letter of February 11, 1271, sent to Mathieu of Vendôme, abbot of St. Denis and regent of France, Philip III, Louis's son and successor, wrote that his late father had gone to Africa "to utterly extirpate there the errors of the infidel Saracens."[25] On the other hand, several contemporary chroniclers, of whom the Sicilian Saba Malaspina was the closest to the scene of events, consider Charles of Anjou, the scheming king of Sicily, to have been the man who diverted Louis's crusade to Tunis. According to this view, adopted by

---

History of the Crusades, vol. 2 (Philadelphia, 1962), pp. 508–17, and H. W. Hazard, "Moslem North Africa, 1049–1394," ibid., vol. 3 (Wisconsin, 1975), pp. 470–76.

[23] Gaufridus de Belloloco, *Vita Sancti Ludovici*, in RHGF 20:21–22; Guillaume de Nangis, *Gesta Sancti Ludovici/Vie de Saint Louis*, in RHGF 20:446–49. For similarly deceiving hints at readiness to convert, made by a Syrian amir in 1239, see Richard, *La papauté*, p. 44.

[24] Gaufridus de Belloloco, p. 23C; Guillaume de Nangis, pp. 460–61. *Les Grandes Chroniques de France* (n. 19 above), p. 281, relate that Louis's choice fell on "frere Andrieu de Lonc Jumel pour ce qu'il savoit partie du langage de Tunes; car aucune foiz, avoit frere Andrieu preechié à Tunes par le commandement le roy de Tunes qui mout l'amoit." On André de Longjumeau, who had served as envoy to Muslim and Mongol rulers, see P. Pelliot, "Les Mongols et la papauté," *Revue de l'Orient chrétien* 28 (1931–32): 3–84; Richard, *La papauté*, pp. 45, 70–74.

[25] "ad partes accesserant Affricanas ad errores infidelium Saracenorum ibidem radicitus extirpandas." *Epistola Philippi regis ad abbatem et monachos S. Dionysii*, in L. d'Achéry, *Spicilegium* (chap. 4, n. 38), 3:669; repeated almost verbatim in Philip's letter to the Dominicans in 1271: Reichert, ed., *Litterae* (chap. 4, n. 59 above), no. 21, p. 81. In an earlier letter, written in the crusader camp at Carthage on September 12, 1270, and addressed to the clergy of France, Philip writes in a language reminiscent of the First Crusade that his father intended to dedicate Africa to the Christian religion, "expulsa barbarie ac nefanda Saracenice gentis eliminata spurcitia": *Raynaldi Annales ecclesiastici*, ed. G. D. Mansi, vol. 3 (Lucca, 1748), p. 268b. For a French version see *Chronique de Primat*, in RHGF 23:62–63.

many modern historians, Charles was intent on making the ruler of Tunis, Muḥammad al-Mustanṣir, pay the tribute he had rendered to earlier rulers of Sicily, and therefore manipulated the French into descending on Tunis.[26]

The two explanations are not mutually exclusive. Charles might indeed have been desirous of having a French army at Tunis rather than in the Orient in order to make al-Mustanṣir yield to his demands, while Louis might have been genuinely interested in re-Christianizing the land of Augustine.[27] In fact, Primat, the most reliable chronicler of that crusade, relates an incident that strongly suggests that the Muslims of Tunis knew that Louis was bent upon their Christianization. On July 27, 1270, three Saracen knights approached the butler of France, announced their intention to become Christians, and were promptly led to the butler's tent. Soon afterward, about one hundred Saracens arrived at the crusader battle line and led the Christians to believe that they, too, had come to ask for baptism. As they were talking, other Saracens suddenly descended on the crusaders and killed sixty foot soldiers. The butler nevertheless continued to believe that the intentions of the first three knights were sincere and let them go, believing their promises to return with many like-minded coreligionists. Of course they never returned, and it transpired that the three

[26] Saba Malaspina, *Rerum Sicularum historia*, in RR.11.SS. 8 (1726), col. 860A. (A critical edition of this chronicle is being prepared by Walter Koller at the MGH, Munich); Pierre Coral, *Majus Chronicon Lemovicense*, in RHGF 21:776AB; *Chronicon Thomae Wykes*, ed. H. R. Luard, in *Annales Monastici*, Rolls Series, 36 (London 1864–69), 4:237; cf. R. Sternfeld, *Ludwig des Heiligen Kreuzzug nach Tunis, 1270, und die Politik Karls I. von Sizilien* (Berlin, 1896), pp. 375–76.

[27] In a letter of November 18, 1270, to Abbot Mathieu of St. Denis, Pierre de Condé reports that Charles of Anjou had urged the crusaders to refrain from initiating hostilities against Tunis until the arrival of his envoy. This has recently been interpreted by Jean Longnon to indicate that Charles "sought to avoid all acts of war against al-Mustanṣir." J. Longnon, "Les vues de Charles d'Anjou pour la deuxième croisade de Saint Louis: Tunis ou Constantinople?" in *Septième centenaire de la mort de Saint Louis: Actes des colloques de Royaumont et de Paris (21–27 mai 1970)* (Paris, 1976), p. 195; Pierre de Condé's letter is printed in d'Achéry, *Spicilegium*, 3:667b. Charles's request to refrain from hostilities has already been noted by Sternfeld, pp. 234–35, 239–40; see also p. 206. But Charles could hardly have intended this state to be of unlimited duration. It is plausible to assume that Charles, then conducting negotiations with al-Mustanṣir over the resumption of tribute payments, intended to use the crusaders' presence to cause al-Mustanṣir to bow to his demands; the sack of Tunis would hardly have furthered Charles's plan to secure a steady flow of tribute from that city to Sicily. Cf. Sternfeld, pp. 234–35; also Hazard, "Moslem North Africa," p. 472, n. 14. On the hopes for al-Mustanṣir's conversion as one of Louis's motives, see the considered opinion of Brunschvig, *Berbérie*, pp. 56–57; also P. Herde, *Karl I von Anjou* (Stuttgart, 1979), pp. 83–87.

had been in league with the attackers who followed on their heels.[28] Primat lays the blame squarely on the butler's shoulders, and makes Louis appear suspicious of the three from the very beginning; but he admits that it was the king who gave the order to let them go. The story, related not without bitterness, rings true; the Muslims seem to have exploited Louis's eagerness to convert them in order to trick his men.[29]

The belief that the conversion of the ruler of Tunis would lead to the Christianization of his subjects should not be considered utterly unrealistic. Evidently Louis expected the people of Tunis to convert, not merely because their ruler would do so, but because the crusader army and the accompanying missionaries would be on the spot. Louis, who threatened in his 1249 letter to the sultan to duplicate in Egypt the recent Christian victories in Andalusia, might have hoped, in 1270, to repeat in Tunis the events of Valencia, where the baptism of an erstwhile Muslim ruler was followed by the conversion of many of his subjects. Still, the resemblance between Louis's plan and Innocent IV's grand concept of a papally initiated expedition to force an infidel ruler to admit Catholic preachers is slight at best. The somewhat pedestrian idea of launching a crusade to help the ruler of Tunis overcome his fears rather brings to mind Jacques of Vitry's expectation in 1217 that upon the arrival of the Fifth Crusade at Acre, Saracens who had hitherto feared the revenge of their coreligionists would gather the courage to convert.[30] (In the next century, this notion is taken up by Jacopo da Verona, a pilgrim who visited Palestine in 1335.)[31]

Closer similarity to Innocent's concept may be discerned in the numerous, almost identically worded accounts of the 1270 peace treaty between al-Mustansir and the crusaders, which report that the ruler of Tunis consented to permit Dominicans, Franciscans, and others to preach the Christian faith freely in monasteries to be erected in all the cities of his realm, and that men wishing to receive baptism might freely do so.[32] These accounts are patently false: The extant Arabic text of the

[28] *Chronique de Primat*, in RHGF 23:48–49; Guillaume de Nangis, in RHGF 23:452–55. See also Sternfeld, p. 243.

[29] Cf. Brunschvig, *Berbérie*, p. 58.

[30] See chap. 3, n. 109 above.

[31] R. Röhricht, ed., "Liber peregrinationis fratris Jacobi de Verona," *Revue de l'Orient latin* 3 (1895): 260.

[32] *Martini Oppaviensis Chronicon*, ed. L. Weiland (1872), in MGH SS 22:474; *Alberti Milioli notarii Regini Liber de temporibus*, ed. O. Holder-Egger (1903), in MGH SS 31:538; Salimbene, *Cronica*, ed. O. Holder-Egger (1905–13), in MGH SS 32:484; anonymous continuator of Gerard Frachet in RHGF 21:5; *Chronique latine de Guillaume de Nangis*, ed. H. Géraud, vol. 1 (Paris, 1843), p. 238; Nicolas Trivet, *Annales sex regum Anglie, 1136–1307*, ed. T. Hog (London, 1845; reprint, Vaduz, 1964), p.

treaty merely grants the Christian "monks and priests" the right to preach and pray "publicly" in their churches.[33] Pierre de Condé, chaplain of Louis IX, reporting on the treaty to Mathieu of St. Denis on November 18, 1270, also mentions only the right of Christians to preach solemnly in their churches; similar formulations appear in the Lives of Louis IX by Primat and Guillaume of Nangis.[34] The false but widespread account of the granting of the right to proselytize is probably taken from an early, no-longer-extant report that attempted to make the treaty of Tunis as palatable as possible to devotees of the crusader idea.[35] (Indeed, another early report goes so far as to claim that the ruler of Tunis consented to pay the salaries of three thousand knights in case fighting should resume in the Levant.)[36] From the present point of view, it is noteworthy that the false report credits the Tunisian crusade with having achieved exactly what Innocent had posited as the goal of his linkage, namely, the forcible opening of an infidel country to Catholic preaching and proselytizing. Whether the author of the original report was familiar with Innocent's formulation, or whether he arrived independently at the concept of crusade as the instrument of opening a country to missionizing, must remain a moot point at least as long as the author's identity remains unknown.

The Impact of the Linkage from Hostiensis to Thomas Fuller

In the realm of theory, the impact of Innocent's linkage may be traced much more clearly. Hostiensis wholeheartedly subscribes to Innocent's view on this particular issue. Indeed his remarks, appearing in the

276; *Bruchstücke aus der Weltchronik des Minoriten Paulinus von Venedig (I. Recension)*, ed. W. Holtzmann, fascicle 2 (Rome, 1927), p. 55 [= Texte zur Kulturgeschichte des Mittelalters, 4]; *Vita Clementis Papae IV, ex MSi Bernardi Guidonis*, in RIS 3, 1:596; Giovanni Villani, *Cronica*, VII, 38, ed. F. Gherardi Dragomanni, vol. 1 (Florence, 1844), p. 367.

[33] The Arabic text was edited and translated by S. de Sacy, "Mémoire sur le traité fait entre le roi de Tunis et Philippe-le-Hardi en 1270 pour l'évacuation du territoire de Tunis par l'armée des croisés," *Mémoires de l'Académie des Inscriptions et Belles-Lettres* 9 (1831): 469 (text), 465 (translation). Text and translation were republished by P. Carrigou-Grandchamp, "Documents relatifs à la croisade de St. Louis (1270)," *Revue Tunisienne* 19 (1912): 450 (text), 453 (translation).

[34] "Et licebit etiam Christianis in locis predictis aedificare Ecclesias, et Ecclesiis solemniter etiam predicare." *Epistola Petri de Condeto ad Mattheum abbatem S. Dionysii*, in d'Achéry, *Spicilegium*, 3:668a; *Chronique de Primat*, in RHGF 32:81; Guillaume de Nangis, *Gesta/Vie*, in RHGF 20:478–79. See also 21:177H.

[35] I shall deal with the false account in a future study.

[36] *Chronicon Marchiae Tarvisinae et Lombardie*, ed. L. A. Botteghi (1914–16), in RIS 8, 3:61.

commentary on the Decretals on which he worked until his death in 1270, amount to a slightly expanded and occasionally reworded version of Innocent's statement.[37] The one substantial change is the addition of the word *praecise* ("absolutely") to Innocent's premise that infidels should not be coerced into accepting the faith.[38] Apparently Hostiensis objects only to the employment of *coactio absoluta*, the physical coercion to undergo baptism.[39] But like Innocent, he regards infidel refusal to admit preachers valid cause for a papally proclaimed war against them.

Surprisingly enough, Johannes de Ancona, the one canonist known to have been active in the crusader East, does not adduce this justification for warfare against the infidel, even though he deals with some of Innocent's arguments immediately preceding the passage in question.[40] Later decretalists adhere to the Innocentian linkage. Joannes Andreae, the great fourteenth-century canonist, simply transcribed into his commentary on the Decretals the statement of Hostiensis—in itself a close paraphrase of Innocent's.[41] Francesco Zabarella (d. 1417), the Paduan canonist who played a major role at the Council of Constance, summarizes Innocent's statement in his *Lectura* on the Decretals; his

[37] Hostiensis, *Commentaria* on X 3.34.8, par. 22–23 (Venice, 1581), p. 128c.

[38]

Innocent IV:	Hostiensis:
Item licet non debeant infideles	Licet enim infideles ad fidem
cogi ad fidem . . .	praecise non cogantur . . .
. . . excommunicando vel	. . . excommunicando vel
compellendo ad fidem . . .	praecise ad fidem compellendo . . .

[39] Cf. Condorelli, *I fondamenti*, p. 129, who attributes the addition of *praecise* to Joannes Andreae. (In reality Joannes merely copied Hostiensis.) On the distinction between *coactio absoluta* and *conditionalis* see chap. 2 above.

It should be noted that somewhat later Hostiensis determines that infidels living in peace with, or subjected to, Christians, "non per bellum, non per violentiam aliquam, sed tantum per praedicationem dicimus converti debere. et si praedicatores non admittant ipsos posse compelli per papam, ut dictum est supra" (*Commentaria* on X 3.34.8, par. 28, p. 128d). It is therefore difficult to see what kind of licit coercion Hostiensis had in mind when he qualified Innocent's blanket rejection of all coercion. Or did he consider the forcible opening of a country to Christian preaching a novel category of *coactio conditionalis*?

[40] Johannes de Ancona, *Summa iuris canonici*, on 3.34. Brugge, Stadsbibliotheek, MS 377, fol. 227ra. On this work, see M. Bertram, "Johannes de Ancona: Ein Jurist des 13. Jahrhunderts in den Kreuzfahrerstaaten," *Bulletin of Medieval Canon Law* NS 7 (1977): 49–64. The author, who lived in the East in the 1260s, has been identified with Giovanni Fazioli: D. Maffei, *Giuristi medievali e falsificazioni editoriali del primo Cinquecento*, Ius commune, Sonderhefte, Texte und Monographien, 10 (Frankfurt/M, 1979), pp. 75–80.

[41] Joannes Andreae, *Commentaria* on X 3.34.8, par. 11, 13 (Venice, 1581), pp. 172d, 173b.

wording indicates that, rather like Hostiensis, he was not quite certain whether to eschew the coercion of infidels into the faith.[42] Archbishop Antonino of Florence (d. 1459), the theologian who decisively contributed to the modification of the medieval teachings on usury, almost literally repeats Innocent's formulation.[43] The Salamancan theologian Francisco de Vitoria laid down in his famous *Relectiones de Indis* of 1539 that when the New World barbarians hinder the Spaniards from announcing the Gospel, it is lawful to wage war on them in order to make Christian preaching possible.[44] And when Thomas Fuller—the first scholar of Sidney Sussex College, Cambridge, to write on the crusades—enumerated in 1638 the "arguments for the lawfulnesse of the Holy Warre," one of them was that "This warre would advance and increase the patrimony of Religion, by propagating the Gospel, and converting of infidels. If any object that Religion is not to be beaten into men with the dint of sword; yet it may be lawfull to open the way by force, for instruction, catechising and such other gentle means to follow."[45]

MILDER THAN INNOCENT

Despite its considerable influence both in the thirteenth century and afterward, the Innocentian linkage was far from universally accepted. While occupying the center of the continuum of attitudes, it was flanked on the one side by those who rejected the crusade, in varying degrees, and on the other side by those who endorsed the crusade but entertained little or no hope of Saracen conversion. At the same time, the popular conception of Christianization, forcible or otherwise, as one of the direct goals of crusading continued to have its exponents.

At the far extreme of what one may call the dovish wing there were the few who considered all religions alternative and roughly equivalent

[42] Franciscus de Zabarellis, *Lectura* on X 3.34.8, par. 5 (Venice, 1502), p. 303a: "Quinto quero an papa potest mandare infidelibus quod admittant predicatores evangelii in terris suis. Inno [centius] quod sic: licet *secundum eum* non debeant infideles cogi ad fidem: quia in hoc omnes libero arbitrio relinquendi sunt et sola dei gratia in hac revocatione valet" (my emphasis).

[43] *S. Antonini archiepiscopi Florentini Summa Theologica*, III.3.2 (De dominio civitatum et regnorum), (Verona, 1740), 3:178.

[44] Franciscus de Victoria, *De Indis recenter inventis et de jure belli Hispanorum in barbaros relectiones*, III. 12, ed. and trans. W. Schätzel (Tübingen, 1952), p. 106. For a discussion of his view and its Innocentian roots see J. Höffner, *Kolonialismus und Evangelium: Spanische Kolonialethik im Goldenen Zeitalter*, 2d ed. (Trier, 1969), pp. 332–51; also, Muldoon, *Popes, Lawyers, and Infidels*, pp. 143–52.

[45] T. Fuller, *The Historie of the Holy Warre*, 4th ed. (Cambridge, 1651), p. 13.

roads to salvation. This genuinely tolerant stance, unheard of among
Catholics of earlier times, was denounced on occasion. The Franciscan
Benoît of Alignan, bishop of Marseilles and enthusiastic supporter of
the crusades, takes issue in a work probably completed in Acre in 1261
with those who believe "that each one may attain salvation in his faith
or law or sect, provided that he considers it good, and given by God,
and his deeds pleasing to God." Benoît explains that those who hold
this opinion have arrived at it by reasoning that it would ill befit God
to permit so few to be saved and so many damned.[46] Such an opinion
might indeed have arisen in crusader Palestine, where a few Catholics
were surrounded by large numbers of Muslims and non-Catholic
Christians; or perhaps it reflected the outlook espoused by the Mongols.[47] But this view need not be explained as a product of local circumstances, for it is denounced also in a tractate written in the 1340s
in southern Portugal.[48] Its reverse is of course the presentation of

[46] Benoît d'Alignan, *Tractatus fidei contra diversos errores*. Rome, Alessandrina 141
(sec. XIV), fol. 187va, Clm 12311 (sec. XV), fol. 150rb: "Contra illos qui credunt
unumquemque in sua fide vel secta salvari et qualiter (Clm: quare) hoc dicunt et qualiter
respondendum (Clm: respondendum sit).

"Item hoc est contra errorem illum qui credit unumquemque in sua fide vel lege vel
secta salvari, dummodo credat esse bonam, et a deo (Clm: et a deo datam) ipsique
placere quod facit. Et hoc dicunt propter paucitatem salvandorum et multitudinem
dampnandorum, quia reputant inconveniens regi regum et domino seculorum, si plures
habet dampnatos in carcere quam sibi salubriter famulantes." (Clm 7454 [sec. XV], fol.
227r-v, has slight differences in wording.)

On this work see M. Grabmann, "Der Franziskanerbischof Benedictus de Alignano
(† 1268) und seine Summa zum Caput Firmiter des vierten Laterankonzils," in *Kirchengeschichtliche Studien P. Michael Bihl OFM als Ehrengabe dargeboten*, ed. I.-M. Freudenreich (Colmar, 1941), pp. 50–64.

[47] Cf. for example the January 1326 letter of Andrea of Perugia, bishop of Zaitun in
Mongol China: "Est enim hec opinio apud eos, sed potius error, quod unusquisque in
sua septa salvatur." *Sinica Franciscana*, ed. A. van den Wyngaert, vol. 1 (Quaracchi,
1929), p. 376. See also the words of Mangu Khan to Guillaume of Rubruck (p. 298).

The Baghdadi Jew Ibn Kammūna, examining in 1280 the tenets of Judaism, Christianity, and Islam, acknowledged the prophethood of Moses, Jesus, and Muhammad,
and argued that Zoroastrians are monotheists and that pagans are brought closer to
God by their idol worship: *Ibn Kammūna's Examination of the Three Faiths: A Thirteenth-Century Essay in the Comparative Study of Religion*, trans. M. Perlmann (Berkeley,
1971), esp. pp. 38–39, 147–48.

[48] "Quod quilibet in secta sua, si bene vixerit, potest salvari, sicut Christiani in fide
sua sancta." Alvarus Pelagius, *Collirium adversus hereses novas*, c. 52, in R. Scholz, ed.,
*Unbekannte kirchenpolitische Streitschriften aus der Zeit Ludwigs des Bayern (1327–1354):
Analysen und Texte*, vol. 2 (Rome, 1914), p. 493. A milder version appears in the
concluding sentence of the *Liber Nicholay*: "Omnes tum unum deum creatorem celi et
terre adorant christiani, Iudei et sarraceni et omnes salvari indubitanter credunt et amen."
The text has been edited by A. d'Ancona, in "Il Tesoro," p. 263. For Wycliffe's belief

Moses, Jesus, and Muhammad as the world's three great impostors, a presentation first attributed in the West to Simon of Tournai (d. 1201).[49] For those who held such views on religion, not only crusading but missionizing must also have seemed a questionable enterprise.

A more restrictive variant of the view attacked by Benoît appears among Cathars. Thus Jean Jaufre of Tignac, sentenced on July 5, 1322, to severe imprisonment because of Albigensian errors, maintained that God loved equally the unbaptized and baptized, Saracens, Jews, and Christians, and all would be equally saved. But the equality envisaged by Jean was an equality among inferiors, since he believed that all adherents of his sect, but only a tiny fraction of all others, would attain salvation.[50]

A less radical stance was taken by Catholics who rejected the crusade as an unchristian act of bloodshed. Surveying anticrusade attitudes in the tractate he submitted to Pope Gregory X on the eve of the Second Council of Lyons of 1274, Humbert of Romans mentions first the contradictors (*oblocutores*) who oppose the anti-Saracen crusade on the grounds that the spilling of blood, even the blood of wicked infidels, does not befit the Christian religion. These *oblocutores*—who, one may add, closely follow in the footsteps of some of the twelfth-century critics of crusading—point to the examples of nonviolence given by Christ, the Apostles, and the martyrs; quote from Scripture and Jerome; and refer to the passages condemning warfare collected by Gratian in the *Decreta*. Later in his tractate Humbert mentions that other *oblocutores* maintain that since God has allowed and continues to allow the crusades to end in disarray or defeat, it appears that it is not His will that Christians proceed in this manner against the Saracens.[51] The arguments of these two kinds of *oblocutores* could and, as will be shown, did converge in the conviction that God let the crusades fail *because* they ran counter to the true spirit of Christianity. Possibly out of rhe-

---

that Saracens "who at the moment of death believe in the Lord Jesus Christ will be judged to be faithful Christians" (a view stated in more general terms by Uthred of Boldon in the 1360s), see Southern, *Western Views*, pp. 76, 82.

[49] Cf. J. Warichez, *Les 'Disputationes' de Simon de Tournai* (Louvain, 1932), pp. xxi–xxii, xxix. See also Alvarus Pelagius, *Collirium*, c. 10, p. 499.

[50] J. Duvernoy, ed., *Le registre d'inquisition de Jacques Fournier, 1318–1325*, vol. 2 (Toulouse, 1965), pp. 110–15. In 1340 in Reichenhall, the priest Rudolf similarly "dixit eciam Iudeum et paganum posse sine baptismo salvari"; he was burned at the stake. *Iohannis abbatis Victoriensis Liber centarum historiarum*, ed. F. Schneider (1909), in MGH Scr. rer. Germ. 36, 2:190; see also p. 218.

[51] Humbertus de Romanis, *Opusculum tripartitum* (chap. 2, n. 79 above), I, 11, 17, pp. 191, 197.

torical considerations Humbert chose to attribute to different characters arguments that in reality were advanced by the same persons.

In the thirteenth and fourteenth centuries, the rejection of the crusade as a violation of Christian morality seems to have been especially vehement among Waldensians and other heretics. Already Alain of Lille (d. 1202) reports that the Waldensians condemn all acts of killing, even if committed in self-defense; and Jacques of Vitry defends the Templars against heretic accusations that they contravene the precepts of Christ by taking up the sword.[52] In the 1260s an anonymous cleric from the region of Passau reports more specifically that the Waldensians consider the pope and all bishops homicides, on account of the wars they conduct against Christians, pagans, and heretics. "And they condemn those who preach the cross, [saying] that the Prussians and the pagans should not be forced to the faith by the sword, but be attracted by preaching."[53] Indeed the Passau cleric himself partly identifies with this view, for elsewhere in his work he states that Christians who force Gentiles into the faith by sword and servitude thereby disparage the crusade.[54] In 1395, the inquisitor Peter Zwicker reports that the Waldensians under the rule of the dukes of Austria condemn the pope for launching expeditions against the Saracens and for giving and preaching the cross against the pagans.[55] Indeed this objection was so prominent a feature among Waldensian and other heretical beliefs that one of the exploratory questions inquisitors were in-

[52] Alain of Lille's citation of Waldensian opinion appears in his *Contra hereticos*, in PL 210:394C–396A; for Jacques of Vitry's defense see chap. 3, n. 105 above.

[53] "Dicunt eciam papam et omnes episcopos esse homicidas. Occasio bella que exercent contra Christianos, paganos et hereticos. Et eos qui crucem predicant, dampnant, quod Pruteni et pagani non sunt gladio cogendi ad fidem sed predicacione alliciendi." Edited in A. Patschovsky and K.-V. Selge, *Quellen zur Geschichte der Waldenser* (Gütersloh, 1973), p. 81. On the anonymous author see A. Patschovsky, *Der Passauer Anonymus: Ein Sammelwerk über Ketzer, Juden, Antichrist aus der Mitte des 13. Jahrhunderts*, Schriften der Monumenta Germaniae Historica, 23 (Stuttgart, 1968), pp. 146–50.

[54] "Peregrinacioni derogant . . . qui gentiles ad fidem cogunt gladio et servitute." W. Preger, "Beiträge zur Geschichte der Waldenser im Mittelalter," *Abhandlungen der K. Bayerischen Akademie der Wissenschaften, Hist. Kl.*, vol. 13, [Denkschriften, 47] (1877), p. 245. The passage appears in the section titled "De occasionibus errorum hereticorum" (pp. 242–45), in which the author enumerates the ecclesiastical misuses that lead people to embrace heresy.

[55] "Item damnant et reprobant D. Apostolicum mittentem bellatores contra Saracenos et crucem dantem vel praedicantem contra quoscunque paganos." I. von Döllinger, *Beiträge zur Sektengeschichte des Mittelalters*, vol. 2 (Munich, 1890), p. 309, no. 69. On Zwicker's report see Patschovsky, *Der Passauer Anonymus*, p. 145, n. 35.

For a heretic from Carcassonne who rebuked the Franciscans for preaching the cross see Döllinger, *Beiträge*, p. 40. For fourteenth-century Albigensians who condemn all killing, including that of infidels, see Duvernoy, *Registre* (n. 50 above), 2:501, 515.

structed to ask of suspects concerned their opinion of the ultramarine crusade.[56] And in an abjuration formula possibly written or used by Benoît of Alignan, the repentant heretic expressly affirms the right of the pope and the bishops to grant indulgences to participants in crusades against "Saracens, and heretics, and impious Christians, or differently, as it will be advantageous to the salvation of souls."[57]

The contrasting of objectionable crusading bent on enforcing Christianization and laudable preaching aimed at voluntary conversion—a contrasting that the anonymous cleric from Passau attributes to the Waldensians—was not done only by heretics. Back in the twelfth century, Ralph Niger expressed the same view, and Isaac of L'Etoile and Walter Map held similar opinions. Although Humbert of Romans does not mention this contrasting among the objections to the crusade, the alternative of peaceful preaching was probably in the mind of those *oblocutores* who, according to Humbert, asked why only the Saracens should be exterminated, and not also Jews, Saracens living under Christian rule, idolaters, Tartars, and other barbarians; since all these were expected to convert as a result of preaching, as Humbert himself writes in his rejoinder, the *oblocutores* probably asked why the unsubjected Saracens should not also be converted rather than exterminated.[58] Three generations later, the English Dominican Robert Holcot (d. 1349) expressly argues against the contention that if the Jews, who delivered Jesus unto death, were not punished with the material sword, surely it is not permissible to fight against the pagans (the context makes clear that the Saracens are meant) with the material sword: Only the spiritual sword, "which is the word of God," should be used against them.[59] Unlike earlier arguments, preaching is con-

[56] Döllinger, *Beiträge*, pp. 320–21, 334.

[57] "Confitemur etiam quod dominus papa et episcopi possunt facere indulgentias, secundum quod fidei et ecclesie ac divino cultui viderint expedire. Et propter hoc approbamus remissiones et indulgentias quas faciunt contra Sarracenos et hereticos, et contra impios xpistianos, vel aliter, prout saluti animarum fuerit oportunum." C. Douais, ed., "Les hérétiques du Midi au treizième siècle: Cinq pièces inédites," *Annales du Midi* 3 (1891): 374–75, doc. II. (The sentence beginning "Et propter hoc approbamus" does not appear in Clm 12311, fol. 271vb.) On the sources of the abjuration formula see W. L. Wakefield, "Notes on Some Antiheretical Writings of the Thirteenth Century," *Franciscan Studies* 27 (1967): 316–17.

[58] Humbertus de Romanis, *Opusculum tripartitum*, I, 15, p. 195; and see also on this point the summary of Humbert's tract in Mansi, *Concilia*, 24:115.

[59] "Pagani non delinquunt contra deum nec deliquerunt plus quam iudei qui eum morti tradiderunt, sed deus pro illis patrem exoravit et Petrum quia unum ex his percussit increpavit, vel saltem eum a tali facto cessare voluit, dicens: Omnis qui gladio percuttit gladio peribit. Et loquebatur ibi de gladio materiali; ergo non licet gladio materiali contra tales pugnare, sed tantum gladio spirituali, qui est verbum Dei." Ro-

trasted here, not with a crusade aimed at forcible conversion, but with all crusades: At long last, mission and crusade become explicitly antithetical. Still later in the century, John Gower will forcefully make his own the contention against which Holcot had argued. Gower, who had still spoken favorably in his *Vox Clamantis* of 1378–81 of fighting the pagans for reasons of faith, and of recovering the Holy Land, definitely rejects the crusade in his *Confessio Amantis* of 1390–93, where the Lover asks,

> I prei you tell me nay or yee,
> To passe over the grete See
> To werre and sle the Sarazin,
> Is that the lawe?

and the Confessor answers,

> Sone myn,
> To preche and soffre for the feith,
> That have I herd the gospell seith,
> But forto sle, that hiere I noght.[60]

Indeed Gower roundly attacks those who preach at home the crusade, and advises them to cross the sea instead and there work for the Saracens' conversion.[61]

More moderate than the rejection of the crusade as essentially unchristian was the charge that it was counterproductive of conversion, a charge diametrically opposed to the Innocentian linkage. In Humbert of Romans' catalog of anticrusade arguments, this contention is presented in the following form: "There are some who say, What's the use of this assault on the Saracens? It does not impel them to convert but rather to oppose the Christian faith. Also, when we are victorious and kill them, we send them to hell, which is against charity. And

---

pertus Holkot, *Super librum Sapientie*, c. 5, lectio 65 (Basel, 1489). Beryl Smalley has shown that Holcot wrote his work after the academic year of 1333–34 and before 1342: *English Friars and Antiquity in the Early Fourteenth Century* (Oxford, 1960), p. 147. For an appraisal of Holcot see the same work, pp. 133–202, and Smalley's "Robert Holcot O. P.," *Archivum Fratrum Praedicatorum* 24 (1956): 9–97.

[60] *Confessio Amantis*, Book III, lines 2487–93, in *The Works of John Gower*, ed. G. C. Macaulay, 4 vols. (Oxford, 1899–1902), 2:293; cf. Book IV, lines 1662–63, 1677–82, 2:346. For Gower's earlier, favorable attitude toward crusading see his *Vox Clamantis*, Book III, lines 307–10, 651–66, 4:115, 125.

[61] *Confessio Amantis*, Book IV, lines 1674–76, 2:346:

> To slen and feihten thei ous bidde
> Hem whom thei scholde, as the bok seith,
> Converten unto Cristes feith.

when we conquer their countries, we have not enough people to settle them, for our men do not want to stay in those parts."[62] Similarly Holcot struggles with the argument that the slaying of pagans is unlawful, since God wants the sinner to convert, not die, and unless miraculously resuscitated, a slain pagan is no longer capable of conversion.[63]

Among contemporary writers whose works are extant, this position is taken by Roger Bacon (d. 1292), the Franciscan *doctor mirabilis* whose scientific activities and relations with his superiors are still somewhat shrouded in myth. Bacon's statement is so close to that of Humbert's sixth kind of *oblocutores* that one may confidently assume that Humbert had it before him. The statement appears in the *Opus Majus*, a work Bacon wrote between 1266 and 1268 to persuade Clement IV of the importance of the sciences for ecclesiastical reform.[64] In the section advocating the study of languages, Bacon argues, inter alia, that they are needed for converting the infidels: Hebrew is necessary for preaching and interpreting Scripture to the Jews in their own language, and the tongues of the Greeks, Ruthenians, and other schismatics and of the Saracens, pagans, Tartars, and other infidels are necessary for preaching the truth in theirs. Bacon asserts that war does not succeed against them, for sometimes the Christians lose, "as often happens Beyond-the-Sea, and especially in the last expedition, namely that of the King of France." And if the Christians are victorious, there are not enough people to defend the occupied territory. As for the infidels, "they are not converted in this way, but slain and sent to hell. Those who survive the wars, [and] their sons, are enraged more and more against the Christian faith because of these wars, and are infinitely removed from the faith of Christ, and roused to do Christians all possible harm. For this reason the Saracens are

[62] ". . . alii dicunt, quae utilitas est in ista impugnatione Saracenorum? Per hoc enim non provocantur ad conversionem, sed potius provocantur contra fidem Christianam. Item quando vincimus et eos occidimus, mittimus eos ad infernum, quod videtur esse contra charitatem. Item quando obtinemus terras eorum, non habemus, qui populent eas et excolant, quia nostrates nolunt in illis partibus remanere." *Opusculum tripartitum*, I, 16, p. 196.

[63] "Movetur questio utrum licitum sit et meritorium alicui christiano aliquem infidelem sicut paganum invadendo per vim occidere. Quod non, quia deus non vult mortem peccatoris sed ut convertatur et vivat. Sed post mortem corporis nequit converti, nisi corpus esset miraculose restitutum et resuscitatum. Ergo talem morti tradere non est consonum divine bonitati." *Super librum Sapientie*, c. 5, lectio 65.

[64] On the apocalyptic angle to Bacon's concern with the promotion of the sciences and ecclesiastical reform see E. R. Daniel, "Roger Bacon and the *De seminibus scripturarum*," *Mediaeval Studies* 34 (1972): 462–67.

becoming impossible to convert in many parts of the world, and especially Beyond-the-Sea. . . . Moreover, faith did not enter this world by arms but through the simplicity of preaching, as is evident." Even today, adds Bacon, many missionaries with but an imperfect knowledge of these languages, using translators, were able to reap a rich harvest; how much more, Bacon implies, would they have succeeded if they had had command of the language of their infidel audiences and their philosophical training had been adequate.[65]

On the basis of this passage, Bacon has been represented as a pacifist opponent of the crusade.[66] This is certainly erroneous. Like most Catholic thinkers of his day, Bacon objects on moral grounds to forcible Christianization; on practical grounds, he also attacks the Innocentian view that war may pave the way for preaching and persuasion; and he eloquently advocates preaching in the native tongues. But Bacon is too much of a realist to assume that such preaching would guarantee the conversion of all infidels. In fact, in the chapter immediately following the one quoted above, he explicitly discusses those infidels who will prove unamenable to preaching, even to Bacon-style preaching "through men wise in all of science, who know languages well or have the best and [most] faithful translators."[67] Indeed the realization that not all infidels will be won over by preaching is quite central to Bacon's thinking: Even in the letter to Clement IV that serves as an introduction to the *Opus Majus*, Bacon dwells on the usefulness of sciences and arts to "the conversion of the infidel and moreover to the reprobation of those who cannot be converted."[68] Against such obstinate infidels Bacon advises launching not only a conventional army but also the *opera sapientie*, the works of wisdom or science. Indeed, he is confident that the obstinate infidels would be much more easily defeated through the application of science than by resort to conventional warfare, because in the latter victory is a matter of chance, whereas the works of wisdom—scientific warfare—based on fixed laws, are efficaciously guided to their targets.[69]

[65] *The Opus Majus of Roger Bacon*, ed. J. H. Bridges, 3 vols. (Oxford, 1897–1900), 3:120–22.

[66] See for instance Throop, *Criticism of the Crusade*, pp. 132–33. For a balanced presentation of Bacon's "philosophy of mission" see E. R. Daniel, *The Franciscan Concept*, pp. 55–56 (but Bacon does not limit the martial use of the *scientiae* to wars of defense).

[67] *Opus Majus*, 3:122.

[68] ". . . scientiarum et artium secreta que sunt Dei Ecclesie utilissima et reipublice fidelium et conversationi [*sic*] infidelium, insuper reprobationi eorum qui converti non possunt." Roger Bacon, *Lettera a Clemente IV*, ed. and Italian trans. E. Bettoni (Milan, 1964), p. 96; cf. also p. 140. For an earlier edition see F. A. Gasquet, "An Unpublished Fragment of Roger Bacon," *English Historical Review* 12 (1897): 502.

[69] "Quinto, ut qui converti non possunt, praesciti ad infernum, reprimantur longe

What does Bacon mean by scientific warfare? The clearest example is found in his discussion of the uses of optics, where he proposes to set up mirrors to cause fires in the ranks of the enemy. "If the men of Acre, and the ultramarine Christians, had twelve such mirrors, they would have expelled the Saracens without bloodshed, and the king of France would not have needed to cross the sea with his army to conquer that land. And when he shall go [again to the East], the master [who built such mirrors] with two others would be more helpful than most, if not all, of his army."[70] Bacon also proposes installing mirrors that would make one army look like many, and thus terrify the infidels.[71] Elsewhere he proposes to employ against the obstinate infidel a scientifically intensified "word power" emanating from the rational soul and capable of altering the substance of the world.[72]

Bacon profoundly abhors bloodshed—he considers Judaism abominable because of the sacrificial slaughter of animals in the Temple.[73] He evidently prefers recourse to the sciences rather than to force of arms in effecting the "reprobation" of infidels unamenable to preaching. Yet Bacon is a child of his age. His rejection of conventional warfare as a means of facilitating conversion is definitely more moderate a stance than that of Innocent IV; but it should not be forgotten that he too professes his eagerness to ensure that "at least the [holy] land with Jerusalem may always remain in Christian possession without fear of loss."[74] And he envisages the employment of scientific warfare for the punishment of unpersuadable infidels or, more bluntly, for

---

magis per vias et opera sapientiae, quam per bella civilia laicorum. Quod enim laicali ruditate turgescit non habet effectum nisi fortuito, sicut videmus in omnibus bellis eorum ultra mare et citra; sed opera sapientiae certa lege vallantur, et in finem debitum efficaciter diriguntur; sicut antiqui principes per sapientes philosophos operati sunt." Roger Bacon, *Compendium studii philosophiae*, in *Fr. Rogeri Bacon Opera hactenus inedita*, ed. J. S. Brewer, Rolls Series, 15 (London, 1859), 1:395.

[70] *Opus tertium*, in *Fr. Rogeri Bacon Opera hactenus inedita*, pp. 116–17. On "specula comburentia omne contumax" see also *Opus Majus*, 2:221.

[71] ". . . et sic pro utilitatibus reipublicae et contra infideles possent hujusmodi apparitiones fieri utiliter et in terrorem." *Opus Majus*, 2:164. Bacon goes on to suggest the production of *apparitiones insolitae* and spy mirrors to be set up high above the enemy, "ut omnia que fierent ab inimicis viderentur," as well as optical devices that would make a small army appear large, and a distant one near, or vice versa (pp. 164–66).

[72] *Opus Majus*, 3:122–25; *Opus tertium*, pp. 95–99. Elsewhere in the *Opus tertium* (p. 86) Bacon expects the rise of a saintly pope by whose merits "pro majori parte convertentur Tartari ad fidem, et Saraceni destruentur." For the context of this expectation see P. Herde, *Cölestin V, 1294 (Peter vom Morrone): Der Engelpapst*, Päpste und Papstum, 16 (Stuttgart, 1981), pp. 191–96.

[73] *Opus Majus*, 2:391.

[74] Ibid., 3:122.

the burning of the contumacious. The advocacy of mirror warfare, like that of push-button warfare in another age, is not the hallmark of the pacifist.

Another contemporary Mendicant, William of Tripoli, goes still further and sees no need for the employment of any arms whatsoever in Christendom's future dealings with the Saracens. William, who concluded his short *De statu Saracenorum* in 1273 at the Dominican convent at Acre, is relatively well informed about the beliefs and history of the Muslims.[75] Like Bacon before him, but more excitedly so, he dwells on the imminent fall of Islam, and relates that the Saracens themselves are convinced that their religion is doomed. One of the prophecies he quotes foretells the death of Sultan Baybars in the very near future, and the victorious spread of the lordship of Christ "up to Caesarea in Cappadocia" within some two years.[76] In addition, he is deeply impressed by the Koranic passages that speak favorably of Jesus and his teachings, and believes that they draw the Saracens closer to Christianity.[77] From these bizarre premises, William arrives at the startling conclusion that the Saracens are on the brink of conversion; after having been, on his own testimony, remarkably successful in baptizing them, he is certain that when told the tenets of Christianity they speedily adhere to them, "and thus, through the simple word of God, without philosophic arguments or military arms, they seek, like simple sheep, the baptism of Christ, and cross over into the fold of God."[78]

William evidently does not believe in the necessity of a crusade at the time he is writing his tractate; but there are no grounds for considering him—as modern historians have—a pacifist opposed to all crusading or to Christian warfare against the Saracens.[79] He is almost certainly identical with the Dominican William of Tripoli who appeared before Pope Urban IV late in 1263 to entreat him to send immediate help to the Crusading Kingdom, and especially to assist in fortifying the castle of Jaffa. Urban, whose letter to Louis IX is the only source on William's mission to the West, presents him as a man

[75] On William and his work see M. Voerzio, *Fr. Guglielmo da Tripoli, orientalista domenicano del sec. XIII, precursore di Fra Ricoldo di Monte Croce* (Florence, 1955).

[76] *De statu Saracenorum* (chap. 4, n. 27 above), cc. XXIII–XXIV, ed. Prutz, pp. 589–90; also c. XLVIII, p. 596. For Bacon's views on this issue see *Opus Majus*, 1:266, 2:389–90, 392; *Rogeri Baconis Moralis Philosophia*, ed. F. Delorme and E. Massa (Zurich, 1953), p. 22.

[77] *De statu Saracenorum*, cc. XXVIII–XLVII, pp. 591–96.

[78] Ibid., c. LIII, pp. 597–98.

[79] Throop's view of William as a missionary pacifist hostile to the idea of the crusade (*Criticism of the Crusade*, pp. 115–22) has been accepted by virtually all later historians of the crusades.

who "does not cease to labor for the welfare of Holy Land, exposing his person to the perils of sea and land."[80] Indeed, in the *De statu Saracenorum* itself there is nothing to hint at a critical attitude toward earlier crusades, or earlier Christian warfare against the Muslims. On the contrary, William speaks of the "glorious" Christian army that ejected the Saracens from Provence, refers to Godfrey of Bouillon "of blessed memory," and speaks approvingly of Edward of England, who "came with three hundred knights to defend the Holy Land."[81] Thus, it is not that he opposes the use of military force on principle or that he considers it, like Bacon, a hindrance to conversion; he merely regards, or presents, it as redundant under the prevailing circumstances as he perceives them, specifically, that Mahomet's law is on the verge of collapse and Saracens convert upon hearing God's simple word.[82]

William's tract survives in seven manuscripts, but it seems to have influenced only Sir John Mandeville (fl. 1356), the author of a widely known compilation of travel accounts.[83] His description of Islam depends on William's and he, too, believes that "sithenes they [the Saracens] arn so neer our trowthe . . . mochel the sonnere they shulde be conuertid vnto our lawe, thoruz prechynge and techynge of cristen men."[84] But Mandeville at the same time calls with considerable emo-

---

[80] "Ceterum, predictum fratrem Guillelmum qui. sicut scire te credimus, non cessat pro dicte terre profectibus laborare, personam suam maris et terre periculis exponendo, et qui ad tuam propter hoc accedit presentiam, regia benignitate recipias." *Registres d'Urbain IV*, no. 473, p. 235. The letter opens with the statement that "frater Willelmus Tripolitanus, ordinis Praedicatorum, nuntius Terre Sancte" was followed by another envoy from the Holy Land, the bishop of Bethlehem (p. 234). It is noteworthy that this bishop is the only crusading prelate mentioned in the *De statu Saracenorum*: c. XVIII, p. 586.

[81] "gloriosa Francorum milicia": c. XVII, p. 585; "tempore felicis recordacionis Godefridi de Boillon": c. XIV, p. 583; "rex Francorum gloriosus Ludovicus de Siria reversus est in Franciam": c. XVIII, p. 585; [Odoardus] "cum CCC militibus ad terram sanctam custodiendam venerat": c. XX, p. 587.

[82] For a similar conclusion see N. Daniel, *Islam and the West*, p. 122; but the inclusion of *De statu Saracenorum*, with only two qualifying sentences added, in a collection of crusade tracts (see below) suggests that the work was not perceived as a piece of anti-crusade propaganda.

[83] The manuscripts are listed in Voerzio, *Fr. Guglielmo*, pp. 38–39.

[84] *Mandeville's Travels: Texts and Translations*, ed. M. Letts, Hakluyt Society, 2, 101–2 (London, 1953), 2:453; see also pp. 455–56. The somewhat shorter French original appears on p. 304. William of Tripoli's influence on Mandeville has been noted by N. Daniel, *Islam and the West*, p. 353, n. 30.

Ugo Monneret de Villard argues that Ricoldo da Monte Croce, who knew William's work, must have been impressed by it even though he never refers to it in his writings: *Il Libro della Peregrinazione nelle parti d'Oriente di frate Ricoldo da Montecroce* (Rome, 1948), pp. 101–3.

tion for the military reconquest of the Holy Land.[85] Evidently he does not share William's confidence in the efficacy of preaching.

This doubt was shared by at least one more reader of William's tract, the anonymous compiler of BN lat. 7470, who appended to it the following sentence: "The Saracens would speedily come to the faith if they would not fear death at the hands of their brethren and would hear [Christian] preaching."[86] The same compilation also contains several crusade plans, all surveyed in a brief introduction in which the compiler prefaces William's optimistic estimate of the impact of preaching on the Saracens with the ominous remark that the tract also describes "how the Saracens could soon be brought to the faith by preaching, *if they were willing to listen to it.*"[87] Evidently the compiler believed, not unlike Innocent IV, that Christian preaching could be expected to bear fruit only after the intervention of Christian force.

A dissociation from crusading still milder than William's combines a recognition of the necessity for armed warfare with the hope that it may somehow be avoided. Thus around 1270 the Provençal troubadour Guillem Daspol expresses the wish that God might inspire the Saracens to recognize their error and convert so that Christians need no longer die in battle with them.[88] And when Pope Nicholas IV called for suggestions on the steps to be taken after the fall of Acre in 1291, one of the plans the archbishop of Canterbury, the Franciscan John Pecham, transmitted in the name of his province called for the dispatch to Syria, before the employment of the material sword, of Arabic-speaking "spiritual warriors" who were to work for the conversion of the enemy. Should these missionaries be martyred, one may confidently hope that Christ will allow miracles that, in their turn, will stir the infidels to embrace the faith "because of the martyrs rather than because of the exhortation of [their] sermons."[89] This and Pe-

---

[85] *Mandeville's Travels*, 1:2, 2:230.

[86] "Sarraceni cito venirent ad fidem si mortem ex parte suorum non timerent et predicationem audirent." BN lat. 7470, fol. 162v; *De statu Saracenorum*, ed. Prutz, p. 598n.

[87] "Tercius tractatus est fratris Guillelmi de Tripoli ordinis predicatorum. In quo agitur de origine progressu et fine Machometi et suorum. Et qualiter secta Saracenorum debet terminari et extirpari et fides Christianorum prevalere. Et in quibus Christus et beata Maria et apostoli et eorum sequaces et fidem immitantes in lege seu Alcoranno Sarracenorum. Et qualiter possent per predicationem cito converti ad fidem nostram si eam audire vellent." BN lat. 7470, fol. lv. "Quomodo Sarraceni si audirent predicatores christianos essent faciles ad convertendum ad fidem Christi." Ibid., fol. 12r.

[88] "Seinhos, aujas, c'aves saber e sen(s)," lines 41–48, in P. Meyer, ed., "Les derniers troubadours de la Provence," *Bibliothèque de l'Ecole des Chartes* 30 (1869): 289.

[89] F. M. Powicke and C. R. Cheney, eds., *Councils and Synods with Other Documents relating to the English Church*, vol. 2, 2 (Oxford, 1964), pp. 1109–10. The suggestion

cham's subsequent suggestions leave no doubt that he did not rule out a crusade; but it is equally clear that he preferred to launch it only as a last resort.

HARSHER THAN INNOCENT

While Waldensians and other heretics, as well as Roger Bacon, William of Tripoli, and the *oblocutores* of Humbert of Romans, espoused views that were milder in varying degrees than those of Innocent IV, there were others who took decidedly harsher stands. It has seldom been noted that one such position was taken by Thomas Aquinas. In a section of the *Summa Theologica* written between 1265 and 1271, Thomas argues, quite in accordance with mainstream Catholic tradition, that infidels should by no means be forced to accept the Christian faith. But, if it be feasible, they should be compelled "not to hinder the faith by blasphemies, evil suasions, or even open persecutions." Then Thomas pointedly adds, "It is on this account that Christ's faithful frequently wage war against the infidels, not indeed to coerce them to believe (for even if they were to defeat them and take them prisoners, they would leave them free [to decide] whether they wished to believe), but in order to compel them not to hinder the faith of Christ."[90] This justification of Christian warfare encompasses that of Innocent, for the refusal to admit Christian preachers is obviously an important form of hindering the Christian faith.[91] But Thomas goes far beyond Innocent, for he presents three broad categories of hindrance—blasphemies, mischievous suasions, and persecutions—that justify warfare against the infidels, categories that could be drawn upon to justify most acts of war against non-Christians.[92] Indeed, since Islam disseminated what a medieval Christian must have considered blasphemy—had not, in Thomas's lifetime, a fellow Dominican imprisoned a Saracen for blaspheming Jesus by denying his divinity?[93]—Islam's very

---

to send out *spirituales ydonei bellatores* might have been influenced by the writings of Ramon Llull (see below).

[90] See Appendix 4/f.

[91] This will be explicitly stated in Cardinal Cajetan's commentary on this passage, also reproduced in Appendix 4/f.

[92] Cf. the refreshingly unbiased essay of B. Altaner, "Glaubenszwang und Glaubensfreiheit in der Missionstheorie des Raymundus Lullus: Ein Beitrag zur Geschichte des Toleranzgedankens," *Historisches Jahrbuch* 48 (1928): 588. (On the other hand, M.-T. d'Alverny presents Thomas as stating merely that one ought to fight the infidels "pour les empêcher de persécuter les chrétiens": "La connaissance," p. 244.) For a recent discussion of Thomas's attitude to war in general see Russell, *The Just War*, chap. 7.

[93] See chap. 4, n. 15 above and Cajetan's examples of blasphemy, Appendix 4/f.

existence, hindering as it did the spread of Christianity, could be construed as a legitimate cause for Christian warfare. In fact, Thomas's
ruling comes very close to the extreme opinion the Franciscan *exemplum* attributes to Francis of Assisi, namely, that the crusade is a just
act of warfare, for the Saracens blaspheme the name of Christ and turn
aside from his worship whomever they can.

In his *Opusculum tripartitum*, Humbert of Romans exhibits a still
more radical attitude. Like Innocent IV, he contends that by refusing
admittance to Christian preachers, the Saracens sin and must be punished—but for Humbert the appropriate punishment is death. Preven-
tion of Christian preaching in order to thwart conversion and submission to Christ has equated the Saracens with the enemies in the parable
in Luke 19:12–27 whom the king executed for refusing to submit to
his rule. And while Aquinas justifies war against infidels who hinder
the faith with their blasphemies, Humbert believes that the Saracens
deserve death for their blasphemies against the Trinity and the fre-
quent abuse of its believers in their *Alcoran*. To live in peace with such
transgressors would be sinful; human laws, as well as evangelical and
apostolic doctrine, call for their removal from the world.[94]

Besides defining the assault on the Saracens as morally imperative,
Humbert also expounds the view, rudimentarily expressed by Bernard
of Clairvaux, that Christian fighting is the only possible answer to
Saracen aggression. Rather like Joachim before him, Humbert argues
that of all the persecutors of the Church, the Saracens are the worst
and most persistent, presenting a physical as well as spiritual danger,
for many Christians tend to accept the undemanding law of Mahumet.
Since there is no hope of converting the unsubjected Saracens, they
must be repulsed by military force.[95] Alluding to the modes of missionary activity outlined in his day, Humbert observes that the Saracens prevent Christian preaching; miracles—here he probably refers to
those expected to occur in the wake of a preacher's martyrdom—do
not take place; and the Saracens are not impressed by saintly Christian
life, since they prefer their own prayers, fasts, alms, and pilgrimages.
Consequently, unless destroyed by Christian or barbarian power—surely
Humbert has here the Mongols in mind—the Saracens will persevere

[94] *Opusculum tripartitum*, I, 14, pp. 194–95. For a more detailed analysis of Humbert's justification of crusading see K. Michel, *Das Opus Tripartitum des Humbertus de
Romanis, O.P.: Ein Beitrag zur Geschichte der Kreuzzugsidee und der kirchlichen Unions-
bewegungen*, 2d ed. (Graz, 1926), pp. 41–48. For a point-by-point summary of Humbert's discourse see Throop, *Criticism of the Crusade*, chaps. 6–7. See also N. Daniel,
Islam and the West, pp. 112–13, 125, 129.

[95] *Opusculum tripartitum*, I, 4–6, 11, pp. 186–88, 191–92.

forever; for as it is often said, just as Mahumet conquered the world by the sword, he will be destroyed by it. (Here Humbert skillfully turns the tables on the critics of the crusade, employing in its defense the verse from Matthew 26 they routinely used in order to attack it.) Moreover, asserts Humbert, it is evident that it pleases God and his saints that the Christians purge the conquered countries of Saracens, for Jacques of Vitry relates in his History that God appeared to Peter the Hermit in a dream and enjoined him to exhort the pope and the princes of the West to rescue the Oriental Christians, and Turpin relates in his letter about the deeds of Charlemagne in Spain that Saint James appeared to Charlemagne in a dream and urged him to liberate Santiago de Compostela from the Saracens.[96] Thus for Humbert the *Historia Karoli Magni et Rotholandi*, a reflection of popular twelfth-century attitudes toward the crusade, becomes a weighty authority for the justification of the crusade. (The dividing line between the realms of *chansons de geste* and theology was evidently much vaguer than modern historians sometimes assume: While Humbert, a former general of the Dominican Order and sometime candidate for the papacy, relies in his plea for a punitive crusade on a work heavily influenced by the Song of Roland, an anonymous German poet of about 1300 has a victorious Christian knight muse whether or not to force baptism on his defeated Saracen rival, and then has him conclude—quite in accordance with the theological consensus of his day—that nobody should be coerced into Christianity, for conversion must be the result of free will.)[97]

The possibility of Muslim conversion is only lightly touched upon in Humbert's tractate. In replying to the *oblocutores* who claim that the crusade provokes the Saracens to oppose the Christians rather than to accept their religion, Humbert admits that one should not expect the crusade to bear direct results in this sphere; yet a sound defeat may cause the Saracens "not to rely so much on their Mahumet." And somewhat later he adds, almost as an afterthought, that one may hope that subjugated Saracens will convert more speedily than the others.[98] In another context he explains that subjugated Saracens can be coerced willy-nilly into attending Christian preaching and therefore one must not despair of them as much as of the others. But it is with considerable reservation that this erstwhile dispatcher of missionaries speaks

[96] Ibid., I, 20, p. 200.

[97] *Reinfrid von Braunschweig*, ed. K. Bartsch, Bibliothek des Litterarischen Vereins in Stuttgart, 109 (Tübingen, 1871), lines 17876–17905. On this work see Wentzlaff-Eggebert, *Kreuzzugsdichtung* (chap. 2, n. 82 above), p. 394.

[98] *Opusculum tripartitum*, I, 16, p. 196.

about the effects of such compulsory attendance: "Now and then some of them convert."[99] With Humbert, Innocent's crusade for free Christian speech has become a crusade aimed, inter alia, at forcing the Saracens to attend Christian preaching; even so, the prospects for their conversion are rather bleak.

For all his radicalism, Humbert presumably concurs with the view of Innocent and Thomas, which goes back to Augustine, that the act of conversion itself must be left to the infidel's free decision. Some of Humbert's contemporaries, however, broke with this view and openly advocated the use of compulsion, thereby drawing closer to the popular attitude that reappeared time and again from 1096 onward. Among men of learning, Bernard of Pavia and Alanus Anglicus may be considered the precursors of this view; but Bernard did not specify the extent of *asperitates* he was willing to tolerate, and Alanus, while not at all vague in his support of compulsion *citra mortem*, hastened to make clear that his was a minority opinion.[100] Ulrich of Strasbourg, by contrast, a pupil of Albertus Magnus and Dominican provincial of Germany in 1272–77, espouses this view forcefully and distinctly. In his main work, the *Summa de bono*, he argues that Biblical events disprove the opinion that men should be brought to the unity of Christ by words, not coercion: Paul was compelled to believe by lightning stroke and blindness, and the children of Israel were often turned back from idolatry through scourges. Ulrich explains that he does not endorse absolute compulsion (*absoluta compulsio coactionis*), for he agrees with Augustine that a man can believe only of his own free will, but he does advocate the compulsion that leads to faith through punishments (*compulsio inductionis per penas*). Such compulsion occurs when the Church subdues Saracens, heretics, or other infidels, and weighs down the yoke of servitude on the defeated if they refuse to believe, so that compelled by human fear, they accept at least a "shapeless faith," which, by habitually hearing its tenets, they will come to cherish.[101] From a practical point of view, the compulsion advocated by Ulrich is identical with the *coactio conditionalis* of Huguccio and In-

[99] Ibid., I, 15, p. 195.

[100] See chap. 2, n. 87 above.

[101] See Appendix 6. My attention was drawn to this work by F. A. von der Heydte, *Die Geburtsstunde des modernen Staates: Ein Beitrag zur Geschichte des Völkerrechts, der allgemeinen Staatslehre und des politischen Denkens* (Regensburg, 1952), pp. 237–38. (Von der Heydte's book, though inexact in places, has received far less attention than it deserves.) On Ulrich see, for instance, W. Breuning, *Erhebung und Fall des Menschen nach Ulrich von Strassburg*, Trierer Theologische Studien, 10 (Trier, 1959); I. Backes, *Die Christologie, Soteriologie und Mariologie des Ulrich von Strassburg*, Trierer Theologische Studien, 29, 1 (Trier, 1975).

nocent III.[102] But while the latter two merely recognized the ex post facto validity of an act of baptism performed under such compulsion, Ulrich expressly advocates its employment.

Similarly, the prominent Franciscan theologian Johannes Duns Scotus (d. 1308), tacitly rejecting Thomas's view, argues that a Christian ruler not only may but ought to take Jewish and infidel children from their parents by force and have them baptized; he advises the ruler to do this with proper caution, lest the parents be forewarned and kill the children to prevent their baptism.[103] And the *doctor subtilis* goes on to say, "Moreover, I believe that it would be a pious deed to coerce the parents themselves with threats and terror to receive baptism and to cling to it thereafter. For even though they would not be true believers in their hearts, it would be still less harmful for them to be unable to keep safely their illicit religion than to be able to keep it freely. Their descendants, if properly brought up, would become true believers by the third or fourth generation."[104] The Dominican Burchard of Strasbourg, who wrote his *Summula iuris* some time before 1311, concurs: "It is asked whether Jews and Saracens may be coerced into being baptized by the carrying off of their sons or property. I answer yes, because they are slaves and have no right to property or sons."[105]

Small wonder, then, that in an age in which eminent theologians like Johannes Duns Scotus or Ulrich endorsed coercion, a merchant

---

[102] See chap. 2, nn. 89–90 above.

[103] *Quaestiones in Quartum Librum Sententiarum*, dist. 4, q. 9 ("Utrum parvuli Judaeorum et infidelium sint invitis parentibus baptizandi"), in *Joannis Duns Scoti Opera Omnia*, new ed., vol. 16 (Paris, 1894), pp. 487–89. Most canonists agreed with the Archdeacon that a ruler may order the baptism of Jewish children: Condorelli, *I fondamenti*, pp. 103–5. Johann of Freiburg, a student of Ulrich—cf. Backes, p. vii—follows Aquinas in rejecting this view: Iohannes Friburgensis, *Summa confessorum* (n.p., 1476), I.4.4. For a present-day view on the issue see Ch. Journet, "Sur le droit de baptiser les petits enfants," *Nova et vetera* 28 (1953): 69–71.

[104] "Imo quod plus est, crederem religiose fieri si ipsi parentes cogerentur minis et terroribus ad suscipiendum Baptismum, et ad conservandum postea susceptum, quia esto quod ipsi non essent vere fideles in animo, tamen minus malum esset eis, non posse impune legem suam illicitam servare, quam posse eam libere servare. Item filii eorum, si bene educarentur in tertia et quarta progenie, essent vere fideles." *Joannis Duns Scoti Opera Omnia*, 16:489. A few lines later Duns Scotus argues that if a few Jews are removed to some island, this would suffice for the fulfilment of the prophecy of Isaiah quoted in Rom. 9:27; all the rest may be converted now.

[105] Burchard of Strasbourg, *Summula iuris*, Clm 7810 (a. 1320), fol. 8rb, Clm 4595 (sec. XIV), fol. 51v: [*De iudeis et sarracenis et servis eorum*] "Queritur an per subtracionem puerorum et rerum possint cogi baptizari. Respondeo sic, quia sunt servi nec habent ius in rebus vel in filiis."

unencumbered by Augustinian tradition explicitly presented forcible Christianization as a goal of the crusade. This was Marino Sanudo Torsello, the Venetian crusade promoter whose *Secreta Fidelium Crucis* dates from the 1310s. Like Jacques of Vitry, whose History is one of his main sources, Sanudo hopes for "the conversion or destruction of the infidels."[106] But more specifically than Jacques, he foresees that after the Christian victory, the infidels—and the schismatics—"will willy-nilly convert, with the sword of the Christians pursuing them."[107]

About three decades later, the old popular cry Conversion or Death will be given full legitimation by a man of learning, the Dominican theologian Robert Holcot. In his commentary on the Book of Wisdom, Holcot determines that the principal aim of the Christians is the Saracens' conversion; the secondary aim is their death, in case they wish to persevere in their malice. Christian preachers should cooperate with Christian warriors, so that the Saracens will be attracted to the faith by the first and, should they refuse to give assent, be slain by the second.[108] Holcot's crisp and definite formulations must have reached a wide audience, for his commentary survives in an exceptionally large

---

[106] "pro conversione vel consumptione infidelium." Marino Sanudo Torsello, *Liber Secretorum Fidelium Crucis*, in J. Bongars, *Gesta Dei per Francos*, vol. 2 (Hanau, 1611; reprint, Jerusalem, 1972), pp. 1, 8, 289–290. Cf. also Sanudo's letter of 1327 edited in A. Cerlini, "Nuove lettere di Marino Sanudo il Vecchio," *La Bibliofilia* 42 (1940): 359.

[107] ". . . sed etiam caeteri undique infideles atque schismatici proculdubio subiugabuntur dominio Christiano, qui ad verum cultum nominis Iesu Christi, eorum nequitias et schisma totaliter delinquentes, velint, nolint convertentur, Christianorum gladio persequente." *Liber Secretorum Fidelium Crucis*, p. 91.

Sanudo also contemplates the possibility of expelling the Saracens (pp. 280–81). In 1337 the archbishop of Tarragona proposed expelling the Saracens from the kingdom of Valencia: E. Baluze, *Miscellanea*, vol. 3 (Lucca, 1762), p. 106. Contemporary canonists and civilists objected to this solution; but it should be noted that the Treaty of Christburg, engineered by a papal legate—the future Pope Urban IV—compels pagan Prussians to choose between baptism or expulsion: H. Patze, "Der Frieden von Christburg vom Jahre 1249," in *Heidenmission und Kreuzzugsgedanke*, p. 457.

[108] "Fideles . . . non debent eorum mortem per se et principaliter et directe intendere, sed per accidens: secundario et indirecte, quia principaliter debent velle eorum conversionem ad fidem. et secundario eorum mortem si velint in eorum malicia perseverare, et sic se conformabunt divine voluntati. . . . Finis principalis intentus eorum est salus et conversio ad fidem. sed finis secundarius est extirpatio. Unde si voluerint credere ñon interficientur. Sic finis principaliter intentus medico est sanare si possit pedem putridum. Et secundo intendit si hoc non possit pedem abscindere. Et quando dicit quod non sunt cogendi ad fidem: dicendum proprie loquendo non possunt cogi ad fidem. possunt tamen cogi desistere a blasphemiis et aliis erroribus. possunt etiam cogi ad quasdam dispositiones previas fidei. Similiter cum bellatoribus debent predicatores assistere ut ex una parte alliciantur et si assentire noluerint feriantur." *Super librum Sapientie* (n. 59 above), c. 5, lectio 65. Cf. N. Daniel, *Islam and the West*, app. F. pp. 322, 392; *The Arabs*, p. 255.

number of manuscripts, both in his native England and on the Continent.[109] Thus with Holcot, a quarter of a millennium after the First Crusade, and after interminable discussions in the schools, the gut reaction of many a common, and not so common, crusader received theological approval at long last.

Finally, at the hawkish extreme of the continuum of opinions, there was the call for the outright extermination of the Saracens unmitigated by any reference to the possibility of conversion. The *Summa universae theologiae*, traditionally ascribed to Alexander of Hales (d. 1245) but not completed until about 1256, lays down that the verse "You shall not allow a witch to live" (Exodus 22:18) applies to heretics and Saracens; therefore they can justly be killed and despoiled by those who wield legitimate power.[110] Similarly Benoît of Alignan, after describing the Saracen view of Paradise in his *Tractatus fidei contra diversos errores*, exclaims that "the absurdities of Machomet . . . are not worthy of debate, but rather are to be extirpated by fire and sword."[111]

THE MANY OPINIONS OF RAMON LLULL

It is hardly surprising that in the course of a lifetime some individuals—Humbert of Romans is an obvious example—changed their opinion on the Saracen question. But it is truly exceptional to encounter a man who ran almost the entire gamut of positions, from rejecting the crusade as essentially unchristian and extolling peaceful persuasion, through simultaneously supporting mission and crusade, to advocating the launching of a crusade against infidels who had refused to convert. This was the Majorcan poet-philosopher Ramon Llull (ca. 1232–1316), the most prolific medieval writer on mission and crusade, who considered Saracen conversion one of his main objectives and wrote on it— in Latin, Catalan, and Arabic—an astonishing number of books and

[109] Smalley, *English Friars* (n. 59 above), p. 142. The Munich Staatsbibliothek alone has six MSS.

[110] "De haereticis vero et Saracenis praeceptum est, Exod. 22, 18: Maleficos non patieris vivere. Ex quo ergo iuste possunt occidi, et iuste poterunt exspoliari." *Alexandri de Hales Summa Theologica*, III, no. 377 II Sol. (Quaracchi, 1948), 4, 2:563. Cf. Elisabeth Gössmann, *Metaphysik und Heilsgeschichte: Eine theologische Untersuchung der Summa Halensis* (Munich, 1964), pp. 394–96.

[111] "Deliramenta ipsius Machometi qui more insanientium et more etiam pecudum locutus est non sunt disputatione digna, sed potius igne ac gladio extirpanda." Edited from Rome, Alessandrina 141, fol. 354va by E. Cerulli, *Il 'Libro della Scala' e la questione delle fonti arabo-spagnole della Divina Commedia*, Studi e Testi, 150 (Città del Vaticano, 1949), p. 415. (It should be noted that the passage beginning with this sentence does not appear in Clm 7454 and Clm 12311.) Cf. N. Daniel, *Islam and the West*, p. 113.

pamphlets, established on Majorca a school for missionaries to the Saracens, received permission to preach at Lucera, endeavored to offer Christian instruction to the sultan of Egypt, and traveled three times to North Africa, possibly meeting his death during the last of these attempts at bringing about Saracen conversion. Sensitive to style to the point of being able to appreciate the beauty of the Koran, emotionally so high-strung that he suffered a severe breakdown in Genoa shortly before embarking on a ship to Tunis, overwhelmed by fear of Saracen retaliation for the preaching he was planning, Llull passionately and eloquently defended every single position he adopted, and his may well be the most effective presentations of most of the opinions then current.[112]

In an early work, the *Llibre de Contemplació en Déu*, written on Majorca between 1271 and 1273, Llull unequivocally expresses his preference for preaching over crusading, and interprets the crusaders' inability to wrest the Holy Land from the Saracens as a sign that crusading does not please the Lord:

> I see many knights who go to the Holy Land beyond the sea, wanting to conquer it by force of arms, and in the end they are all brought to naught without obtaining their aim. Therefore it seems to me, O Lord, that the conquest of that Holy Land should not be done but in the manner in which You and Your apostles have conquered it: by love and prayers and the shedding of tears and blood.
>
> As it seems, O Lord, that the Holy Sepulcher and the Holy Land beyond the sea should preferably be conquered by preaching rather than by force of arms [*per predicacio mills que per forsa*

---

[112] For a recent survey of the literature on Llull see R. Brummer, *Bibliographia Lulliana: Ramon-Llull-Schriftum, 1870–1973* (Hildesheim, 1976). Of the many modern biographies of Llull, the most useful is that by E. W. Platzeck, *Raimund Lull: Sein Leben— Seine Werke—Die Grundlagen seines Denkens*, 2 vols. (Düsseldorf, 1962–64), 1:3–59. For the dates of Llull's works, I rely on Platzeck, 2:3–84; for the sake of convenience, all works will also be quoted by their number on Platzeck's list (e.g., Pla 292 will refer to Llull's last work).

On Llull's breakdown at Genoa and his attempt to go to the sultan, see *Vita coaetanea* (Pla 208), cc. 20, 34, ed. H. Harada, in *Raimundi Lulli Opera latina*, vol. 8, Corpus Christianorum, Continuatio mediaevalis, 34 (Turnhout, 1980), pp. 284–85, 295. The remark "dictamen Alcorani est valde pulcrum" appears in *De acquisitione Terrae Sanctae* (Pla 165), ed. E. Kamar, in *Studia Orientalia Christiana: Collectanea* 6 (1961): 119; see also *Liber de fine* (Pla 134), Clm 10543 (sec. XV), fol. 130r: "Et sic vocant verbum dei alcoranum, dictamine vero multum ornatum est." For a similar appreciation of the Koran's style see Ricoldo da Monte Croce's *Improbatio Alcorani*, quoted by Monneret de Villard, *Il Libro*, pp. 103–4.

darmes], the holy monk-knights should go forward, O Lord, buttress themselves with the sign of the cross, fill themselves with the grace of the Holy Spirit, and go preach to the infidels the truth of Your Passion, and shed for Your love all the water of their eyes and all the blood of their bodies, just as You have done out of love for them!

So many knights and noble princes had gone to the land beyond the sea, O Lord, to conquer it, that if this manner would have pleased You, surely they would have wrested it from the Saracens who hold it against our will. This indicates, O Lord, to the holy monks that You hope every day that they do out of love for You what You did out of love for them; and they can be sure and certain that should they throw themselves into martyrdom out of love for You, You shall hear them out in all they want to accomplish in this world in order to give praise to You.[113]

This is an eloquent—and coherent—formulation of some of the arguments of Humbert of Romans' *oblocutores*, in words echoing those of Joachim of Fiore. And yet a few chapters later Llull claims that Jesus empowered the Christians to constrain some captive Saracens, as well as some Jews, and teach them by force (*per forsa*) the tenets of Christianity. After having heard and understood them out of fear of the Christians, "like a child who has to recite his lesson out of fear of his teacher," all or some of these trainees will convert, and subsequently work for the conversion of others.[114] Evidently, Llull's advocacy of preaching allows, even at this early stage, for a liberal recourse to *asperitates* in the course of persuasion.

Later in the decade, some time between 1275 and 1281, Llull composed at Montpellier the *Ars iuris*, one of his few excursions into the

---

[113] *Llibre de Contemplació en Déu* (Pla 2), chap. 112, nos. 10–12, in *Obres de Ramón Lull*, 20 vols. (Palma de Mallorca, 1906–38), 4:58–59; *Liber Contemplacionis in Deum*, in *Raymundi Lulli Opera*, ed. I. Salzinger, 10 vols. (Mainz, 1721–42), 9:250. Cf. Altaner, "Glaubenszwang," pp. 598–99.

[114] *Llibre de Contemplació*, chap. 346, no. 18, in *Obres de Ramón Lull*, 8:374; *Liber Contemplacionis*, in *Raymundi Lulli Opera*, 10:488; French translation from the Catalan original by R. Sugranyes de Franch, *Raymond Lulle, docteur des missions* (Schöneck-Beckenried, 1954), p. 124 (but "que destrenya alcuns sarraíns" does not mean "pour libérer quelques Sarrasins"; in Llull's writings and elsewhere, *destrènyer* denotes 'posar en destret, en situació difícil,' and 'obligar per la força': A. M. Alcover et al., *Diccionari Català-Valencià-Balear*, 10 vols. [Palma de Mallorca, 1930–62], s.v. Indeed, Llull's Latin version [p. 488] has "potestatem constringendi aliquos saracenos"). Elsewhere in this chapter Llull approves of defensive war: *Llibre de Contemplació*, chap. 346, no. 21, p. 376; *Liber Contemplacionis*, p. 489; Sugranyes de Franch, p. 126.

Ars iuris, MS C (see p. 225), fol. 161v.

field of law.[115] In this short treatise, hitherto unnoticed by students of Llull's thought on mission and crusade, Llull expresses a view that closely resembles that of Innocent IV. It is indicative of Llull's interest in the subject that his discussion takes up the better part of three chapters while Innocent had stated his case in just three sentences. Using his ubiquitous circles, figures, and symbols, Llull lays down that the pope is bound to send wise and devout preachers fluent in the infidels' languages. Should the infidels refuse to hear the preaching of the faith by the Catholics, the emperor is bound to wage war against them in order to make them amenable to preaching. Somewhat later Llull attempts to prove that infidels should not be compelled to accept the Catholic faith against their will.[116] In sum, Llull translates here Innocent's linkage into his own, idiosyncratic idiom.

In the *Doctrina pueril*, written in Catalan at Montpellier between 1282 and 1287, still other motifs make their appearance. Some wise Saracens do not believe in Mafumet's prophethood, writes Llull, and might easily convert if they were preached to, and their conversion would set an example to the Saracen rank and file.[117] Here Llull echoes the wishful thinking of Jacques of Vitry, Roger Bacon, and William of Tripoli. His subsequent statement that "the Apostles converted the world by preaching and shedding tears and blood and much travail and cruel deaths, and the land the Saracens hold they had converted,"

---

[115] Pla 28. My attention was first drawn to this little work by F. A. von der Heydte, *Die Geburtsstunde*, p. 243.

[116] The pertinent passages are edited in Appendix 7.

[117] *Doctrina pueril* (Pla 42), chap. 71. nos. 10–11, ed. G. Schib (Barcelona, 1972), pp. 164–65. Cf. *De acquisitione Terrae Sanctae*, ed. Kamar, pp. 117–19.

elaborates an idea expressed in his *Llibre de Contemplació* and recalls Walter Map's remark that by preaching the Apostles conquered countries the sword subsequently lost.[118] And when Llull later writes that Christians have the power to teach the Catholic faith *per forsa* to some Jewish and Saracen children living under their rule, so that they may in turn convert their brethren, he draws close to Johannes Duns Scotus, the difference being that Llull apparently believes that forcible education in Christianity will lead to voluntary baptism.[119]

Still more incongruous statements appear in Llull's novel *Blanquerna*, also written during his stay in Montpellier in 1282–87. In a famous chapter, Llull mounts a forceful attack on the crusade: He has an envoy of the Egyptian sultan appear at the papal court and read a letter in which the sultan expresses his amazement that the Christians attempt to conquer the Holy Land after the manner of the prophet Mafumet, who conquered by force of arms, and are not willing to follow the manner of Jesus and the Apostles, who converted the world by preaching and martyrdom. The sultan also expresses the opinion that because the pope and the Christians do not follow in the footsteps of their "initiators" (*començadors*), God does not want them to possess the Holy Land.[120] The argument is, of course, an old one—only a few years earlier it was used by the Egyptian Muslim polemicist al-Qarāfī— but never before had it been so dramatically presented, with the sultan branding the pope as a follower of the Prophet.

In Llull's novel, the effect is immediate, and the pope inaugurates a well-organized effort at converting the infidels by preaching and persuasion, sometimes by enforced persuasion along the lines already familiar to the readers of the *Llibre de Contemplació* and the *Doctrina pueril*. Thus the pope proposes that some of the Jews and Saracens living in the lands of the Christians should be assigned to study, under pain of punishment, Latin and Holy Scripture, and after having gained

[118] *Doctrina pueril*, chap. 71, no. 12, p. 165.

[119] "Molts jueus e sarraÿns són en la senyoria dels cristians, qui no han conexença de la fe catòlica, e los cristians han poder que a ·lguns infants, fills dels infeels, la mostren per força, per tal que n'agen conexença, e que per la conexença agen consciència d'estar en error, per la qual consciència és possible cose que convertesquen d'altres." *Doctrina pueril*, chap. 83, no. 4, pp. 194–95. In *Obres de Ramón Lull*, 1:155, this passage ends with "es possíbol cosa que s convertesquen e que n convertesquen daltres," which is to be preferred. It should be noted that the entire passage is lacking in the two Munich MSS of the Latin version of the work, Clm 10548 (sec. XIV), fol. 47ra, and Clm 10549 (sec. XIV–XV), fol. 76vb.

[120] *Libre de Blanquerna* (Pla 44), chap. 80, no. 1, in *Obres de Ramón Lull*, 9:295; French translation in Sugranyes de Franch, "Un texte de Ramón Lull," pp. 105–6, and *Raymond Lulle*, p. 99.

proficiency, they should be freed and honored, so that they may convert others.[121] Missionaries are sent to the unsubjugated infidels. When those of a certain province refuse to listen to the preachers and throw them out, the cardinal in charge has recourse to the secular arm and orders that all those who refuse entrance to "the holy Christians who want to preach the word of God" be subdued by force of arms; the Christian warriors are to refuse a truce with any infidel who does not suffer the Christians to demonstrate the truth of the Catholic faith. This is, of course, the Innocentian linkage in action; not surprisingly, in Llull's fictional world "so great was the power of the Christians that the infidels of that land consented to be preached to, and were allowed a truce as long as they would permit the Christians to preach in their land and convert the infidels."[122] But Llull, who obviously takes delight in devising divergent scenarios, immediately afterward tells of a Saracen king who was not willing to have Christian preachers enter his country, and had the friars expelled. When the latter came to the cardinal, he told them that they had dishonored the "power of the will," and declared that the king's corporeal power should be overcome by much loving and honoring of the Passion of God and by holy men who clandestinely or overtly go among the infidels until by their perseverance the corporeal power would be defeated by the spiritual.[123] Here Llull sounds like Francis in the *Regula non bullata*, presenting life in humility among the Saracens as one mode of missionary work. Yet the reader of *Blanquerna* is in for still another surprise: Elsewhere in the novel, two Christian kings wage war against each other, and the pope induces them to make peace and go on a crusade, the one against the Saracens of the Levant, the other against those of the Occident, with both ultimately to join forces and descend on the Saracens of the south.[124] Evidently shocked by so much incongruity, the author of a dissertation presented to a German university in 1911 was of the opinion that this crusade is a "grobe Inkonsequenz."[125] But Llull, who is intent upon exploring ever more possibilities, swiftly attaches to this expedition many Arabic-speaking friars whose purpose is to attempt to convert the Saracens before the two kings kill them

---

[121] *Libre de Blanquerna*, chap. 80, no. 5, p. 298. For a similar suggestion see Llull's *Tractatus de modo convertendi infideles* (Pla 66), ed. Jacqueline Rambaud-Buhot, in *Beati magistri Raimundi Lulli Opera Latina*, fascicle 3 (Palma de Mallorca, 1954), p. 104.

[122] *Libre de Blanquerna*, chap. 87, no. 4, pp. 339–40.

[123] Ibid., n. 5, p. 340.

[124] Ibid., chap. 81, nos. 3–6, pp. 304–6.

[125] A. Gottron, *Ramon Lulls Kreuzzugsideen* (Berlin and Leipzig, 1912), p. 11.

and send their souls to eternal hellfire: a repetition of Louis IX's crusades as they might have appeared to a distant observer.

In another work of fiction, The Book on the Psalm Quicumque vult, or the Book of the Tartar and the Christian, which was written somewhat later than *Blanquerna* but still between 1282 and 1287, Llull seems to be more seriously concerned with the dilemma of force and persuasion. The scene is set once more at the papal court, the place where Llull would have liked to have had his say but rarely if ever did. Two clerics are engaged in a dispute, the first contending that it is better to spread Christianity through knowledge and martyrdom than with sword in hand, the second retorting that it would be preferable if a mighty king wrought continuous destruction upon the infidels, for in that case the latter would quickly convert and obey the Catholic church. The work concludes with Llull awaiting the pope's decision on which of the two approaches "is more useful to the Church and pleasing to God, and whether the two are necessary."[126]

Llull's own answer, in the coming years, was to place the crusade in the service of mission. Under the impact of the fall of Acre in 1291, he wrote a series of crusading pamphlets in which he outlined, occasionally in great detail, the military as well as the missionary tactics to be employed. The crusader army he envisages always includes numerous linguistically and theologically trained preachers. Even before the victorious conclusion of the crusade, the preachers will engage in missionizing among the Saracen prisoners of war, disputing with them, and forcing them willy-nilly to read "the book called *Alquindi*" (which is, of course, the Letter of al-Kindī), the book called Telif, and, not surprisingly, one of Llull's own books.[127] After the definite defeat of the Saracens, the preachers would, of course, have many more opportunities for missionizing. Yet even in this period in which Llull favors a combination of mission and crusade, he occasionally voices a clear preference for the former, as in an exhortation of 1296 to Boniface VIII and his cardinals in which he states that preaching is the easier means for conversion of the Saracens *and* recovery of the Holy Land.[128]

[126] *Liber super psalmum 'Quicumque vult' sive liber Tartari et Christiani* (Pla 46), in *Raymundi Lulli Opera*, ed. Salzinger, 4:30. Cf. Altaner, "Glaubenszwang," p. 602.

[127] For the missionizing among Saracen prisoners see *Liber de fine*, ed. A. Madre, in *Raimundi Lulli Opera latina*, vol. 9, Corpus Christianorum, Continuatio mediaevalis, 35 (Turnhout, 1981), p. 283. For an attempt at identifying the book called Telif, see C. H. Lohr, "Ramon Llull, *Liber Alquindi* and *Liber Telif*," *Estudios Lulianos* 12 (1968): 145–60.

[128] *Liber de articulis fidei sive liber apostrophe* (Pla 78), in *Raymundi Lulli Opera*, ed. Salzinger, 4:57; *Tractatus de modo convertendi infideles* (n. 121 above), p. 109.

Llull's insistence on enforced instruction in Christianity, a motif that first made its appearance in the *Llibre de Contemplació*, led to his appeal in 1299 to Jaume II of Aragon for the promulgation of an edict obligating the Jews and Saracens of his realm to attend public disputations that he, Llull, intended to hold. In a decree of October 30, 1299, Jaume allowed him to preach in the synagogues and mosques of the realm, and obliged the infidels to attend the sermons, though not to engage in polemics; in other words, the king chose to reissue the 1242 order of his grandfather, Jaume I. In 1301 Llull asked Henry II Lusignan of Cyprus for a similar order, but was turned down.[129] The reluctance of crusader rulers to further conversion apparently outlasted their expulsion from the Syro-Palestinian mainland. In later years Llull continued to advocate this method, which a modern expert on Llull rather euphemistically presents as a manifestation of "some limits to Llull's tolerance."[130]

In the *Liber de fine*, a crusade-and-mission plan that Llull presented in 1305 to Jaume II, who later passed it on to Pope Clement V, there appears a radical, hitherto unnoticed departure. Llull writes that the leader of the crusade should send some of the Arabic-speaking friars accompanying the expedition to the chiefs of the Saracens to inform them that should they be willing to revert to the Catholic faith, they will be given (that is, confirmed in the possession of their) castles and cities. The friars should present the arguments for the truth of Christianity; if the Saracens should be unwilling ("to revert to the faith," one obviously ought to supply on the basis of the passage's structure), the friars are to tell them that perpetual warfare will be waged against them, with the sword of the Christians stirring, tearing asunder, and slaying them.[131] Some twenty years earlier, in the imaginary discussion

---

[129] Altaner, "Glaubenszwang," pp. 603–5; the proposal to hold sermons for Jews and Saracens on Saturdays and Fridays, respectively, submitted in 1311 to the Council of Vienne (Pla 207a), has been printed by E. Longpré, "Deux opuscules inédits du B. Raymond Lulle," *La France Franciscaine* 18 (1935): 153.

On Jaume I's order of 1242 see chap. 4 above; on the forced sermon and disputation as techniques of Christianization see R. Chazan, "The Barcelona 'Disputation' of 1263: Christian Missionizing and Jewish Response," *Speculum* 52 (1977): 829–30, 838.

[130] J. N. Hillgarth, *Ramon Lull and Lullism in Fourteenth-Century France* (Oxford, 1971), p. 25, n. 109. Other "limits," like teaching the faith *per força* to children, go unmentioned.

[131] "Adhuc: Aliqui de fratribus ante dictis, scientibus arabicum, transmittantur principibus Saracenis et aliis infidelibus, sicut dixi, per regem dominum bellatorem. Et illis dicant, quod dominus rex bellator castra et ciuitates dabit eis, si uelint reuerti ad nostram fidem catholicam sacrosanctam. Et eis monstrarent nostrae fidei rationes; et si nolint, dicant eis, quod ordinatum est in perpetuum contra eos, quod bellatoris ensis erit mouens, scindens et interficiens ante dictos." *Liber de fine*, ed. Madre, p. 283. I would like to

at the papal court in which one cleric advocated bringing the infidels into the faith through preaching and the other by having a Christian army wreak havoc among them, Llull has the pope decide between the two choices; now, well into his seventies, and probably less confident of the efficacy of preaching, Llull adopts, to some extent even literally, the standpoint of the second cleric, with the sole difference being that Llull looses his Christian soldiers only after the Saracens have been given the chance to convert through persuasion.[132]

In 1311, nearly eighty years old, Llull repeats this idea in a somewhat vaguer form in his Disputation between Peter the Cleric and Ramon the Fantast. The Church, Ramon tells his interlocutor, has at its disposal two swords, the corporeal and the spiritual, to lead all the infidels to the way of truth. Therefore, the pope should first send to the Saracens, Turks, and Tartars wise and discreet men who are ready to die, to show them their errors and lead them to baptism. Then, if they should resist, he may, and indeed must, employ the secular sword against them.[133] Thus the old Llull realizes, like Roger Bacon before

---

thank Dr. Alois Madre, of the Raimundus-Lullus-Institut at Freiburg/Br. for having placed a transcription of this passage at my disposal some time before the publication of his critical edition.

In calling upon the Saracens to *revert* to the Catholic faith Llull seems to adhere to the view that the Saracens had been Christian before the advent of Muhammad.

[132] Cf. the above quoted words of Llull in the *Liber de fine* with those of the second cleric: "nunquid esset potius, esse ordinatum et positum expresse, ut aliquis maximus rex esset deputatus in perpetuum successive, qui cum magno exercitu Christianorum devastaret et destrueret infideles; nam si hoc sciretur in nationibus infidelium, cito converterentur, et obedirent Catholicae ecclesiae." *Liber super psalmum 'Quicumque vult'*, p. 30.

[133] "Nam universa catholicorum Ecclesia duos gladios habet, ut in evangelio dictum est, scilicet gladium corporalem, ensem videlicet, et spiritualem, scilicet scientiam et devotionem. Cum istis autem duobus gladiis sufficeret Ecclesia omnes infideles ad viam reducere veritatis. Primo, si papa sapientes et discretos, mortem sustinere paratos, apud Sarracenos, Turcos et Tartaros mitteret, qui infidelibus suos errores ostenderent et sanctae fidei catholicae veritatem aperirent, ut ipsi infideles ad sacrum regenerationis lavachrum venirent; deinde si resisterent, tunc papa contra ipsos procurare deberet gladium saecularem. Licitum et debitum est talem esse ordinationem, et qui in aliquo contra ordinationem est, phantasticus est et culpabilis, atque per consequens inordinatus." M. Müller, ed., "Raymundi Lulli Disputatio Petri Clerici et Raymundi Phantastici" (Pla 210), *Wissenschaft und Weisheit* 2 (1935): 322. It is noteworthy that in his perceptive essay on Llull's attitude toward persuasion and coercion, Bertold Altaner, who was not aware of the formulation in the *Liber de fine*, deduced on the basis of this single passage that Llull, in contradiction of his earlier views, came to endorse forcible Christianization: "Glaubenszwang," pp. 608–9. This passage, as well as that in the *Liber de fine*, demands the modification of the repeatedly expressed view of Ramon Sugranyes de Franch that Llull endorses the use of force only in order to safeguard free Christian preaching: Sugranyes de Franch, "Un texte de Ramón Lull," p. 102; *Raymond Lulle*,

him, that some infidels will prove unresponsive to preaching; but while Bacon counseled combating them with the *opera sapientie*, the old Llull occasionally comes close to recommending, as a last resort, a course of action that the author of *Blanquerna* had characterized as "la manera de lur profeta Mafumet."

In May 1312 Llull is in Montpellier, on his way back from the Council of Vienne. In his *De locutione angelorum* he describes how "lying in his bed wishing to fall quite asleep" he considered the council's decisions, and especially the acceptance of his proposals to set up chairs for the teaching of the infidels' languages, and to transfer the confiscated property of the Templars to the Knights Hospitaller to enable them to maintain a permanent naval force against the Saracens. "Ramon was very glad," he writes, "because on account of the aforesaid ordinance the Saracens can be easily defeated and overcome and, once overcome, the entire world will be easily converted, for they are the ones who hinder the universe."[134] Then, two months later, in July 1312 on Majorca, a sudden volte-face: In the *De participatione Christianorum et Sarracenorum*, Llull again considers these two decisions of the council—and decides to propose to Frederick III of Sicily that he, together with the ruler of Tunis, organize Christian-Saracen disputations, "and perhaps by such manner there could be peace between Christians and Saracens."[135] Does this mean that the octogenarian finally arrived at a definite renunciation of the crusade? Some modern students of Llull's thought are inclined to think so.[136] But this is not the case. In the *De civitate mundi*, a work Llull wrote in Messina in May 1314 shortly before leaving for Tunis, he has Justice declare that the Empire's duty is to defend, sword in hand, the Roman Church

pp. 82, 86; and "Els projectes de creuada en la doctrina missional de Ramon Llull," *Estudios Lulianos* 4 (1960): 280, 286. On Llull's shift from considering the crusade as a means of opening the way to missionaries to his fully endorsing it, see also M. Batllori, "Teoria ed azione missionaria in Raimondo Lullo," in *Espansione del Francescanesimo*, pp. 196, 203–4.

[134] Pla 213. Passage edited from Clm 10495 (sec. XIV), fol. 223r, by Gottron, *Ramon Lulls Kreuzzugsideen*, p. 49, n. 5. On Llull's role at Vienne see B. Altaner, "Raymundus Lullus und der Sprachkanon (can. 11) des Konzils von Vienne (1312)," *Historisches Jahrbuch* 53 (1933): 210–12, 216–19.

[135] "et forte per talem modum posset esse pax inter christianos et sarracenos habendo talem modum per universum mundum non quod christiani vadant ad distruendum sarracenos nec sarracini christianos." Preface to *De participatione Christianorum et Saracenorum* (Pla 214), ed. Helene Wieruszowski, "Ramon Lull et l'idée de la Cité de Dieu," *Estudis franciscans* 47 (1935): 110. For similar proposals in Llull's earlier writings see Sugranyes de Franch, *Raymond Lulle*, pp. 69–70.

[136] Gottron, p. 49; Altaner, "Raymundus Lullus," p. 218; and especially Hillgarth, *Ramon Lull*, p. 130.

against infidels and schismatics, against unjust Christians, "and against the infidels who hold the Holy Land."[137] The last work Llull wrote on Christian soil before his final departure for the lands of the Saracens thus includes a clear affirmation of the crusade. True, in the *De civitate mundi* Justice is not allowed to have her way and destroy the world: The Dignities of God impose a compromise that takes into account the views of Mercy, Grace, Humility, and Piety. But even so, Justice is permitted to destroy "the disobedient ones."[138]

In his last years Llull did not devise a new crusading project; neither did he pen another plan for converting the Saracens. The closing scene of *De civitate mundi* provides a clue to this sudden silence. When Justice urges Ramon to go to the Curia and to Christian rulers and announce the decisions of the Dignities, he excuses himself, pleading that he had been several times to the Curia and to numerous rulers, and had written many books, all to no avail. Indeed he was derided and beaten and ridiculed as a fantast. Therefore he has now decided to go to the Saracens and see whether he can lead them back to the holy Catholic faith. (He promises, though, to write down the decisions of the Dignities and send them to the Curia and to several rulers.)[139] This is, of course, a literary device, but the sentiment rings true. The old man, now well in his eighties, at last gives up his attempts to propagate crusade and mission at the gates of the great of Catholic Europe, and decides in a final, possibly desperate act to hurl at the Saracens the not-inconsiderable force of his intellect, perhaps also the ultimate testimony to his faith. The speech of Justice proves that he did not come to renounce the crusade; he merely decided to retreat to the one course of action upon which he could embark without outside assistance.

MISSION AND CRUSADE IN THEIR AGE OF DECLINE

When the Dominican missionary Ricoldo da Monte Croce, in Mongol-occupied Baghdad in 1291, heard of the fall of crusader Acre, he

---

[137] *De civitate mundi* (Pla 269), ed. J. Stöhr, in *Raimundi Lulli Opera latina*, vol. 2 (Palma de Mallorca, 1960), p. 197.

[138] *De civitate mundi*, p. 200.

[139] Ibid., pp. 200–201. For an earlier stage of Llull's dissatisfaction with the impact of his activities see, for instance, the *Liber natalis pueri parvuli Christi Jesu* (Pla 187), written in Paris in 1311, ed. H. Harada, in *Raimundi Lulli Opera latina*, vol. 7, Corpus Christianorum, Continuatio mediaevalis, 32 (Turnhout, 1975), p. 72. For a laical sketch of Llull I would like to refer to an item unlisted in any learned work, namely, Aldous Huxley's short story "The Death of Lully."

composed his bitter Epistle to God, in which he complained that neither Dominic and Francis, nor Louis of France and other kings and barons, had succeeded in subduing the beast Machomet; on the contrary, it was continuing to devour Christians and coerce them to deny their faith.[140] Others must have shared the realization that neither mission nor crusade had proved equal to the task of solving the Saracen question: In 1311 Llull takes issue with the twin arguments that the princes had failed to reconquer the Holy Land and the preachers reaped little fruit.[141] As far as the unsubjugated Muslims were concerned, these appraisals of crusading and missionizing were undoubtedly accurate.

Nevertheless, both mission and crusade continued to have some advocates throughout the fourteenth century. In about 1310, Ricoldo—his confidence evidently restored—wrote an *Improbatio Alcorani* intended to facilitate missionary work, and in another tract, the *Libellus ad nationes orientales*, he expressed the opinion that it is easier to convert Saracens than Jews or Oriental Christians.[142] From time to time some missionaries left for the lands of Islam: For instance, in 1320 three English Dominicans, intent on preaching to the Saracens, obtained a letter of recommendation from Edward II to the king of Cyprus, and in 1383 the councilors of Valencia city granted thirty florins to the Franciscan Nicolás Espital, who left to preach the faith in Muslim Granada.[143] And some martyrdom-seeking Franciscans brought death upon themselves by publicly assailing the Prophet, for instance, in Jerusalem in 1391.[144] The crusade continued to have its attractions,

---

[140] R. Röhricht, ed., "Lettres de Ricoldo de Monte Croce," *Archives de l'Orient latin* 2 (1884): 268–69. Back in 1287, Bishop Guillaume of Amiens wryly observed that in no country had the Mendicants succeeded in establishing Christianity: H. Denifle and E. Chatelain, eds., *Chartularium Universitatis Parisiensis*, vol. 2 (Paris, 1891; reprint, Brussels, 1964), no. 543, p. 15.

[141] Müller, ed., "Raymundi Lulli Disputatio," p. 323.

[142] *Improbatio Alcorani*, in PG 154:1042A (the Byzantine statesman and scholar Demetrius Cydones translated the work into Greek about 1360, thereby acknowledging the West's preeminence in anti-Islamic polemic); the relevant passage from the *Libellus* appears in A. Dondaine, "Ricoldiana: Notes sur les oeuvres de Ricoldo da Montecroce," *Archivum Fratrum Praedicatorum* 37 (1967): 163.

[143] T. Rymer, *Foedera*, vol. 3 (London, 1706), p. 851; G. Palanca, "Misión de Fr. Nicolás Espital, O.F.M., al reino de Granada en 1383," *Archivo Ibero-Americano* 4 (1915): 431–32.

[144] See chap. 3, n. 99 above. The Franciscans who settled on "Mount Zion" in 1335 were allowed to celebrate Divine Office there, but not "Sarracenis publice praedicare": *Ludolphi de itinere Terrae Sanctae Liber*, ed. F. Deycks, Bibliothek des litterarischen Vereins in Stuttgart, 25 (Stuttgart, 1851), p. 77. For a public sermon on the Mount, which took place in about 1358 "coram omnibus Saracenis advenientibus" and did not entail

and not only for noblemen: Among the volunteers who flocked to Avignon in 1309 to take part in the Crusade of Rhodes, there were no fewer than forty burgesses from the Westphalian town of Soest.[145] In 1364, when Peter I of Cyprus crisscrossed Catholic Europe organizing the crusade that was to sack Alexandria one year later, the knights and burgesses of Esslingen and Erfurt offered to join.[146] And while the actual military expeditions were few and mostly limited in scope, there was a great proliferation of crusade plans. Some of them, possibly under Llull's influence, aimed also at Saracen conversion. In his On the Recovery of the Holy Land, written about 1306, the French pamphleteer Pierre Dubois advances inter alia the eccentric proposal that especially trained Catholic girls be given in marriage to Saracen chiefs and encouraged to lead them toward baptism. Intent on manipulating for his purposes the strains purportedly inherent in Saracen polygamy, Dubois argues that these wives, knowing that their husbands' baptisms would entail their passage into monogamy, would strive the more zealously for their conversion.[147] Again, toward the end of a detailed crusade plan written in early 1312, Bishop Guillaume Durant of Mende suggests that before the departure of the crusade, learned preachers should leave for Outremer and Greece. Should the infidels receive them well, the preaching may bear much fruit; "should they refuse to receive them, they may be more rightfully attacked."[148] The dispatch of preachers in advance of the crusade recalls Archbishop Pecham's suggestion of 1292; the more rightful Catholic assault in the

---

punishment, see J. Smet, ed., *The Life of Saint Peter Thomas by Philippe de Mézières* (Rome, 1954), p. 81. For a succinct survey of Mendicant activity in Egypt and Syria during this period see Richard, *La papauté*, pp. 261–65.

[145] H. Lahrkamp, "Nordwestdeutsche Orientreisen und Jerusalemwallfahrten im Spiegel der Pilgerberichte," *Oriens Christianus* 40 (1956): 117–18. On commoner participation in Louis IX's oriental crusade see B. Z. Kedar, "The Passenger List of a Crusader Ship, 1250: Towards the History of the Popular Element on the Seventh Crusade," *Studi Medievali* 3.13, 1 (1972): 267–79. See also Riley-Smith, *What Were the Crusades?* pp. 62–65.

[146] Runciman, *A History* (chap. 1, n. 56), 3:442.

[147] Petrus de Bosco, *De recuperatione Terrae Sanctae*, in J. Bongars, *Gesta Dei per Francos* 2:336.

[148] Guillaume Durant, *Informacio brevis super hiis que viderentur ex nunc fore providenda quantum ad passagium*. BN lat. 7470, fol. 123r, lower margin: "Item quod ante generale passagium premitterentur ultra mare et in greciam multi religiosi et seculares bene literati et bone vite ad predicandum infidelibus. Nam ex hoc posset sequi, spiritu sancto cooperante, magnus fructus si eos reciperent. Et si nollent recipere, possent iustius impugnari." For a short summary of Durant's plan, see A. S. Atiya, *The Crusade in the Later Middle Ages* (London, 1938), pp. 68–70.

wake of infidel refusal amounts to an unmeticulous restatement of the Innocentian linkage.

No novel conceptions of the relationship between mission and crusade were proffered in this age, which witnessed the decline of both. But as so often happens, ideas that remained vague or disconnected while the issue was live and pressing now achieved their mature formulation. It has already been seen that Robert Holcot about 1340 and John Gower some fifty years later gave well-rounded expression to two extreme, diametrically opposed views on mission and crusade, the one explicitly advocating Christianization at the point of the sword, the other coupling a full endorsement of preaching with complete rejection of crusading. Holcot, in addition, lucidly pinpointed the reason for the inevitable collision between Catholic preaching and the Islamic legislation against blasphemy: "It is not possible," he explains, "to teach the life of Christ except by destroying and condemning the law of Machomet."[149] The issue of preaching by invective was squarely faced when, some time before 1345, Franciscans formally discussed the *quaestio* whether a Christian may preach in a mosque and attack there the law of Machomet.[150] And when in 1326 Andrea of Perugia, the Franciscan bishop of Zaitun in Mongol China, observed that "we can preach [here] freely and safely, yet none of the Jews and the Saracens does convert," he must have realized that the Islamic prohibition against Christian missionizing was not the only reason for the missionaries' lack of success among Saracens.[151] Perhaps it dawned upon him that work among adherents of that self-confident high culture, Islam, was doomed to fail wherever the preaching was not backed by power.

But while extreme views on mission and crusade were expressly formulated, it was the Innocentian conception of crusade paving the way for mission that remained the most influential. Transmitted from one generation to another through the channels of canon law and theology, studied at the universities, enjoying the aura of authority, obviously congruent with mainstream patristic thought, and sufficiently consonant with the hard fact that the only Muslim countries to be-

[149] "Saraceni sunt tales qui predicatores fidei non admittunt, imo in lege eorum cautum est quod quicunque predicaverit contra legem Machometi occidatur. Et ideo de eis non est spes conversionis, cum fides sit ex auditu, auditus autem per verbum Dei, Ad Roma. X. Non enim est possibile docere vitam Christi nisi destruendo et reprobando legem Machometi." *Super librum Sapientie*, c. 5, lectio 65.

[150] *Passio fratris Livini gallici*, in Golubovich, *Biblioteca* (chap. 4, n. 8 above), 4:390–92; cf. N. Daniel, *Islam and the West*, pp. 121–22.

[151] "Et nos predicare possumus libere et secure; sed de iudeis et saracenis nemo convertitur; de ydolatris batizzantur quam plurimi, sed batizzati non recte incedunt per viam christianitatis." Wyngaert, ed., *Sinica Franciscana* (n. 47 above), p. 376.

APPENDIXES

1. Processing Information about Muhammad

(a) *A Carolingian View of Islam*

Paschasius Radbertus, Expositio in Matheum, BN lat. 12298 (sec. XII), fol. 81v. PL 120:804 (faulty).

Et ne quis michi obiciat Sarracenos, qui multa regna terrarum nutu Dei suis occuparunt armis et dominantur pene ubique in Christianis, quasi ad eos evangelium Christi necdum pervenerit: pervenit quidem et receperunt Dei noticiam, sed male seducti a quibusdam pseudo-apostolis, ut ita loquar Nicholai discipulis, propriam sibi tam ex veteri testamento quam et ex novo condiderunt legem, ac si sub unius Dei cultu, nec tamen nobiscum nec cum Iudeis quippiam sentire volentes, omnia perverterunt. Qui, /81vb/ dum cupiunt universa suo dominio subiugari, nec querunt quem quisque deum colat, sed ut eis tantum-modo serviatur. A quibus forte quia primum iusto Dei iudicio susce-perunt spiritum erroris, ut multi putant, suscipiendus est Antichristus. Quorum assensu ac dominio tanta poterit peragere, qualia et quanta in apokalipsi Iohannis manifeste leguntur.

205

(b) *Adaptations of the Anastasian Text*[1]

Anastasius Bibliothecarius, *Chronographia Tripertita*, in *Theophanis Chronographia*, ed. C. de Boor, vol. 2 (Leipzig, 1885), pp. 209–10.

Landulfus Sagax, *Historia Romana*, ed. A. Crivelucci, vol. 1 (Rome, 1912), p. 134.

Docuit autem auditores suos, quod, qui occidit inimicum vel ab inimico occiditur, in paradisum ingrediatur. paradisum vero carnalis cibi ac potus et commixtionis mulierum perhibebat fluviumque vini ac mellis et lactis et feminarum non praesentium sed aliarum et mixturam multorum annorum futuram et affluentem voluptatem nec non et alia quaedam luxuria et stultitia plena, compati tamen invicem et auxiliari patienti.

Docuit autem auditores suos, quod qui occidit inimicum uel ab inimico occiditur, in paradysum ingrediatur. Paradysum uero carnalis cibi ac potus et commixtionis mulierum perhibebat fluuiumque uini ac mellis et lactis et feminarum non presentium daliarum [*sic*] *et mixturam multorum annorum futuram et affluentem uoluptatem nec non et alia quedam, luxuria et stultitia plena, compati tamen inuicem et auxiliari patienti.*

[1] See also the relevant part of Hugh of Fleury's first redaction, Appendix 1/c below.

Frutolf of Michelsberg,
Chronicon Universale, ed.
G. Waitz (1844), in
MGH SS 6:153.

Sigebert of Gembloux,
Chronica, ed.
L. C. Bethmann (1844), in
MGH SS 6:323.

Docuit autem auditores suos,
quod qui occidit inimicum,
vel occiditur ab inimico,
paradysum ingreditur;
paradysum vero carnalis cibi
ac potus et commixtionis
mulierum perhibebat capacem,
fluvium quo*que vini* et *mellis*
et lactis ibi esse

    et affluentem
voluptatem multaque *alia*
luxuria et stulticia
plena, quae stultis videbantur
delectabilia ideoque credibilia.

Hic docebat,
quod hi *qui inimicum* occidunt
vel qui *ab inimico* occiduntur,
paradisum ingrediantur.
Paradisum vero esse *carnalis cibi*
ac potus;
      ibique esse
fluvium vini, lactis ac
mellis, et mixturam *feminarum non*
presentium, sed aliarum multo tempore

futuram, et affluentem
voluptatem, et multa huiusmodi.
Hic est Muhammad, cui gentiles adhuc
cultum deitatis adhibent.

207

(c) *Hugh of Fleury's Two Redactions*

First redaction, 1109
BN lat. 4963 (sec. XII), fol. 96r–97r

Second redaction, 1110

A BN lat. 14625 (sec. XII), fol. 70ra–70va
B BN lat. 5013A (sec. XII), fol. 112v–113r
C BN lat. 4963B (sec. XIII), fol. 41va–42ra
V Vat. Reg. lat. 545 (sec. XII), fol. 64r-v.[2]

Verum per idem tempus Cyrus Alexandrinus episcopus, et Sergius Constantinopoleos patriarcha, Monothelitarum heresim predicabant. A quibus depravatus Heraclius

Interea vero augustus Heraclius aberravit a catholica fide.

augustus post tantas victorias aberravit[a] a catholica fide. Unde divino iudicio Agareni, qui et Sarraceni dicuntur, Himmaro[b] duce eius imperium graviter ceperunt lacerare. Nam Himmarus[c] Damaschum[d] et /A 70rb/ regionem Phenicis et Iherusalem totamque Syriam[e] occupavit et Antiochiam comprehendit. Promotus est etiam Mauhias a prefato ty /C 41vb/ ranno pretor et amiras[f] totius regionis que est ab Egypto[g] usque ad Euphraten[h]. Hac preterea tempestate Sarraceni qui et Turci

Tunc Agareni qui et Sarraceni /96v/ dicuntur, Muameth pseudopropheta eis ducatum prebente, a suis sedibus exierunt et imperium Heraclii graviter devastare ceperunt. Muameth autem

dicuntur, Muhamet pseudopropheta eis ducatum prebente, a suis sedibus exierunt et imperium Heraclii graviter devastare ceperunt. Porro iste Muhamet[i] Sarracenorum et Arabum princeps et

pseudopropheta erat Ismahelita.
 Qui cum in primeva etate sua mercator existeret, pergebat

pseudopropheta fuit de genere Hismael[j] filii Abrahe[k]. Qui cum in primeva etate sua esset mercator, pergebat

[a] ob erravit B   [b] Hymmaro B Himaro C Hunmaro V
[c] Hymmarus B Humarus C Hunmarus V   [d] Damascum BC   [e] Siriam B
[f] amyras B   [g] Egipto B   [h] Eufraten C   [i] Muamet C   [j] Hysmael B
[k] Habrahe B Abrae C

[2] On the importance of this manuscript see N. Lettinck, "Pour une édition critique de l'*Historia Ecclesiastica* de Hugues de Fleury," *Revue Bénédictine* 91 (1981): 386–97.

frequenter cum camelis suis apud
Egiptum et Palestinam. Conversabatur
itaque cum Iudeis et Christianis et
tam novum quam vetus testamentum
sepe colloquens eis callide rimabatur;
sed et incantatores adiens magus
perfectissimus effectus est.

Contigit etiam ut ingrederetur Corozaniam
provintiam. Cuius provintie domina
Cadigan nominabatur. Que cum diversas
species, quas secum Muameth attulerat,
miraretur, cepit ei familiarius
adherere. Tunc Muameth sumpta fiducia
penes illam, cepit eam dementare,
et incantationum suarum
prestrictam fantasmate, paulatim
in errorem inducere. Cepit enim
predicare quod ipse esset Messias,
quem esse venturum Iudei expectant,
et astruebat sibi testimonia
de utroque testamento. Suffragabantur
quoque ei tam incantationum prestigia
quam calliditatis eius ingenia copiosa.
Igitur hac opinione non solum potens
mulier decepta est, sed et omnes
Iudei, ad quos fama eius pertingere

poterat, catervatim ad eum confluebant,
ita ut ei crederent et religionem
mandatorum eius quasi legislatoris
susciperent, Moysi lege postposita.
Confluebant etiam ad eum Sarraceni
cum Iudeis. Tunc cepit novas quasdam
leges fingere et eis tradere.
In quibus erat insertum creatorem
Deum esse precipue colendum
et circuncisionis ritum penitus
observandum. Amenitatem etiam paradisi
suis promittebat auditoribus et
astruebat *paradysum carnalis cibi*

frequenter cum camelis suis apud
Egyptum[l] et Palestinam et conversabatur
cum Iudeis et Christianis a quibus
tam novum quam vetus didicit testamentum;

sed et magus
perfectissimus effectus est.
Et cum hac illacque[m] discurreret,
contigit ut Corozaniam[n] ingrederetur
provinciam. Cuius provintie domina
Cadigam[o] nominabatur. Que cum diversas
species, quas secum Muamet[p] attulerat,
miraretur, cepit ei /V 64v/ familiarius
adherere. Quam Muamet[q]

incantationum suarum
prestrictam fantasmate, cepit astu paulatim
in errorem inducere, dicens ei
quod ipse esset Messias,[r]
quem esse venturum adhuc[s] Iudei expectant.

Suffra /B 113r/ gabantur verbis
eius tam incantationum prestigia
quam calliditatis eius ingenia copiosa.
Qua opinione non solum potens
mulier decepta est, sed et omnes
Iudei, ad quos fama eius pertingere
poterat, ad eum cum /A 70 va/
Sarracenis catervatim confluebant,
attoniti tanta novitate rei.

Quibus cepit novas
leges fingere et eis tradere,
adhibens ipsis legibus testimonia
de utroque testamento. Quas leges
Ysmahelite[t] suas appellant,[u]
eumque suum legislatorem esse fatentur.

[l] Egiptum B   [m] illac B
[n] Corrozaniam B Gorozaniam C   [o] Cadigan AC   [p] Muamet C
[q] Muhameth A Muamet C Muameth V   [r] Messyas B   [s] om. B
[t] Ismahelite B Hismahelite C   [u] suas esse dicunt B

ac potus vini scilicet *lactis et mellis,*
et commixtionis mulierum /97r/ habere
sufficientiam utpote *affluentem*
*voluptat*ibus omnium delitiarum.
Docebat quoque illum esse Dei amicum
qui legis ipsius inimicum interficeret.

Igitur prefata mulier videns hominem
Iudeorum et Sarracenorum pariter
contubernio vallatum, existimare cepit
in eo divinam latere maiestatem,
et cum esset vidua assumpsit sibi eum
in maritum. Sicque Muameth totius
provintie illius obtinuit principatum.

Tunc prefata mulier videns hominem
Iudeorum et Sarracenorum pariter
contubernio vallatum, existimabat
in illo divinam latere maiestatem,
et cum esset vidua assumpsit eum sibi
maritum. Sicque Muameth[v] tocius
provincie illius optinuit principatum.
Demum vero Arabes ei adherentes
regnum Persidis ceperunt infestare
ac postmodum orientalis imperii fines
usque ad Alexandriam super Heraclium[x]
invadere. Post hec vero Muameth[y]

Sed cum iam incredibiliter illum
fortuna ditasset et extulisset,
cepit cadere epilentica
passione. Quod cernens Cadigan cepit
omnino contristari quod nupsisset
huiusmodi inpurissimo et epilentico viro.
Quam ille placare desiderans, quasi
religiosis sermonibus demulcebat eam dicens:
quia visionem Gabrihelis angeli
loquentis mecum comtemplor et non ferens
splendorem vultus eius,
defitio et cado. Tunc curavit
mulier interrogare Christianos atque
Iudeos utrum esset aliquis angelus
qui Gabrihel vocaretur. Illi vero
responderunt quod angelus Gabrihel
sepe a Deo mitteretur hominibus sanctis.

cepit cadere frequenter epilentia[z]
passione. Quod Cadigan[aa] cernens opido
tristabatur eo quod nupsisset
inpurissimo homini et epilentio.[bb]
Quam ille placare desiderans, talibus
sermonibus demulcebat dicens:
quia Gabrielem[cc] archangelum
loquentem mecum contemplor et non ferens
splendorem vultus eius, utpote carnalis
homo, deficio /C 42ra/ et cado.

Emanavit ergo a muliere ad omnes
viri discipulos quod ex ore angeli
suam illam susciperet legem,
quam populo dabat.

Credidit ergo mulier
et omnes Arabes et Hismahelite[dd]
quod ex ore archangeli Gabrihelis[ee]
illas susciperet[ff] leges,
quas suis discipulis dabat,
eo quod Gabrihel[gg] archangelus sepe
a Deo mittatur hominibus sanctis.

---

[v] Muhamet B Muameth CV   [x] Eraclium C   [y] Muhamet B Muamet C Muameth V
[z] epilentica V   [aa] Cadigam B   [bb] epilentico V   [cc] per Gabrielem C Gabrihelem V
[dd] Hismaelite B   [ee] Gabrielis B Michaelis C   [ff] suscipere C   [gg] Gabriel BC

(d) *The Spanish Note on Mahmeth and Hugh of Flavigny*

Spanish Note
ed. M. C. Díaz y Díaz, in *Archives d'histoire doctrinale et littéraire du Moyen Age* 45 (1970): 157–58.

Hugh of Flavigny, *Chronicon*, ed. G. H. Pertz (1848), in MGH SS 8:323.

Exortus est Mahmeth haeresiarches
tempore *Heraclii* imperatoris, *anno imperii* ipsius septimo. . . .
Quum esset pusillus,
factus est cuiusdam *viduae*
subditus; *quumque* in negotiis
cupidus foenerator discurreret,
coepit Christianorum conventibus
assidue *interesse*, et ut erat
astutior tenebrae filius, coepit
nonnulla collationibus Christianorum
memoriae commendare, et inter suos
brutos Arabes
cunctis *sapient*ior esse.

Anno Heraclii imperii 5 natus est
Mahamet,

qui *cum esset* infantulus, defunctis patre
et matre, adhesit *viduae* quae et
nutriebat. *Cumque* adolevisset

cepit per scolas *christianorum*
ire et auditoriis *interesse*, et

quae ibi audiebat,
domi hominibus gentis suae
referebat. At illi mirabantur
iam tum in eo *sapient*iam,
cum audirent ab eo quae audierant.
Die igitur quadam,
cum reverteretur ab auditorio,
obviam habuit diabolum habentem
os aureum,
et dicentem se *esse Gabrielem
archangelum*, missum a Deo ad ipsum,
ut praedicaret *genti suae* quae
audierat et sciebat.
Tunc *cepit
praedicare* Mahamet,

. . . Mox erroris spiritus
in speciem vulturis ei apparens,
os aureum sibi ostendens,
angelum Gabrielem esse dixit,
et ut propheta
in *gente sua* appareret impetravit.
Quumque repletus esset tumore
superbiae, *coepit*
inaudita brutis animalibus *praedicare*,
et quasi ratione quadam,
ut ab *idol*orum cultu recederent,
et Deum corporeum in coelis *adorarent*,
insinuavit.

ut derelinquerent *idol*a manu facta
et *adorarent* creatorem
qui fecit quae sunt.
Cumque plures adhererent illi
et ut propheta eum haberent,
congregatis qui secum erant
arma sumpsit,
et ut rex et propheta quos poterat
sibi subiciebat,
et regnavit in Damasco,
et caput regni eius
Babylonia civitas fuit.

Arma sibi credentibus assumere iubet
. . .

. . . apud Damascum Syriae urbem
regni principium fundaverunt.

211

2. LETTERS OF GREGORY IX ON MISSIONIZING AND THE CONVERSION OF SLAVES

a. *Gregory IX to the Patriarch of Jerusalem and to the Commanders of the Military Orders.*
Viterbo, July 28, 1237

Archivio Segreto Vaticano, Reg. Vat. 18, fol. 311r, no. 173. *Cartulaire général de l'Ordre des Hospitaliers de St.-Jean de Jérusalem (1100–1310)*, ed. J. Delaville Le Roulx, vol. 2 (Paris, 1897), p. 513, no. 2168 (reconstruction of the copy sent to the Knights Hospitaller); *Acta Honorii II (1216–27) et Gregorii IX (1227–41) e registris Vaticanis aliisque fontibus*, ed. A. L. Tautu (Città del Vaticano, 1950), no. 228, pp. 307–8 (faulty). Po 10424. *Reg. Greg. IX*, ed. Auvray, no. 3792 (summary).

Patriarche Jerosolimitano apostolice sedis legato, archiepiscopis et episcopis et ceteris ecclesiarum prelatis in Syrie partibus constitutis, presentes litteras inspecturis.

In transmarinis partibus sepe sepius accidisse dicitur, quod multi sclavorum qui habentur ibidem, amorem catholice fidei pretendentes, ad hoc solum sacramentum baptismatis perceperunt ut, obtenta libertate que secundum[a] terre consuetudinem talibus indulgetur, abirent in viam gentium extra Dei notitiam positarum. Hac igitur de causa, necnon ex eo quod aliqui ex vobis et quidam religiosi partium earundem nolunt huiusmodi sacramenti pretextu sclavos ammittere, ipsis petita humiliter baptismi gratia denegatur. Verum cum ex hoc, non absque Redemptoris offensa et scandalo timentium Dominum nimis saluti depereat animarum, m[andamus] q[uatenus] illos saltem[b] ex sclavis eisdem qui pure et simpliciter propter Deum ascribi[c] fidelium collegio cupiunt et deposcunt, in servitute pristina permansuri, baptiçari[d] libere permittatis; circa ipsos[e] quibus facultatem adeundi ecclesiam et percipiendi sacramenta ecclesiastica concedatis,[f] illud humanitatis studium exercentes, quod et divine voluntati sit placitum, et fidei proferat incrementum. Datum ut supra.[3]

In e[undem] m[odum] Magistro et Fratribus Hospitalis Jerosolimitan.
In e[undem] m[odum] Magistro et Fratribus Militie Templi.
In e[undem] m[odum] Preceptori et Fratribus Hospitalis Sancte Marie Teutonicorum Jerosolim. in Accon.[4]

[a] super   [b] om.   [c] adscribi   [d] baptizari   [e] illos   [f] concesseritis

---

[3] The previous letter has "Datum Viterbii, V kal. Augusti, anno undecimo."

[4] The version preserved by the Dominicans and printed in *Bullarium*, ed. Ripoll and Bremond (chap. 4, n. 21 above), 7:15, no. 221, has a different protocol and eschatocol, and exhibits variants a through f, as indicated above.

b. *Gregory IX Grants the Crusading Privilege to
Franciscan and Dominican Missionaries in Outremer.
Lateran, March 4, 1238*

Archivio Segreto Vaticano, Reg. Vat. 18, fol. 365r-v, no. 446. Po 10525.
Reg. Greg. IX, ed. Auvray, no. 4153 (summary).

Universis fratribus minoribus et predicatoribus per terram ultramarinam
consti[tutis].

Credentes quod non minus in oculis Redemptoris habeatur acceptum infideles ad fidem divini verbi propositione convertere antequam[a] armis Sarracenorum perfidiam expugnare, vobis, qui in terra ultramarina ad conversionem
paganorum vel aliorum verbo seu sancte laboratis conversationis exemplo, illam concedimus veniam peccatorum, que in eiusdem terre succursum venientibus, in generali concilio est concessa. Datum Laterani, IIII nonas Martii,
anno undecimo.[5]

[a] quam

c. *Gregory IX to the Patriarch of Jerusalem and
His Suffragans. Lateran, March 9, 1238*

Archivio Segreto Vaticano, Reg. Vat. 18, fol. 365r, no. 440. *Reg. Greg. IX*,
ed. Auvray, no. 4147 (excerpt).
Eisdem.[6]

Intelleximus quod nonnulli in regno Jerosolimitano, habentes sclavos et alios
Sarracenos in servos, ipsis, quia magis possessiones quam animas diligunt,
facultatem audiendi verbum Dei vel suscipiendi sacramentum baptismatis penitus
interdicunt. Et licet tibi, frater patriarcha, super hoc alia vice direxerimus scripta
nostra, sumptis quibusdam occasionibus nichil exinde facere voluisti. Quod-
circa m[andamus] q[uatenus] singuli in propriis diocesibus, omni occasione
cessante, huiusmodi infidelium dominos, ut ipsos saltem semel in mense ac in
precipuis festivitatibus predicationem audire ac sacrum baptisma suscipere, in
servitute pristina moraturos; et conversorum dominos, quod eosdem conversos confiteri peccata sua, et eisdem festivitatibus ac diebus dominicis officiis
interesse permittant, aliquo privilegio vel indulgentia non obstante, mo[nitione]
pre[missa] per cen[suram] ec[clesiasticam], ap[pellatione] postpo[sita],
com[pellatis], mandatum nostrum taliter impleturi, quod çelatores animarum,
sicut vos esse credimus, merito comprobemini, nosque vobis super hoc aliter
scribere non cogamur. Datum ut supra.[7]

[5] The version preserved by the Dominicans and printed in *Bullarium*, ed. Ripoll and
Bremond, 1:99, has a different protocol and eschatocol, and exhibits a single—but noticeable—variant, as indicated above.

[6] The previous letter was addressed "patriarche Jerosolimitano apostolice sedis legato
et eius suffraganeis."

[7] The previous date is "VII idus Martii, anno undecimo."

d. *Gregory IX to William of Modena, His Legate in Livonia.*
Lateran, March 9, 1238

Archivio Segreto Vaticano, Reg. Vat. 18, fol. 363v, no. 427. Po. 10529. *Reg. Greg. IX*, ed. Auvray, no. 4124 (summary).

Episcopo quondam Mutinensi apostolice sedis legato.

Cum lux vera que illuminat omnem hominem venientem in hunc mundum vocat aliquos[a] ad ammirabile[b] lumen suum, ut relicto gentilitatis errore fidem Domini nostri Iesu Christi recipiant per baptismum, debent renati huiusmodi ex aqua et spiritu sancto favorem et gratiam apud Christicolas invenire, ut et fideles çelari[c] conversionem infidelium videantur et infideles ad fidem emulatione laudabili provocentur. Cupientes igitur fidem catholicam propagari, m[andamus] q[uatenus] si quos de servili conditione seu alias[d] alterius ditioni subiectos ad baptismi gratiam, Domino inspirante, contigerit convolare, a dominis[e] eorumdem Christianis, videlicet religiosis vel secularibus, in favorem fidei Christiane de onere servitutis facias aliquid relaxari, et dari eis liberam facultatem confitendi peccata, adeundi ecclesiam, et divina officia audiendi, indulgentia seu privilegio aliquo non obstante.

Datum Laterani VII idus Martii, pontificatus nostri anno undecimo.[8]

[a] aliquot   [b] admirabile   [c] zelari   [d] alios   [e] domnis

e. *Gregory IX to the Bishop of Majorca.*
Lateran, January 26, 1240

Archivio Segreto Vaticano, Reg. Vat. 19, fol. 149 [143]r, no. 224. *Reg. Greg. IX*, ed. Auvray, no. 5063 (summary).

Eidem.[9]

Insinuantibus dilectis filiis populo Maioricarum accepimus, quod plures ex Sarracenis servis eorum quos capiunt, ut aufugere valeant, baptismi percipiunt sacramentum, et sic, non absque gravi dampno fidelium, in statum pristinum dampnabiliter relabuntur. Quare nobis humiliter supplicarunt ut eis, quod huiusmodi baptiçatos ut servos possidere valeant, concedere curaremus. Nos igitur, eorum supplicationibus inclinati, m[andamus] q[uatenus] consideratis circumstantiis universis, super hoc provideas prout animarum saluti et terre statui videris expedire.

Datum Laterani VII kal. Februarii, pontificatus nostri anno tertiodecimo.

f. *Gregory IX to the Bishop of Majorca.*
Lateran, April 24, 1240

Archivo de la Catedral, Palma de Mallorca. Liber privilegiorum, fol. 2a.

---

[8] The version printed in *Liv-, Est-, und Curländisches Urkundenbuch*, ed. F. G. von Bunge, vol. 1, 1 (Reval, 1853), no. 158, col. 203–4, has a different protocol and eschatocol, and exhibits variants a through e, as indicated above.

[9] The previous letter was addressed "episcopo Maioricensi."

J. Miralles and M. Rotger, eds., "Cartulario del primer obispo de Mallorca," *Bolletí de la Societat Arquelógica Luliana* 13 (1910–11): 159, no. 35. (I would like to thank Señor Antonio Mut, director of the Archivo del Reino de Mallorca, for putting at my disposal a photocopy of this entry.)

Gregorius nonus concessit episcopo Maioricensi ut possit concedere populo Maioricensi quod baptizatos servos suos valeant vendere, prout sibi videbitur expedire. Datum Laterani ut supra.[10]

3. URBAN IV ON SARACENS AND JEWS ASKING TO CONVERT AT ACRE. ORVIETO, JULY 26, 1264

Archivio Segreto Vaticano, Reg. Vat. 29, fol. 198v, no. 975. O. Posse, *Analecta Vaticana* (Innsbruck, 1878), p. 35, no 427 (summary); *Reg. Urbain IV*, ed. J. Guiraud, no. 1925 (summary).

Patriarche Jerosolimitano apostolice sedis legato. Nonnulli, sicut accepimus, Sarraceni pauperes et Judei, converti ad unitatem ecclesie cupientes, ad civitatem Acconensem accedunt et postulant baptiçari. Verum licet donum baptismatis consequantur, tamen quia, paupertatis mole depressi, non habent unde possint in vite necessariis sustentari, prius quam catholice fidei doctrinam suscipiant, abire sinuntur. Nec interdum aliqui eorum in huiusmodi proposito perseverant, quin immo ad errores solitos redeunt, in obprobrium nominis christiani. Unde cum in exaltationem et augmentum fidei cedere dinoscatur, cum tales de gentilitatis errore ad Dominum convertuntur, et si eos resilire contingat, quodammodo cedat in ipsius fidei detrimentum, f[raternitati] t[ue] m[andamus] q[uatenus] super hiis apponas salubre remedium; illis quos taliter converti contigitur, saltem per aliquos dies in quibus catheçiçari valeant et in fidei doctrina formari, ab ecclesiis vel monasteriis Acconensis civitatis et diocesis facias, per te vel per alium seu alios, in vite necessariis secundum quod expedire videris provideri. Contra[dictores] etc. usque compescendo. Non obstante si aliquibus a sede apostolica sit indultum, quod inter[dici] vel excom[municari] nequeant aut sus[pendi] per litteras apostolicas non facientes plenam et expressam de indulto huiusmodi mentionem. Datum apud Urbemveterem, VII kal. Augusti, anno tertio.

4. JUSTIFYING ANTI-SARACEN WARFARE: FROM ERMOLD THE BLACK TO THOMAS AQUINAS

a. *Ermold the Black, "Poem on Louis the Pious," Book 1, lines 287–98*

Ermoldi Nigelli Carmina, ed. E. Dümmler (1884), in MGH Poetae Latini 2:14.

> Tum soboles Caroli sapienti haec edidit ore:
> 'Accipite hoc animis consilium, proceres.

---

[10] The previous date is "VIII kal. Madii pontificatus eiusdem anno XIIII."

Si gens ita deum coleret, Christoque placeret,
Baptismique foret unguine tincta sacri,
Pax firmanda esset nobis, pax atque tenenda,
Coniungi ut possit relligione deo.
Nunc vero execranda manet, nostramque salutem
Respuit, et sequitur daemonis imperia.
Idcirco hanc nobis pietas miserata tonantis
Servitii famulam reddere namque valet.
Nunc nunc actutum muros properemus et arces,
O Franci, ut redeat pristina vis animis.'

b. *Bernard of Clairvaux, "In Praise of the New Chivalry"*

De laude novae militiae, III, 4, in *S. Bernardi opera*, ed. J. Leclercq and H. M. Rochais, vol. 3 (Rome, 1963), p. 217.

Non quidem vel pagani necandi essent, si quo modo aliter possent a nimia infestatione seu oppressione fidelium cohiberi. Nunc autem melius est ut occidantur, quam certe relinquatur virga peccatorum super sortem iustorum, ne forte extendant iusti ad iniquitatem manus suas.

c. *Bernard of Clairvaux, Call for the Second Crusade*

J. Leclercq, ed., "L'encyclique de Saint Bernard en faveur de la croisade," *Revue Bénédictine* 81 (1971): 299, and "A propos de l'encyclique de Saint Bernard sur la croisade," ibid. 82 (1972): 312 (corrections). [A somewhat different reading, with no reasons given for the changes, appears in J. Leclercq and H. Rochais, eds., *S. Bernardi opera*, vol. 8 (Rome, 1977), pp. 316–17.]

Si Iudaei penitus atteruntur, unde iam sperabitur eorum in fine promissa salus, in fine futura conversio? Plane et gentiles, si essent similiter subiugati, in eo quidem iudicio essent exspectandi similiter quam gladiis appetendi. Nunc autem cum in nos esse coeperint violenti, oportet vim vi repellere eos, qui non sine causa gladium portant.

d. *Oliver of Cologne, Letter to the Sultan*

Epistola salutaris regi Babilonis conscripta, ed. H. Hoogeweg, in *Die Schriften des Kölner Domscholasters Oliverus* (Tübingen, 1894), pp. 299–300.

Si gens tua doctrinam Christi et praedicatores eius publice admitteret, ecclesia Dei gladium verbi Dei libenter ei mitteret et ad consortium fidei catholice gaudens invitaret. Sed quoniam aliud remedium non invenit contra potentiam Sarracenorum, lex catholicorum principum gladio materiali ad defensionem Christianitatis et iuris sui recuperationem licenter utitur. Nam vim vi repellere omnes leges et omnia iura permittunt.

e. *Innocent IV on the Christian Right to Preach*

Apparatus to X 3.34.8

A   Vat. lat. 1443 (sec. XIV), fol. 228vb
B   Clm 6350 (sec. XIV), fol. 166va
C   Vat. Urb. lat. 157 (sec. XV), fol. 130ra-rb
D   Clm 15704 (sec. XV), fol. 159va-vb
E   ed. Lyons, 1525, p. 165a
F   ed. Frankfurt/M., 1570, p. 430cd

Item licet non debeant infideles cogi ad fidem, quia omnes libero[a] arbitrio relinquendi sunt et sola Dei gratia in hac vocatione[b] valeat. XLV.[c] d. de Iudeis.[11] tamen mandare potest papa infidelibus quod admittant predicatores evangelii in terris sue iurisdictionis, nam cum omnis creatura rationabilis facta sit ad Deum laudandum. Senten. lib.II.di.prima c. et si queritur in fine.[d][12] quare[e] si ipsi prohibent predicatores[f] hoc[g] predicare, peccant et ideo puniendi sunt.

In omnibus autem predictis casibus et in aliis ubi licet pape eis aliquid mandare,[h] si non obediant[i] sunt compellendi[j] brachio seculari et[k] indicendum est bellum contra eos per papam et non per alios, nisi ubi quis[l] de suo iure[m] contendit. Nec est contra II.q.I. multi.[13] ubi dicitur quod non pertinet ad nos iudicare de hiis qui[n] foris sunt,[o] quia intelligitur quod non debemus eos iudicare[p] excommunicando vel compellendo[q] ad fidem, ad quam sola Dei gratia vocantur. XLV.[r] d. de Iudeis. . . .[14]

Sed dices nunquid et[s] eodem[t] modo debet papa admittere[u] illos qui vellent predicare legem Macometi.[v] Respondeo non.[x] Non enim ad paria debemus eos nobiscum iudicare,[y] cum ipsi sint in errore et nos in via veritatis, et hoc pro constanti tenemus.

[a] liberi C   [b] vacatione D   [c] XLI. C   [d] Senten.II.l.d.I. in fine A Senten. II.1.d.I se B l.d.I. in fine D Senten.II.d.I.si queritur EF   [e] om. BEF   [f] predicatoribus C   [g] om. EF   [h] mandare eis aliquid B aliquid eis mandare CD   [i] hobediant A et si non obediant CD   [j] compellendi sunt EF   [k] om. AD et etiam C   [l] per alios ubi aliquid B per alios ubi quis EF   [m] iure suo BDEF   [n] que BD   [o] sint D   [p] iudicare eos B   [q] compellendo eos C   [r] XL. ABCD   [s] om. D   [t] Sed dicet mihi quod eodem B   [u] admiscere B amittere D   [v] Mathometi A Machometi CDEF   [x] om. D   [y] iudicare nobiscum C

[11] D.45 c.5.
[12] Peter Lombard, *Sententiae*, II.1.6, in PL 192:653: "Et si quaeritur ad quid creata sit rationalis creatura, respondetur: Ad laudandum Deum."
[13] C.2 q.1 c.18.
[14] D.45 c.5.

APPENDIX 4

f. *Thomas Aquinas, "Utrum infideles compellendi sint ad fidem"*

Secunda Secundae Summae Theologiae, qu. 10, art. 8, in *S. Thomae Aquinatis Opera omnia*, vol. 8 (Rome, 1895), pp. 89–90.

... Respondeo dicendum quod infidelium quidam sunt qui nunquam susceperunt fidem, sicut gentiles et Iudaei. Et tales nullo modo sunt ad fidem compellendi ut ipsi credant: quia credere voluntatis est. Sunt tamen compellendi a fidelibus, si facultas adsit, ut fidem non impediant vel blasphemiis, vel malis persuasionibus, vel etiam apertis pesecutionibus. Et propter hoc fideles Christi frequenter contra infideles bellum movent, non quidem ut eos ad credendum cogant (quia si etiam eos vicissent et captivos haberent, in eorum libertate relinquerent an credere vellent): sed propter hoc ut eos compellant ne fidem Christi impediant.

In his authoritative commentary, written between 1507 and 1522, Cardinal Cajetan explicitly refers to the prohibition of Christian preaching:

In eodem articulo octavo considera diligenter causam iustam belli contra infideles, et compulsionis eorum: ne scilicet fidem Iesu Christi impediant aliquo trium modorum: scilicet vel blasphemiis, puta dicendo mala de Christo Iesu aut Sanctis eius aut Ecclesia eius; vel persuasionibus inducendo nostros ad infidelitatem; vel persecutionibus, sive in communi, ut quotidie videmus Turcas invadere Christiani nominis gentes, vel in particulari, si Christianos aut praedicatores fidei occidant. Et fabrica super illam quoniam ad impedimenta fidei spectat quod non sufferunt in terris suis praedicationem publicam fidei, quod praemiant abnegantes Christum et accedentes ad eorum fidem, et alia huiusmodi.

g. *A Franciscan* Exemplum *on Francis and the Sultan*

L. Oliger, ed., "Liber exemplorum fratrum minorum saeculi XIII," *Antonianum* 2 (1927): 251; spelling and punctuation altered to conform with the original, Vat. Ottob. lat. 522, fol. 250v.

Aliam questionem idem soldanus fecit ei dicens: Deus vester docuit in evangeliis suis malum pro malo vos non debere reddere, non deffendere pallium, etc. Quanto magis ergo non debent Christiani terras nostras invadere? etc. Vos, inquit beatus Franciscus, non videmini totum legisse Christi domini nostri evangelium. Alibi enim dicit: Si oculus tuus scandalizat te, erue eum et prohice a te, etc. Per quod quidem docere nos voluit, nullum hominem esse ita carum nobis, vel ita propinquum, etiam si carus nobis fuerit quasi oculus capitis, quin separare, eruere et penitus eradicare debeamus, si nos a fide et amore Dei nostri conetur avertere. Unde propter hoc Christiani vos et terram quam occupastis iuste invadunt, quia blasphematis nomen Christi, et ab eius cultura quos potestis avertitis. Si autem velletis creatorem et redemptorem cognoscere, confiteri et colere, diligerent vos quasi se ipsos. Mirantibus quoque astantibus in responsionibus eius.

5. JOACHIM OF FIORE: THREE PASSAGES ON CRUSADING

This tentative edition is based on the following manuscripts:

A   Milan, Biblioteca Ambrosiana H 15, inf. misc. (sec. XIII–XIV), fol. 131ra-rb, 146ra-rb, 159ra

C   Rome, Biblioteca Casanatense 1411 (sec. XIV), fol. 117rb-va, 142rb-va, 164vb–165ra

T   Todi, Biblioteca Comunale, Cod. 43 (sec. XIII, 2d half), fol. 130ra-rb, 157ra-rb, 181va-182ra

Tr Troyes, Bibliothèque municipale, MS 249 (sec. XIII), fol. 99vb–100ra

V   Vatican, Chig. A. VIII. 231 (sec. XIV), fol. 99va-vb

These and other MSS of the *Expositio in Apocalypsim* have been listed by Marjorie Reeves, *The Influence of Prophecy*, pp. 512–13. In the printed edition of Venice 1527 (reprint, Frankfurt/M., 1964), the passages in question appear on pp. 134d–135a, 164d–165a, 191d–192b.

(a) [Pars tercia]

Decem cornua que vidisti decem reges sunt qui regnum[a] *necdum acceperunt*[b] *sed una hora tanquam reges regnum accipiunt post bestiam.*[15] Et paulo post:[c] *hii odient fornicariam et desolatam facient eam*[d] *et nudam et carnes eius manducabunt et ipsam igne concremabunt. Deus enim dedit in corda eorum ut faciant quod illi placitum est ut dent regnum suum bestie donec consumentur verba Dei. Et mulier quam vidisti est civitas magna que habet regnum super reges terre.*[16] O utinam poneret ad cor verba hec[e] urbs superba et non presumeret de aquis multis,[17] id est[f] de[g] multitudine

C 117va   populorum suorum. Utinam / vel hoc cor eius concuteret[h] quod nuper accidit regi suo et multitudini populorum qui fuerunt cum eo, quomodo defecerunt in via nemine persequente, et vix pauci homines de tam mul-

A 131rb   tis potuerunt evadere, ut discat omnis ecclesia sanctorum non dari victoriam multitudini armatorum, / sed reliquiis fidelis populi qui conten-

Tr 100ra   dunt in fide. Dictum est autem / quod siccande essent[i] aque Eufrates *ut prepararetur*[j] *via regibus ab ortu solis.*[18] Et[k] quod sine gemitu dicendum non est, iniciatio quedam terribilis iam precessit super eo, scilicet quod nuper accidit super inclito[l] illo exercitu Frederici magni et potentissimi imperatoris, et aliis exercitibus populi christiani, qui transeuntes mare in

T 130rb   / infinita multitudine, vix in paucis reliquiis pene sine[m] effectu remearunt ad propria. *Ab ortu* autem *solis via regibus* illis[n] preparari dicta est, quia magna tribulatio que presens est a parte orientis incepisse dinoscitur.[o]

[15] Apoc. 17:12.

[16] Apoc. 17:16–18.

[17] Cf. Apoc. 17:1: "ostendam tibi damnationem meretricis magnae quae sedet super aquas multas."

[18] Apoc. 16:12.

Non enim videre possum quomodo hoc verbum allegorice intelligi[p] queat, sicut et multa alia, nisi forte dicamus terram Jherosolimitanam[q] vocari spiritualiter ortum solis, quia ibi ortus est sol iusticie, Christus Deus noster. Igitur *equestris exercitus*[19] quem vidit in visione Johannes, falsos illos christianos designat, et regnum pariter Sarracenorum, quod licet videamus proficere in regnum novum, quod designatum est in pedibus statue quam vidit in visione Nabuchodonosor rex, *de plantario tamen ferri* ortum est,[20] id est[r] de illo regno[s] Sarracenorum, quod initiatum est a Mahomet.[t] Et hoc quod[u] summopere notandum credidi, ne quis me arguat bis[v] ducere[x] ad conflictum gentem Sarracenorum, id est[y] in duobus temporibus, quarto scilicet et sexto, non est contrarium vel absurdum, quia capud[z] unum bestie quod[aa] quasi mortuum visum fuit, revixit iterum[bb] a mortuis,[21] et visum est quod fecisset deteriora mala quam que[cc] fecerat a principio. Non est alienum a fide quia[dd] in illa visione Nabuchodonosor aurum quidem positum est semel, argentum semel, es[ee] similiter / semel, ferrum autem non semel sed bis, et[ff] dictum est quod duo regna ultima essent ferrea, licet sequens *mixtum luto*[gg] et quod alterum ex altero orietur.[22] Hec idcirco dico, quia duo ista ultima regna locum habent[hh] inter conflictus septem angelorum de quibus agimus in quarto scilicet[ii] et sexto tempore, ceteris tribus regnis ab hac communione seclusis.

V 99vb

[a] regnum etc. A   [b] om. Tr   [c] Et post A   [d] eam etc. usque que habet regnum super reges terre A   [e] hec verba V   [f] de aquis suis hoc est CTTrV   [g] om. Tr   [h] concuteret cor eius CTTr converteret cor eius V   [i] erunt A   [j] preparetur CTTrV   [k] om. T   [l] insolito A   [m] sine pene A   [n] illius TV   [o] dignoscitur T   [p] om. C   [q] terra Ierosolimitana A   [r] hoc est CTTrV   [s] illo regno T   [t] Moameth CV Moamech T Mahometh Tr   [u] quidem CTTrV   [v] his C hiis T   [x] dicere V   [y] hoc est CTTrV   [z] caput C   [aa] vel Tr   [bb] iterum revixit CTTrV   [cc] om. A   [dd] quod A   [ee] hes Tr   [ff] sed et C   [gg] luce T   [hh] regna ultima habent locum CTTrV   [ii] videlicet CTTrV

(b) [*Pars quarta, distinctio quarta*]

. . . quia omnia capita visa sunt mortua, visum est quod bestia penitus[a] esset mortua. Verumptamen non est ita, quia aliud demonstratur in fine. Mortua sunt[b] revera cetera, *unum* vero non fuit mortuum sed *quasi* mortuum.[23] Nam quis audivit unquam[c] a tempore illo[d] quo in manu Romanorum contriti sunt Judei pro legis sui tuitione, eos contra[e] Christianos arma levasse? Quis aliquod paganorum regnum pro[f] cultura ydo-

[19] Apoc. 9:16.   [20] Dan. 2:41.
[21] Cf. Apoc. 13:3.   [22] Cf. Dan. 2:32, 41, 43.
[23] Cf. Apoc. 13:3.

lorum post Juliani obitum adversus christianos pugnasse? Quis Gothos et Guandalos et Longobardos conversos tandem ad catholicam fidem, ad rigorem antique perfidie remeare persensit? Saracenorum vero ex tot annis semel inchoata[g] perfidia perseverat in malo et ubique christianum nomen impugnare pro viribus non desistit. O quot milia christianorum in eorum manibus data sunt et quam multos et quam variis tormentis[h] cruciant in odium crucifixi. Capud[i] istud mori non potuit usque ad presens, vivit usque adhuc, ut[j] operetur adhuc[j] mortem multorum, ut perficiat dum advivit[k] opera regis sui. Sed cur se illud Johannes *quasi* mortuum vidisse[l] perhibuit? Forte futurum est ut capud illud christiani et predicando[m] magis quam preliando usque pene ad defectum et interitionem[n] perducant, et iterum resumptis viribus ad pristinam redeat feritatem.[o] Si completum non[p] est, brevi temporis spacio[q] utrumque poterit consummari. Sed non deerit forsitan qui completum existimet materialibus armis, nequaquam extimans contempnenda[r] que ante annos aliquot[s] in ecclesia acciderunt. Anno enim[t] ut fertur 1015[u] incarnacionis dominice signum in aere satis apparuit ammirandum, stellas scilicet innumeras circumquaque discurrere et velud in modum avium / aerias[v] semitas pervagari. Quo precedente signo ad exortacionem Urbani pape christia/ni undique commoti statuerunt ire ultra mare ad liberandum sepulcrum, quod et factum est. Tanta vero post hec data est[w] audacia christianis, ut iam pene paganorum multitudinem crederes annullatam et veluti ad nichilum Christo prevalente redactam. Ut enim multa in uno perstringam: christianis qui ultramarinas partes sunt aggressi,[x] Sarraceni qui erant in Egipto prestiterunt tributa, Constantinopolitanis hii qui possidebant Asyam. Affrica et que prope sunt civitates a rege Scilicie capte,[y] christianos ceperant habere colonos.[24] Reges Hyspaniarum sepe[z] de hostibus triumphabant.[aa] Quis igitur tot victoriis de gente illa indomabili glorificatos cerneret[bb] christianos et non secure capud bestie extimaret defunctum? Ac[cc] si quis sano capite circumspicere sufficiat,[dd] videmus in hac die quantulecumque pacis, gentes in circuitu nostro intumescere quasi mare et capud quod erat quasi mortuum, restitutum pristine sanitati,[ee] undique ad cedendas victimas, / undique ad occidendum et devorandum[ff] paratum, facturum quod per eum Dominus[gg] faciendum prescivit. Si vero ut supra diximus completum nondum est, possibile est alio ordine sine mora compleri. Spiritualis enim[hh] sensus huic opinioni magis assentire videtur, scilicet[ii] quod adhuc non sit completum, sed[jj] alio[kk] et sollempniori ordine[ll] sine mora complendum.

C 142va

T 157rb

A 146rb

[a] visum est de bestia quod penitus CT   [b] sunt enim CT   [c] unquam audivit CT
[d] om. T   [e] om. C   [f] et pro CT   [g] ut inchoata C   [h] et quam
multis ac variis tormentis A   [i] caput C   [j-j] om. C   [k] adiuvat C
[l] se vidisse A   [m] ut apud illud christiani prevaleant et predicando CT
[n] intentionem T   [o] veritatem C   [p] nondum CT   [q] spacio temporis CT

[24] This seems to be the only mention of Catholic settlers in the African territories conquered by Roger II.

^r contemplanda C contempnendo T   ^s aliquot annos C annos aliquos T
^t etenim CT   ^u m^oxv^o CT   ^v aerias CT   ^w om. C   ^x aggressi
sunt CT   ^y capte a rege Scilicie C Sicilie T   ^z se C   ^{aa} triumphant T
^{bb} cernerent C   ^{cc} Aut T   ^{dd} sufficeret CT   ^{ee} sospitati CT
^{ff} ad devorandum C   ^{gg} Dominus per eum C   ^{hh} autem CT   ⁱⁱ videlicet CT
^{jj} set C   ^{kk} aliud alio A   ^{ll} modo A

(c) [*Pars sexta, distinctio prima*]

Et facta sunt inquit *fulgura et voces et tonitrua et terremotus factus est*
magnus, qualis numquam fuit ex quo homines esse ceperunt^a *super terram*
talis^b *terremotus sic magnus.*^{b 25} Quando^c vult Deus per successiones temporum mutare statum^d ecclesie ut alia post alia secundum quod scriptum

T 181vb   est consumentur,^e precedunt ante annos aliquot^f / fulgura miraculorum,
voces exortacionum,^g tonitrua spiritualium eloquiorum, sive ut somp-
nolenti quique ac desides excitentur a sompno mortis, sive ut tam ipsi
quam alii intelligant quod novum aliquid facturus sit Dominus super
terram. Puto tamen quod hec signa ceperunt iam olim precedere tem-
poribus^h nostris. Nam et viri sancti precesserunt nos ante non multos
annos,ⁱ qui miracula facerent et qui verbis exortatoriis^j non paucis populum Domini^k ad penitentiam provocarent. Si tamen fuerunt aliqui qui
audirent et cogitarent^l et dicerent in corde suo, quod est hoc, ut qui
norunt diiudicare faciem celi et terre signa quoque temporum presenti-
rent, sed quia dura et terrena corda hominum non possunt sentire nisi

C 165ra   virgam, ecce percussio satis / gravis secuta est in populo nequam, ecce
terremotus factus est magnus. Mota quippe sunt^m corda populorum ex
hiis que acciderunt et commota sunt a mari usque ad mare in omni
potestate et regno occidentalis ecclesie, que aliquid adhuc esse videtur,
zelantibus universis pro iniuria regis sui et cupientibus ulcisci de genti-
bus infidelibus, queⁿ ablato^o signaculo fidei nostre polluunt usque^p adhuc templum sanctum eius. Zelati sunt multi et moti sunt, non animo
solum^q sed et corpore. Quare ergo non profecerunt? Puto pro eo quod
in zelando non rectum ordinem tenuerunt. Oportuerat enim illos con-
siderare primo quam ob causam id passi sumus, quam ob causam tradita
sint sancta nostra in manus extraneas, in manus infidelium gentium^r que
ignorant Deum. Ne forte qui fecit^s aliquando flagellum de resticulis et
eiecit de templo vendentes et ementes,²⁶ ipse nunc pro simili^t culpa con-
gregaverit gentes *in congregationem unius fascis*²⁷ et utatur eis pro flagello
contra nos, eiciens nos iterum de domo sua que facta est a populo *spe-*
*lunca latronum.*²⁸ Quid enim si gentes infideles permittuntur ad tempus

²⁵ Apoc. 16:18.
²⁶ Cf. Joan. 2:15: "et cum fecisset quasi flagellum de funiculis omnes eiecit de tem-
plo."
²⁷ Isa. 24:22.
²⁸ Matt. 21:13, Marc. 11:17, Luc. 19:46.

possidere^u domum ipsam, de qua nos turpiter eiecti sumus, ut Dominus ostendat^v in nobis, qui non servamus^w promissum, multo amplius fore pollutam quam in eis qui nichil promiserunt, si quomodo confundamur, vel isto modo, et agnoscamus vel sero reatum nostrum? Prius enim

T 182ra oportebat nos ipsos pugnare^x contra nos, ut pur/garemus fletibus delicta nostra; et sic premissa satisfactione, si adhuc urgeret necessitas, procedere secure ad bellum, habentes ipsum quem offendimus, Deum vivum placatum, tutorem propicium et^y ducem belli. *Magnus igitur^z terremotus factus est* nimis pro hiis^aa que acciderunt, et quod eo deterius est, nimis^bb magna pro culparum meritis instabilitas animorum. Defecit enim fides et veritas de terra, ubique *motus,*^cc quia ubique scissura. Recedit frater a fratre et proximus a proximo suo, ita ut nichil sit solidum, nichil stabile^dd super terram. Et licet^ee *terremotus* ille *magnus*^ff adhuc post dies aliquot^gg futurus sit, signa tamen motionis illius ac si presencia iam tenemus, et initia pre solito manifesta dolorum future tempestatis vastitatem precurrunt.

^a homines fuerunt CT   ^b-b om. A   ^c Quomodo C   ^d factum A   ^e consumuntur T   ^f aliquos T   ^g exhortationum T   ^h in temporibus CT
^i annos ante A   ^j exhortatoriis T   exortacionis A   ^k Deum C
^l recogitarent CT   ^m sunt quippe C   ^n qui CT   ^o oblato T   ^p om. C
^q solum animo CT   ^r gentium infidelium CT   ^s se et C   ^t sua A
^u possidere ad tempus CT   ^v ostendat Dominus CT   ^w observamus C
^x pungnare C   ^y ac CT   ^z ergo CT   ^aa eis A   ^bb om. CT   ^cc motio CT
^dd sit stabile CT   ^ee quamvis CT   ^ff magnus ille A   ^gg aliquos T

6. Ulrich of Strasbourg: *compulsio inductionis per penas*
Summa de Bono VI, 3, 6

P   BN lat. 15901, fol. 120vb–121rb
V   Vat. lat. 1311, fol. 166va

Domino etiam Ihesu Christo *data est omnis potestas in celo et in terra,* Mathei xxviii,[29] et hoc propter humilitatem passionis propter quam *in nomine* eius debet flecti *omne genu celestium terrestrium et infernorum,* ad Philippenses ii°.[30] Et ideo de regno eius, quod est ecclesia, dicitur Dan. ii: *In diebus regnorum illorum suscitabit Deus celi regnum quod non dissipabitur in eternum, et regnum eius alteri populo non tradetur* et minuet *et*

P 121ra *consumet* omnia *regna hec, et ipsum stabit / in eternum.*[31] Et Dan. vii: *Dedit ei potestatem et honorem et regnum et omnes populi tribus et lingue servient ipsi*^a.[32] Et in Psalmo de rege filio regis dicitur quod^b *adorabunt eum omnes reges*^c etc.[33] Et hac auctoritate rex noster Christus eos qui ad

[29] Matt. 28:18.   [30] Phil. 2:10.
[31] Dan. 2:44.   [32] Dan. 7:14.
[33] Ps. 71:11.

verbi eius vocationem regno[d] subdi contempserunt, iussit compelli ad intrandum per fidem in regnum ecclesie, Luc. xiiii.[34] Et ideo dicit Augustinus ad Vincentium: *Neminem ad unitatem Christi esse cogendum* sed *verbo esse agendum. Sed hec opinio mea non tantum ex verbis contradicentium sed* etiam[c] *demonstrantium superatur exemplis*,[35] scilicet in Paulo, qui percussione et cecitate compulsus est credere, Actuum ix,[36] et in Nabuchodonosor, Dan. v°.[37] Et sepe Dominus populum Israel per flagella revocavit ab ydolatria. Non loquimur autem hic de absoluta compulsione coactionis, quia sic vere dicit Augustinus, quod cetera potest homo facere nolens, sed *credere nonnisi volens.*[38] Sed loquimur de compulsione inductionis per penas, et hoc fit cum ecclesia expugnat Sarracenos et hereticos et alios infideles, et super victos iugum servitutis aggravat si credere nolunt,[f] ut saltem[g] hoc humano timore compulsi fidem suscipiant informem, ut per consuetudinem audiendi et tractandi ea que fidei sunt,[h] facilis et delectabilis eis fiat[i] fides, que prius ex dissuetudine fuit eis[j] irrationabilis et odiosa.[39] Unde dicit Gregorius: *Si rusticus tante*[k] *perfidie et obstinationis fuerit, ut ad Deum minime venire consentiat, tanto pensionis onere gravandus est, ut ipsa exactionis sue pena compellatur ad rectitudinem festinare.*[40] Quapropter patet bella[l] ecclesie iusta esse non solum contra ipsos infideles, sed etiam contra omnes receptores et defensores et cooperatores, et ideo ecclesia iuste possidet ipsos victos in

P 121rb servos et terras / eorum occupat. Nec tenetur ad restitutionem de quocunque dampno eis illato et qui occidunt resistentes non sunt rei homicidii, sed potius tamquam Christo[m] militantes merentur eternum premium. Et in laude eorum convenit dici illud Iudicum[n] v: *Qui sponte obtulistis de Israel animas vestras ad periculum, benedicite Domino*;[41] et infra: *Quia propria voluntate obtulistis vos discrimini, benedicite Domino.*[42] Eadem enim est[o] ratio iustitie de toto orbe terrarum quem Dominus dedit ecclesie,[p] que fuit de terra promissionis quam dedit Deus populo Israel.

[a] ei P   [b] om. V   [c] gentes P   [d] eius regno V   [e] et V   [f] si credere nolunt *bis* V   [g] om. P   [h] sunt fidei V   [i] fiat eis V   [j] om. V   [k] tanta P   [l] hec bella V   [m] pro Christo V   [n] Judith V   [o] om. V   [p] om. V

[34] Cf. Luc. 14:16–23.

[35] Augustine, Ep. 93, no. 17, in PL 33:329–30; here quoted from C.23 q.6 c.3.

[36] Act. 9:3–18.

[37] Dan. 5:20–21.

[38] Augustine, *Tractatus in Iohannis evangelium*, XXVI, 2, ed. R. Willems, Corpus Christianorum, Series Latina, 36 (Turnhout, 1954), p. 260.

[39] Cf. C.23 q.6 d.p.c.4.

[40] *Reg. Greg. I*, IV, 26, in MGH Epp. 1:261; here quoted from C.23 q.6 c.4.

[41] Judic. 5:2.

[42] Judic. 5:9.

7. RAMON LLULL: THREE *questiones* ON PREACHING, WARFARE, AND CONVERSION

Ars iuris (Pla 28)   Montpellier, 1275–81

The printed edition of Rome 1516 abounds in gross misunderstandings and is of little worth. Clm 10654 (sec. XVII), which was partially utilized by von der Heydte in *Die Geburtsstunde des modernen Staates* (Regensburg, 1952), renders the text into humanistic Latin. The present, tentative edition is based on the following manuscripts:

A   Clm 10514 (sec. XIV), fol. 51r, 56v–57r, 59r-v
B   Clm 10534 (sec. XV), fol. lv–2r, 15r–16v, 22r–22v
C   Clm 10538 (sec. XV), fol. 141r–142v, 147v–148r, 161v–162r

B 2v;
C 162r

Figura iuris in duas dividitur.[a] Prima est quadrangularis assituata in circulo, composita de duobus quadrangulis, ut in se patet. . . . / Primus quadrangulus est compositus de quatuor litteris, scilicet[b] A.B.C.D.

A   in hac arte significat Deum
B   unum hominem
C   Ius
D   alium hominem.

Secundus quadrangulus compositus est[c] de quatuor litteris, scilicet[d] E.F.G.H.

E   significat animam B, et
F   corpus B, et
G   significat corpus D,[e]
H   animam D. . . .

[a] dividitur partes B   [b] om. C   [c] est compositus C   [d] om. A   [e] D et A

Duodecimo queritur, utrum papa teneatur de iure mittere predicatores ad infideles.[a]

Inter nos et infideles est differentia quoad EH et quoad FG; quoad EH, quia nos sumus in veritate et ipsi sunt in falsitate; quoad FG, quia mutue non[b] intelligimus nos per lingagium. Sed ista differentia que est inter nos et ipsos est in contrarietate,[c] et est maior quoad EH quam quoad FG. Unde si papa non tenetur[d] mittere predicatores ad infideles, sequeretur quod non teneretur contrarietatem que est inter nos et ipsos convertere in concordantiam quam habere debemus in A, quod est inconveniens maximum, et[e] impossibile et contra bonitatem / magnitudinem etc. sui officii;[f] ergo de iure tenetur.

B 15v

Principium fidei nostre[g] est Christus benedictus et dominus papa est[h] eius vicarius et medium coniunctionis,[i] ut fides nostra exaltetur, et suus finis consistit in convertere infideles et predicare in omni tempore,[j] cum in[k] omni tempore A sit recolibile et intelligibile[l] et amabile, et quia A est magnum[m] in sua recolibilitate etc. Ideo[n] papa de tota sua magnitudine potestatis bonitatis etc. quam habet ratione officii sui, tenetur zelare fidem. Unde patet quod tenetur[o] mittere predicatores infidelibus, alioquin eius officium / esset in privatione magnitudinis bonitatis potestatis etc. quoad principium medium et finem, quod est impossibile.

C 141v

Officium pape est maius quoad EH quam quoad FG, et maius quoad A quam ad EH, et sic papa de iure tenetur multiplicare bonitatem magnitudinem[p] magis in EH quam in FG. Ideo[q] patet quod tenetur mittere predicatores ad infideles ut maioritas sui officii non defficiat in magnitudine bonitatis durationis potestatis, atque ut A non defficiat magnitudini officii pape.

Si papa tenetur mittere predicatores infidelibus, multiplicatur C[r] quoad fidem spem caritatem iusticiam prudentiam et fortitudinem. Ista[s] multiplicatio erit per differentiam concordantiam principii medii et[t] finis et maioritatis in equalitate bonitatis magnitudinis etc. fidei spei[u] etc. et hoc patet per se. Et ideo sequitur quod papa tenetur mittere predicatores scientes ydioma[v] / infidelium, sapientes et devotos, ut multiplicatio virtutum non pereat, et quod[x] materia quam papa habet sub potestate bonitatis sue actionis non sit ociosa.

B 16r

[a] Questio. Utrum papa de iure teneatur mittere predicatores ad infideles. Solucio. A
[b] om. A   [c] et ipsos cum contrarietate A   [d] teneretur A   [e] etiam A
[f] officii sui A   [g] nostre fidei B   [h] om. B   [i] coniunctionis B   [j] in convertere et predicare infideles et hoc in omni tempore A in convertere infideles etc. omni tempore C   [k] om. C   [l] om. A   [m] magnus AC
[n] Et ideo A   [o] teneretur A   [p] et magnitudinem B   [q] Et ideo A
[r] E: ABC, C:Clm 10654, fol. 30v and ed. Rome, 1516, p. XV.   [s] Et ista A
[t] om. A   [u] et spei B   [v] ydiomata A   [x] ut A

Tertiodecimo[a] queritur, utrum imperator teneatur de jure pugnare contra infideles.[b]

Differentia maior est in concordantia de EH quam de FG, et per consequens in[c] contrarietate, unde[c] cum inter nos et infideles sit major differentia et contrarietas quoad EH quam quoad FG, ex eo quia inter nos et ipsos est contrarietas quoad A, ideo / imperator tali modo debet debellare infideles, quod[d] propter contrarietatem que est inter nos et ipsos quoad FG, non destruatur concordantia que potest esse inter nos et ipsos in A quoad EH,[e] nec etiam concordantia quam cum ipsis habere possumus quoad AFG.

C 142r

A 57r

In/fideles sunt materia in qua fideles[f] possunt per majus medium servire A[g] ut ipsos ad finem ad quem sunt creati reducant.[h] Et ideo imperator non debet esse[i] contra illum finem in materia de FG. Verumtamen si infideles sunt rebelles audire predicationem et ostensionem fidei[j] a catholicis, tunc imperator tenetur impugnare ipsos ut forma materiam[k] disponat[l] ad predicationem.

Majoritas[m] major est in EH quam in FG et sic de jure[n] imperator

tenetur impugnare infideles[o] magis quoad EH quam quoad FG, ut substantialiter[p] majoritas conservetur in EF[q] et minoritas in accidentibus.
B 16v Verumtamen[r] / ipsos[s] quoad FG impugnare tenetur,[t] ut illa terra que
adquisita fuit per predicationem, recuperetur et magnitudo officii imperatoris non sit contra magnitudinem bonitatis etc. A.[u]

Posito principio medio fine maioritate et equalitate bonitatis magnitudinis etc.[v] officii imperatoris in concordantia de AEHFG, declaratur
quod imperator de jure tenetur impugnare[x] contra infideles ut superius
dictum est, quia potestatem habet pugnandi; que potestas est bona magna
etc. et sic est principium pugnandi medium[y] et finis. Et si pugnat sunt
C 142v principia[z] media et fines etc. / supradicta in maioritate et concordantia,
et si non pugnat sunt in minoritate et contrarietate sui officii. Unde
patet quod imperator de jure tenetur pugnare contra infideles.

[a] Terdecimo B   [b] Questio. Utrum . . . infideles. Solucio. A   [c-c] om. B
[d] quam A   [e] CH A   [f] catholici A   [g] Deo B   [h] om. A   [i] om. BC
[j] fidem BC   [k] materia B   [l] ut forma et materia disponant C   [m] ad
predicationem majoritatis C   [n] om. BC   [o] infideles et de iure B   infideles de jure C   [p] substantialis BC   [q] in EF conservetur C   [r] verum B
[s] om. A   [t] om. A   [u] bonitatis etc. officii B bonitatis etc. C   [v] etc. A   C
[x] pugnare A   [y] etiam medium A   [z] principium B

A 59v Vicesimo primo queritur, utrum aliquis debeat venire invitus ad fidem.[a]

Suppono quod B sit homo catholicus et quod D sit infidelis. Inter
BD[b] est differentia et hec differentia est in contrarietate quoad A, quia
inter AB[c] est concordantia, inter[d] AD est contrarietas. Concordantia autem digna est quod sit in magnitudine bonitatis etc. Et sic B non debet
cogere D quod credat A cum minoritate bonitatis magnitudinis etc., que
minoritas esset si D coactus baptizaretur.

Finis quare sunt BD est A, et hoc quia[e] est recolibile intelligibile et
amabile et sic A[f] est principium medium ipsorum BD. Unde sequitur
quod BD debent A frui et servire[g] cum forma et materia debent esse
disposita[h] ad illam fruitionem que indisposita esset in EH si H[i] cogere-
tur in coactione G. Nec transiret[j] D per medium coniunctionis caritative
necque[k] cum fide et sic[l] defficerent ei principium et finis et[m] in privando
sibi libertatem B non esset effective cum forma fidei caritatis etc.; quare
D non debet compelli.

Majoritas substantialiter maior est in E quam in F et sic de HG et
quia A est recolibile[n] etc. cum maioritate bonitatis libertatis etc. et non
cum minoritate,[o] ideo B non debet compellere D in G sed in H per
B 22v predicationem, osten/dendo veritatem[p] fidei catholice etc.[q] Et B debet
C 148r sustinere mor/tem quoad F, ut per predicationem possit reducere H ad
A, et debet[r] facere bona D quoad G ut per illa H inducatur ad diligen-
dum A.

BD magis possunt[s] concordare et coequare in coniunctione de EH
quam in coniunctione de FG, et hoc[t] quoad principium medium et fi-

227

nem, quod patet manifeste. Unde sequitur quod B debet inducere D ad viam veritatis discurrendo per maioritatem concordancie principii medii et[u] finis substantie et equalitatis[v] bonitatum magnitudinum perfectionum etc. EH contra minoritatem ipsius H, quod[x] H reducatur in minoritate[y] per coactionem G. Et de hoc habemus exemplum in apostolis Christi qui per istum modum infideles ad viam veritatis reduxerunt. Quare apparet quod infideles non debent compelli venire ad fidem catholicam inviti.[z]

[a] Questio. Utrum aliquis debeat compelli venire invitus ad fidem. Solucio. A
[b] B et D. C   [c] A et B. C   [d] et inter A   [e] in A. A   [f] om. A
[g] fini servire A   [h] cum forma sub qua forma debet esse materia disposita A
[i] B. C   [j] Non transeunte A   [k] nec B   [l] sicut A om. C   [m] etiam A
om. C   [n] E est rationabile C   [o] minoritate etc. C   [p] de veritate A
[q] om. A   [r] debet reducere HA etiam debet A   [s] se possunt A   [t] de hoc C
[u] om. A   [v] equalitate C   [x] *fortasse* quam?   [y] unitate BC   [z] quod
infidelis non debet compelli invitus venire ad fidem catholicam A

Alexander, P. J. "Byzantium and the Migration of Literary Motifs: The Legend of the Last Roman Emperor." *Medievalia et Humanistica* NS 2 (1971): 47–68.

———. "The Diffusion of Byzantine Apocalypses in the Medieval West and the Beginnings of Joachimism." In *Prophecy and Millenarianism: Essays in Honour of Marjorie Reeves*, edited by Ann Williams, pp. 53–106. London, 1980.

———. "Medieval Apocalypses as Historical Sources." *American Historical Review* 73 (1967–68): 997–1018.

Alphandéry, P. "Mahomet-Antichrist dans le Moyen Age latin." In *Mélanges Hartwig Derenbourg*, pp. 261–77. Paris, 1909.

Altaner, B. *Die Dominikanermissionen des 13. Jahrhunderts: Forschungen zur Geschichte der kirchlichen Unionen und der Mohammedaner- und Heidenmission des Mittelalters.* Habelschwerdt, 1924.

———. "Glaubenszwang und Glaubensfreiheit in der Missionstheorie des Raymundus Lullus: Ein Beitrag zur Geschichte des Toleranzgedankens." *Historisches Jahrbuch* 48 (1928): 586–610.

d'Alverny, Marie-Thérèse. "La connaissance de l'Islam au temps de Saint Louis." In *Septième centenaire de la mort de Saint Louis: Actes des colloques de Royaumont et de Paris (21–27 mai 1970)*, pp. 235–46. Paris, 1976.

———. "La connaissance de l'Islam en Occident du IXᵉ au milieu du XIIᵉ siècle." In *Settimane di studio del Centro italiano di studi sull'alto medioevo*, vol. 12, pp. 577–602. Spoleto, 1965.

———. "Deux traductions latines du Coran au moyen âge." *Archives d'histoire doctrinale et littéraire du moyen âge* 22–23 (1947–48): 69–131.

———. "Pierre le Vénérable et la légende de Mahomet." In *A Cluny: Congrès scientifique, 9–11 juillet 1949*, pp. 161–70. Dijon, 1950.

Amari, M. *Storia dei Musulmani di Sicilia*, edited by C. A. Nallino, 3 vols. Catania, 1933–39.

d'Ancona, A. "Il Tesoro di Brunetto Latini versificato." *Atti della R. Accademia nazionale dei Lincei: Memorie della classe di scienze morali, storiche e filologiche* 4.4 (1888): 111–274.

Arnold, T. W. *The Preaching of Islam: A History of the Propagation of the Muslim Faith.* 2d ed. London, 1913.

Atiya, A. S. *The Crusade in the Later Middle Ages*. London, 1938.

Balard, M. "Remarques sur les esclaves à Gênes dans la seconde moitié du XIIIᵉ siècle." *Mélanges d'archéologie et d'histoire publiés par l'Ecole Française de Rome* 80 (1968): 627–80.

Balme, F. "La province dominicaine de Terre-Sainte de janvier 1277 à octobre 1280.," *Revue de l'Orient latin* 1 (1893): 526–36.

Batllori, M. "Teoria ed azione missionaria in Raimondo Lullo." In *Espansione del Francescanesimo*, pp. 187–211.

Berchier, H., Courteaux, Annie, and Mouton, J. "Une abbaye latine dans la société musulmane: Monreale au XIIᵉ siècle." *Annales E.S.C.* 34 (1979): 525–47.

Berry, Virginia. "Peter the Venerable and the Crusades." In *Petrus Venerabilis (1156–1956): Studies and Texts Commemorating the Eighth Centenary of His Death*, edited by G. Constable and J. Kritzeck, pp. 141–62. Rome, 1956.

Bertram, M. "Johannes de Ancona: Ein Jurist des 13. Jahrhunderts in den Kreuzfahrerstaaten." *Bulletin of Medieval Canon Law* NS 7 (1977): 49–64.

Beumann, H. "Kreuzzugsgedanke und Ostpolitik im hohen Mittelalter." In *Heidenmission und Kreuzzugsgedanke*, pp. 121–45.

Bigalli, D. "Giudizio escatologico e tecnica di missione nei pensatori francescani: Ruggero Bacone." In *Espansione del Francescanesimo*, pp. 151–86.

Blanke, F. "Die Entscheidungsjahre der Preussenmission (1206–1274)." In *Heidenmission und Kreuzzugsgedanke*, pp. 389–416.

Borgolte, M. *Der Gesandtenaustausch der Karolinger mit den Abbasiden und mit den Patriarchen von Jerusalem*. Münchener Beiträge zur Mediävistik und Renaissance-Forschung 25. Munich, 1976.

Browne, L. E. *The Eclipse of Christianity in Asia: From the Time of Muhammad till the Fourteenth Century*. Cambridge, 1933.

———. "The Patriarch Timothy and the Caliph al-Mahdi." *Moslem World* 21 (1931): 38–45.

Brundage, J. "Holy War and the Medieval Lawyers." In *The Holy War*, edited by T. P. Murphy, pp. 99–140. Columbus, 1976.

Brunschvig, R. *La Berbérie orientale sous les Ḥafsides: Des origines à la fin du XVᵉ siècle*. Vol. 1. Paris, 1940.

Bulliet, R. W. *Conversion to Islam in the Medieval Period: An Essay in Quantitative History*. Cambridge, Mass., and London, 1979.

Burns, R. "Christian-Islamic Confrontation in the West: The Thirteenth-Century Dream of Conversion." *American Historical Review* 76 (1971): 1386–1434.

————. *Islam under the Crusaders: Colonial Survival in the Thirteenth-Century Kingdom of Valencia.* Princeton, 1973.

————. "Journey from Islam: Incipient Cultural Transition in the Conquered Kingdom of Valencia (1240–1280)." *Speculum* 35 (1960): 337–56.

————. *Moors and Crusaders in Mediterranean Spain: Collected Essays.* London, 1978.

Bussi, E. "La condizione giuridica dei musulmani nel diritto canonico." *Rivista di storia del diritto italiano* 8 (1935): 459–94.

Cahen. C. "Le commerce d'Amalfi dans le Proche-Orient musulman avant et après la Croisade." *Comptes-rendus de l'Académie des Inscriptions et Belles-Lettres,* 1977: 291–300.

————. "Note sur l'accueil des chrétiens d'Orient à l'islam." *Revue de l'histoire des religions* 166 (1964): 51–58.

Canard, M. "Quelques 'à-côté' de l'histoire des relations entre Byzance et les Arabes." In *Studi orientalistici in onore di Giorgio Levi della Vida,* 1:98–119. Rome, 1956.

————. "Les relations politiques et sociales entre Byzance et les Arabes." *Dumbarton Oaks Papers* 18 (1964): 33–56.

Cardini, F. "Gilberto di Tournai: Un francescano predicatore della crociata." *Studi Francescani* 72 (1975): 31–48.

————. " 'Nella presenza del Soldan superba': Bernardo, Francesco, Bonaventura e il superamento dell'idea di crociata." *Studi Francescani* 71 (1974): 199–250.

Citarella, A. O. "The Relations of Amalfi with the Arab World before the Crusades." *Speculum* 42 (1967): 299–312.

Colbert, E. P. *The Martyrs of Córdoba (850–859): A Study of the Sources.* Washington, D.C., 1962.

Coll, J. M. "San Raymundo de Peñafort y las Misiones del Norte Africano en la Edad Media." *Missionalia Hispanica* 5 (1948): 417–57.

Condorelli, M. *I fondamenti giuridici della tolleranza religiosa nell'elaborazione canonistica dei secoli XII–XIV: Contributo storico-dogmatico.* Milan, 1960.

Courtois, Ch. "Grégoire VII et l'Afrique du Nord: Remarques sur les communautés chrétiennes d'Afrique au XIe siècle." *Revue historique* 195 (1945): 97–122, 193–226.

Cowdrey, H.E.J. "Cluny and the First Crusade." *Revue Bénédictine* 83 (1973): 285–311.

————. "Pope Urban II's Preaching of the First Crusade." *History* 55 (1970): 177–88.

Creutz, R. "Additamenta zu Konstantinus Africanus und seinen Schülern Johannes und Atto." *Studien und Mitteilungen zur Geschichte des Benediktiner-Ordens und seiner Zweige* 50 (1932): 420–42.

———. "Der Arzt Constantinus Africanus von Montekassino: Sein Leben, sein Werk und seine Bedeutung für die mittelalterliche medizinische Wissenschaft." *Studien und Mitteilungen zur Geschichte des Benediktiner-Ordens und seiner Zweige* 47 (1929): 1–44.

———. "Der Cassinese Johannes Afflacius Saracenus, ein Arzt aus 'Hochsalerno.'" *Studien und Mitteilungen zur Geschichte des Benediktiner-Ordens und seiner Zweige* 48 (1930): 301–24.

———. "Die Ehrenrettung Konstantins von Afrika." *Studien und Mitteilungen zur Geschichte des Benediktiner-Ordens und seiner Zweige* 49 (1931): 25–44.

Cutler, A. "The First Crusade and the Idea of Conversion." *Muslim World* 58 (1968): 57–71, 155–64.

———. "The Ninth-Century Spanish Martyrs' Movement and the Origins of Western Christian Missions to the Muslims." *Muslim World* 55 (1965): 321–29.

———. "Peter the Venerable and Islam (review article)." *Journal of the American Oriental Society* 86 (1966): 184–98.

———. "Who Was the 'Monk of France' and When Did He Write?" *al–Andalus* 28 (1963): 249–69.

Daniel, E. R. "Apocalyptic Conversion: The Joachite Alternative to the Crusades." *Traditio* 25 (1969): 127–54.

———. "The Desire for Martyrdom: A *Leitmotiv* of St. Bonaventure." Franciscan Studies 32 (1972): 74–87.

———. *The Franciscan Concept of Mission in the High Middle Ages.* Lexington, Ky., 1975.

———. "Roger Bacon and the *De seminibus scripturarum.*" *Mediaeval Studies* 34 (1972): 462–67.

Daniel, N. *The Arabs and Mediaeval Europe.* London and Beirut, 1975.

———. *Islam and the West: The Making of an Image.* Edinburgh, 1960.

———. "Learned and Popular Attitudes to the Arabs in the Middle Ages." *Journal of the Royal Asiatic Society*, 1977: 41–52.

Defourneaux, M. *Les Français en Espagne aux XIe et XIIe siècles.* Paris, 1949.

Delorme, F. "De praedicatione cruciatae saec. XIII per Fratres Minores." *Archivum Franciscanum Historicum* 9 (1916): 99–117.

Dérumeaux, P. "Saint Bernard et les Infidèles." In *Mélanges St. Bernard: XXIVe Congrès de l'Association bourguignonne des sociétés savantes*, pp. 68–79. Dijon, 1953.

Dufourcq, Ch.-E. "Les relations du Maroc et de la Castille pendant la première moitié du XIIIe siècle." *Revue d'histoire et de civilisation du Maghreb* 5 (juillet 1968): 37–62.

Dunlop, D. M. "A Christian Mission to Muslim Spain in the Eleventh Century." *al-Andalus* 17 (1952): 259–310.

Egidi, P. *La colonia saracena di Lucera e la sua distruzione*. Naples, 1912.

Elm, K. "Franz von Assisi: Busspredigt oder Heidenmission?" In *Espansione del Francescanesimo*, pp. 69–103.

Erdmann, C. *The Origin of the Idea of Crusade*, translated by M. W. Baldwin and W. Goffart. Princeton, 1977.

Espansione del Francescanesimo tra Occidente e Oriente nel secolo XIII: Atti del VI Convegno Internazionale di Studi Francescani, Assisi, 12–14 ottobre 1978. Assisi, 1979.

Franke, F. R. "Die freiwilligen Märtyrer von Cordova und das Verhältnis der Mozaraber zum Islam (nach den Schriften von Speraindeo, Eulogius, und Alvar)." *Gesammelte Aufsätze zur Kulturgeschichte Spaniens* 13 (1958): 1–170.

Fritsch, E. *Islam und Christentum im Mittelalter: Beiträge zur Geschichte der muslimischen Polemik gegen das Christentum in arabischer Sprache*. Breslau, 1930.

Funk, P. *Jakob von Vitry: Leben und Werke*. Leipzig and Berlin, 1909.

Gabrieli, F. "La politique arabe des Normands de Sicile." *Studia islamica* 9 (1958): 83–96.

Gauss, Julia. "Anselm von Canterbury und die Islamfrage." *Theologische Zeitschrift* 19 (1963): 250–72.

———. "Toleranz und Intoleranz zwischen Christen und Muslimen in der Zeit vor den Kreuzzügen." *Saeculum* 19 (1968): 362–89.

Gemelli, Pia. "Giacomo da Vitry e le origini del movimento francescano," *Aevum* 39 (1965): 474–95.

Glazik, J. *Die Islammission der russisch-orthodoxen Kirche*. Missionswissenschaftliche Abhandlungen und Texte, 23. Münster, 1959.

Goitein, S. D. "Contemporary Letters on the Capture of Jerusalem by the Crusaders." *Journal of Jewish Studies* 3 (1952): 162–77.

———. *Palestinian Jewry in Early Islamic and Crusader Times in the Light of the Geniza Documents*. Jerusalem, 1980 (in Hebrew).

González Palencia, A. "Toledo en los siglos XII y XIII." In *Moros y cristianos en España medieval: Estudios historico-literarios*. Madrid, 1945.

Gottron, A. *Ramon Lulls Kreuzzugsideen*. Berlin and Leipzig, 1912.

Grabmann, M. "Der Franziskanerbischof Benedictus de Alignano († 1268) und seine Summa zum Caput Firmiter des vierten Laterankonzils." In *Kirchengeschichtliche Studien P. Michael Bihl OFM als Ehrengabe dargeboten*, edited by I.-M. Freudenreich, pp. 50–64. Colmar, 1941.

———. "Die Schrift: De rationibus fidei contra Saracenos Graecos et Armenos ad Cantorem Antiochenum des heiligen Thomas von Aqui." *Scholastik: Vierteljahresschrift für Theologie und Philosophie* 17 (1942): 187–216.

Graf, G. *Geschichte der christlichen arabischen Literatur*. Vol. 2, *Die Schriftsteller bis zur Mitte des 15. Jahrhunderts*. Studi e Testi, 133. Città del Vaticano, 1947.

Haverkamp, A. "Zur Sklaverei in Genua während des 12. Jahrhunderts." In *Geschichte in der Gesellschaft: Festschrift für Karl Bosl*, edited by F. Prinz et al., pp. 160–215. Stuttgart, 1974.

Hehl, E.-D. *Kirche und Krieg im 12. Jahrhundert: Studien zu kanonischem Recht und politischer Wirklichkeit*. Monographien zur Geschichte des Mittelalters, 19. Stuttgart, 1980.

Heidenmission und Kreuzzugsgedanke in der deutschen Ostpolitik des Mittelalters, edited by H. Beumann. 2d ed. Darmstadt, 1973.

Heisig, K. "Die Geschichtsmetaphysik des Rolandliedes und seine Vorgeschichte." *Zeitschrift für romanische Philologie* 55 (1935): 1–87.

Herde, P. "Christians and Saracens at the Time of the Crusades: Some Comments of Contemporary Medieval Canonists." *Studia Gratiana* 12 (1967): 361–76.

von der Heydte, F. A. *Die Geburtsstunde des modernen Staates: Ein Beitrag zur Geschichte des Völkerrechts, der allgemeinen Staatslehre und des politischen Denkens*. Regensburg, 1952.

Hillgarth, J. N. *Ramon Lull and Lullism in Fourteenth-Century France*. Oxford, 1971.

Holt, P. M. "Qalawūn's Treaty with Acre in 1283." *English Historical Review* 91 (1976): 802–12.

Hübinger, P., et al. "Die lateinische Christenheit und der Islam im Mittelalter." In *Geschichte in Wissenschaft und Unterricht*, Beiheft 1965: 20–24.

Huygens, R.B.C. "Les passages des lettres de Jacques de Vitry relatifs à Saint François d'Assise et à ses premiers disciples." In *Hommages à Léon Herrmann*, pp. 446–53. Collection Latomus, 44. Brussels, 1960.

Kahl, H.-D. "Bausteine zur Grundlegung einer missionsgeschichtlichen Phänomenologie des Hochmittelalters." In *Miscellanea Historiae Ecclesiasticae: Congrès de Stockholm, 1960*, pp. 50–90. Bibliothèque de la Revue d'histoire ecclésiastique, 38. Louvain, 1960.

———. "Compellere intrare: Die Wendenpolitik Bruns von Querfurt

SECONDARY LITERATURE

im Lichte hochmittelalterlichen Missions- und Völkerrechts." In *Heidenmission und Kreuzzugsgedanke*, pp. 177–274.

———. "Zum Ergebnis des Wendenkreuzzugs von 1147." In *Heidenmission und Kreuzzugsgedanke*, pp. 275–316.

Kedar, B. Z. "Canon Law and the Burning of the Talmud." *Bulletin of Medieval Canon Law* NS 9 (1979): 79–82.

———. "Gerard of Nazareth, A Neglected Twelfth-Century Writer in the Latin East: A Contribution to the Intellectual and Monastic History of the Crusader States." *Dumbarton Oaks Papers* 37 (1983): 55–77.

———. "Muslim Conversion in Canon Law." In *Proceedings of the Sixth International Congress of Medieval Canon Law, Berkeley 1980*, edited by S. Kuttner and K. Pennington, pp. 321–332. Città del Vaticano, 1985.

Khoury, A.-Th. *Polémique byzantine contre l'Islam (VIIIᵉ–XIIIᵉ s.)*. Leiden, 1972.

———. *Les théologiens byzantins et l'Islam: Textes et auteurs (VIIIᵉ–XIIIᵉ s.)*. Louvain and Paris, 1969.

Knoch, P. *Studien zu Albert von Aachen. Der erste Kreuzzug in der deutschen Chronistik*. Stuttgart, 1966.

Kritzeck, J. "Moslem-Christian Understanding in Mediaeval Times." *Comparative Studies in Society and History* 4 (1961–62): 387–401.

———. *Peter the Venerable and Islam*. Princeton, 1964.

Kuttner, S. *Kanonistische Schuldlehre von Gratian bis auf die Dekretalen Gregors IX*. Studi e Testi, 64. Città del Vaticano, 1935.

Lacam, J. *Les Sarrazins dans le haut moyen–âge français: Histoire et archéologie*. Paris, 1965.

Lamma, P. *Momenti di storiografia cluniacense*. Rome, 1961.

Lavagnini, B. "Siracusa occupata dagli Arabi e l'epistola di Teodosio Monaco." *Byzantion* 29–30 (1959–60): 267–79.

Leclercq, J. "Gratien, Pierre de Troyes et la seconde croisade." *Studia Gratiana* 2 (1954): 585–93.

———. "Saint Bernard's Attitude toward War." In *Studies in Medieval Cistercian History*, edited by J. R. Sommerfeldt, vol. 2, pp. 1–39. Kalamazoo, Mich., 1976.

———. "La vie et la prière des chevaliers de Santiago d'après leur règle primitive." *Litúrgica* 2 (1958): 347–57.

Lemmens, L. "De sancto Francisco Christum praedicante coram sultano Aegypti." *Archivum Franciscanum Historicum* 19 (1926): 559–78.

Levi della Vida, G. "La corrispondenza di Berta di Toscana col califfo Muktafi." *Rivista storica italiana* 66 (1954): 21–38.

Lévi-Provençal, E. *L'Espagne musulmane au Xᵉᵐᵉ siècle: Institutions et vie sociale*. Paris, 1932.

———. *Histoire de l'Espagne musulmane*. 3 vols. Paris, 1950–53.

Lévi-Provençal, E. "La 'Mora Zaida,' femme d'Alphonse VI, et leur fils, l'infant don Sancho." In *Islam d'Occident: Etudes d'histoire médiévale*, pp. 137–51. Paris, 1948.

Lewis, B. *The Muslim Discovery of Europe*. New York and London, 1982.

Liauzu, G. "La condition des musulmans dans l'Aragon chrétien aux XIe et XIIe siècles." *Hespéris-Tamuda* 9 (1968): 185–200.

Lopez, R. S. "A propos d'une virgule: Le facteur économique dans la politique africaine des papes." *Revue historique* 198 (1947): 178–88.

Lotter, F. *Die Konzeption des Wendenkreuzzugs: Ideengeschichtliche, kirchenrechtliche und historisch-politische Voraussetzungen der Missionierung von Elb- und Ostseeslawen um die Mitte des 12. Jahrhunderts.* Vorträge und Forschungen, Sonderband 23. Sigmaringen, 1977.

Luppi, B. *I Saraceni in Provenza, in Liguria e nelle Alpi Occidentali.* Bordighera, 1952.

Lupprian, K.-E. *Die Beziehungen der Päpste zu islamischen und mongolischen Herrschern im 13. Jahrhundert anhand ihres Briefwechsels.* Studi e Testi, 291. Città del Vaticano, 1981.

Malvezzi, A. *L'Islamismo e la cultura europea.* Florence, 1956.

Manselli, R. "La *res publica christiana* e l'Islam." In *Settimane di Studio del Centro italiano di studi sull'alto medioevo,* vol. 12, pp. 115–47. Spoleto, 1965.

———. "La Terza Età, *Babylon* et l'Anticristo mistico." *Bullettino dell'Istituto Storico Italiano per il Medio Evo e Archivio Muratoriano* 82 (1970): 47–79.

Mayer, H. E. *The Crusades*, translated by J. Gillingham. New York and Oxford, 1972.

Meredith-Jones, C. "The Conventional Saracen of the Songs of Geste." *Speculum* 17 (1942): 201–25.

Metlitzki, Dorothée. *The Matter of Araby in Medieval England.* New Haven and London, 1977.

Meyendorff, J. "Byzantine Views of Islam." *Dumbarton Oaks Papers* 18 (1964): 113–32.

Michel, K. *Das Opus Tripartitum des Humbertus de Romanis, O.P.: Ein Beitrag zur Geschichte der Kreuzzugsidee und der kirchlichen Unionsbewegung.* 2d ed. Graz, 1926.

Monneret de Villard, U. *Il Libro della Peregrinazione nelle parti d'Oriente di frate Ricoldo da Montecroce.* Rome, 1948.

Mor, C. G. "Intorno a una lettera di Berta di Toscana al Califfo di Bagdad." *Archivio storico italiano* 112 (1954): 299–312.

Muldoon, J. "*Extra Ecclesiam non est imperium*: The Canonists and the

Legitimacy of Secular Power." *Studia Gratiana* 9 (1966): 551–80.

——. *Popes, Lawyers, and Infidels: The Church and the Non-Christian World, 1250–1550*. Philadelphia, 1979.

Musca, G. *L'emirato di Bari, 847–871*. Bari, 1964.

Pellegrini, L. "Le missioni francescane sotto Alessandro IV (1254–1261)." *Studi Francescani* 64 (1967): 91–118.

Platzeck, E. W. *Raimund Lull: Sein Leben—Seine Werke—Die Grundlagen seines Denkens*. 2 vols. Düsseldorf, 1962–64.

Plocher, Marianne. "Studien zum Kreuzzugsgedanken im 12. und 13. Jahrhundert." Ph.D. diss., University of Freiburg, 1950.

Prawer, J. *Crusader Institutions*. Oxford, 1980.

——. *Histoire du royaume latin de Jérusalem*. 2 vols. Paris, 1969–70.

——. *The Latin Kingdom of Jerusalem: European Colonialism in the Middle Ages*. London, 1972.

Prutz, H. *Kulturgeschichte der Kreuzzüge*. Berlin, 1883.

Rajna, P. "San Francesco d'Assisi e gli spiriti cavallereschi." *Nuova Antologia: Rivista di Lettere, Scienze ed Arti* 327 (1926): 385–95.

Reeves, Marjorie. *The Influence of Prophecy in the Later Middle Ages: A Study in Joachimism*. Oxford, 1969.

Reeves, Marjorie, and Hirsch-Reich, Beatrice. *The Figurae of Joachim of Fiore*. Oxford, 1972.

Richard, J. *L'esprit de la croisade*. Paris, 1969.

——. *The Latin Kingdom of Jerusalem*, translated by Janet Shirley. Amsterdam, 1979.

——. *La papauté et les missions d'Orient au moyen âge (XIIIᵉ–XVᵉ siècles)*. Rome, 1977.

——. "La politique orientale de Saint Louis: La croisade de 1248." In *Septième centenaire de la mort de Saint Louis: Actes des colloques de Royaumont et de Paris (21–27 mai 1970)*, pp. 197–207. Paris, 1976.

Riley–Smith, J.S.C. "Crusading as an Act of Love." *History* 65 (1980): 177–92.

——. *What Were the Crusades?* London, 1977.

Röhricht, R. "Die Kreuzpredigten gegen den Islam: Ein Beitrag zur Geschichte der christlichen Predigt im 12. und 13. Jahrhundert." *Zeitschrift für Kirchengeschichte* 6 (1883–84): 550–72.

Roscher, H. *Papst Innocenz III und die Kreuzzüge*. Göttingen, 1969.

Rotzetter, A. "Kreuzzugskritik und Ablehnung der Feudalordnung in der Gefolgschaft des Franziskus von Assisi." *Wissenschaft und Weisheit* 35 (1972): 121–37.

Rousset, P. *Histoire des croisades*. Paris, 1957.

Rousset de Pina, J. "L'entrevue du Pape Alexandre III et d'un prince sarrasin à Montpellier, le 11 avril 1162: Notes sur les relations islamo-chrétiennes à la fin du XIIe siècle." In *Etudes médiévales offertes à A. Fliche*, pp. 161–85. Publications de la Faculté des Lettres de l'Université de Montpellier, 4. Montpellier, 1953.

Runciman, S. "The Decline of the Crusading Idea." In *Relazioni del X Congresso Internazionale di Scienze Storiche*, 3:637–52. Florence, 1955.

Russell, F. H. *The Just War in the Middle Ages*. Cambridge, 1975.

Sahas, D. J. *John of Damascus on Islam: The "Heresy of the Ishmaelites."* Leiden, 1972.

Schack, Dietlind. *Die Araber im Reich Rogers II*. Berlin, 1969.

Scheeben, H. C. "Dominikaner oder Innozentianer?" *Archivum Fratrum Praedicatorum* 9 (1939): 237–97.

Schwinges, R. C. *Kreuzzugsideologie und Toleranz: Studien zu Wilhelm von Tyrus*. Monographien zur Geschichte des Mittelalters, 15. Stuttgart, 1977.

Smalley, Beryl. "Robert Holcot O.P." *Archivum Fratrum Praedicatorum* 24 (1956): 9–97.

Sommerville, R. "The Council of Clermont and the First Crusade." *Studia Gratiana* 20 (1976): 324–37.

Southern, R. W. *Western Views of Islam in the Middle Ages*. Cambridge, Mass., 1962.

Stein, S. *Die Ungläubigen in der mittelhochdeutschen Literatur von 1050 bis 1250*. 1933. Reprint. Darmstadt, 1963.

Sternfeld, R. *Ludwig des Heiligen Kreuzzug nach Tunis, 1270, und die Politik Karls I. von Sizilien*. Berlin, 1896.

Sugranyes de Franch, R. "Els projectes de creuada en la doctrina missional de Ramon Llull." *Estudios Lulianos* 4 (1960): 275–90.

———. *Raymond Lulle, docteur des missions*. Schöneck-Beckenried, 1954.

———. "Un texte de Ramón Lull sur la croisade et les missions." *Nova et Vetera* 21 (1946): 98–112.

Thomson, R. M. "William of Malmesbury and Some Other Western Writers on Islam." *Medievalia et Humanistica* NS 6 (1975): 179–87.

Throop, P. A. *Criticism of the Crusade: A Study of Public Opinion and Crusade Propaganda*. Amsterdam, 1940. Reprint. Philadelphia, 1975.

Toynbee, A. *Constantine Porphyrogenitus and His World*. London, 1973.

Turki, A. "La lettre du 'Moine de France' á al-Muqtadir billāh, roi de Saragosse, et la réponse d'al-Bāŷī, le faqīh andalou." *al-Andalus* 31 (1966): 73–153.

Vasiliev, A. A. "The Iconoclastic Edict of the Caliph Yazid II, A.D. 721." *Dumbarton Oaks Papers* 9–10 (1956): 23–47.

van der Vat, O. *Die Anfänge der Franziskanermissionen und ihre Weiterentwicklung im nahen Orient und in den mohammedanischen Ländern während des 13. Jahrhunderts.* Werl/Westf., 1934.

Verlinden, Ch. *L'esclavage dans l'Europe médiévale.* Vol. 1, Brugge, 1955. Vol. 2, Gent, 1977.

Voerzio, M. *Fr. Guglielmo da Tripoli, orientalista domenicano del sec. XIII, precursore di Fra Ricoldo di Monte Croce.* Florence, 1955.

Waas, A. *Geschichte der Kreuzzüge.* 2 vols. Freiburg, 1956.

Waltz, J. "Historical Perspectives on 'Early Missions' to Muslims." *Muslim World* 61 (1971): 170–86.

———. "Muḥammad and the Muslims in St. Thomas Aquinas." *Muslim World* 66 (1976): 81–95.

———. "The Significance of the Voluntary Martyrs of Ninth-Century Córdoba." *Muslim World* 60 (1970): 143–59, 226–36.

Warren, F. M. "The Enamoured Moslem Princess in Orderic Vital and the French Epic." *Publications of the Modern Language Association of America* 29 (1914): 341–58.

van den Wyngaert, A. "Frère Guillaume de Cordelle, O.F.M." *La France Franciscaine* 4 (1921): 52–71.

These pertinent works appeared while the present book was in the press or after its original publication:

Brundage, J. A. "St. Anselm, Ivo of Chartres, and the Ideology of the First Crusade." In *Les mutations socio-culturelles au tournant des XIe–XIIe siècles. Études anselmiennes,* pp. 175–87. Paris, 1984.

Cahen, C. *Orient et Occident au temps des Croisades.* Paris, 1983.

Kedar, B. Z. "Ungarische Muslime in Jerusalem im Jahre 1217." *Acta Orientalia Academiae Scientiarum Hungaricae* 40 (1986): 325–27.

Luttrell, A. "Le origini della parrocchia a Malta." In *Pievi e parrocchie in Italia nel basso medioevo (sec. XIII–XV). Atti del VI Convegno di Storia della Chiesa in Italia (Firenze, 21–25 sett. 1981),* 2:1187–1198. Rome, 1984.

Rotter, E. *Abendland und Sarazenen. Das okzidentale Araberbild und seine Entstehung im Frühmittelalter.* Berlin and New York, 1986.

Sénac, P. *L'image de l'autre. L'Occident médiéval face à l'Islam.* Paris, 1983.

Siberry, Elizabeth. *Criticism of Crusading, 1095–1274.* Oxford, 1985.

Urvoy, D. "La pensée religieuse des Mozarabes face à l'Islam." *Traditio* 39 (1983): 419–32.

INDEX

Library of Congress Cataloging in Publication Data

Kedar, B. Z.
  Crusade and mission.

  Bibliography: p.
  Includes index.
  1. Missions to Muslims. 2. Crusades. I. Title.
BV2625.K43 1984   266′.2′0917671   84-3403
ISBN 0-691-05424-X
ISBN 0-691-10246-5 (pbk.)